Publication of this book has
been generously assisted by a grant from
The Carl and Lily Pforzheimer Foundation, Inc.

THE GOTHAM LIBRARY
OF THE NEW YORK UNIVERSITY PRESS

The Gotham Library is a series of original works and critical studies, published in paperback primarily for student use. The Gotham hardcover edition is primarily for use by libraries and the general reader. Devoted to significant works and major authors and to literary topics of enduring importance, Gotham Library texts offer the best in literature and criticism.

Comparative and Foreign Language Literature:
Robert J. Clements, Editor
Comparative and English Language Literature:
James W. Tuttleton, Editor

The Evidence of the Imagination:

Studies of Interactions between Life and Art in English Romantic Literature

Edited by
Donald H. Reiman, Michael C. Jaye, and Betty T. Bennett, *with the assistance of* Doucet Devin Fischer and Ricki B. Herzfeld

New York · New York University Press · 1978

Library of Congress Cataloging in Publication Data
Main entry under title:

The Evidence of the imagination.

Includes bibliographical references and index.
1. English literature—19th century—History and criticism—Addresses, essays, lectures. 2. Romanticism—England—Addresses, essays, lectures. I. Reiman, Donald H. 1934—II. Jaye, Michael C., 1941—
III. Bennett, Betty T. 1935—
PR457.E9 820'.9'007 77-14673
ISBN 0-8147-7372-9
ISBN 0-8147-7373-7 pbk.

Manufactured in the United States of America

To Kenneth Neill Cameron
Scholar, Teacher, Friend

And behold! thrones were kingless, and men walked
One with the other even as spirits do,
None fawned, none trampled . . .
And women, too, . . .
Speaking the wisdom once they could not think.

Contents

Foreword

There are several quite compelling reasons why The Carl and Lily Pforzheimer Foundation, Inc., is pleased to participate in the publication of *The Evidence of the Imagination.*

In well deserved recognition of his long and distinguished career as a teacher and as a scholar, this volume is dedicated to Kenneth Neill Cameron.

A number of contributors to the volume have been closely associated in a variety of ways with The Carl H. Pforzheimer Library, administered and maintained by The Carl and Lily Pforzheimer Foundation, Inc., which encourages and supports scholarly research and publications. The essays herein themselves not only exemplify careful historical and textual scholarship that has been a hallmark of The Carl H. Pforzheimer Library's own research programs, but the thematic focus of the volume, emphasizing as it does human elements in the creation and effect of literature, accords fully with the purposes of the Pforzheimer Foundation. Since some contributors were colleagues or students of Kenneth Cameron during his years at New York University, it seems especially fitting that this book is published by New York University Press.

Finally, as President of the Pforzheimer Foundation, my own warm feelings towards Kenneth Cameron are not only those of a continuing friend, but also those of a delighted colleague in the work of The Carl H. Pforzheimer Library.

Kenneth Neill Cameron was chosen by the late Carl H. Pforzheimer to be the Editor of *Shelley and his Circle* and resident researcher at The Carl H. Pforzheimer Library because my parents found him to be a man with a broad background of scholarly dedication and acumen who also recognized Shelley and his writings as living forces in modern society. For Kenneth Cameron—and for his students and colleagues who are glad to honor him in this volume—the study of humane letters remains a "humanly" important experience.

Poetry, like government, education, and other vital human activities, is much too important to leave solely to the experts. Laymen who value great artistic achievements have not only a right but a duty to insist that they not be excluded from the precincts of poetry by self-appointed professional guardians. Wordsworth wrote in his Preface to *Lyrical Ballads,* "The Poet writes under one restriction only, namely, the necessity of giving immediate pleasure to a human being possessed of that information which may be expected from him, not as a lawyer, a physician, a mariner, an astronomer, or a natural philosopher [to which list we may well add, a literary critic] but as a Man."

The highest dedication to the growth of knowledge can, we believe, be combined with a full commitment to human ideals. In this belief, The Carl and Lily Pforzheimer Foundation, Inc., is pleased to participate in this volume of humane scholarship.

Vigil Hill
August 1977

Carl H. Pforzheimer, Jr.

Acknowledgments

The editors wish to express their thanks not only to the friends, colleagues, and former students of Kenneth Neill Cameron who ultimately contributed to *The Evidence of the Imagination,* but to several others who offered various kinds of help and suggestions at the inception of this volume, including Gina M. Luria, M. Roxana Klapper, Charles J. Clancy, Leon Edel, Ralph Anthony Manogue, John Rogers Maynard, Sudie Nostrand, Gordon N. Ray, M. L. Rosenthal, and Lewis M. Schwartz. Members of the staff of The Carl H. Pforzheimer Library have assisted in various ways: Mihai H. Handrea and Robert Yampolsky answered reference and bibliographical questions; Carol E. Czernicki, Margaret Finan, Eileen Silverman, and Meryl Marcus assisted with a voluminous correspondence; and Ricki B. Herzfeld and, especially, Doucet Devin Fischer, from beginning to end played an active, vital role in the creation of this volume, corresponding with various contributors; reading, checking, and (by their suggestions) improving many of the contributions; copyediting the volume; and counseling and assisting the editors in ways too numerous to describe. Paul Magnuson and John J. Lavelle also came to the editors' aid in particularly crucial moments.

To the directors of The Carl and Lily Pforzheimer Foundation, Inc., and especially its President, Carl H. Pforzheimer, Jr., we are grateful both for early encouragement and support and for a subvention in support of publication. We appreciate also advice from the Foundation's legal counsel, Martin F. Richman of Barrett, Smith, Schapiro, Simon, and Armstrong.

Finally, we thank James W. Tuttleton, Editor of the Gotham Library, and Malcolm Johnson, Director of New York University Press, and his staff (especially Despina Papazoglou) for expeditiously transforming the completed manuscript into a published book.

17 January 1978

Donald H. Reiman
Michael C. Jaye
Betty T. Bennett

Introduction

Donald H. Reiman

The subtitle given to this volume does not represent an attempt to fence in or to delimit either the subject matter or the methodologies employed in the following studies. Rather, it hints at their place within the act of communication that is the work of literature. Whatever linguistic, semantic, or aesthetic theories may be current, such doctrines cannot change the basic facts of the literary venture. First, a human being living in a particular place and time, stimulated by individual circumstances, puts words together in an order determined in part by that artist's experience, in part by the supposed expectations of the specific audience he/she is addressing (whether that audience be one friend, all fellow poets, or an entire nation), in part by the denotations, connotations, past associations (public and private), sounds, and appearance of the words themselves, in part by grammatical, syntactical, and rhetorical concerns, and in part by the requirements of the form (tragedy or sonnet) in which he/she chooses to embody these ordered words. Second, the words are transmitted from the form in which the author (or a scribe) first committed them to paper (or tape recorder or the memory of an auditor); they are transcribed by others, printed or engraved or recorded, reprinted, possibly miscopied, and eventually read and/or heard by human beings living in a variety of times and places and with their own personal experiences. The words (and the punctuation marks and spacing—or the pauses and intonations) read and/or heard by this audience may differ somewhat from those the writer first wrote or uttered; certainly the significance and associations of individual words, phrases, or even subjects will differ vastly from one reader or hearer to another. The communication of a literary work thus embodies three distinct elements—an elusive author, a mutable text, and an ever-changing audience.

Whatever one's epistemology, psychology, or semiotics may be, three separate functions must be performed by students of literature. The first is to ascertain, by a study of the transmission of the text, what words—in what order and with what emphasis—the poet approved as his poem. This is the task of the textual critic.[1] Second, the specialist literary historian, beginning with this authoritative text, examines the life and works of the author and the history and culture of his/her times to determine what forces shaped the creation of the particular literary work, at what audience it was directed, and what the work should have meant to that intended audience.[2] The final task of the specialist scholar is thus to provide a detailed explication of the literary work in the light of the author's life, his other works, his times, and all of the past that was alive for him. Third, the general critic—beginning, ideally, with the authoritative text of the work of art and a full understanding of its probable intended meaning, as provided by specialized literary researchers—reacts to the literary work in the present tense, elucidating it for modern readers and evaluating its continuing relevance. Each reader performs this role of general critic in everything he/she reads, but a few people (Edmund Wilson comes to mind) make a useful career of assisting others with this task.

For the broadest sort of successful work—Swift's *Modest Proposal* or Shelley's *Hellas*—the general critic may be able to work reasonably well without too much help from specialists, but the history of literary taste is strewn with the disasters that result when ignorant critics meet such difficult literary masterpieces as *Songs and Sonnets, King Lear, The Tempest, Paradise Lost,* "Ode: Intimations of Immortality," "Kubla Khan," *Prometheus Unbound, Moby Dick,* or *Ulysses.* We now fully value these works, but others to which neither specialists nor critics have devoted sufficient attention, either to unravel complexities or unveil beauties, continue to lack what will someday appear to be a just appreciation of their merits. As Jerome J. McGann has reminded us, formalistic understanding and appreciation of a work of art is not enough: no author (or work) can be made the judge in his own case.[3] It is not enough to say: "the poet aimed at this effect and achieved it; therefore it is a successful work of art." Sympathetic understanding is, however, a necessary first step in relating literary texts to living men and women, and such understanding most often comes from specialists who have immersed themselves in the lives, times, and art of particular authors.

Whatever general hierarchy of literary excellence or relevance general critics may devolve must be based on a solid understanding of the works of art within the biographical and historical contexts that generated their creation. The specialist, unearthing evidence to elucidate the work of imagination that he finds worthy of attention, neither surrenders his own appreciation and enjoyment of great art nor attempts to substitute his function as scholar for that of critic. But the chief task of the specialist scholar is to produce understanding so that the evaluation of all critics can be a just one; he is like a detective assembling the evidence, the merits of which lawyer-like general critics will argue before a jury of humanistic readers.

The papers in this volume are the work of specialist literary scholars who delve into various aspects of the social and political context, language, biography, and textual history to clarify the place of individual works in the contexts of their creation. Two papers, those by Marcelle Thiébaux and William Walling, focus on the fate of works in the hands of their intended audiences, seeking the causes of various readers' failure to assess accurately the significance of the corpus of writings of Wollstonecraft and Peacock. Michael C. Jaye and G[eoffrey] M. Matthews have added contributions from their on-going studies of the literary significance of the manuscripts of Wordsworth and Shelley respectively, and in so doing they radically alter our understanding of some less-studied poems. Eileen Sanzo, Carl Woodring, and Paul Magnuson examine in detail particular themes and use of language in works by Blake and by Wordsworth, relating these appearances in poetry to changes taking place simultaneously in British social, intellectual, and aesthetic history. Joyce Hemlow and Marion K. Stocking, drawing on their years of research into the Burney family and the family of Claire Clairmont respectively, examine in detail actual people and events that were creatively transformed by Lamb in "The Wedding" and Henry James in *The Aspern Papers.* John J. Lavelle explores Shelley's relationship to the Pythagorean tradition, and Betty T. Bennett traces the influence of the political ideals of Wollstonecraft, Godwin, and Percy Bysshe Shelley upon the historical novels of Mary W. Shelley, thereby distinguishing them from Scott's historical romances. David V. Erdman, Irene Tayler, and I explore various aspects of the proposition that the motive force behind Wordsworth's poetry is much less "philosophical" than many critics have assumed and much more a working out of the poet's own personal crises. Besides analyzing a number of poems that have never been explored in this light, we variously account for strengths and weaknesses in Wordsworth's poetry on the basis of his resolutions of those psychological upheavals. Leslie A. Marchand measures changes in Byron's beliefs and attitudes by analyzing the course of his friendship with Francis Hodgson, a theologically orthodox clergyman who repeatedly attempted to "save" Byron from his humane skepticism. Finally, in what may be the most far-reaching paper in the volume, Aileen Ward considers Keats's changing ideals of fame, social utility, and poetic greatness in order to identify a pattern of growth and maturity that scholar-critics have hitherto overlooked.

In almost every paper the specialist's exceptional grasp of the context—the time and place, historical and intellectual, in which the creative artist worked—adds a dimension first to the facts relating to the particular writer and the works discussed and, ultimately, to the modern reader's appreciation of the author's achievement. And this growth in appreciation stretches beyond merely formalistic considerations to encompass the human dimension that relates the experience of the writer and his artistic shaping of that experience to the living concerns of the reader. If a poet "is a man speaking to men," then such humane examination of the mortal entanglements and struggles of the writers of the Romantic era should add to the resonance of their highly individual voices. If poetry is "the record of the best and happiest moments of the happiest and best minds," then the external history of these minds and these moments has an educative and humanizing function lower than, but akin to, the imaginative poetic records themselves.

As teachers of literature, one of our tasks is always to convince those who choose to study with us that the discipline we profess bears some significant relationship to the lives that both we and they lead.[4] If these students come to believe (however unjustly) that teachers of literature are either esthetes worshiping a précieuse formalism or savages rhetorically destroying one another in a world of egos red in tooth and claw, then they will see that we have nothing new to teach them. But if we can, not only through our writings but also through the attitudes embodied in our professional and private lives, show that great literature stretches and ennobles the commonplaces of our existence and provides us with momentary stays against confusion, then the study of literature will take its rightful place as the most "practical" of disciplines and the heights of these great arguments may come to be recognized as more important than the bottom line.

NOTES

1. The methods which the textual critic should use have been so fully, lucidly, and sanely set forth by G. Thomas Tanselle, in "The Editorial Problem of Final Authorial Intention," *Studies in Bibliography,* 29 (1976), 167-211, that anything I might say about them here would be inadequate.
2. This aspect of the scholar's function has been explored by E. D. Hirsch, Jr., first in his excellent essay on "Objective Interpretation," *PMLA,* 75 (1960), 463-479 and, in greater detail, in *Validity in Interpretation* (New Haven: Yale University Press, 1967). In *The Aims of Interpretation* (Chicago: University of Chicago Press, 1976), Hirsch carries the inquiry beyond "meaning" (or accurate knowledge) to "significance" (or value).
3. "Formalism, Savagery, and Care; or, The Function of Criticism Once Again," *Critical Inquiry,* 2 (1976), 605-630.
4. For a powerful indictment of the failure of college teachers of English to perform this essential duty, together with a description of the practical consequences of their failure, see Carl Woodring, "Beyond Formalism, Beyond Structuralism: Jobs" *ADE and ADFL Bulletins,* Special Joint Issue: "Employment and the Profession" (September 1976), 1-5.

Periodical Short Titles and Abbreviations

(Though most short reference titles are given by individual contributors within their notes, the following standard abbreviations are used in various papers.)

ELN:	*English Language Notes*
ELH:	*ELH: A Journal of English Literary History*
K-SJ:	*Keats-Shelley Journal*
MLQ:	*Modern Language Quarterly*
PMLA:	*PMLA: Publications of the Modern Language Association of America*
SIR:	*Studies in Romanticism*
TLS:	(London) *Times Literary Supplement*
WC:	*The Wordsworth Circle*

Blake and the Symbolism of the New Iron Age

Eileen Sanzo

One of the most frequently used sets of images in Blake's great prophetic books, and one of the most neglected in critical commentaries on the books, is that of Los's furnaces and forges, his hammer and anvil, his metallurgy. Certainly these images gripped Blake's imagination, for they appear with a compelling power, frequency, and intensity. The iron-making image connected with Los often appears in the text close to and in contraposition with an image of the weaving industry associated with his Emanation, Enitharmon. Los's furnaces of Bowlahoola and Enitharmon's looms of Cathedron are the foundry and factory of the new industrial age, mythicized by Blake and thus made heroic. In the industrial city of Golgonooza, "namd Art & Manufacture by mortal men,"[1] "Cathedrons Looms are builded. and Los's Furnaces."[2] In making Los, who is his hero and personal representative, "Lord of the Furnaces,"[3] a laborer in the new age of work, Blake dignifies the work of the common person in an age of industrial oppression and revolutionary struggle. It is through Bowlahoola and Cathedron that the archetypal city of Golgonooza will be built up, the imperfect city of the contemporary world, the raw material which is to be transformed through labor into the utopian city of the New Jerusalem. It is through "Mental Fight"[4] or labor "in brotherhood & Love"[5] that the iron gray London (and "the City of Golgonooza ... is the spiritual fourfold

London" [6]) will be turned into the golden Jerusalem; meanwhile the work struggle in this imperfect city goes on:

> Therefore Los stands in London building Golgonooza
> Compelling his Spectre to labours mighty
> (*J.* 10.17-18)

In reference to the Spectre, Blake means that Los compels all aspects of his divided self to work together and to the utmost:

> Yet ceasd he not from labouring at the roarings of his Forge
> With iron & brass Building Golgonooza in great contendings
> Till his Sons & Daughters came forth from the Furnaces
> At the Sublime Labours
> (*J.* 10.62-65)

The sons and daughters are the fruits of his labor, the first fruits of utopia.

Blake recognized that industrialism could be used to benefit man in providing the physical basis for utopia, but his ambition was for a future beneficial to all mankind, not for the aggrandizement of a greedy few, or for the prolongation of the tyranny of the rich in Britain. In the contemporary period, however, industrialism was but a system for an even greater oppression of the poor—and on a massive scale—because the new inventions were linked to the old, prevailing philosophy. It is well known that Blake was protesting the abuses of contemporary industrialism, but what is being noted here is that he chooses the industrial processes themselves as cultural symbols, and iron in particular, to represent the age.

Iron-making, for Blake, symbolizes the iron-heartedness and iron rigidity which sanctioned the exploitation of the poor in the factories and also on the battleground, for he believed that Britain's wars in the eighteenth and early nineteenth centuries were waged for economic empire. It was iron-making after all that supplied both the factory machinery and weapons. Representing this mythically, he draws a parallel between contemporary industrial Britain and the pride, power and ultimate ruin of ancient Egypt, which flourished upon slave labor just as "Albions Druid

Sons" practiced human sacrifice in another way in Blake's day. The image of brick-making, an industry of contemporary London as well as ancient Egypt, is first selected and then it is associated with iron-making:

> Minute Particulars in slavery I behold among the brick-kilns
> Disorganiz'd, & there is Pharoh in his iron Court:
> And the Dragon of the River & the Furnaces of iron.
> Outwoven from Thames & Tweed & Severn awful streams
> Twelve ridges of Stone frown over all the Earth in tyrant pride
> Frown over each River stupendous Works of Albions Druid Sons
>
> (*J.* 89.17-22)

Iron-making in eighteenth-century Britain was still dependent upon its rivers and streams,[7] and the Thames, Severn, and Tweed represent symbolically the tributaries that watered the Surrey Weald iron area, the Birmingham iron region, and the Stirling iron area. The assertive "tyrant pride" of the twelve ridges of stone that frown over all the earth could well represent both the pyramids and the new iron technology made possible by the stone blast furnaces. Thus the blast furnace is both a contemporary actuality and a powerful symbol of the age. It represented, at the same time, the work system, the iron factory "Wheels of Enitharmon," and the wars carried on with iron ordnance made in the foundry and factory. The working man and woman were thus forced to perpetuate their own slavery by their work:

> Loud sounds the Hammer of Los, loud turn the Wheels of Enitharmon
>
> . . . .
>
> . . . Los lifts his iron Ladles
> With molten ore: he heaves the iron cliffs in his rattling chains
> From Hyde Park to the alms-houses of Mile-end & old Bow
>
> (*M.* 6.27-31)

Los and Enitharmon represent men and women who worked as much as sixteen to eighteen hours a day at the factory and foundry at a time when there was as yet no labor legislation to protect them, lived in starvation, and worked amid the stench and the uproar of the machinery. If Los and Enitharmon were thrown out of work, their five-year-old child might have a job. If Los and Enitharmon were very fortunate, they would grow old, not like the multitude of London street beggars, but in "the Alms-houses of Mile-end & old Bow." [8]

In a sense the industrial age could be called a new iron age, for iron dominated the period. That is, at any rate, how Blake designates the age symbolically, for the iron image grips and compels his imagination, and in the prophetic books, furnaces, forges, pulleys and chains, hammers and anvils are poetically everywhere in London, the capital city of the industrial world, stretched across the city's own iron darkness:

> Loud sound the Hammer of Los, & loud his Bellows is heard
> Before London to Hampsteads breadths & Highgates heights To
> Stratford & old Bow: & across to the Gardens of Kensington
> On Tyburns Brook: loud groans Thames beneath the iron Forge
> Of Rintrah & Palamabron of Theotorm [on] & Bromion, to forge the instruments
> Of Harvest: the Plow & Harrow to pass over the Nations
> (*M.* 6.8-13)

The harvest will be the millennium, when the destitution of the period; the political oppression, symbolized by the reference to the hangings at Tyburn, the institutions, represented by the poor-houses at Stratford and old Bow, will be superseded by the work efforts toward social justice by Los and his sons symbolically laboring at the furnace and forge. Thus iron-making is a symbol with two faces: it can represent for Blake the oppression of the industrial age or it can represent the labors of man the maker guided by true utopian vision.

It is no coincidence that Blake, so sensitive to the contemporary world, chooses the images of iron and textile-making in a period when iron and textile products are Britain's chief exports. Iron is central to the period, for all the other industries and the new inventions depended upon it.[9] In the middle of the eighteenth century, 18,000 tons of iron were produced each year; in 1788, 68,000 tons a year. After that date the manufacture of iron soared to 125,400 tons of pig iron in 1796 and 250,000 tons in 1806.[10] Blake was aware of the dominance of iron in his age when he chose it as a major image and symbol. It would not be out of keeping for him to recognize similarities between his own age, a kind of new iron age, and an ancient period such as the first iron age.

Blake often drew parallels between his own times and ancient periods, such as the Egyptian, which, as we have seen, he associated with the iron age. The historical tradition concerning the wars and massacres of the ancient iron age was accessible to Blake in the eighteenth century. He knew, in particular, the work of the eighteenth-century mythagogue Jacob Bryant and may have engraved some of the plates for his volumes *New System, or an Analysis, of Ancient Mythology.*[11] Bryant writes that the golden age soon deteriorated through bloodletting and writes of the heroes of the iron age that they "are found to be continually engaged in wars and murders: and, like the specimens exhibited of the former Ages, these are finally cut off by one another's hands, in acts of robbery and violence: some for purloining oxen; others for stealing sheep; and many for carrying away the wives of their friends and neighbours." [12] The modern scholar Mircea Eliade writes that the historic tradition concerning the ancient iron age was that it was of all ages "the most tragic and most debased," a time characterized by an "uninterrupted succession of wars and massacres," by "mass slavery and by almost universal impoverishment." [13] There are many parallels with the new iron age, as depicted by Blake. Iron used by ancient tribes for plunder suggests the iron technology that fostered what Blake considered Britain's wars of empire of the eighteenth and nineteenth century. In fact, both the ancient iron age and the new iron age depended upon human sacrifice; the ancient iron age, upon ritual sacrifice; the new iron age, upon the bloodshed in the wars and also the expendability of the lives of the poor under industrialism. In the ancient world, tribes like the Assur laid down explicit rules for human sacrifice in the smelting process.[14] The primordial idea of creation out of nothing, an idea more appropriate to the mythical golden age than to the iron age, was displaced until we see a stage reached, according to Eliade, where "creation or fabrication will be inconceivable without previous sacrifice."[15] The new iron age, as depicted by Blake, also believed in the necessity for human sacrifice; it was in fact argued that factory owners could not pay a living wage or reduce working hours and still be competitive and it was maintained that Britain could not wield its power and empire without such sacrifice.

One instance of explicit human sacrifice in Blake occurs in *The Four Zoas* and is then repeated in *Jerusalem;* Luvah, representing revolutionary France ("For Luvah is France: the Victim of the Spectres of Albion"[16]), is burned with the ore in the blast furnace, like the victim during ancient smelting:

> Luvah was cast into the Furnaces of affliction & sealed
> And Vala fed in cruel delight, the furnaces with fire
> Stern Urizen beheld urg'd by necessity to keep
> The evil day afar, & if perchance with iron power
> He might avert his own despair; in woe & fear he saw
> Vala incircle round the furnaces where Luvah was clos'd
> (*F.Z.* 2. page 25, 40-44; page 26, 1)

The furnace in which Luvah was sacrificed was the contemporary industrial blast furnace, for the idea of unsealing it and letting the molten metal run into channels is peculiar to the blast furnace[17]:

> Then were the furnaces unseald with spades & pickaxes
> Roaring let out the fluid, with molten metal ran in channels
> (*F.Z.* 2. page 28, 7-8)

Urizen, watching as Luvah burns, represents Britain's ruling class witnessing the course of events in revolutionary and post-revolutionary France. He is intent on keeping the "evil day" of social revolution in Britain far off, hoping to avert it through "iron power," literally through iron weapons manufactured in his factories and foundries, where, as "great Work master,"[18] he exercises an iron rule over the workers. The "voice of Luvah," representing the suffering of the poor in England and France, cries out from "the furnaces of Urizen"[19]:

They have surrounded me with walls of iron & brass, O Lamb
Of God clothed in Luvahs garments
(*F.Z.* 2. page 27, 9-10)

The Lamb of God, Christ the victim, is identified in the present age with suffering industrial man.

Urizen, the "great Work master," is linked through eighteenth-century metallurgy to the wars in America and Europe:

Thus Urizen in self deceit his warlike preparations fabricated
And when all things were finishd sudden wavd among the Stars
His hurtling hand gave the dire signal thunderous Clarions blow
And all the hollow deep rebellowed with the wondrous War

But Urizen his mighty rage let loose in the mid deep
Sparkles of Dire affliction issud round his frozen limbs
Horrible hooks & nets he formd twisting the cords of iron
And brass & molten metals cast in hollow globes & bor'd
Tubes in petrific steel & rammd combustibles & wheels
And chains & pullies fabricated all round the heavens of Los

Judging from the present, the future of the new age of iron technology seems dark:

. . . All futurity
Seems teeming with Endless destruction never to be repelld
(*F.Z.* 8, page 101 first portion, 26-29;
page 100 second portion, 26-31;
page 101 second portion, 30-31;
The Poetry and Prose, p. 359)

Urizen seems often identified with iron. The very name Urizen seems to have, in addition to "your reason" and "horizon,"[20] the additional connotation of "iron." The sound patterns of iron and Urizen are close, and Blake, like Joyce, enjoyed multiple sound puns. Iron is often associated with unyielding tyranny in Blake's work. Urizen, with his "awful Law," [21] was like "Jupiter of the Greeks, an iron-hearted tyrant." [22] Urizen writes with "his iron pen" [23] in "books of iron and brass," [24] the Bible and all law rigidly interpreted. Possibly they are also the commercial account books of the "great Work master"? In *The Book of Urizen,* iron chains bind Urizen, who is himself the agent of mental and physical constriction.

However, not only Urizen, but his enemy Los, "Lord of the Furnaces," is associated with iron and Los is a sympathetic personality, the builder of Golgonooza and thus Jerusalem through his iron-making. Just as the ancient iron age made advanced agricultural implements possible, it seems that the industrial age, which oppresses man, possesses the potentiality, according to Blake, of blessing man. What is lacking in man's use of industrial power, what is needed if it is to be used to build Jerusalem, is the shaping vision of "Brotherhood." [25] Industrialism must be used for man and not against him. Thus the iron-hearted Urizen must be converted to the persuasion of the golden Los (Sol). It is indeed a kind of alchemy, and the new iron age must be transformed once more to the mythical golden age. Blake combined the classical myth of the ancient age of gold with the Judeo-Christian symbolism of the recovery of Eden in the new Jerusalem, the golden city with "golden arches" [26] and "pillars of gold," [27] built by "golden Builders." [28] The ancients treasured gold because it represented the sun, which, Blake read in Bryant's account of mythology, was the universal and primordial deity of early man. Los, the sun, was traditionally associated in English poetry with the Christian Son, who was for Blake the "Universal Man," [29] humanity united in "brotherhood & Love." [30] Iron Urizen, the ruling class and tyrannous individual Reason, must be united, identified with Los, Sol, the Son, the Universal Man, humanity united in brotherhood. Thus at the end of *Jerusalem,* in the attainment of utopia, iron Urizen is linked with the south, the sun and gold; while golden Los, under his alternate name of Urthona,[31] is linked with the north, formerly the land of snow and hail and stony, frozen Urizen, and now a place of industrial dynamism:

. . . bright beaming Urizen
Layd his hand on the South & took a breathing Bow of carved Gold

. . . .

Urthona Northward in thick storms a Bow of Iron terrible thundering.
(*J.* 97.7-11)

Thus opposites are reconciled in the unity of the one Universal Man. There is to be for industrial man a personal and social alchemy, symbolized by the fusion of the Zoas, Los and Urizen, a fusion represented by Blake, not by the medieval alchemical furnace, but rather in the industrial blast furnace, the "Furnaces of affliction." [32] Industrial discovery and power can be used for man to achieve utopia and thus the new iron age can be alchemized into the new golden age, the iron-dark city of the contemporary world into golden Jerusalem.

In *The Book of Urizen,* Urizen is "hiding in surgeing/ Sulphureous fluid his phantasies," [33] while Los is struggling with him throughout the book. Sulfur was one of the chief elements used in alchemy; Eliade writes that there was a "belief, widespread in the Middle Ages, that ores are generated by the union of two principles, sulphur and mercury," [34] and that sulfur is mentioned hundreds of times in the pages of Greek alchemists.[35] Blake knew the alchemical tradition through reading Paracelsus and Boehme. In Plate 12 of *The Book of Urizen,* we see the figure of Urizen immersed in the "Sulphureous fluid," while one print of this plate, according to David Erdman, reads, "I labour upwards into futurity." [36] Blake sees the industrial iron age so laboring to emerge, through the furnaces of affliction, into the new golden age of love and brotherhood.

NOTES

1. *Milton,* Plate 24, l. 50, *The Poetry and Prose of William Blake,* ed. David Erdman (Garden City, N.Y.: Doubleday and Co., 1970), p. 119. Unless otherwise indicated, all subsequent references are to this edition. Citations to the engraved books *(Milton, Jerusalem, Urizen,*

etc.) are by plate and line numbers. Citations to *The Four Zoas* are by "Night," page of the manuscript (as given in Erdman's text), and line.

2. *Jerusalem* 59.23. (Hereafter cited as *J.*)
3. *J.* 8.26.
4. *Milton* 1. "And did those feet," 13. (Hereafter cited as *M.*)
5. *The Four Zoas* Night 8, page 103, 9. (Hereafter cited as *F.Z.*)
6. *M.* 20.39-40.
7. The Carron Company in Stirlingshire "specialized . . . above all, in ordnance and other war materials. Their great guns, . . . 'were cast solid, and bored by a drill worked by the whole force of the River Carron.'" F.C. Dietz, *An Economic History of England* (New York: H. Holt, 1942), p. 341.
8. Along Mile-end Road, approaching Bow Road, there were three almshouses, each holding approximately ten men living on a daily pittance. Henry Wheatley, *London Past and Present* (London: J. Murray, 1891), II, 542.
9. Frederick Austin Ogg, *Economic Development of Modern Europe* (New York: Macmillan, 1918), p. 137.
10. H. de B. Gibbins, *Industry in England,* 11th ed. (New York: Scribner's, 1925), pp. 353-354; and T.S. Ashton, *Iron and Steel in the Industrial Revolution* (1924; rpt. New York: A.M. Kelley, 1968), p. 95.
11. S. Foster Damon, *A Blake Dictionary* (New York: E.P. Dutton, 1971), p. 61.
12. *New System, or an Analysis, of Ancient Mythology* (London, 1774-1776), III, 168-169.
13. Mircea Eliade, *The Forge and the Crucible,* trans. Stephen Corrin (New York: Harper and Row, 1971), p. 67.
14. Ibid.
15. Ibid., p. 31.
16. *J.* 66.15.
17. Walter Gale, *The British Iron and Steel Industry: A Technical History* (Newton Abbot, Devon.: David and Charles, 1967), p. 23.
18. *F.Z.* 2, page 24, 5.
19. *F.Z.* 2, page 26, 4.
20. Damon, p. 419.
21. *F.Z.* 1, page 12, 17.
22. Letter "To: William Hayley," 23 October 1804, *The Poetry and Prose,* p. 702.
23. *F.Z.* 6, page 71 (second portion), 35.
24. *F.Z.* 6, page 70 (first portion), 3.
25. *J.* 96.28.
26. *J.* 27, "The fields from Islington," 11.
27. Ibid., 10.
28. Ibid., 25.
29. *F.Z.* 1, page 3, 6.

30. *F.Z.* 8, page 103, 9.
31. Los is called frequently the Spectre, or other self, of Urthona.
32. *F.Z.* 2, page 25, 40.
33. *The Book of Urizen* 10.13-14.
34. Eliade, p. 48.
35. Ibid., p. 147.
36. *The Illuminated Blake,* annotated by David Erdman (Garden City, N.Y.: Doubleday, 1974), p. 194.

Wordsworth as Heartsworth; or, Was Regicide the Prophetic Ground of Those "Moral Questions"?

David V. Erdman

In recent decades Wordsworth scholarship has gained immensely in sophistication and in altitude but seems somewhat to have lost political if not historical focus.[1] The greatly increased precision of text, the extensive scrutiny of biographical detail, and the judicious estimation of Wordsworth's life, thought, and works have all but transformed our understanding of his poetry. Yet in the fitting of his life into his times there has not been commensurate advance. George McLean Harper, in areas where his factual information has not proved faulty, still affords the soundest full-length portrait of Wordsworth as an Englishman politically inspired, oriented, and buffeted. Important correctives have been supplied by Carl Woodring in his book on Coleridge's politics and in his chapter on Wordsworth's; and by E. P. Thompson in his Schweitzer Lecture of 1969, "Disenchantment or Default? A Lay Sermon," dealing with the flight to Germany of 1798 and restoring the contemporary quality of two spots of time in 1797 and 1798. Recently Paul Sheats has brought the early and politically crucial poetry (and life) into the open air of common day, free of upmanship and fashionable mystique.[2]

More particularly for the period of our concern, the poet's residence in France, Rudolf Storch is investigating the transformations in Wordsworth's life and poetry energized by the French Revolution and its sequelae and has already published an analyis of *The Borderers* as "a document of the mental revolution" described in Book X of *The Prelude.* Mark Reed's *Chronology of the Early Years* has codified the biographical and some of the historical particulars required to give precision to such documenting.[3]

What I wish to do here is to put Wordsworth's drama of 1796-1797, *The Borderers,* beside Books IX and X of *The Prelude* (of 1805)—both entitled "Residence in France"—in an attempt to bring some specificity into our reading of the *Prelude* account and to bring down from the clouds of abstraction the debate over the politics of *The Borderers,* which has too often raged inconclusively over definitions of Godwinism.[4] In Book X (829ff.) Wordsworth quietly draws upon his unpublished drama, using the words of its villain, Oswald,[5] to define one extreme of revolutionary "Philosophy," the idea of building "social freedom" exclusively by "One guide, the light of circumstances, flash'd / Upon an independent intellect." Wordsworth goes on to describe the ways in which the "shock" given to ancient institutions and old opinions by the revolution in France had been felt by "the minds of all men" so that his own mind had been "both let loose, / Let loose and goaded" (861-864). Having, as he believed, the temperamental balance of a nature both joyful and melancholy yet withal happy, Wordsworth had enough self-confidence to probe boldly "the living body of society / Even to the heart." "I took the knife in hand," he writes; "I push'd without remorse / My speculations forward; yea, set foot / On Nature's holiest places." And he offers someday to write a "dramatic Story" the lively "Shapes" of which will convey

> What then I learn'd, or think I learn'd, of truth!
> And the errors into which I was betray'd
> By present objects, and by reasonings false
> From the beginning, inasmuch as drawn
> Out of a heart which had been turn'd aside
> From Nature by external accidents,
> And which was thus confounded more and more,
> Misguiding and misguided.
>
> (X.882-889)

Wordsworth had, of course, already written *The Borderers,* a drama in which the actions and dramatis personae (story and shapes) convey the truth and errors of a moment of history chosen as analogous to the interregnum which the poet witnessed in France in 1792 (and perhaps 1793).[6] The hero, named Marmaduke in the final version, represents the "I" of the passage quoted, "an amiable young man" (according to the play's Preface: *PW,* I, 345-349) betrayed by misconstruing "present objects" and by the false reasonings of the villain Oswald (whom Wordsworth compares to Iago), whose role it is to make attractive the reasonings which appear to justify killing in the name of revolutionary justice but which can be shown by the dramatist to be false from the beginning.

From the first scene onward Oswald is presented as a willful liar as well as a schemer who falsifies evidence and suborns witnesses. This is a dramatic way of showing up false reasoning—not by presenting a bona fide political philosopher (Godwin or anyone else) but by exposing the reasoner as criminal, or diabolic.[7] Patently, Oswald represents a strong outside influence on the Wordsworth of 1792. But in *The Prelude* the poet represents himself as having been both the misguider and the misguided, i.e. both Oswald and Marmaduke, and in his Preface to the drama he gives primary attention to the psychology of the villain in a process that may be understood as what Blake called the annihilation of the Selfhood, both recognition and rejection of the satanic in oneself, "the errors into which I was betray'd." In the context of the *Prelude* passage just quoted, Wordsworth is saying that his own heart had been turned aside from Nature in the sense that he had been led into the unnatural position (for an Englishman) of sympathizing with France, his country's natural (traditional) enemy and, after the war broke out in early 1793, of unnaturally praying for and rejoicing in the anticipated defeat of his own country.

In the drama and its Preface the external accidents that turned aside Wordsworth as Oswald are identified as betrayal "into a great crime" (Oswald, "deceived" and "betrayed" by the crew of his naval transport, had marooned an "innocent" man, his Captain, on a desert island) by the "spirit of enterprise in a tumultuous age." The Preface mentions lack of "solid principles of genuine benevolence" as the flaw in his character. In the drama the specifics indicate a parallel to justifying regicide or parricide: Oswald had been tricked into taking the initiative in the marooning, misled into believing the captain guilty of besmirching his honor; but the crew's wish to be rid of "a tyrannic Master" whom "all hated" was genuine enough: the crime was their conspiracy to kill him, "at any cost" (IV.1689-1760). Wordsworth as Marmaduke, the amiable young man, is betrayed by similar "external accidents" plus the love of a loving woman, his difference from Oswald being the possession of a benevolent heart, source of his weakness but potential salvation.

In *The Prelude* the accidents which turn Wordsworth's heart aside from Nature—a turning which precedes and opens him to the false reasoning—may be identified as his residing in France, his listening to the humanitarian comments on the war against poverty of that fine warrior Michel Beaupuy (and of others less fine, presumably, the Oswald type), and—we come now to what was central, for the poet himself, to the whole business—his falling in love with and taking to his bosom a French woman with beautiful eyes, Annette Vallon. Wordsworth hints at the intimate and inseparable connections between his French love and his French politics not only in *The Borderers* but also in the story of Vaudracour and Julia that he inserted into *The Prelude,* Book IX, just at the point where he ought to be telling of his love of Annette, which he chose to keep from public view. A later analogue is the Solitary's story in *The Excursion.* In the first two of these three tales the hero is drawn by love to murder: Vaudracour (a punning self-definition as Heartsworth: il vaut du coeur) slays one of his tyrannous father's myrmidons; Marmaduke decides upon, fecklessly attempts, and then accidentally achieves the murder of the baron Herbert, the father of his beloved Idonea. In the Solitary's story, pure accident of disease kills his *two* infants and beautiful wife in quick succession, though before that catastrophe the Solitary's story is the happiest extensive "shape" given to the Annette and Caroline story, being written at the furthest remove from it and freest of guilt. (That two of these tales may have been "true stories" of other people has little to do with Wordsworth's use of them as emblems of his own experience.) [8]

The parallels in the "Vaudracour and Julia" story [9] are clear if we posit that Julia's father's house equals France, that her lover's father's house equals England. "Vaudracour . . . hie[d]/Back to his Father's house . . . to obtain a sum of gold" (IX.646-648) means Wordsworth went back to England (in December 1792, just before his daughter Caroline was born) to raise money. Violence (compare the outbreak of hostilities between England and France in January) for which Vaudracour shares the guilt of a "Murderer" (killing a man to be with Julia, but landing in jail instead) then forces him to stay "Quietly in his Father's House" (698) "nor take/One step to reunite himself with her"—i.e., Wordsworth is compelled to stay in England, away from Annette, before the birth of Caroline.[10] *Yet* Vaudracour sneaks back to his love's house for a happy but precarious and hazardous meeting with mother and child, which I take as confirmative evidence for the inference that Wordsworth paid a clandestine visit to France in October 1793, after the war was in motion.[11]

The Vaudracour story, as analogue, must be partly fantasy, for Vaudracour is present at his child's birth and even manages a two months' visit; but what Wordsworth needed was a vehicle for the essential relationship and predicament of his story, not a point-for-point duplication of it. In the Marmaduke-Idonea analogue, we shall see, no infant is born or even conceived, and yet the poet parallels the essentials—even the infant—symbolically. Some years ago George Meyer observed of the hero of *The Borderers* that "Marmaduke's innocence is less dubious than Othello's, and his crime is [superficially] not so great," and then asked, "What is there . . . that hinders Marmaduke from continuing his active, benevolent life as a guardian of the poor and innocent . . . ? Why . . . does Marmaduke not compensate the affectionate and faithful Idonea for the loss of her father by marrying her and endeavouring to make felicitous the remaining years of her life?" [12] Marmaduke, though he originally willed the death of her father as an act of revolutionary justice, had not, finally, meant to let him die on the heath; it was only that he walked off absent-mindedly with Baron Herbert's knapsack of food and water (thereby repeating, if without sustained malice, Oswald's marooning of his captain on a barren rock).[13] What fatally estranges the lovers is Idonea's recognition of her father's knapsack hanging on Marmaduke's shoulder. The playwright could have managed affairs differently, to a different conclusion. But to answer Meyer's question bluntly,

Marmaduke cannot have Idonea (or Vaudracour, Julia, and their daughter) because William could not have Annette and their daughter Caroline.

Further, the reason Marmaduke cannot continue his active life may lie in the psychology impelling Wordsworth to choose to become a recluse after September 1795, if not sooner. In *The Recluse* as finally written, Wordsworth explains that he is putting aside his hope to write heroic poetry and—he puts this first—his other hope, a "forwardness of soul which looks" toward "the Warrior's Schemes" in "the Cause / Of Liberty endangered." It is not very clear what schemes Wordsworth entertained in the line of fighting for Liberty, but Marmaduke's actions on this level are fairly explicit. Idonea's father is a dispossessed baron. (Annette's family were royalists [14] and her "father," the King of France, was dispossessed.) Marmaduke's active republicanism is what sets him against his beloved's father. (Wordsworth's set him against Annette's royal father, and probably against her actual father.) Thus the debate over the justice and necessity of the dethronement, trial, and execution of Louis XVI is recapitulated in the central moral conflict in *The Borderers.* Most of the arguments between villainous Oswald and gullible Marmaduke concern the justification of the trial and execution of Baron Herbert, Idonea's father; they could be source-hunted in the arguments for the trial and execution of Louis, central topic of public—and private—debate during the whole of Wordsworth's residence in Paris in 1792.[15] King Louis had been dethroned (dispossessed) in August, while Wordsworth was with Annette; his rule had been replaced by a Republic in late September (Wordsworth, joyous about this event in *The Prelude,* is presumed to have attended the celebration at Orleans on 21 September); the King was called to trial by the new Convention, after demonstrations by the Paris Commune on 19 October, not long before Wordsworth arrived in Paris; and his trial was continuing, in mounting tension, when Wordsworth left for London in late November or December.[16] The misgivings of Marmaduke are all the misgivings of the true heart, the true nature, the man with a *soul.*

The gothic settings and agonized tones of the "trial" of Baron Herbert, however, suggest a correspondence with the time of Wordsworth's later visit to France (contemplated or actual) during the Terror of 1793, which is described in *The Prelude* as personally traumatic (though ostensibly witnessed only from across the English Channel, since *The Prelude* does not mention a later visit to France).[17]

> Through months, through years, long after the last beat
> Of those atrocities [of 1793-94] . . .
>
> I scarcely had one night of quiet sleep
> Such ghastly visions had I of despair
> And tyranny, and implements of death [the lanterne, the guillotine],
> And long orations which in dreams I pleaded
> Before unjust Tribunals, with a voice
> Labouring, a brain confounded, and a sense
> Of treachery and desertion in the place
> The holiest that I know of, my own soul.
> (X.371-381)

Just as something in the poet's soul tells him this is all against nature, something in Marmaduke's soul tells him (cf. II.776-786) that he is doing an atrocious thing. In the play he takes an unconvincingly long time to be convinced by his soul, against the reasoning and the challenges of Oswald and his own mind. The invented plot is not big enough to hold the real one and all its "long orations which in dreams I pleaded." But (as Storch says) it *feels* right.[18]

I am a benevolent man, says Wordsworth in the persona of Marmaduke, and yet look what treachery and desertion of humanity my humane actions and principles have carried me to! "Never once / Had I thought ill of human kind, or been / Indifferent to its welfare," says Wordsworth in the persona of the Poet of *The Prelude* (X.831-833); yet I swallowed all this in the name of Liberty!

In *The Prelude* he attributes the first tremendous "subversion" of his "moral nature" (X.234-235) not to the experiences of 1792 but to the war which his own country launched against the new Republic (in response to the guillotining of Louis in January 1793).[19] "And now the strength of Britain was put forth / In league with the confederated Host . . ." (230-231). He had not anticipated the effect of this "shock." Although aware that his "native Rulers" looked "upon regenerated France" with "ungracious eyes," he had never "foretasted the event" (234, 243-245, 249). The poet of the love story knows that Vaudracour's aristocratic "father" is a cruel tyrant but insists that Vaudracour himself, even after he has slain one of the armed men, "instruments of ruffian power" sent by his father to seize him, has "never once" entertained an unfilial or unkind thought (IX.712-716). In the 1820 revision, we are asked to believe that even after his act of deadly wrath against his father's henchmen (soldiers? recruiting officers?) "no sense / Of hasty anger rising in the eclipse / Of true domestic loyalty, did e'er / Find place within his bosom." The "persevering wedge of tyranny" separates the lovers, but (in both versions) Vaudracour rebukes Julia for coupling "with his Father's name some words / Of vehement indignation." [20]

The extravagance of the protest emphasizes the force of the shock and the extravagance of the recoil. The minds of "ingenuous Youth" were quite released, by the "ravage of this most unnatural strife" (251), from obedience to habit, custom, law. It was a time

> In which apostacy from ancient faith
> Seem'd but conversion to a higher creed,

—the creed which Oswald urges the ingenuous Marmaduke to act upon—

> A time in which Experience would have pluck'd
> Flowers out of any hedge to make thereof
> A Chaplet in contempt of his grey locks
> (X.284-290)

—not appreciating how fine a chaplet grey locks *are.*

In *The Borderers* the error, symptomatic of an interregnum which the villain and hero share, is a contempt for the grey locks of Experience. In this sense grey-headed father Herbert is Custom, Law, Ancient Faith, the Constitution (in Burke's sense): and only in this wide sense is the king significant to Wordsworth. His expressed feeling about the execution of King Louis amounts to sorrow that the evil and guilty tyrant from whom the French liberated themselves happened to have been a human being. (That, in the "Letter to the Bishop of Llandaff," written soon after the event—and before his French experience of October 1793 and its nightmare tribunals which cast doubt backward upon the "senseless" wisdom of the guillotine.[21])

At one point Marmaduke is shown as giddy with his "higher creed," and the playwright lets his words symbolically expose his regicidal thoughts. Marmaduke starts to argue that a King or General is nothing different from the "carcasses" he strews the meadow with; but he then collapses into wondering whether a king slaughtering multitudes—and an idler who sits in the sun and "floats kingcups in the brook" (symbolically flings off the heads of kings, i.e. by theoretical justification of regicide) are not "both fools, or wise alike, / Each in his way?" (III.1228-1239).

Some critics write as though *The Borderers* represented a struggle going on in the poet's mind while he wrote it. But the text hardly supports such a reading. Wordsworth as the author of this play has a firm grip on moral questions—however much he may have reopened and reformulated them later. The social framework of the plot, the signaled moral assumptions of the speeches and the action, all imply an end to social experiment. The self-governing band of defenders of the people during a hiatus of royal power, once they have shaken off the ruthless Oswald and his victim Marmaduke, are not about to establish a truly free commonwealth. Rather, everyone but Oswald is happy to learn that good King Henry is restoring barons (especially father Herbert) to rightful ownership of the land; that good old English law and religion are to be restored, after this troubled "interregnum."[22] Marmaduke seems to lack the momentum of confidence in any future for the troops or for himself; all he manages at the end is to dissociate himself from—not to prevent—further bloodshed, as we shall see.

Wordsworth himself must only temporarily have reached such a collapse of morale before he found the strength to write this play. We are told in *The Prelude* that, after the sensational news of August 1794 that *"Robespierre was dead"* (a moment corresponding to the fall of Oswald in the play), Wordsworth had hopes that "the young Republic" would irresistibly succeed and that a spirit of "unambiguous peace at home" (in France, hence also in England) would triumph (X.542 ff.; 583-592). By the time he began writing *The Borderers,* having come out of his dejection of the early months of 1796, he was ready with unmistakable moral answers. His struggle over good and evil, bodied forth in the play, is presented as a warning example against presumptuous (and futile) killing in the guise of revolutionary action.

It is not in his flawed debate with Oswald, but in sober conversation with his faithful comrade in arms that Marmaduke observes:

> Lacy! we look
> But at the surfaces of things; we hear
> Of towns in flames, fields ravaged, young and old
> Driven out in troops to want and nakedness;
> Then grasp our swords and rush upon a cure
> That flatters us, because it asks not thought.
> (II.1029-1034) [23]

In the next Act it is Oswald who expresses the contextless afterthought:

> Action is transitory—a step, a blow,
> The motion of a muscle ....
> Suffering is permanent, obscure and dark ....

This is "Truth," Marmaduke knows, because "I feel it" (III.1539-1545).

The contrary "truths" of Jacobinical levelling and of "justice" that combine the functions of judge, jury, and executioner in one person, the leader of the band, are all shown us on the stage to be false. And when, in the last Act, Marmaduke cracks up (as signified by an echo of Orestes and the flies: "Buzz, buzz, ye black and winged freebooters" (V.1992), he is revealing the moral perspective which had been that of Idonea's father all along. The play should be staged—by any company so bold—with much striding about and grasping and rattling of swords (in the beginning) by these defenders of the victims of want and nakedness.

The rank and file of the revolutionary band are good honest folk, and Marmaduke as their Leader, before his corruption by Oswald, was as the Preface tells us "an amiable young man." But we see the Leader flattered, by the manifest villain, into thinking his judgment is sound. It is Oswald who defines the Band as one which "you've collected for the noblest ends . . . / To guard the Innocent." But when we hear the troops, without their leader, preparing impatiently to "strip the Scottish Foray / Of their rich Spoil, ere they recross the Border" (I.2-3), we may be troubled at the language. The "rich Spoil" they are after (to recover it for the Innocent English) sounds less like bread seized from the poor than like the loot of rich estates or shops. From the dispossessed Herbert's point of view, which we are ultimately invited to accept, Marmaduke the Freebooter "Doth prey alike upon two distracted Countries, / Traitor to both" (I.209-210). For Wordsworth and his audience the two countries were, of course, England and France. All Marmaduke's evidence as to the sins and evil intentions of Baron Herbert (and of the sinister character of "that cold voluptuary . . . [Lord] Clifford," to whose lust Herbert is allegedly betraying the virgin Idonea, Marmaduke's intended) is hearsay evidence, supplied by Oswald or by wretches whom he has suborned, or by his forgery.[24] Oswald gives Marmaduke another earful every time he weakens.

Let us go back in imagination to the days in 1792 when Wordsworth was getting instruction from officer Beaupuy about the ravaged victims of tyranny: "'Tis against *that* / Which we are fighting" (IX.518-519). The victims were real, not stage-managed. But the consequence was to arouse the poet's sympathies and commitment to the cause. And then he fell in love and quite lost his tourist status. But only in a sinister transposition does Oswald take the place of Michel Beaupuy. The tragedy is far advanced. Wordsworth has now moved on to Paris, so to speak, and come under the spell of a more ruthless spokesman, possibly Robespierre but more probably a composite suggested by some of his Jacobin admirers. There was an actual "Colonel" John Oswald, who seems to have known people in practically any of the radical groups Wordsworth is likely to have entered, from those around Tom Paine and Brissot to the journalists Carra and Gorsas to the

Girondists turned Montagnard in 1793—but there is matter enough about John Oswald for another essay; it need be said here only that the leadership role of Wordsworth's Oswald makes him a kind of Robespierre (as Robespierre is defined in *The Prelude*).[25]

When Marmaduke and Oswald come right down to the trial and execution of "the arch-impostor," the latter's term for Baron Herbert, Marmaduke is inspired by Oswald to depart from the troop's usual practice of assembling the whole "Camp" as a revolutionary tribunal. Temporarily under the good influence of honest lieutenant Lacy, Marmaduke is able to imagine a tribunal of citizens gathered from the "Country round" ("*here* . . . Men alone are Umpires" and "Reason" can use her eyes) (II.1118-1122). But even while putting this grandly—"He shall be brought / Before the Camp, and would that [the] best and wisest / Of every country might be present" (II.1125-1127)—Marmaduke betrays the democratic ideal.

In the first place, his *wish* that the best and wisest might be present is an admission that they will not be. Secondly, he speaks not of judging or trial but only of execution. "There / His crime shall be proclaimed" (1128). Marmaduke's own individual judgment (with Oswald at his elbow) has already sentenced the baron to death. The multitude are to take the guilt as proved: "and for the rest / It shall be done as Wisdom shall decide." Presumably the best and wisest would have been in on the sentencing, not the finding of guilt. Yet here we are also shown Marmaduke's better, if weaker, impulse: he is not quite sure that the crime deserves death; or rather, he only weakly resists taking the role of executioner. Indeed his "weakness" is his potential salvation (and Herbert's). Like Hamlet unable to slay the King at his prayers, Marmaduke is unable to "lift the avenging steel" at the sight of Herbert's face. (This is their first meeting; he discovers that the face is human, that it even looks like the face of his beloved!)

> . . . it put me to my prayers,
> Upwards I cast my eyes, and, through a crevice,

—the scene calls for a dungeon within a ruined castle—

Beheld a star twinkling above my head,
And, by the living God, I could not do it. *(Sinks exhausted.)*
(II.987-990)

The weakness in good Marmaduke is essentially his inexperience of villains—and the effect of the general absence of law and order. In the last act we are pretty well prepared (as a good English audience) to recognize that the freebooters are not revolutionaries except by accident. The end of the interregnum means all is well again in England: Idonea expects her beloved Marmaduke to marry her and help her father dispense benevolence to the people.

My Father soon
Shall sun himself before his native doors;
The lame, the hungry, will be welcome there.
(III.1627-1629)

Even when she learns of Herbert's death, we wish the playwright would let them embrace, and he does what he can. At the very end it is Marmaduke who commends his former comrades to protect "the Lady" who has, from the fact that she was brought up in poverty, become "worthier of that noble birth, / Whose long-suspended rights are now on the eve / Of restoration" (V.2301-2305). His "tragedy" is that he is deranged by his derangement, a misfit like the Ancient Mariner.

As Marmaduke finally catches up with the audience (and his troop) in recognizing the villainy of Oswald, he finds himself incapable of any decisive action but retirement. "There are men / Who with bare hands would have plucked out thy heart / And flung it to the dogs," he says to Oswald, but having drawn him "towards the Cottage," he stops short at the door (V.2260). Thus he stops short of haling his evil counselor, in turn, to a tribunal of the people. "But I forgive thee," reads the first draft; the final draft is closer to the "yielding up" of 1796: "but I am raised / Above, or sunk below, all further sense / Of provocation." The Band do, nevertheless, "rush upon Oswald and seize him." That Marmaduke is not sunk but raised, in some degree, he indicates by declaring this "A rash deed!" and resigning his command.

Nevertheless, in leading Oswald to the cottage door he has, in effect, flung him "to the dogs," repeating the earlier inadvertent starving of Herbert on the heath. Retrospectively, Wordsworth's spectator role and departure during the trial of King Louis and his willing but leaving to others the assassination of Robespierre are matched in the successive relations of irresponsible responsibility to these two deaths: "Suffering is permanent, obscure and dark."

Long before Marmaduke understands what he is doing, he has helped the audience to do so. In Act I, with allusions to King Lear lucid in madness, he points to the female beggar who has told him what we know are lies about abandonment by her father, and cries out: "Come hither, Fathers, / And learn what nature is from this poor Wretch!" (443-444). The dramatic irony is that he understands the duty of a father toward a child better, in this false situation, than he has been able to recognize his own duty toward Father Herbert, as child or son-in-law to be. In a moment, in a flash, but sotto voce, he recognizes the sanctity of Fatherhood, hedged by as much divinity as a King:

> Mar. (to himself): Father!—to God himself we cannot give
> A holier name; and, under such a mask . . . .

—i.e., to find a pander such as he thinks Herbert to be, acting under the mask of Father to destroy the innocent, gives him a sense of basic disturbance:

> Oswald, the firm foundation of my life
> Is going from under me; these strange discoveries
> Looked at from every point of fear or hope,
> Duty or love—involve, I feel, my ruin.
> (I.543-550)

Compare the "unnatural strife / In my own heart" (X.251) felt by Wordsworth when the land of his fathers warred against France, producing a sense of treachery in his soul which, looked at from every point of fear or hope, led to his (temporary) ruin or despair. Consider the passage in which he speaks of pushing "without remorse" his speculations into "Nature's holiest Places" (X.877):

Thus I fared
Dragging all passions, notions, shapes of faith,
Like culprits to the bar, suspiciously
Calling the mind to establish in plain day
Her titles and her honours, now believing,
Now disbelieving,

—like Marmaduke dragging one suspected imposter about, then another—

endlessly perplex'd
With impulse, motive, right and wrong, the ground
Of moral obligation ...

(Here he is looking from every point, and the rest of the passage hardly needs remarking upon as parallel to Marmaduke's perplexity, despair, and remorseful retirement):

... what the rule
And what the sanction, till, demanding *proof*
And seeking it in everything, I lost
All feeling of conviction, and, in fine,
Sick, wearied out with contrarieties,
Yielded up moral questions in despair. ...

"The proofs," cries Marmaduke to Oswald, about the plot that trapped *him* into marooning an innocent, "you ought to have seen / The guilt—have touched it—felt it at your heart—/As I have done" (IV.1769-1771). But Marmaduke's failure to recognize a Father had led to the erosion of his whole system of values.

In Act II Oswald exclaims, when apprehended by the honest Wallace, "That subtle Grey-beard—/ I'd rather see my father's ghost" (1018-1019). And the play could end here, for the news is that King Henry has "Dissolved the Baron's League" and is sending sheriffs "to reinstate / The genuine owners of [seized] Lands and Baronies." Marmaduke almost instructs his troops, who are ready with their swords, *not* to grasp them "and rush upon a cure." Instead he concludes with an ironic enigma which only the attentive audience will comprehend, for Marmaduke fails to grasp his own words' meaning:

> The deeper malady is better hid;
> The world is poisoned at the heart.
> (II.1033-1036)

The troop, at least, understand him to mean Herbert's false heart, and in the sinister presence of Oswald they vie with one another in "manful" resolution: "Hew him down, / And fling him to the ravens," says simple Lacy. "Are we Men, Or own we baby Spirits?" [26] taunts Oswald. Yet the right conclusion, *we* know, is that the cure does lie in the goodness in every man's heart, a goodness in which we must have ancient faith. The utterance reveals the depth of Wordsworth's perplexity as it was when he was Marmaduke. And the same irony is expressed in Act IV: "We all are of one blood, our veins are filled / At the same poisonous fountain!" We know, what he should know, that the very opposite is the truth about our one blood. After Herbert's death, Marmaduke, unhinged, speaks truly:

> He is at peace;
> His body is at rest; there was a plot,
> A hideous plot, against the soul of man:
> It took effect—and yet I baffled it,
> In some degree.

The revolutionary condemnation of Baron Herbert, based on faulty perception and false evidence, was a plot to destroy Ancient Faith, which Marmaduke baffled to the degree that he withdrew his conscious will from the act of execution. He also baffled "in some degree" the consequences in his own soul when, after judging the false Oswald rightly, he refused to lift his own sword. Yet Herbert and Oswald were both killed, and Marmaduke was indelibly implicated. The counterparts of Herbert and Oswald in the historical arena, King Louis and perhaps Robespierre, died in similar ways, by revolutionary condemnation and by the stabs of fellow revolutionaries, respectively. But whereas the arguments for regicide occupy most of the discussion in *The Borderers,* while the reasons for killing Oswald are made so manifest that their expression takes few words, in *The Prelude* the regicide, which filled the air of Paris during Wordsworth's stay in 1792, is scarcely mentioned while the reasons to justify the assassination of a revolutionist turned tyrant fill much of Book X. But we are getting ahead of the story.

A reader attentive to the many signals identifying Oswald as a Robespierre that run through the play will recognize in the final stabbing of the calculating alienator a parallel to the fall of the real Robespierre, the news of which filled Wordsworth with immense relief in 1794. At the distance of *The Prelude* of 1805, the poet could not sustain Marmaduke's ennobling disapproval of someone else's "rash act." This act was one of justified revenge, he felt—or more exactly had felt in 1794, with an emotion rekindled as he wrote. "Great was my glee of spirit," he confesses, "great my joy / In vengeance, and eternal justice, thus / Made manifest" (X.540-542). Furthermore, in *The Prelude* he permits himself to hint darkly (but without disapproval) at having, when he was in France, considered assassinating or assisting the assassination of the man he called "chief Regent" of the Jacobin "Tribe of Moloch" (X.469-470). He had been willing to sacrifice himself "for cause so great" (136), and he "called to mind" the school debates justifying the great assassins of "tyrannic Power," Brutus and Harmodius (the latter an unsuccessful hero) (159-168). Such were the "Warrior's Schemes" mentioned in *The Recluse,* there defined as incited by "the Cause of Liberty endangered" (748).[27]

These hints, it must be noted, are scattered confusingly through Book X—presumably in consequence of Wordsworth's decision to conflate his return to England in December 1792 with his return about a year later, after a visit during which he saw (as he told Carlyle) an opponent of Robespierre guillotined. Thus he omitted mention of the second visit and return. If, however, we are mistaken about a second visit, he may have wished to give the persona of *The Prelude* an experiential presence in Paris during the ascendancy of Robespierre. It would have been in that later period, of a month or two surrounding 7 October 1793, the day of the execution of Gorsas—a man he describes early in Book IX as one of the journalists of 1791 who were "Powers, / Like earthquakes" giving "shocks repeated day by day" (IX.178-181)—not the autumn of 1792, that Wordsworth had nightmares of pleading "Before unjust Tribunals" (X.378).

Actually he puts his account of the Jacobin Terror and these nightmares immediately after his account of watching the British fleet assemble in Portsmouth (in August 1793), and so in the right place chronologically; but he lets us assume that his account of the Terror is as a witness from abroad, that he is in England all this time. And he puts his remarks about assassination back before the 1792 departure, even though that places them, improbably, before the *shock* of January-February 1793 and in the period when we are to suppose he remained an "ingenuous Youth" untroubled by doubts of the success of the cause of Liberty so acute as to require the assassination of a leader. With our curiosity aroused, we can see that the poet manages his account of the month or two he spent in Paris in October-November 1792 in such a way as to *rehearse in it* the later Robespierrean ascendancy. The frightening thing of 1792 was "those September Massacres, / Divided from me by a little month" and only made dreadful—at the time they had induced the spirit that won the battle of Valmy—by memory, dwelling upon "tragic fictions" and "mournful" chronicles, and the poet's working himself up with the thought that "The earthquake is not satisfied at once" (X.64-75). Writing long after the event, he can easily imagine his fears in Paris in 1792 as preparing the mental state of 1793, when he more truly (it would seem) felt "Defenceless as [in] a wood where tigers roam" (82). Then he anticipates the dread of Robespierre by giving as his next memory the sound of hawkers "Bawling, *Denunciation of the crimes / Of Maximilian Robespierre,*" the speech of Louvet, 29 October in which Louvet demanded Robespierre's head. Wordsworth doesn't quite make the latter point, but his observation that "Louvet was left alone without support / Of his irresolute Friends" implies that no one took the cue. Well, of course, this may be the cue that started Wordsworth's own thoughts of assassination. The case against such an inference comes from the relative detachment indicated in the *Prelude* account of this period (it was Louvet, after all, who was being terroristic in his advocacy, not Robespierre, while no one was being so in act), and from the plot of *The Borderers*—to single out the matter under discussion now.

Insofar as the character of Oswald is given traits or principles suggestive of Robespierre, it is to be inferred that by the time of writing the play Wordsworth loathed him. But it is also to be inferred that he had spent some time under the fascination and inspiration of his ruthless leadership.[28] (Wordsworth's later confession of having grieved for Buonaparte has been recognized as implying an earlier time when he had high hopes of Buonaparte as a revolutionary savior.) He has been accused of having little knowledge of Robespierre, since he calls him the leader "of the atheist crew" (458), whereas he was a deist; yet the demonstration of Oswald's "atheism" is Robespierrean enough, suggesting a variety of natural religion comparable to Robespierre's worship of a Supreme Being. The troops come to suspect that Oswald is in league with "imagined Beings" or "infernal fiends" (1154-1158): compare the *Prelude*'s "devilish pleas" and "blasts from hell" (X.311, 315). Even the death of Oswald, by stabbing, suggests the death of Robespierre as first (erroneously) reported.[29]

At the news of that death, Southey is said to have felt as though he had lost a father, and we might put it that Wordsworth had lost a hero whom he had grown to hate.[30] The tremendous relief of his "Hymn of triumph" (X.544) seems to express a triple relief: that someone else had taken the cue, that the poet himself had not had to play the Brutus nor need reproach himself for not having done so, and that the world was now at last released from the false leadership (if we take Wordsworth's Oswald as its representative "shape") which he had to an almost fatal extent trusted, then seen as atheistic, nay diabolic. The themes of regicide and parricide reverberate in the play (as perhaps in real life) as though explosions at both ends of a double tether. (In the play, Oswald iterates the theme by insisting that Marmaduke must "stab" Herbert because forsooth *he* is a "Parricide" [894-895].)

Wordsworth's slipping back to Jacobin France in October (or September) 1793 despite naval war preparations—he could have made arrangements for a boat to make the trip, while he and William Calvert were spending a summer month in the Isle of Wight in view of the English fleet—required trustworthy contacts in France and in Paris, and a very strong commitment or concern.[31] How strong, we may detect in the camouflaged allusions to Annette and their infant, for whose birth he had not been able to stay the year before.[32] In the Vaudracour and Julia story, he returns to his beloved's house for a blissful domestic moment. While their infant daughter is nursing at one breast, he pillows his face on the other. "Julia, how much thine eyes / Have cost me!" (IX.817-818). That, in *The Prelude.* In the earlier work, only three years after the event, in Marmaduke's outcry,

> Mysterious God,
> If she had never lived I had not done it!

Wordsworth is letting himself say: I should never have entangled myself in the mazes of revolutionary justice if I hadn't fallen in love with Annette and been around to hear Beaupuy and Robespierre, and (it may be) the actual Oswald. And finally, under the mask of tragedy, he permits an even more hateful outburst. Idonea's father had rescued her when an infant from the flames of a burning city (179-181). Marmaduke at his tether's end cries out to her: "Oh! would that thou hadst perished in the flames!" And there is an outcry of still deeper anguish, if we take it that Wordsworth had returned to France to see his own child. When Marmaduke is demonstrating his machismo of sang froid about kings and carcasses to an admiring Oswald, he enunciates a sentiment that leaves even Oswald breathless: "Now for the corner-stone of my philosophy:" it is that, on such provocation "as this earth yields" (i.e., without appeal to any divine tribunal), a man worth his salt "could . . . chuck his babe beneath the chin, / And send it with a fillip to its grave" (III.1240-1243).

In such moments our hero is wishing he had never gone to France. The judging and killing dramatized is not of *his* father, not of George III, and indeed in 1796 Wordsworth still felt great contempt for George: his unpublished imitation of Juvenal, in his letters to Wrangham, is replete with contempt of "Kings and Sons of Kings" and stresses how "ripe for the block" some English kings had been. It was Louis XVI, Annette's king, essentially outside the orbit of his British loyalties, upon which he fell back when writing *The Borderers.* (In the Juvenalian satire, he was dismissive: "Let Bourbon spawn her scoundrels / Be my joy the embryo Franklin in the printer's boy." [33])

The Borderers, then, may be read as a play about the events of 1792-1793 in France, moralized by a dramatic version of the poet's agonized reappraisals of 1795-1796. Reed (p. 174 and n. 20) demonstrates that Wordsworth's crisis about moral questions was concluded before the middle of 1796 and that the tragedy was possibly begun in July but really in motion by 24 October when Dorothy reports the poet "ardent in [its] composition." It is instructive to note what else was happening that October. On the sixth it was announced that a delegation headed by Lord Malmesbury was to be sent to negotiate peace with France. His credentials were signed on the thirteenth. Edmund Burke, who had reiterated his fulminations against "Regicide" France as recently as the past February, now published (in the *Morning Post* of 19 October) his first "Thoughts on the Prospect of a Regicide Peace," fiercely attacking the negotiation.

That leaves four or five days for the provocation to reach Wordsworth, to produce his ardor to tell the story, to dramatize the "shapes" of the moral lessons of the great tragedy of the regicide. Would he have agreed with Burke in preferring loud war to peace with the Regicide Republic? Not at all. But the tragedy purges his soul of the impulse to feed on a day of vengeance for any armed men. And it contributes "in some degree" (to quote Marmaduke) to the baffling of a hideous plot "against the soul of man." The father—Herbert or Louis—"is at peace." Seize not the sword to prey alike on both "distracted Countries."

When Wordworth in 1802 ("Calais, August 15, 1802") contrasts the joyless birthday "festival" of "young Buonaparté" as Consul for life with the "prouder time" witnessed by the poet himself at the happy dawn of the Revolution, we are apt to take in stride the line defining that time, "The senselessness of joy was then sublime!" But another point of contrast is given: truly happy is he who can sound *himself* for knowledge of man's destiny and ground of hope. If the tribunals were unjust and fearsome, in retrospect the joy had been "without thought," senseless. Wordsworth does not give us what in our ardent youth we may wish him to give. He memorializes the bliss but refuses it the chaplet of wisdom. During the first years of his "Residence in France" he felt close to springs of joy and to gleams like the flashing of a shield, of hope for Man. But in the greyer years he restructured his life's course to find for it such springs in spots of childhood and pre-revolutionary youth as to manage to bypass the interregnum, scorn consuls and popes and kings and killers of kings, traveling through the events of storm-tossed France "only as they were storm / Or sunshine to my individual mind, / No further" (X.105-106). The "spots of time" that nurtured that mind, that self in which could be sounded the sources of true happiness for self and mankind, include the moment near Tintern Abbey, where the "waters, rolling from their mountain-springs" with an *inland* murmur, are above the ebb and flow of the tide, above "the fretful stir . . . and the fever of the world," a moment when he could act "more like a man / Flying from something that he dreads, than one / Who sought the thing he loved." And recollecting the moment five years after, he can somehow fall asleep in body, can recollect the moment but not what it was he dreaded, what it was he loved and sought. In fact the senselessness of joy is available by recollecting "what I was" when the cataract was like a passion and there were "a feeling and a love, / That had no need of a remoter charm / By thought supplied . . . ." In 1793!

Is it uncharitable to notice that Julia's costly eyes have been, during these five long years, supplanted by the "wild eyes" of his sister Dorothy?

The Borderers, offered as a sacrifice on the altar of peace with France, did succeed as a purgation, for some years at least, of Wordsworth's warlike spirit. It dispelled the bad dreams of unjust tribunals that had succeeded to the sublime "senselessness of joy." There is no brandishing of swords in the *Lyrical Ballads. The Recluse* was meant to put aside the Warrior. And the poem that became *The Prelude* was undertaken to cure the poison at the heart of man by establishing a faith to overcome despair about France. A time would come, nevertheless, when the poet who had been able, as an ingenuous Marmaduke, to admire the Jacobin Robespierre, would bring himself again to acknowledge Carnage as God's Daughter (in the "Thanksgiving Ode" of 1816, for Waterloo).

The poetry that reaches our hearts and minds today, however, belongs to that long and vigorous period of hope in a peaceful intellectual victory over "indifference and apathy / And wicked exultation" (II.450-451); of a struggle sustained, despite "dereliction and dismay" on every side, by a poet who despaired not of our nature but retained a "more than Roman confidence" in the availability of natural sources of "joy / And purest passion" for the "uneasy" human heart (II.457-466).

NOTES

1. The first draft of this paper was prompted by Chapter 5 of George Wilbur Meyer's *Wordsworth's Formative Years* (Ann Arbor: University of Michigan Press, 1943) dealing with *The Borderers.* Meyer was concerned with what he saw as an important but "merely" strategical "shift of emphasis" in Wordsworth's politics of social reform, "from the evil caused by monarchical institutions, to the good that resides in the hearts of common men," and demonstrated that in *The Borderers* "there is scarcely a trace remaining of his hatred of monarchy and his zeal for a democratic form of government" (pp. 218-219).
2. G. M. Harper, *William Wordsworth: His Life, Works, and Influence,* 3rd ed. (1929; rpt. New York: Russell, 1960); Carl Woodring, *Politics in the Poetry of Coleridge* (Madison: University of Wisconsin Press, 1961); Chapter 4, "Wordsworth," in *Politics in English Romantic Poetry* (Cambridge: Harvard University Press, 1970); and, especially on *The Borderers,* pp. 14-19 of *Wordsworth,* 2nd ed. (Cambridge: Harvard University Press, 1968); Thompson's article in *Power and Consciousness,* ed. Conor Cruise O'Brien and William Dean Vanech (New York: New York University Press, 1969), pp. 149-181; Paul D. Sheats, *The Making of Wordsworth's Poetry, 1785-1798* (Cambridge: Harvard University Press, 1973).
3. R. F. Storch, "Wordsworth's *The Borderers:* The Poet as Anthropologist," *ELH,* 36 (1969), 340-60. His book, *The Poetry of Man,* is in the press. Mark L. Reed, *Wordsworth: The Chronology of the Early Years, 1770-1799* (Cambridge: Harvard University Press, 1967), provides an extremely helpful compilation but too compendious to include all the pertinent evidence for each dating. An excellent but neglected study, which I have come upon too late to make use of in this paper, is Jonathan Bishop's "Wordsworth and the Spots of Time" *(ELH,* 26, 1959, 45-65), a collation of *The Prelude*'s spots that includes Entering London, The Night in Paris, and Robespierre's Death (as those passages are called for convenience) and, by singling out elements each has in common with the other, suggests arresting psychological and political interrelations.
4. For a good survey of recent criticism, see Sheats, *The Making of Wordsworth's Poetry,* pp. 120-121 and 274 (note 16). For an essay urging us to regard Wordsworth's play as an impressive work of art, see W. J. B. Owen, "*The Borderers* and the Aesthetics of Drama,"

Wordsworth Circle, 6 (1975), 227-239. The text I cite of *The Prelude* is the 1805 version, as given in the 1960 revised impression of the Ernest de Selincourt edition (Oxford: Clarendon Press).

5. I take the names of the characters (and the text cited) from the final manuscript version, as given in *The Poetical Works of William Wordsworth,* ed. E. de Selincourt, I (Oxford: Clarendon Press, 1940). Oswald was first Danby, then Rivers; Marmaduke was Ferdinand, then Mortimer; Idonea was Matilda in the two earlier drafts. On Oswald's name, see below. (The five-volume de Selincourt-Darbishire edition of the *Poetical Works* [Oxford: Clarendon Press, 1940-1954] is hereafter cited as *PW.)*
6. *The Borderers,* written two years after the fall of Robespierre, was described by Wordsworth, in 1842, as a study of the perversions of human nature witnessed "During my long residence in France, while the revolution was rapidly advancing to its extreme of wickedness . . ." *(PW,* I, 342). If Wordsworth left France for good in December 1792 (but see below), then the extreme to which the revolution was advancing was the condemnation and guillotining of King Louis. If he returned for a visit in October 1793, as appears likely, the extreme was the terror identified in his mind with the ascendancy of Robespierre. In either case the soul-searching of the poet culminated in 1796–1797 in the writing of the play. See *Prelude* I.127-133 in reference to that period.
7. Emphasis on Oswald's "philosophy" (Godwinian or otherwise) tends to ignore his simple dishonesty. Sheats (pp. 274-275) notes that "Emphasis on the modernity of Rivers' skepticism may obscure the fact that he is enslaved." "This is not to say that he does not incorporate powers and aspirations that Wordsworth (and Godwin) admired, but that he perverts these to justify 'a great crime.' " (The phrase is from Wordsworth's prefatory essay of ca. 1799: *PW,* I, 345.) Leslie F. Chard, II, in *Dissenting Republican: Wordsworth's Early Life and Thought in their Political Context* (The Hague: Mouton 1972), p. 212, n. 49, opines: " . . . Wordsworth was not interested in presenting a good Godwinian, or a bad one; rather he is portraying the inevitable consequences of any form of Godwinism"! Chard traces the theme of "misused power" to the English Republicans, whose influence on Wordsworth is his primary concern.
8. Wordsworth claimed in 1820 that the facts of the story of Vaudracour and Julia "are true; no invention . . . was needed"; de Selincourt *(Prelude,* p. 297) observes that the "fates of these two lovers were sufficiently like and sufficiently unlike those of Wordsworth and Annette to tell Coleridge . . . the state of his own feelings at the time." Helen Maria Williams' *Letters written in France in 1790, containing Memoirs of Mons. and Madame F.* "tells a story corresponding in its main outlines to that of Vaudracour and Julia" (ibid., p. 323). E. P. Thompson has called my attention to the "facts" of the story of

the Solitary as those of the life of John Thelwall; for a more personal parallel to some of the Solitary's experiences, see Donald H. Reiman, "Poetry of Familiarity," pp. 166-167.

9. The later version, published separately in 1820 and not included in the 1850 *Prelude,* is basically the same in plot; in language and moral tone it is considerably less sympathetic to Julia and the "delirious hour" of love (redefined as an "unguarded moment that dissolved / Virtuous restraint").

10. Wordsworth "was represented by proxy at the baptism . . . at Orleans on December 15" (Harper, p. 93). Insensitivity to the indications in the Vaudracour-Julia story seems to underlie reconstructions of the William-Annette story such as those of Read and Bateson, thus criticized by Sheats (p. 268): "To ask, with Herbert Read, 'Why did he desert her as soon as the child was born?' . . . or to imagine with F.W. Bateson, Annette's 'reproachful eyes' following Wordsworth across Salisbury Plain in the summer of 1793 . . . is to indict Wordsworth on the basis of conjecture." There must be an element of conjecture, of course, in any reconstruction, but Sheats's own is more firmly based: "Wordsworth portrayed the love of Vaudracour for Julia in terms virtually identical with those he used to describe his own commitment to the Revolution. Both causes invited an impassioned investment of trust and hope, and offered a reality that surpassed fiction. . . . The after effect of both relationships, moreover, was to place Wordsworth in ardent opposition to 'law' and 'custom' on behalf of the values to which he . . . appealed at the close of *Descriptive Sketches* [composed during the summer and fall of 1792]. Given the spirit of that poem, it is probable that he committed his love for Annette to the keeping of the mighty powers that guided the Revolution—nature, love, and truth—and that he parted from her, in October 1792, in hope and trust that they soon would be reunited as man and wife" (see page 76 and following). (Here the reference is to his leaving Blois for Paris in October 1792; on page 79 a typographical error has Sheats saying that Wordsworth paid "a flying visit to France in October of 1792," meaning 1793.) Considering Wordsworth's probable feelings that drew him to make that visit, Sheats asks, "How could he respond to letters like the following, which Annette sent in March 1793?" and translates her French: "Come, my love, my husband, and receive the tender embraces of your wife, your daughter. . . . Her little heart often beats against my own; I seem to feel her father's . . . soon . . . I shall say to her: 'Caroline, in a month, in a fortnight, in a week, you are going to see the most beloved of men . . ." (p. 78). The scene is reenacted in IX.785: "Vaudracour / (This heard I from one present at the time) / Held up the new-born Infant in his arms / And kiss'd, and bless'd, and cover'd it with tears. . . ." It is odd that Reed makes no mention of this letter in the *Chronology.*

11. Reed (p. 147) is fairly certain: "There seems little chance that W was not in Paris at the time of the death of Gorsas." But the evidence is even stronger than he supposes. Alaric Watts's story that an "old republican" named Bailey had warned Wordsworth in Paris that his life was in danger because of his connection with the Mountain, "whereupon W had 'decamped with great precipitation'," is garbled but perhaps not from confusing Mountain and Girondins; he may have said, knowing of the looming round-up of all Englishmen, "even though you have friends among the Mountain." The biographical tradition that Wordsworth in Paris associated with "the" Girondins (formulated in Christopher Wordsworth's *Memoirs)* accepts a somewhat false model. Some of his associates may have been Girondists one day and Montagnards the next; one of them may have been John Oswald (see below). Reed also neglects the evidence of Wordsworth's mistaken account of Beaupuy as having perished on the Loire *(Prelude* IX.430-436), remarked upon by James R. MacGillivray in *TLS,* 12 June 1930, p. 496 ("Wordsworth in France"); it is helpful not only as further confirmation but as suggesting a date of return. MacGillivray's reconstruction is worth quoting at some length: "On Oct 27, 1793 (twenty days after the execution of Gorsas at Paris) . . . by the borders of the unhappy Loire . . . Brigadier-General Beaupuy was severely wounded . . . rumour spread . . . that he was dead. The battle [was fought] at Chateau-Goutier . . . about 21 miles north of the Loire . . . in a straight line from Paris to the Breton Coast. . . . Now if Wordsworth did find his way through to Paris in September 1793, saw the execution of Gorsas on 7 October, fled from Paris soon after, spent a few days with Annette and her baby at Blois or Orleans, and then returned toward the coast, he would be just passing through La Vendee at the end of October when the report of Beaupuy's death was abroad. . . . Even the realistic 'with snow upon the ground' [IX.730] may be taken from Wordsworth's actual experience, for the *Gentleman's Magazine* (1793, p. 970) records temperatures below freezing for several days at the end of October 1793 when it would seem that Wordsworth was finding his precarious way back to the French coast. . . ." We may add that he could have heard that another revolutionary commander in the Vendee had recently been killed, Colonel John Oswald, and no mistake.
12. *Wordsworth's Formative Years,* p. 201.
13. Compare the poet's insistence that Vaudracour never felt a moment of anger at his father's tyranny (see note 20 below).
14. "I have found evidence," says Harper, (I, 141), "that Annette belonged to a royalist family, and it may well be that the objection to the permanent bond of marriage with a foreign lad of twenty-two, a republican, a free-thinker, and poor, came as much from the side of her relatives as of his." Curiously Wordsworth reverses the scales,

making Vaudracour an aristocrat and Julia "plebian" (emphatically so in the 1820 version).

15. For an extensive analysis of the debates, with texts of representative speeches, see Michael Walzer, ed., *Regicide and Revolution: Speeches at the Trial of Louis XVI* (Cambridge: Cambridge University Press, 1974).
16. Dorothy Wordsworth's letter from Forncett dated 22 December 1792, of which only a fragmentary transcript survives: "William is in London; he writes to me regularly . . . ," seems to imply that he has been in London for some time (see Reed, pp. 138-139), and Reed puts the probable date of his leaving Paris as late November. But it just possibly implies that he writes "regularly" from wherever he happens to be and has just come to London.
17. Emile Legouis, *The Early Life of William Wordsworth,* tr. by J. W. Matthews (New York: E. P. Dutton, 1918), pp. 270, 276, held that Robespierre's Reign of Terror "gave birth to Wordsworth's tragedy" and interpreted the play as "Godwin's argument for the necessity of extirpating all the human feelings read in the lurid light of '93," with Oswald standing in that light as a *"Montagnard* . . . surrounded by weak and virtuous *Girondins."* Meyer (p. 180) agreed that the play takes on "increased significance if the reader brings to it an intimate knowledge of the events of the early years of the French Revolution, especially of the Terror under Robespierre; Wordsworth himself suggests as much in the Fenwick note to the play." But Meyer had to take issue with Legouis' picture of Godwin, and never returned to that lurid light.
18. "The way Marmaduke is persuaded of Herbert's 'guilt' is clumsy and improbable, but this does not matter, because it *feels* right that Marmaduke should be so persuaded" (Storch, p. 345). Storch is focusing on what is "psychologically correct": "The important part of the plot is that he hovers between the urge to 'punish' the old man, and the filial piety which prevents him from executing the death sentence." The clumsiness, in the focus I am suggesting, represents the playwright's attempt to make sure that everyone in the audience sees that Marmaduke is mistaken, that he is being trapped.
19. Wordsworth makes no direct allusion to the act of regicide; so Reed properly leaves it out of his chronicle. Yet the items Reed does list are untrue to Wordsworth's own point of view (except perhaps in later years). Reed gives simply "Feb 1 France declares war on England"; then "Feb 11 . . . England declares war on France." Even on the level of public events, these should be preceded by: 21 Jan Louis XVI sent to the guillotine; 28 Jan British Parliament votes to prepare for war with France and dismisses the French ambassador. The February entries would then fall into place as France's response to the aggressive vote of 28 January, the fact that staggered the "minds of all ingenuous Youth" of Wordsworth's generation (X.233).

For the British rulers' impatience to attack as soon as the execution occurred, see William T. Laprade, *England and the French Revolution* (Baltimore: 1909), pp. 116, 121.

20. *Prelude* IX.712-716; 1820 "Vaudracour and Julia" lines 166-171.
21. "Any other sorrow for the death of Louis," says Wordsworth, "is irrational and weak. In France royalty is no more; the person of the last anointed is no more also, and I flatter myself I am not alone, even in this *kingdom,* when I wish [that] his posterity are never restored to a throne" *(Prose Works,* I, 33). The "Letter" was written in explicit contempt and indignation at Bishop Watson's betrayal of the cause of humanity in condemning the French republicans for the execution of Louis. Dated the day after the news reached London, Watson's recanting paragraphs were published 30 January and Wordsworth's "Letter" (extant in a somewhat unfinished draft and never published by Wordsworth) seems to have been written within the next few weeks. Reed accepts a modern tradition of dating the letter as late as June, but W. J. B. Owen and Jane Worthington Smyser, in *The Prose Works* (Oxford: Clarendon Press, 1974), I, 20-21, argue convincingly for "February or March."
22. See II.677-683; 721-725; 1022-1025.
23. " . . . it asks not thought." Compare "The Senselessness of Joy . . ." *(PW,* III, 111).
24. Critics tend to accept Baron Clifford (who remains off stage) at Oswald's evaluation of him as a "cold voluptuary" and "Monster"; yet we should be impressed by the fact that Idonea and Herbert were approaching him without fear, until Oswald interfered. Indeed the point of I.344-345 ff., "would I had gone with her as far / As the Lord Clifford's Castle," seems to be that Herbert would have trusted Clifford, who had "expressed / Compassion for me" and whose "influence is great / With Henry, our good King." Clifford "might / Have heard my suit, and urged my plea at Court"; he gets put off by the evil power of Oswald. Herbert does not know Clifford well, has perhaps never met *him,* and has heard that he has moods, wilder (presumably) as well as "milder," but faltering under the eye of Oswald, and distracted by the "riotous noise" of a village wedding (shades of the Ancient Mariner's guest), mumbles "no matter I do not like the man" (early draft), or "No matter—he's a dangerous Man" (final draft)—as Oswald's "plot requires" (see I.329-331; 344-350; 369). Honest Lacy is also (in the early draft) tricked (at a moment when he thinks Oswald's "words are reason!") into judging Clifford from the wildness of his castle: "Clifford! who ever heard of this wild castle / And doth not know him?" (II.1094; 1103-1105 [B]). The audience is to understand that Lacy and Herbert are making the same mistake about Clifford that Marmaduke is making about Herbert.
25. "It was [John] Oswald, an English Jacobin, who seems to have

suggested the idea of the terrible 'Loi des Suspects' to the Convention and even advocated a more extreme measure still, namely to *put to death* every suspected man in France. This suggestion, emanating from a vegetarian (for Oswald had adopted the diet of the Brahmins after some years spent in India), drew from Thomas Paine the ironical remark, 'Oswald, you have lived so long without tasting flesh that you have now a most voracious appetite for blood' *(Letters of Redhead Yorke,* 1906 edition, p. 71)." Nesta H. Webster, *World Revolution* (Boston: Small, Maynard & Co., 1921), p. 76 and n. The "law of suspects" was adopted on 19 September 1793; in October it began to be applied to the Girondists, the first being A. J. Gorsas, whose execution Wordsworth told Carlyle he had witnessed, thinking "Where will it *end,* when you have set an example in *this* kind?" See Mary Moorman, *William Wordsworth, A Biography: The Early Years 1770-1803* (Oxford: Clarendon Press, 1957), corrected 1967, p. 240. Robespierre himself had opposed the broad concept of that "law," approving the killing of leaders only. In other words, the real Oswald was perhaps closer than the real Robespierre to Wordsworth's Oswald. The latter comes on stage with "a bunch of plants in his hand" and reminds us again of his vegetarianism in his last entrance (see I.44-45; V.2245). John Oswald was a sensational figure; his career is strikingly matched by that of Wordsworth's villain. There is not room here for an extensive comparison, but for some choice contemporary reports, see Burton R. Pollin, "Permutations of Names in *The Borderers,* or Hints of Godwin, Charles Lloyd, and a Real Renegade," *WC,* 4 (1973), 31-35.

26. II.1066-1073. The characterization of the troops is exceptional here; for the moment even the honest rank and file are carried away by Oswald's spell—just when Marmaduke is recovering from it.
27. A bland introduction of the theme of tyrannicide appears in Book IX in Wordsworth's praise of Beaupuy, his instructor in the revolutionary cause. Beaupuy, going into action, is compared to Dion, pupil of Plato in "philosophic war." The term sounds mild, but the "Deliverer's glorious task" for which Plato's conversation "ripen'd" Dion (as, we may understand, Beaupuy's conversation ripened Wordsworth) was a mission, with other "Adventurers in Arms," to assassinate Dionysius the "Sicilian Tyrant" (415-425). This was, of course, to grasp the sword *with* thought. Did perhaps Wordsworth imagine his voyage to France in 1793 in similar terms?
28. Consider the implications of X.178-181, 746-752, and especially X.417: "I Felt a kind of sympathy with power" (suggested by W.J.B. Owen in personal communication).
29. The first news was that Robespierre was stabbed by fellow deputies (later that he was shot); he was half dead when guillotined. One version of the death of Col. John Oswald, (on 14 September 1793) is that he was killed by his own troops (J. G. Alger, *Englishmen in the*

French Revolution, London, 1889, I, 76-77). However much Wordsworth may have had the real Oswald in mind, though, he would not have considered him a target for assassination; Oswald could not have been the chief, to whom "opposition" seemed required (X.130).

30. This observation of the complexity of the response is made by Carl Woodring *(Politics in the Poetry of Coleridge,* pp. 194-195) after noting Coleridge's heartache at the necessary fall of Robespierre: ". . . Coleridge's disappointment with Robespierre belonged to an emotional identification with him that later generations have been unable to grasp—have apparently dreaded to touch. His poetry dealing with Robespierre should be read [as should *Prelude* X] in the light of John Poole's story . . . that Coleridge reacted with shock to the news of the tyrant's fall. His companion Southey 'actually laid his head down upon his arms and exclaimed, "I had rather have heard of the death of my own father." ' " We should be willing to grasp the similar complexity in Wordsworth's explanation of the intensity of his wishes and the strength and perturbation of his thoughts when he considered acting the Brutus against the "tyrannic Power" in X.177-187.
31. Reed (p. 148, n. 16) questions Mary Moorman's interpretation of X.259-264 as a reference to the English defeat at Hondeschoote, 8 September 1793; but the next English defeat was at Toulon in December, too late for the context. Thus the calculation that Wordsworth was still in Wales on 15 September should stand. Indeed, the "unworthy service" on which the fleet which Wordsworth and Calvert had been watching in Portsmouth harbor was to sail was to take reinforcements to the Duke of York at Dunkirk, embarkation port for that unfortunate battle of Hondeschoote (the fleet, known as Lord Moira's transport, was delayed beyond its expected arrival of 28 August.) As far as the fleet's passivity is evidence of the time of Wordsworth's departure from the Isle of Wight, that departure could be middle rather than early August.
32. The lines that refer to the summer of 1793 have been misinterpreted in their autobiographical significance. Mary Moorman (I, 223), quoting X.243-254 to the effect that the attack of Britain "upon regenerated France" lay like a weight on Wordsworth's heart, "at enmity with all the tenderest springs / Of my enjoyments," misses the allusion—for so it must be—to Annette and the tender infant daughter and reads the poet as a poor Susan longing for the waterfalls and winds (tender springs?) of his darling Hawkshead.
33. Lines 72 ff., 80, 125-126 of the Juvenalian satire, in letters to Francis Wrangham; written "almost certainly in the spring or summer of 1796." *Early Letters* (rev.), 172-177.

William Wordsworth's Alfoxden Notebook: 1798

Michael C. Jaye

William Wordsworth's Alfoxden Notebook holds a significance far greater than its physical appearance and scrawled contents would suggest.[1] Measuring 4 x 6¼ inches, this reddish brown pocket-size notebook, with drafts entered between late January through March of 1798 on ten of the remaining twenty-one leaves and on the end papers, yields evidence of that turning point in English poetry when Wordsworth's imaginative powers rose toward a new poetic.[2] Although many of the passages in the Notebook were published in the *Poetical Works* in 1949, Geoffrey Hartman was the first to emphasize their centrality to any study of the evolution of Wordsworth's poetry and to explain their neglect: "they have attracted relatively little notice because they appear to be overflows from 'The Ruined Cottage' rather than a new departure."[3] Since Hartman's recognition of their importance, Jonathan Wordsworth and Paul Sheats have contributed valuable studies of some of the passages; and Mark Reed has, within the limits imposed by his *Chronology,* provided an excellent description of the manuscript and its contents.[4] No one, however, has yet focused on the Alfoxden Notebook as a document itself.

Most of the poetry in the Notebook is fragmentary and lacks the textual integrity and the finality of authorial design that would normally make it the object of intrinsic criticism. Yet this was poetry Wordsworth drafted at the high point of the *annus mirabilis* (1797-1798) when, as Helen Darbishire notes, Wordsworth and Coleridge "met every day, sharing their ideas and kindling each other to poetry."[5] The Alfoxden Notebook constitutes a primary record of Wordsworth's creative impulses in early 1798, experimentally seeking various modes of apprehending the self, and ultimately making these the subject of poetry.[6]

The Alfoxden Notebook makes another claim for our attention: it preserves the traces of the creative imagination in first flow. Perhaps no more unusually than any other draft manuscript, yet heightened by the significance of a new direction in Wordsworth's poetry, the Alfoxden Notebook holds both the struggling transcription of creative thought in the immediacy of conception and the poet's revisionary attempts to reshape his initial visionary utterance. Transcription, the stilling of creative energy into verbal symbol, frequently caused the poet physical and psychological pain, for transcription records but also interrupts the flow of the creative imagination. The physical and mechanical act of the driving hand preserves but also turns that creative flow into the stasis of a rigid inscription alien to its source. Wordsworth's oft-discussed concern with the inadequacy of language possibly has its root in crises immanent in poetic creation, the translation of energy into sign.[7] Yet, if transcription runs the danger of stilling creative energy, the stillness of sign holds the flow of thought and allows it to be returned to aurality. And, as Wordsworth fully recognized, transcription of initial creative thought was a necessary prologue to re-formation, to a discipline of form and coherence:

> That patience which, admitting no neglect,
> By slow creation, doth impart[s] to speach
> Outline and substance even, till it has given
> A function kindred to organic power,
> The vital spirit of a perfect form.
>
> (*Prelude,* p. lvi)

Finally, manuscripts such as the Alfoxden Notebook not only reveal the activity of poetic imagination, but they also present the most accurate evidence of the poet's intention, unrevised by redactions in prefaces, letters, or conversation, and less fugitive than the intention established through biographical events or poetry composed earlier.

Between the publication of *An Evening Walk* and *Descriptive*

Sketches in 1793 and Wordsworth's initial work in the Alfoxden Notebook in January of 1798, his most important achievements included "Salisbury Plain," an early version of "The Ruined Cottage" limited to the story of Margaret's domestic tragedy, and *The Borderers,* revised for the stage in late 1797. "Salisbury Plain," like so many of Wordsworth's ambitious attempts, underwent continuing revision until it emerged as "Guilt and Sorrow." [8] The rejection of *The Borderers* by Covent Garden during Wordsworth's visit to London in December, 1797, naturally disappointed him; [9] but the expansion of "The Ruined Cottage," embraced under the all-encompassing scheme of *The Recluse* in early 1798, opened new possibilities for poetic development as he began to sketch the character of the Pedlar in the Alfoxden Notebook.[10] The rejection of *The Borderers* may have freed Wordsworth from any further concern over adapting his poetic sensibilites to an established audience. Once rid of expectations of an easy popular success, he could experiment without a nagging consciousness of what would or would not gratify the depraved taste of a sensationalized public. Of course, this movement into new modes of poetic experience meant that Wordsworth would have to create and educate his own audience by continued apologia and explanation; [11] but these new modes of experience, like the Copernican and Kantian revolutions earlier, would ultimately usurp an established cultural context.

The vitality of Wordsworth's work during these early months of 1798 moved his poetry in diverse ways at once. The Alfoxden Notebook records his attempts at various lyrical forms and modulations of dramatic voice—"The Thorn," "Andrew Jones," "A Whirl-Blast from Behind the Hill," "Away, Away It is the Air," and "A Little Unpretending Rill"—attempts leading to one strong mode of expression in Wordsworth's poetry and finding early public display in *Lyrical Ballads,* 1798.[12] But another and essentially more potent voice emerged in the Alfoxden passages—a voice increasingly concerned with autobiographical identity, exploring the psychological basis of human behavior which lay in childhood experience. At first, Wordsworth drew cautiously upon his own experiences, partly clothing them in the fabrication of the Pedlar's identity. But the process of touching the recesses of memory for the material of poetry, once begun, led inevitably in less than a year through "Tintern Abbey" to the beginnings (at Goslar, Germany, in late 1798) of the autobiographical account of the growth of the poet's mind in *The Prelude.* At the same time, Wordsworth incorporated his sensuous perception of the natural world as part of his exploration of the phenomena of the mind. And this exploration developed and sustained a moral vision threatened by the collapse of his social revolutionary hopes.

Autobiographical poetry was not new to Wordsworth in early 1798. Carol Landon has admirably traced a number of early passages foreshadowing some of the subjects of *The Prelude;* [13] and, of course, a generous definition of "autobiographical" might include much of Wordsworth's poetry written before 1798. Yet by the criteria established in "Tintern Abbey" or *The Prelude,* most of the poetry Wordsworth wrote before 1798 is only slenderly autobiographical. Not only do the passages lack the direct and charged language of a man speaking to other men, but they rarely make the present consciousness of experience their subject; nor does the speaker in these passages seek to trace in their lineaments the process of his own growth, the epistemological or ontological basis for his present consciousness of himself, the meaning residing in his own experience, or the moral characteristics of his identity as man and poet.

The dominant Wordsworthian voice being formed in the Alfoxden Notebook, like the voice of the narrator in "The Thorn," becomes the implicit subject of the poetry; [14] yet unlike the dramatic persona of "The Thorn," the voice of autobiographical experience is the voice of a poet-speaker, an early form of the philosopher-poet envisioned by Coleridge. The identity of the poet-speaker and the subject matter of autobiography form a reciprocal relationship: to become a poet-speaker necessitates locating or shaping an anterior identity. For Wordsworth, this involved a complex representation of consciousness becoming reflexive by considering its own past, displacing a narrative of past events with a present drama of consciousness that apprehends slowly or swiftly, now receding now coming near, a located point in the past.

The first remaining leaf [15] in the Alfoxden Notebook contains drafts of "The Old Cumberland Beggar"—one of Wordsworth's earliest attempts at developing the theme central to his conception of moral epistemology: "The Child is father of the Man." Although Wordsworth began drafting his description of the beggar in "Old Man Travelling" a year earlier, the new energy informing his work in early 1798 provides the impetus for his return to the subject and a major expansion of his earlier fragments. His Alfoxden drafts emphasize the causal link between childhood experience and adult morality. They descriptively present an instinctual childhood response to solitary and rejected figures in society, figures who in their almost primitive and austere lines seem to arise out of the natural world, to breed perpetual benediction, so that finally a moral landscape rises out of the human one:

> Some there are
> By their good works exalted, lofty [souls *del.*]
> *minds*
> And meditative, in which reason falls
> Like a strong radiance of the setting sun
> On each minutest feeling of the heart
> Illuminates, and to their view bring forth
> In one harmonious prospect, mind[s] like these
> In childhood from this man perchance received
> A thing more precious far than all
> that [whi *del.*] books
> Or the solicitudes of love can do
> That first mild touch of sympathy and thought
> In which they found their kindred with a world
> Where want & sorrow were.
>
> (*PW,* IV, 237-238, ll. 105-116)

The clarity of the copy in the Notebook suggests that Wordsworth was working from an earlier draft, but the few revisions in the manuscript text typify the perfecting tendency, the "slow creation" seeking "perfect form" long after spontaneity has had its say. Wordsworth's emendation of "soul" to "mind" represents one kind of revision he frequently makes. In the context of the line, "minds" are more likely to be "meditative" than "souls," and the change prefigures the later line, "mind[s] like these." Such precision often escapes the poet's control in the rush of composition. And though one may observe Wordsworth's continuing ambiguity in the use of such abstract nouns as "mind/soul" or "things/objects," his habit of revision does indicate some attempt to discriminate their usage, even if in the early stages of composition he uses them interchangeably.[16] Whatever public priority Wordsworth assigned to spontaneous or extempore composition, his manuscript practice, and we have so far seen only minor examples, showed the need for the stilling of sound so that the retrospective revisionary faculty might "impart to speach/ Outline and substance even."[17]

The appearance of a solitary outcast in "The Old Cumberland Beggar" represents no new departure in Wordsworth's poetry; we glimpse such figures as early as *An Evening Walk,* and fuller portraits appear in "Salisbury Plain." They continue to be integral to Wordsworth's poetry, recurring exempla of his moral vision, as his drafting of the discharged soldier passages in Alfoxden illustrates. What is new is the choice of an early autobiographical experience as the basis for a sustained poem. What is new is a poem wherein the child's confrontation with the outcast beggar stimulates future moral growth because the child, impressionable, instinctually sympathetic, perceiving them both in a bond of humanity, finds his "kindred with a world/ Where want & sorrow were." As he later told Isabella Fenwick, Wordsworth located the source of "The Old Cumberland Beggar" in his own childhood experience: "Observed, and with great benefit to my own heart, when I was a child" *(PW,* IV, 445). Nonetheless, the voice that speaks in the Alfoxden drafts of this poem is not yet that of the poet-speaker, for the narrator makes no claim for autobiographical authenticity, describing rather than participating in the human moral drama. The narrator's detachment from what he sees, even while he knows the immediacy of closure in "want & sorrow were," may partly be compensatory response, assuring authorial control or allaying authorial anxiety over the subjective source of the poem. Yet within the Alfoxden Notebook itself, the natural landscape eventually dominates the human landscape as a generative force of moral or imaginative power, and the authorial voice eventually abandons detachment to insist on presence.

Wordsworth's emphasis on the child's "natural education" in "The Old Cumberland Beggar" bears on the development of "The Ruined Cottage." It must have been soon after writing "The Old Cumberland Beggar," if not while writing it, that Wordsworth turned again to his childhood experiences to sketch the childhood of the Pedlar.[18] In earlier versions of "The Ruined Cottage," the narrator and Pedlar are strangers; but in the version drafted in early 1798 they are old friends. In fact, a somewhat later version of "The Ruined Cottage," "We are dear Friends; I from my childhood up / Had known him" *(PW,* V, 405-406), echoes "The Old Cumberland Beggar": "Him from my childhood have I known" (1. 22).[19] The narrator of "The Ruined Cottage," like the narrator of "The Old Cumberland Beggar," recognizes the beneficent influence enjoyed by the child instructed in moral law through early contact with such solitary figures.

Wordsworth's approaches to autobiographical revelation in the Alfoxden Notebook, the alternate voices through which he attempted expression, are as consequential as his concern with the shaping experiences of childhood. As he drew the portrait of the Pedlar in the Alfoxden Notebook and other manuscripts of the same period, he increasingly identified with the character. In later years Wordsworth recalled, "the character I have represented in his person is chiefly an idea of what I fancied my own character might have become in his circumstances" (Fenwick note, *PW,* V, 373). His description of the Pedlar's childhood, founded upon his own memories of childhood or imagined experiences which he wished to associate with his own childhood, formed the model for his views on "natural education"—so much so that he later incorporated whole sections from the Pedlar's childhood into the autobiographical *Prelude.* Nominally, the narrator of the Pedlar's childhood preserves a subject-object distinction, speaking of the Pedlar as "he." Wordsworth's easy revision of "he" to "I" in adapting these passages for *The Prelude* suggests that the narrator's distance here, unlike his real distance in "The Old Cumberland Beggar," is fictive. The pressure of sustaining such fictive distances found relief in other evolving texts in the Alfoxden Notebook.

Within a few months, an urgency to cite memory and to sound the personal past, to subsume subject through the lyrical dimension of a poet-speaker in whom a risk-taking "I" supplants a fictive "he," moves through the Alfoxden Notebook to "Tintern Abbey" and the beginnings of *The Prelude.* One seeks the genesis of this urgency in the uncertain relationships between life and art. Did Wordsworth first decide, for instance, to create a psychologically convincing history for a "silent poet" such as the Pedlar and then search his own past experiences for material to substantiate the portrait? Or, at this critical juncture in Wordsworth's own life, were previously suppressed experiences not to be denied, although deflected in the narrator's "he"? Life's complex interaction with art is always problematic, but the singular circumstances of Wordsworth's life in early 1798 certainly helped to loose the flood of memory: perspective gained as he approached his twenty-eighth year; his disappointment over *The Borderers;* his rejection of Godwinism and the recent proposal by Tom Wedgwood in the autumn of 1797 that he and Coleridge run a school under "modern" principles; [20] his care and observation of little Basil Montagu; [21] his decision, made at Coleridge's urging, to compose a great "philosophical poem," *"The Recluse or views of Nature, Man, and Society" (Early Letters,* p. 214) with the expanded "Ruined Cottage" as a part; the ready potential of the Pedlar as a character for whom a childhood could be created; and the impetus of creative energy experimenting with many new and exciting modes of expression. And as important as any of these circumstances, there was Dorothy's steady influence, her readily borrowed powers of concretely expressed observation, and Coleridge's enthusiastic promptings.

The composition of "A Night-Piece" on what was the first leaf (a stub remains with initial letters of many lines) and the inside end paper marks a quickly assimilated stage in the evolution of Wordsworth's poetry. The poem, nearly complete and certainly a major achievement, heralds the dominant motifs of Wordsworth's greatest poetry: it almost conflates the speaker's "I" with its "he," the "musing man"; it sketches the paradigm of the mind's engagement with the natural world, unfolding revelatory experience; it makes of the natural world a symbolic landscape wherein motion is analogue to the mind's interior motion and where particularity of description struggles with indeterminacy of meaning.

Beth Darlington is probably correct in her estimate that, despite Wordsworth's claim of having composed the poem extempore, he was indebted to Dorothy's Journal description of 25 January 1798:

> The sky spread over with one continuous cloud, whitened by the light of the moon, which, though her dim shape was seen, did not throw forth so strong a light as to chequer the earth with shadows. At once the clouds seemed to cleave asunder, and left her in the centre of a black-blue vault. She sailed along, followed by the multitudes of stars, small, and bright, and sharp. Their brightness seemed concentrated (half-moon).[22]

The initial letters on the first stub show a version of the poem closely corresponding to the text in the Christabel Notebook (except as noted, the Christabel text is used throughout this discussion). The Alfoxden text appropriates Dorothy's description, but it is a text, as drafts on the end paper (facing the first stub) reveal, very much in the process of revision:

spread out
a broad & undetermined orb [spread out *del.*]
[*an undetermined del.*]

Dimly discovered checquering not the ground

Built round by those huge clouds
retains its
force

Still
[And *del.*] deepens its interminable depth

Built round by those white clouds
enormous clouds

The opening lines of the Christabel version, although they do not incorporate the revisions offered by the Alfoxden end paper (the revisions related to the closing lines are incorporated), also make blank verse of Dorothy's prose description:

The sky is overspread
With a close veil of one continuous cloud
All whitened by the moon that first appears,
A dim seen orb, yet chequers not the ground
With any shadow,—

Wordsworth's clear debt to Dorothy for the particularity of his description of the natural world also emphasizes the primacy of the transforming imagination that creates a drama where before there was only a pointing at things. So, too, his dependence on Dorothy's descriptions should make apparent his greater independence—his disengagement from the tradition of descriptive nature poetry. "A Night-Piece" escapes the constraint of static description by making a way for the subliminal drama of mind and world, by making motions of the natural world analogues to the mind's interior motions:

At last, a pleasant, instantaneous light
Startles the musing man whose eyes are bent
To earth. He looks around, the clouds are split
Asunder, and above his head, he views
The clear moon, and the glory of the heavens.
There, in a black-blue vault she sails along
Followed by multitudes of stars, that small
[& bright *del.*]

[*within that del.*] *vault*
And bright, and sharp, along the gloomy [vault *del. pencil*]
[*chasm del. pencil*]

Drive as she drives. How fast they wheel away!
Yet vanish not. The wind is in the trees,
But they are silent: still they roll along
[*chasm del.*]
Immeasurably distant, and the [vault *del.*]
vault
[The deep blue vault *del.*]
[And the vault built round by those white clouds *del.*]
Built round by those white clouds, enormous clouds,
Still deepens its interminable depth.
At length the vision closes, & the mind
Not undisturbed by the deep joy it feels,
Which slowly settles into peaceful calm,
Is left to muse upon the solemn scene.

(Christabel Notebook)

"A Night-Piece" presages Wordsworth's future lyrical dramas of the mind's interaction with the natural world, the mind turning in on itself in the flux of immediate consciousness and sensation. By beginning with the tranquil frame of the nocturnal experience, "A Night-Piece" anticipates the emphasis Wordsworth was to place on darkness fostering heightened moods of perception, on still sight leading to insight: obscurity nurturing vision in the opening of the discharged soldier episode; beginning to see again from within the shadow of "Tintern Abbey's" "dark sycamore"; vision emerging from the physical or psychological dark, dreariness, gloom, shadow, or mist of the seminal episodes in *The Prelude.* Sensuous experience is the catalyst for the mind's revelation. But in this poem, the mind does not half-create, sends no "auxiliar light" to bestow new splendor on the moon. Yet because of the mind's awareness of its own sensation of the landscape's motion, the poem conveys a consciousness of motion in an interior landscape. As in so many of Wordsworth's experiences with nature, tranquillity gives way to energy, passivity to activity, initiating a progression of sensations and tensions which are resolved into a "peaceful calm" of temporal suspension. Experience moves explicitly outward and tacitly inward; perception of the "deep" of the external physical universe has its corollary in the stirring of the "deep" within man. Stars drive, "How fast they wheel away! / Yet vanish not!" and the mind drives, wheeling, "Not undisturbed by the deep joy it feels." The chiaroscuro effect of the natural world, unfolding the "black-blue vault" in reflexive motions of clouds, stars, and moon, parallels the perception of obscure depths in the self, unfolding sensation, consciousness, and the energy of "deep joy." Finally, all that can be known or apprehended as an intrinsic reality is the motion itself within the "black-blue vault" of the interior landscape and toward an implied but hidden center.

The transitional line, "At length the vision closes," distances the speaker, shifting tense and perspective from a record of immediate sensation to retrospection. The line holds a comprehensive ambiguity, making doubtful whether it is the vision of the world or the self which "closes." Yet the ambiguity reinforces the reader's sense of multiple experiences: the visual perception of the external world and the psychological visionary sensation of the internal self, and the motions of these. In fact, the poem has been informing the reader of an unseen reciprocity between the narrator and the "musing man," as well as between the mind of man and nature. The internal process shadows, at times trails, the external process. The moon, barely concealed, suddenly intrudes, "a pleasant instantaneous light"; "deep joy" intrudes and disturbs (illuminates) the mind; the narrator intrudes his retrospective illumination. At all these points, motion is stilled: "settles into calm." As in "The Solitary Reaper," the speaker's shift of tense is a turning, a countermotion against the directional force of the poem. Paradoxically, the nominal distancing of the voice at the end of the poem is a closure of distance confirming a sense of the self observing the self, detaching itself from its own experience in order to represent its obscure apprehension of its own interminable depths.

The poetics of "A Night-Piece" anticipates Wordsworth's discrimination in the Preface between the objectivity and clarity of fact, analytically known, and the truth of poetry directly apprehended through passion.[23] Poetry, especially poetry that reaches toward the ideal of the sublime, gains its effect, as Coleridge frequently noted, through indistinctness.[24] "A Night-Piece," for instance, continually shifts its center of meaning by dislocating its chronology. Although the reader tacitly identifies externality and internality, a play of indistinction prevents resolution. Even the intrusion of the narrator at the close, seeming to settle the irresolution in favor of interior process, is attended by ambiguity. And here Wordsworth's poetic indeterminancy of meaning is meaningful: inability to locate scene or its time-center in either mind or nature makes the event pervasive.[25] Indeed, this view of the poem's process illustrates what Jonathan Wordsworth has rightly ascribed to the poet's philosophical concern at this time—a concern with the one life indeterminately rolling through all things, including the mind of man.[26]

But a lack of thematic or referential clarity is different from a lack of experiential clarity. Thematic clarity depends on distinction, often spatial isolation of the object or thought perceived. Experiential clarity depends on prolonging the temporal experience, perceiving its inclusivity through diffusion and radiating pervasiveness. As Hartman suggests in his discussion of the halted traveler, this clarity is a discrimination in motion—a sudden stilling of movement, a suspension or extension of temporal experience.[27] Thus in "A Night-Piece" the instantaneous gleam that surprises the traveler stills motion. So, too, and more essentially for the reader's experience of the poem, the final interposition of the narrator's voice stills the motion of the poem.

Wordsworth had no vocabulary, no psychological or psychoanalytical terminology, to delineate sharply the self perceived. But his task was to create a vocabulary and syntax, a recurring way of saying through passion and feeling, that would mediate the sense of self. The division between the durational sense of self and the object-ridden nature of language is expressed and partly overcome because recurrence in poetic speech recreates temporality, while ambiguities in the language of feeling suggest depths rather than locate a specific but limited meaning. Wordsworth rightly avoided the analytical mode, the language of empiricism, and instead relied upon a recurring way of speech for the mind's awareness of its own being. He created a familiar language of obscure apprehensions aspired to in verbs that imply intrinsic ways of knowing through increasing or decreasing velocities of motion: intensity, rapidity, conflict, floating, suspension. As Donald Davie points out, the energy of verbs counteracts referential obscurity and communicates much of the power of Wordsworth's poetry.[28] Such active verbs of motion dominate "A Night-Piece." They become a language for primary and passionate knowledge through which, in their recurrence in his own canon, the poet seeks to establish words "not only as symbols of the passion, but as *things,* active and efficient, which are of themselves part of the passion." [29] But such motion verbs are only part of this vocabulary. Equally important are those strong abstract nouns and adjectives that create meaning repetitiously and syntagmatically in context with the verbs, stilling their motion or subsuming their energy.[30] "Still they roll along" embraces the paradox of stillness with motion. "Deep joy" is the pervasive energy informing life; "calm" resolves the cycle of experience begun in tranquillity into a more pervasive tranquillity. Ways of saying reciprocally evolve ways of perceiving. Thus in "A Night-Piece" and throughout the Alfoxden Notebook Wordsworth begins to establish the significant themes of his poetry by discovering their language.

On the second leaf of the Notebook we see one of Wordsworth's earliest attempts to speak in his own voice, making his own past the subject of his poetry. The Notebook preserves the first drafts of the autobiographical discharged soldier episode, which in 1804 was to be incorporated as part of *The Prelude* (IV.363-504).[31] These early drafts of the discharged soldier combine both lyrical and narrative elements. In them Wordsworth observes how the dual powers of the natural world and human distress become beneficent agents in his spiritual development. Here, in contrast to "The Old Cumberland Beggar," a natural landscape conditions moral sensitivity before the speaker's confrontation with the discharged soldier; but the episode departs significantly from Wordsworth's earlier work in giving prominence to the "I" in the poem. Unlike the earlier unhappy personal histories in "Salisbury Plain" and "The Ruined Cottage," the episode recites no full story of distress and misfortune. Nor does Wordsworth intrude a Godwinian tirade against wars of oppression or unjust institutions, though these evils may be implied. Instead, he emphasizes the human, redemptive counterpoint of sympathy between men. The soldier speaks in the flat language of stoic piety:

> My trust is in the god of heaven
> And in the eye of him that passes me.
> (Alf. Nb.; cf. *Prelude* IV.494-495)

Because the soldier lacks character dimension, the reader's attention fastens on the reaction of the first-person speaker, who, illustrating the empathic bond between men under the kindly auspices of nature, finds his "kindred with a world / Where want & sorrow were." His usefulness ended, the indifferent institutions of society cast the soldier aside. But the speaker, whose moral will has evolved through his contact with the natural world, directs the soldier to the natural philanthropy of those living simply and closely to the natural world:

> behind yon wood
> A labourer dwells an honest man & kind
> He will not murmur should we break his rest
> And he shall give you food if food you need
> And lodging for the night.
> (Alf. Nb.; cf. *Prelude,* p. 537)

In other Alfoxden passages (leaves 5v and 6r) Wordsworth traces this empathic nexus between men to a silent intercourse with a natural world that maintains the primacy of instinct over language:

> Why is it we feel
> So little for each other but for this
> That we with nature have no sympathy
> *things*
> Or with such [idle objects *del.*] as have no power to hold
> Articulate language.

A line drawn horizontally below this fragment would seemingly signal a stilling of thought, an exhaustion of the creative impetus. However, this seeming closure is overrun by a succeeding surge of creative flow:

> And never for each other shall we feel
>
> *?feel*
> As we may feel till we [have *del.*] sympathy
>
> With nature in her forms inanimate
>
> *?Or such things ?as*
> With objects such as have no power to hold
>
> Articulate language. In all forms of things
>
> There is a mind.[32]

A few months later, in "Tintern Abbey," Wordsworth holds the thought in his most powerful metaphor:

> For I have learned
> To look on nature, not as in the hour
> Of thoughtless youth; but hearing oftentimes
> The still, sad music of humanity.

The opening lines of the discharged soldier episode as recorded in the Christabel Notebook, some version of which stood in the Alfoxden Notebook, establish a distinctive psychological pattern in Wordsworth's poetry:

> I love to walk
>
> Along the public way when for the night
>
> Deserted in its silence it assumes
>
> A character of deeper quietness
>
> Than pathless Solitudes. . . .
>
> . . . .

. . . .   On I pass'd
Tranquil, receiving in my own despite
                    I slowly pass'd along
Amusement as [from time to time *del.*]
From such near object as from time to time
            the slumber of the sense
Quiescent, and disposed to sympathy
With an exhausted mind worn [by *del.*] out by toil
And all unworthy of the deeper joy
Which waits on distant prospect cliff or sea
The dark blue vault or universe of stars.

(Cf. *Prelude* IV.364-384)

As in "A Night-Piece," isolation, silence, darkness, quiescence are pre-revelatory. The indistinct blending of the mind and the world, the dim sense of infinitude within, "deeper joy," and without, "dark blue vault," sound again the vocabulary of self-apprehension. The "I" of the dramatic lyric begins to speak with no division of speaker from character. He shifts to a retrospective distancing, but then becomes present in his own past experience. The recitation of that experience mounts to a lyric celebration: the senses become confused and consciousness of self is lost and then the self is more deeply apprehended in a vision of the imagination:

[While in such vacant mood I wandered on *del.*]
Thus did I steal along that silent road
My body from the stillness drinking in
A restoration like the calm of sleep
But sweeter far. Above, before, behind,
Around me all was peace and solitude,
[*My eyes upon the earth I moved along del.*]
I looked not round, nor did the solitude

Speak to my eye but it was heard & felt
Oh! happy state! what beauteous pictures now
Rose in harmonious imagery—they rose
As from some distant region of my soul
And came along like dreams yet such as left
Obscurely mingled with their passing forms
A consciousness of animal delight
A self-possession felt in every pause
And every gentle movement of my frame.

(Chr. Nb.; cf. *Prelude* IV.385-399)

Silence and solitude inform the self, are "heard & felt." "Silence," as Victor Zuckerkandl observes, is not the absence of sound, but "a condition of sound";[33] for Wordsworth, silence is frequently the primal condition of sound. As with the "musing man" of "A Night-Piece" or the figure "with forehead bent / Earthward" in the ascent of Snowdon, a mesmerizing physical process, "My eyes upon the earth I moved along," surrenders the surface activity of consciousness to the interpenetration of forces from the depths of mind and world. Quiescence now yields to discovery, as forms become motion suspended within the temporal experience of a dream. In this still motion, the speaker apprehends himself:

what beauteous pictures now
Rose in harmonious imagery—they rose
As from some distant region of my soul
And came along like dreams yet such as left
Obscurely mingled with their passing forms
A consciousness of animal delight
A self-possession felt in every pause
And every gentle movement of my frame.

Whence arise these forms? Wordsworth's revision, "As from some distant region of my soul," suggests both interpenetration and the obscure starting-points of reality: these forms rise from outside the mind, within the mind, and in the reciprocal play of mind and nature. As in "A Night-Piece," revelatory experience culminates in a sense of self-possession akin to calm. The speaker apprehends his being as at one with the flow of motion—an apprehension Wordsworth ultimately expressed in "Westminster Bridge":

> Ne'er saw I, never felt, a calm so deep!
> The river glideth at his own sweet will.

When the lyrical drama of the mind's reciprocity with the natural world finally passes to the more traditional narrative of the discharged soldier, the design of the poem fulfills its implicit argument: the speaker's interaction with nature cleanses, instructs, restores an instinctual moral sense, and prepares him for empathic response to the vicissitudes of the human world. In the discharged soldier, Wordsworth goes somewhat beyond the reflective halfway house of "A Night-Piece," receding from the physical "glad animal movements" of childhood, approaching the pure transcendental experience involving a complete loss of self.

The Alfoxden Notebook holds other initial explorations of transcendental experience. One such fragment (leaf 6r), perhaps intended for the Pedlar, describes a transfiguration into prophetic perception:

> Transfigured by his feelings he appeared
> Even as a prophet—one whose purposes
> Were round him like a light—sublime he seem'd
> One to whom solitary thought had given
> The power miraculous by which the soul
> Walks through the world that lives in future things.
> (Cf. *PW,* V, 413)

Another fragment, written immediately below this (separated by a horizontal line), projects a pervasive soul unifying indeterminate, interacting "modes of being":

Of unknown modes of being which on earth
Or in the heavens or in the heavens & earth
Exist by mighty combinations, bound
Together by a link, & with a soul
Which makes all one.[34]

As we have seen in "A Night-Piece" and the discharged soldier, the strongest examples of Wordsworth's development in the Alfoxden Notebook comprehend the reciprocity between mind and nature. One passage especially, "He wandered there," undergoes numerous revisions before emerging as a tentatively established text. While the passage seems originally intended for the Pedlar, a later version in MS. 18a is simply headed "Fragment." Finally, in 1799 Wordsworth severed part of the passage for inclusion in the Two-Part *Prelude* (cf. Parrish, *The Prelude, 1798-99,* pp. 152-155) and, with his usual economy, in 1804 he used the remainder for Book VII.720-729. The multiple versions of this passage in the Notebook and its ultimate inclusion (like the discharged soldier) in *The Prelude* demonstrate how forces of revision dominate the text from its beginning, often deconstructing in order to reconstruct it, as the poet imposes subsequent intention upon previous intention.

The passage takes its origin from sound, a reference dominant throughout the Alfoxden Notebook, where diminution of sound or even silence is invoked as the purest condition of aural perception and of intrinsic knowledge of the world of things. As I conjecture, Wordsworth first drafted this fragment on leaf 3v:

[?]
Oh listen listen how [sounds *del.*] that wind away

While the last touch they leave upon the sense

Tells they ?have

the [?]
[Hush they are ?coming—they have passd *del.*]

[And ?run *del.*] [35]

Then, immediately above, he pursued the effects of sound upon the solitary mind:

> Not for whateer there is of power in sounds
> That make their dim abode in distant
> To breathe an elevated mood by form
> Or imaged unprofaned.

In their incipient struggle for expression, the lines lack syntactic completion, yet Wordsworth has recorded a central concept in evocative language: sounds "breathe an elevated mood," communicating power undistorted and undiluted by sight, "by form / Or imaged unprofaned." Moreover, Wordsworth opens with the suspended "Not for whateer," a characteristic way of saying that compels syntactical completion and in which we hear the recurrent "Not for this" and "Nor perchance" of "Tintern Abbey" and the elemental beginning of *The Prelude*'s "Was it for this." In the first burst of composition, however, the referent for "Not for whateer" is undefined, "distant" lacks a substantive to modify, image is written "imaged," and the periodic structure fails.

In the next stage of composition, perhaps within moments, Wordsworth cancels the four lines and writes above them an expanded description, identifying subject and setting:

> [There would he *del.*] wander in the storm and there
>
> *Would feel*
> [He felt *del.*] whateer there is of power in sounds
>
> To breathe an elevated mood—by form
>
> Or image unprofaned of sounds that are
>
> The ghostly language of the antient earth
>
> Or make their dim abode in distant winds.[36]

Further down the page, where space was left below the two earlier drafts, Wordsworth continues the passage:

There would he stand

still
[Beneath *del.*] In the [warm *del.*] covert of some
?lonesome rock

Or
Would gaze upon the moon untill its light

Fell like a strain of music on his soul

And seem'd to sink into his very heart.[37]

Juxtaposing the second section with the first part of the passage, Wordsworth dramatizes different dimensions of his quest through the sensations for the hiding places of the world's power. The stillness of motion and sound in the second part counterpoints the movement of the wanderer and the inherent force of the storm. While the second section balances the response to sound in the first part with a response to light, it also extends the metaphorical argument of the passage. The more contemplative posture accommodates the transposition of light to sound ("a strain of music") and, as both images fuse through the tactile dimension of weight passing through the senses, the wanderer is transfigured. While light-to-sound-to-feeling penetrates the "dim abode," some essential source of previously unknown being, the "very heart," stirs.

On the next page (leaf 4r), Wordsworth develops the passage still further:

He lov'd to contemplate

aged
The mountains and the antient hills
stand
to [feed *del.*]

[His spirit in their solitudes *del.*]

And feed his spirit in their solitudes

(Cf. *PW,* V, 413)

And above this, with a horizontal line separating them, Wordsworth drafts a related fragment:

> The mountain's outline and its steady forms
> Gave simple grandeur to his mind nor less
> The changeful language of its countenance
> Gave movement to his thoughts and multitude
> With order and relation.
> (Cf. *Prelude,* p. 566)

Finally, on a page following three stubs, the various parts of the passage are revised, expanded, and joined together (leaf 5r and 5v). The first two lines now yoke the violent and tranquil aspects of nature:

> In storm and tempest and beneath the beam
> Of quiet moons he wanderd there—and there

Revising the opening lines, Wordsworth cancels "he wandered there" in the second line, and makes it the opening half line:

> *he wanderd there*
> In storm and tempest and beneath the beam
>
> Of quiet moons [he wandered there *del.*]—and there
>
> Would feel whateer there is of power in sound,
>
> To breathe an elevated mood, by form
>
> Or image unprofaned—[38]

The second part of the passage also undergoes change, abandoning the metaphor of light as "a strain of music" while synthesizing components of both parts:

> Or image unprofaned—there would he stand
> [Listening to sounds b *del.*]
> Beneath some rock, listening to sounds that are
> The ghostly language of the antient earth
> Or make their dim abode in distant winds
> Thence did he drink the visionary power.

Much of the dramatic force of the original counterpoint between the first and second parts is diminished by their synthesis, but Wordsworth then creates a dramatic "I" who considers the effect of such an experience on future experience:

> I deem not profitless these fleeting moods
> Of shadowy exaltation not for this
>
> That they are kindred to our purer mind
> And intellectual life but that the soul
> Remembring how she felt but what she felt
> Remembring not retains an obscure sense
> Of possible sublimity at which [?her ?thought *del.*]
> [Een from the very dimness of the thing *del.*]
> With growing faculties she doth aspire
> With facul[ties] still growing, feeling still
> That whatsoever point they gain—There still
> Is something to pursue.
>
> *they still*
>
> *Have something to*

Here Wordsworth establishes a pattern of description followed by analysis that he is to employ as a fundamental structure of *The Prelude;* the alternating voices enact a dialectic of two distinct modes of knowledge: the faculties of imaginative recreation and analytical retrospective understanding. Donald Davie has commented on the obscurity of the passage, citing F.R. Leavis' censure: "the verse, evenly meditative in tone and movement, goes on and on, without dialectical suspense and crisis or rise and fall." [39] Again, clarity here is primarily experiential; even so, the lines yield their thought, though perhaps with difficulty.[40] The significance of past experiences (previously described) lies in their future effect. Their immediacy or specific quality may be lost, but their emotional resonance, though indistinct, is indestructible and is capable of resurrection—a process reasserted in the Preface's discussion of "emotion recollected in tranquillity" and almost paraphrased in Wordsworth's description of the sublime: "Power awakens the sublime either when it rouses us to a sympathetic energy & calls upon the mind to grasp at something towards which it can make approaches but which it is incapable of attaining—yet so that it participates force which is acting upon it" *(Prose Works,* II, 354). The soul retains from its penetration by natural forces a power to recall "how she felt," "an obscure sense / Of possible sublimity," though denied specificity, "what she felt / Remembring not." This conjunction of power and deprivation stirs memory; the soul moves with incremental power to locate its source in emotional intensity and pervasive calm; it becomes in its attempt to recapture the past most like the thing it seeks, a correspondent creative and penetrating force.[41]

The reader has all along been aware of the intrinsic identity of the speaker and his fictive "he" (the fiction is abandoned altogether in *The Prelude).* But the presence of the "I" in this passage defines the effective subject: the speaker's pursuit of a past event (the soul) pursuing yet another past event. That is the argument or plot line of the passage, the drama spoken *about.* But there is another drama being enacted, the interior lyrical drama of the speaker striving to sustain a presence, to voice a language of imminent self-description, which is simultaneous with his language of narrative. Throughout his exploration of the interrelationship between the mind of man and nature, Wordsworth uncovers a reciprocating universe in which, implicitly, the mind of man, his reflexive consciousness, is the most readily apprehensible reciprocal element. The poet's utterance enacts the motions it names—the reciprocities between things in the world, between man and nature, within the mind of man, and ultimately between immediate consciousness and language which expresses that consciousness. The drama of the speaker's presence is most active when language refers back to an interior motion that it cannot fully capture. Hence the ambiguities of "things," "modes," "form," "soul," "mind," "joy," for example, point to an interior motion which language can never fully contain but can only "sound" toward: "the mind's / Internal echo of the imperfect sound" *(Prelude* I.64-65).

In the drama of the poet's argument, a moment in the past locates a still earlier moment and moves it into a reciprocal relationship. In the lyrical drama of the speaker's presence, language locates this past event, and moves it out of its stillness into a reciprocal relationship with the present, making this located past the reflex of present consciousness. Here, drama centers on the struggle of the speaker's voice to capture two motions at once: the argument or plot narrative of the past event and the active presence of immediate consciousness. This transcription of the speaker's presence—of consciousness checking itself, countering, and resuming its flow—is known primarily through its aural qualities, through hesitation and resurgence in speech (the spaces between phrases) as well as in the ambiguities of articulate language.

This present voice of the speaker rising in the midst of past experience, like the rising of the voice of imagination in the Simplon Pass episode, falls back to its recitation of past events and their consequences: narrative and argument regain ascendency over dramatic lyricism. Nature's penetration of the mind unknowingly shapes human intellect, imposing an organic order and intrinsic sense of the sublime through a power not to be found in society, human intercourse, or conventional education. Wordsworth had first written:

The mountain's outline and its steady forms
Gave simple grandeur to his mind nor less
The changeful language of its countenance
Gave movement to his thoughts and multitude
With order and relation.

While revising, Wordsworth lets stand the last three lines with their emphasis on inarticulate language and directional impetus of natural phenomena, but composes a significant transition and amplifies his characterization of the process molding the human mind:

But from these haunts

lonesome
Of [untamed *del.*] nature he had skill to draw

A better & less transitory power
An influence now he drew a better power

habitual
less transient
An influence more permanent. To his mind
The mountain's outline and its steady form
?imprint
Gave simple grandeur and its presence shaped
The measure and the prospect of his soul
To majesty, such virtue had these forms
[Perennial and *del.*]
aged hills
Of mountains and the nor less
their counten
The changeful language of [its countenance *del.*]
Gave movement to his thoughts and multitude
With order & relation.

(Leaves 5r, 5v; cf. *Prelude,* pp. 566-67)

Wordsworth deletes "untamed," for he no longer is speaking of storms and tempest but of tranquil nights as well; "lonesome," salvaged from the cancelled line, "In the still covert of some lonesome rock," reinvokes the necessary condition of solitude preparatory to seminal experiences with nature. Most significant, however, are the newly added first three lines which depict the adolescent as no longer merely the subject of random sense perceptions, but as one who had now achieved the skill to select nature's most valuable and permanent impressions.

The passages examined so far concentrate on the necessary passivity of the mind during its first contacts with nature. The senses are stimulated to a point of intensity, and then, as if annihilated by their own activity, fall away—opening the mind or soul to direct and unmediated presences of nature. Three fragments in the Notebook continue this exploration of passivity as a prime requisite for communion with the natural world:

There is a holy indolence
Compared to which our best activity
Is oftimes deadly bane
They rest upon their oars
Float down the mighty stream of tendency
calm
In a [dark *del.*] mood of holy indolen[ce]
A most wise passiveness in which the heart
Lies open and is well content to feel
As nature feels and to receive her shapes
As she has made them.[42]

Another fragment on the preceding page (leaf 3v) reads:

Some men there are who like insects &c
dart and dart against the mighty
stream of tendency others with
no vulgar sense of their existence
To no vulgar end float calmly
down.
(Cf. *PW,* V, 413)

The effects of following "the mighty stream of tendency" are expressed in an heretofore unpublished fragment, where in an oblique light nature lays bare her beauty—a gift given to the soul already reconciled with its own nature:

One evening when the sun was setting low
And with unusual clearness he perceived
The exceeding beauty of this earth and felt
The loveliness of Nature.[43]

Although Wordsworth in the Alfoxden Notebook concentrates on the mind's passivity in the presence of natural forces, he also begins to trace another psychological pattern: one in which the mind, losing its passivity, acts as both subject and object in an increasing state of tension, open to receive impulses from the natural world but also remitting its own impulses into the world and into the depths of its own interior. As George Mead observes, "One senses the self only insofar as the self assumes the role of another so that it becomes both subject and object in the same experience."[44] This approach to the sublime state, as Wordsworth notes in his fragmentary "Essay on the Sublime," involves awareness of "intense unity" through a suspension or extinction of "the comparing power of the mind" *(Prose Works,* II, 353-354). We have seen in the "He wandered there" passage the discriminating faculty of the adolescent mind. But in early 1798 Wordsworth was already drafting descriptions of an imaginative faculty whose extrinsic motion interfuses the power of the mind with the power flowing through the universe of things. Thus Wordsworth describes the growing powers of the Pedlar's imagination in early 1798 (lines he transferred to *The Prelude* as self-description):

> To every natural form, rock, fruit and flower
> Even the loose stones that cover the highway
> He gave a moral life, he saw them feel
> Or linked them to some feeling.
> *(PW,* V, 388, ll. 276-279; cf. *Prelude* III.124-144)

After a period of childhood tutelage under nature, the mind of man becomes a partner in the "*active* universe." This interdependent relationship, suggested in lines from "Tintern Abbey" ("both what they half-create,/ And what perceive"), finds ultimate expression in a mixture of exegesis and celebration when Wordsworth drafts Part II of the Two-Part *Prelude* in late 1799. Wordsworth's revisions are noteworthy:

> Emphatically such a Being lives
>
> An inmate of this *active* universe.
>
> From Nature largely he receives nor so
>
> Is satisfied but largely gives again

For feeling has to him imparted strength
[For *del.*] powerful in all sentiments of grief
And

Of exultation fear & joy his mind

Even as an agent of the one great mind

Creates, creator & receiver both

[*Acting del.*] *but in alliance with*
[Working but in the spirit of the works *del.*]

Which it beholds.[45]

In what appears to be one of the relatively later fragments in the Alfoxden Notebook (leaf 6v), Wordsworth delineates the entire range of the mind's response to nature: from passive inclination, to interaction, to the mind coming back into itself as the secret hiding place of power:

To gaze
On that green hill and on those scattered trees
And feel a pleasant consciousness of life
In the impression of that loveliness
Untill the sweet sensation called the mind
[Into itself and all external things *del.*]
[?Flo *del.*]
Into itself by image from without
Unvisited; and all her reflex powers
Wrapp'd in a still dream forgetfulness

I lived without the knowledge that I lived
Then by those beauteous forms brought back again
To lose myself again as if my life
Did ebb & flow with a strange mystery.

Passive sensuous perception quickly yields to tranquillity, a "holy indolence" and "pleasant consciousness of life." Emotional experience then excites the imaginative faculties, and the mind, incorporating external influences, penetrates further and further into itself. Sight becomes insight, and as in previous descriptions, motion is held in stillness; but here the mind undergoes experience independent of external stimuli:

> Untill the sweet sensation called the mind
> Into itself by image from without
> Unvisited; and all her reflex powers
> Wrapp'd in a still dream forgetfulness.

Self-apprehension resides in pervasive calm—the durational sense of the self's flow, prolonged, suspending the "comparing power of the mind."

Wordsworth's drafting of the poem suggests his intention to distinguish the autonomy of the imagination. Having apparently started to write "all external things / Flo[? wed into the mind]," he caught himself and described the opposite—the mind in independent act, creating its own perceptions "by image from without / Unvisited." As the space in the manuscript before the last four lines may suggest, these lines are a retrospection imposed upon previous retrospection wherein the present voice had moved to self-apprehension:

> I lived without the knowledge that I lived
> Then by those beauteous forms brought back again
> To lose myself again as if my life
> Did ebb & flow with a strange mystery.

But even the last four lines quickly become present flow, the recurrent "again" intertwining the voice of the poet-speaker with the past-become-present, creating another indeterminacy of meaning by describing present interior motion as well as the motion of past experience. So the voiced word makes all experience a present without a past and without anticipation of an end, creating a present fullness of time to wrap any other time "in a still dream."

In this passage as well as in other passages we have seen, Wordsworth renders the discovery of self in the saying of self, for when the act of self-apprehension becomes the implicit subject of a poem, dualities of "I" and "it," subject and object, self and language, merge. The poem is no longer about something other (a narrative *about*), but realizes itself and thus its subject matter in the act of speaking. Whether a passage seeks to locate the self in a historical past, in a moment of interaction between mind and world, or in the motions of reflexive consciousness, the poet's language points powerfully and passionately toward the interior drama of consciousness, and, paradoxically, succeeds in part because his language fails wholly to capture the self in statement. Yet the act of speaking validates the poet's identity in each utterance: I am that I am. In this sense, the poet speaking, fusing poetic speech act and subject matter, voice and word, constitutes not a mimesis of reality, but a real act in the real world.

In the Alfoxden Notebook Wordsworth has left a partial record of his evolving creative imagination: There we see him working out basic themes and ways of saying. The experiences beginning to be explored in the Alfoxden Notebook and other manuscripts of this period are first attempts at expressing types of human experience which were to become the most vital elements in Wordsworth's poetry. These attempts gain their complex fulfillment through interior perspective, through making into a present record of immediate consciousness—the mind of man shaped by nature shaped by mind. As Wordsworth drew these early descriptions of the mind's encounter with the natural world, he found a moral landscape rising out of the natural one and began in earnest to examine those experiences which shaped the life of a poet. Some of these he unfolded to account for the Pedlar's character in early 1798, but within a few months he expressed them more directly in "Tintern Abbey" and in early drafts of *The Prelude.*

Above all, Wordsworth was founding a mode of self-apprehension inextricably interfused in a mode of poetic speech. He anticipated in poetry what Henri Bergson was later to express as a philosophical principle:

> There is one reality, at least, which we all seize from within, by intuition and not by simple analysis. It is our own personality in its flowing through time—our self which endures.[46]

It was his "own personality in its flowing through time," his "self which endures" which Wordsworth began to "seize from within," and seizing, said in the Alfoxden Notebook.

NOTES

1. I am indebted to the Trustees of Dove Cottage Library for permission to examine and to quote from the manuscripts. The Alfoxden Notebook is renumbered Dove Cottage MS. 14. For the dating and description of the Notebook, see Mark Reed, *Wordsworth: The Chronology of the Early Years* (Cambridge: Harvard University Press, 1967), pp. 321-322 (hereafter cited as *Chronology: Early Years); The Prelude,* ed. Ernest de Selincourt, 2nd ed. rev. by Helen Darbishire (Oxford: Clarendon Press, 1959), pp. xxv-xxvi (hereafter cited as *Prelude);* and *The Poetical Works of William Wordsworth,* ed. E. de Selincourt and Helen Darbishire. 2nd ed., 5 vols. (Oxford: Clarendon Press, 1952-1959), V, 340-342 (hereafter cited as *PW).* Beth Darlington has edited texts of "A Night-Piece" and the discharged soldier passage in "Two Early Texts," *Bicentenary Wordsworth Studies in Memory of John Alban Finch,* ed. Jonathan Wordsworth (Ithaca: Cornell University Press, 1970), pp. 425-448 (hereafter cited as *Bicentenary Studies).* Since this study was completed, Stephen Parrish's excellent edition of *The Prelude, 1798-99* (Ithaca: Cornell University Press, 1977) appeared, enabling me to check some difficult readings in the Notebook.
2. Of the twenty-one leaves, four are blank (one recto and one verso of other leaves are also blank), five are given over to German exercises and a German translation of "The Two April Mornings" (see *PW,* IV, 69), one to a late draft of "The Ruined Cottage" (see *Chronology: Early Years,* p. 322), and one to a quotation from Richard Payne Knight's *The Progress of Civil Society* (Dr. Robert Woof of the University of Newcastle-upon-Tyne has kindly identified the source of this quotation; see note 17 below). At least twenty-four stubs remain where leaves have been torn or cut out of the Notebook. Some of these can be identified as having material related to "A Night-Piece," *PW,* II, 208, the discharged soldier episode, and "The Ruined Cottage." Many of the original drafts in Wordsworth's hand were copied by Dorothy into other notebooks, particularly the Christabel Notebook (Dove Cottage MS. 15) and MS. 18a (Dove Cottage MS. 16).

   I do not center my discussion on some of the poetry in the Notebook which does not bear on my argument—most notably, drafts of "The Thorn," "A Whirl-Blast from Behind the Hill," "Away, Away It is the Air," and "Andrew Jones" (see *PW, II, 240, 127-128; PW,* IV, 357-58; *PW,* II, 463).
3. *Wordsworth's Poetry: 1787-1814* (New Haven: Yale University Press,

1964), p. 163. Hartman's brilliant and seminal analysis of some of these passages puts all other discussions in his debt.

4. For Reed's description see note 1 above. Jonathan Wordsworth traces the relationship between autobiographical experience and the shaping of the Pedlar's character and emphasizes Wordsworth concern during this period with "the One Life in Nature" in *The Music of Humanity: A Critical Study of Wordsworth's Ruined Cottage* (London: Nelson, 1969), pp. 16-18, 157-162, 171-173, 206, 256. Sheats, in *The Making of Wordsworth's Poetry: 1785-98* (Cambridge: Harvard University Press, 1973), pp. 164-183, sees the experiences with nature as a "psychological ambush that is benign," and deftly examines the stylistic and psychological patterns in Wordsworth's poetry of this period.
5. *The Poet Wordsworth* (1950; rpt. Oxford: Clarendon Press, 1966), p. 85.
6. Much of my discussion follows lines already established by Albert O. Wlecke in his analysis of the "structures of Wordsworth's consciousness as these are exhibited or implied in his poetry," *Wordsworth and the Sublime* (Berkeley: University of California Press, 1973), p. 13.
7. David Perkins offers the finest discussion of Wordsworth's creative process in *Wordsworth and the Poetry of Sincerity* (Cambridge: Harvard University Press, 1964), pp. 61-107. But see also Wordsworth's letter to Coleridge of December 1798, detailing the "uneasiness" and "pain" felt during the initial work on *The Prelude* in *The Letters of William and Dorothy Wordsworth: The Early Years, 1787-1805,* ed. E. de Selincourt, 2nd ed. rev. by Chester L. Shaver (Oxford: Clarendon Press, 1967), p. 236 (hereafter cited as *Early Letters).*
8. See *The Salisbury Plain Poems of William Wordsworth,* ed. Stephen Gill (Ithaca: Cornell University Press, 1975).
9. See *Early Letters,* pp. 194-197; but see also Wordsworth's remarks years later to Isabella Fenwick that he was not disappointed, *PW,* I, 343.
10. Wordsworth announces *The Recluse* on 6 March 1798: "My object is to give pictures of Nature, Man, and Society. Indeed I know not any thing which will not come within the scope of my plan. If ever I attempt another drama, it shall be written either purposely for the closet, or purposely for the stage. There is no middle way. But the work of composition is carved out for me, for at least a year and a half to come." *(Early Letters,* p. 212.)
11. Some of Wordsworth's most damning comments on contemporary taste and his own measure of the need to educate his audience are found in the 1800 Preface, *The Prose Works of William Wordsworth,* ed. W.J.B. Owen and Jane Worthington Smyser, 3 vols. (Oxford: Clarendon Press, 1974), I, 128-130 (hereafter cited as *Prose Works);* in the "Essay, Supplementary to the Preface," *Prose Works,* III, 80-84; in the fragmentary essay on "The Sublime and the Beautiful," *Prose Works,* II, 360; and in *The Letters of William and Dorothy Wordsworth:*

The Middle Years, 1806-1811, ed. E. de Selincourt, 2nd ed. rev. by Mary Moorman (Oxford: Clarendon Press, 1969), pp. 145, 150, 194-195. See also, Nathaniel Teich's study, "Evaluating Wordsworth's Revolution: Romantic Reviewers and Changing Taste," *Papers on Language and Literature,* 11 (1975), 106-123.

12. See Stephen Parrish's fine study, *The Art of the Lyrical Ballads* (Cambridge: Harvard University Press, 1973), especially his discussion of the narrator's voice as the subject of "The Thorn," pp. 97-114.
13. "Some Sidelights on *The Prelude,*" *Bicentenary Studies,* pp. 359-376.
14. See Parrish, above, n. 12.
15. I apply the term *leaf* exclusively to those leaves still intact in the Notebook. Editorial emendations are enclosed in square brackets. Deletions are enclosed in square brackets and indicated by *del.* Revisions are indicated by italics. ? indicates a conjectured word; [?] indicates an illegible word. Transcriptions of passages from the notebooks which include interlined corrections or emendations have been printed with extra space between the lines so that the reader may see at a glance to which lines the interlined words appertain.
16. In one instance in MS. JJ (Dove Cottage MS. 19) Wordsworth wrote, "The soul of man is fashioned & built up" (Parrish, *Prelude, 1798-99,* p. 83), but by the time the line appears in the Two-Part *Prelude* "soul" becomes "mind" (Parrish, *Prelude, 1798-99,* p. 233). Elsewhere in the Alfoxden Notebook (leaf 5v), Wordsworth writes, "Or with such idle objects as have no power to hold," then cancels "idle objects," substituting "things" in what looks like swift response to the line's having too many feet; however, he also takes care to provide an alternate reading for the line when it recurs later in the text as "With objects such as have no power to hold," adding above, "Or such things as."

    Robert Langbaum suggests that "the words *soul* and *imagination* are used interchangeably" in *The Prelude,* "The Evolution of Soul in Wordsworth's Poetry," *PMLA,* 82 (1967), 270. Wlecke comments, "It can generally be said that 'mind' in Wordsworth, when seen under the aspect of its own eternity, is frequently characterized by the poet as 'soul.' " *(Wordsworth and the Sublime,* p. 151.)
17. See Perkins, above, pp. 77-83. Dorothy's letter of 5 March 1798 indicates both the accomplishments and difficulties of composition during this period: "His faculties seem to expand every day, he composes with much more facility than he did, as to the *mechanism* of poetry, and his ideas flow faster than he can express them" *(Early Letters,* p. 200).

    Wordsworth's concern with the problems of blank verse and the language of poetry is indicated by a note (inverted leaf 20r and 20v) he copied out of Richard Payne Knight's *The Progress of Civil Society* (London: G. Nicol, 1776):

Dr. Johnson observed, that in blank verse, the language suffered more distortion to keep it out of prose than any inconvenience or limitation to be apprehended from the shackles & circumspection of rhyme. Boswells life Vol. 1st p. 584.

This kind of distortion is the worst fault that poetry can have; for if once the natural order & connection of the words is broken, & the idiom of the language violated, the lines appear manufactured, & lose all that character of enthusiasm & inspiration, without which they become cold & vapid, how sublime soever the ideas & images may be which they express.

(Knight, p. 71)

A horizontal line is drawn beneath the transcription in the Notebook and a note follows:

These lines occur a few pages before the preceding note.
See, of Reviews & Baviads in despite,
Each month new swarms of Bavius's write

(Knight, p. 65)

I am greatly indebted to Dr. Robert Woof of the University of Newcastle-upon-Tyne for identifying the source of this passage. Knight's first paragraph is a direct quotation from Boswell (cf. *Life of Johnson,* ed. G. Birkbeck Hill, 2nd ed. rev. by L. F. Powell [Oxford: Clarendon Press, 1934], II, 124). Wordsworth appears not only to be interested in the difficulties of blank verse, but to share Knight's interest in poetry which would convey "enthusiasm & inspiration," "the natural order & connection of the words," and "the idiom of the language"—an interest which fully emerges in the 1800 Preface.

18. See John A. Finch, " 'The Ruined Cottage' Restored: Three Stages of Composition," *JEGP,* 66 (April, 1967), 191-195.

19. A stub in the Alfoxden Notebook indicates that a draft of lines 30-52 of MS. B of "The Ruined Cottage" *(PW,* V, 379-380) once stood there. It seems likely from stubs and fragments in the Notebook that Wordsworth's first efforts to draft the childhood of the Pedlar were made in the Alfoxden Notebook and were almost immediately followed by work that resulted in MS. B of "The Ruined Cottage." See Finch, above, p. 195; Reed, *Early Years,* p. 321; and Jonathan Wordsworth, *The Music of Humanity,* pp. 16, 158.

20. David V. Erdman in his essay, "Coleridge, Wordsworth, and the Wedgwood Fund," *BNYPL,* 60 (September and October 1956), 425-443, 487-507, suggests that Tom Wedgwood's proposal in September 1797 spurred Wordsworth's interest in the psychological questions relating to the development of the child's mind and was "the precipitating 'vibration' that released the spontaneous overflow of a

thousand springs and sources, experiential, literary, theoretical" (p. 506).

21. The plan Wedgwood put forward was calculated to produce a John Stuart Mill, with all the attendant suffering recorded in Mill's *Autobiography.* Wordsworth, though sharing the view that childhood determined the man, rejected Wedgwood's mechanistic views on external controls and the supremacy of reason. Here he was not reacting to theory, but to his own experiences as a child and especially to his continuing observation of little Basil Montagu. The role of young Basil is often neglected in considering the development of Wordsworth's poetry. Yet long before Wedgwood's proposal, the Wordsworths' letters indicate that their *system* for rearing children is to have no *system,* no external impositions of rational order, but to let nature shape its own organic order: "You ask to be informed of our system respecting Basil; it is a very simple one, so simple that in this age of systems you will hardly be likely to follow it. We teach him nothing at present but what he learns from the evidence of his senses. . . . He knows his letters, but we have not attempted any further step in the path of *book learning.* Our grand study has been to make him *happy* in which we have not been altogether disappointed" *(Early Letters,* p. 180; see also, pp. 166, 221-222).
22. See Beth Darlington's "Two Early Texts," *Bicentenary Studies,* pp. 425-448. See also, *Journals of Dorothy Wordsworth,* ed. Mary Moorman (London: Oxford University Press, 1971), p. 2.
23. "Poetry is the most philosophic of all writing: it is so: its object is truth, not individual and local, but general, and operative; not standing upon external testimony, but carried alive into the heart by passion." *Prose Works,* I, 139. Cf. Wordsworth's comparison of poetry and science, *Prose Works,* I, 140-141. See James Scoggins' discriminating study of the Preface, especially the distinction between the fact of science or understanding and the truth of poetry, in "The Preface to *Lyrical Ballads:* A Revolution in Dispute," in *Studies in Criticism and Aesthetics, 1660-1800: Essays in Honor of Samuel Holt Monk,* ed. Howard Anderson and John S. Shea (Minneapolis: University of Minnesota Press, 1967), pp. 395-397.
24. See J. A. Appleyard's review of Coleridge's various comments on indistinctness, *Coleridge's Philosophy of Literature: The Development of a Concept of Poetry* (Cambridge: Harvard University Press, 1965), pp. 86-93.
25. For discussions of the problematical in Wordsworth's poetry, see J. Hillis Miller's "The Still Heart: Poetic Form in Wordsworth," *NLH,* 2 (1970), 297-310, and "The Stone and the Shell: The Problem of Poetic Form in Wordsworth's Dream of the Arab," in *Mouvements premiers études critiques offertes à Georges Poulet* (Paris: Librairie José Corti, 1972), pp. 125-147.
26. *Music of Humanity,* p. 184 ff.
27. *Wordsworth's Poetry,* pp. 3-18. See Murray Krieger, "The Ekphrastic

Principle and the Still Movement of Poetry; or *Laokoön* Revisited," *The Play and Place of Criticism* (Baltimore: Johns Hopkins University Press, 1967), pp. 105-128.

28. *Articulate Energy: An Enquiry into the Syntax of English Poetry* (New York: Harcourt, Brace and Co., 1958), pp. 106-116. Paul Sheats's fine analysis of "A Night-Piece" calls attention to the "Powerful emphasis [which] falls . . . on the verbs that denote the motion and power of the moon" *(The Making of Wordsworth's Poetry,* p. 165).
29. Note to "The Thorn," *PW,* II, 513. But see also Wordsworth's comments on learning German, *Early Letters,* pp. 249-250.
30. Perkins, with characteristic discernment, observes that Wordsworth "develops a personal language of recurrent images or symbols, a language that allows an otherwise impossible depth of association or meaning, and that forces us to read the whole of his work before we can master any part" *(Poetry of Sincerity,* p. 107).
31. Some doubt exists as to whether the episode actually occurred in 1788 or 1789; see Reed, *Early Years,* pp. 87, 95. *The Prelude* places the experience in Wordsworth's eighteenth year. Possibly, as *Prelude,* p. 538, suggests, it was meant to form part of *The Recluse.* Only lines relating to *Prelude* IV.450-468 and fragments on the dog howling "to the murmur of the village stream" (see *Prelude,* pp. 536-537) survive in the Notebook. As Beth Darlington *(Bicentenary Studies,* pp. 428-429) indicates, stubs preceding the passage in the Notebook confirm that a more complete version once existed there, including lines relating to *Prelude* IV.364-399, 442-448. This early version of the discharged soldier served as the basis for the poem copied into the Christabel Notebook. The Christabel version was in turn revised and copied in MS. 18a, which, in turn, was used for the composition of *The Prelude* in 1804. In both the Christabel and 18a Notebooks, the passage is headed "Fragment."
32. Cf. *PW,* V, 340. By March 1798, Wordsworth adapted these lines for inclusion in "The Ruined Cottage," though perhaps with a loss of their original power:

> Not useless do I deem
> These quiet sympathies with things that hold
> An inarticulate language; for the man
> Once taught to love such objects as excite
> No morbid passions no disquietude
> No vengeance, and no hatred needs must feel
> The joy of that pure principle of love
> So deeply that unsatisfied with aught
> Less pure and exquisite he cannot choose
> But seek for objects of a kindred love
> In fellow-natures and a kindred joy.
> *(PW,* V, 400-401)

33. Zuckerkandl asks, "May we not assume that it was the sounds in nature–the sound of wind, of water in all its forms, of electric discharges, the rustling of leaves rather than the sight of their growth and fall–which aroused in sensitive minds the idea of a nature alive in all its parts?" *Sound and Symbol,* trans. Willard R. Trask, Bollingen Series XLIV (New York: Pantheon, 1956), p. 2.

34. Cf. *PW,* V, 340-341. Part of this fragment is used a few months later in the composition of the stolen boat episode in Book I of *The Prelude:*

    Unusual was the power
    Of that strange sight for many day[s] my brain
    Workd with a dim & undetermin'd sense
    Of unknown modes of being
    (See Parrish, *Prelude,* 1798-99, pp. 85-91)

    The rest of the fragment forms a description of the Pedlar in MS. B of "The Ruined Cottage":

    By such as have observed the curious links
    With which the perishable hours of life
    Are bound together, and the world of thought
    Exists and is sustained.
    (*PW,* V, 383-384, ll. 187-190)

35. The fragment is developed on leaf 9r:

    right opposite
    The central grove I loved to stand & hear
    The wind come on & touch the tree & then
    Elicit all proportion of ?sweet airs
    As from an instrument
    (Cf. *PW,* V, 342)

    For Wordsworth's reaction to sound see Raymond D. Havens, *The Mind of a Poet* (1941; rpt. Baltimore: Johns Hopkins University Press, 1967), II, 292-293. Wordsworth writes in the Christabel Notebook:

    The ear hears not & yet I know not how
    More than the other senses does it hold
    A manifest communion with the heart.
    (Cf. *PW,* V, 343 and 481 n.)

    The dominance of sound throughout the Alfoxden Notebook is clearly indicated by its central presence in many fragments or episodes. The draft of "The Thorn" (leaf 7r) begins with the storm: "A summit where the stormy gale / Sweeps through the clouds from vale to vale." On the bottom of the preceding leaf (6v), Wordsworth drafts some lines, possibly related to "The Thorn," seeming to question the absence of "the still, sad music of humanity":

> Are there no groans in breeze or wind
> Does ?misery leave no ?track behind
> Why is the earth without a ?shape & why
> Thus silent is the sky

Another fragment (leaf 8r) has the sound of the sheep breaking the silence:

> lovely as the fairy day
> Which one hour after sunset the sea gains
> From the bright west when on the bare hill-top
> Scarce distant twenty paces the sheep bleats
> Unseeing and darkness covers all the vales
> (Cf. *PW,* V, 341)

A single line on the other side of the leaf (8v) reads: "The echoes beat the rocks as if with wings." At the bottom of the same page, Wordsworth drafts another passage where sound is heard in stillness and then continues the passage (leaf 9r) with sound as an architectonic metaphor:

> and beneath the star
> Of evening let the steep and lonely path
> The steep path of the rocky mountain side
> Among the stillness of the mountains hear
> The panting of thy breath.
> Where truth
> [leaf 9r begins]
> Whe
> Like some fair fabric in romantic glory
> Built by the charm of sounds & symphonies
> Uplifts her fair proportions at the call
> Of pleasure her best minister.—
> (Cf. *PW,* V, 341, 342)

On the closing end paper, Wordsworth drafts three lines toward "There is a little unpretending rill":

> little
> [There *del.*] is a brook
>
> A brook that bustles down its stony path

And makes a never-failing melody
(Cf. *PW,* III, 4, 419)

Two drafts of lines from the discharged soldier exist in the Notebook on the dog howling "to the murmur of the village stream" (leaf 2r, 21v; cf. Darlington, *Bicentenary Studies,* pp. 445-446). Still another passage (leaf 7v) is drafted on the sound of dogs breaking the "stillness of the moon" (cf. *PW,* V, 341). And, of course, there is the draft of "A Whirl-Blast from Behind the Hill" (leaf 7r and 7v), *PW,* II, 127-128.

36. Compare the young Pedlar's desire for nature in her violent forms:

he was o'er power'd
By Nature, and his mind became disturbed,
And many a time he wished the winds might rage
When they were silent
(*PW,* V, 384)

Or these added lines:

When they were silent; far more fondly now
Than in his earlier season did he love
Tempestuous nights the uproar and the sounds
That live in darkness;
(*PW,* V, 384 n.)

"Andrew Jones," though not in lines extant in the Alfoxden Notebook, describes a similar experience:

I love upon a stormy night
To hear those fits of slender song
Which through the woods and open plains,
Among the clouds or in the rains,
The loud winds bear along.
(*PW,* II, 464)

For Wordsworth's early descriptions of storms, see Carol Landon, "Some Sidelights on *The Prelude,*" *Bicentenary Studies,* pp. 364-372.

37. Although this last image is cancelled as part of this passage, it reappears in MS. JJ of *The Prelude:*

The soul of man is fashioned & built up
Just like a strain of music
(Cf. Parrish, *The Prelude, 1798-99,* p. 83)

38. MS. 18a omits "he wandered there" entirely, leaving a blank space in the second line. MS. RV of *The Prelude* is the first to change "he" to "I" throughout, making it Wordsworth's own adolescent experience. MS. RV solves the problems of transition and fills the blank caused by the deletion of "he wandered there" in the following way:

> I would walk alone
> In storm & tempest or in starlight nights
> Beneath the quiet heavens and at that time
> Would feel. . . .
> (Cf. Parrish, *The Prelude, 1798-99,* pp. 193-195)

39. Davie, *Articulate Energy,* pp. 109-112; F. R. Leavis, *Revaluation* (1936; rpt. London: Chatto & Windus, 1959), p. 162.
40. A fragment in the Christabel Notebook of uncertain date (between 1798 and 1800), expresses the same thought:

> we to Nature and her impulses
> [? ? *del.*]
> Of our whole being made free gift, and when
> Our trance had left us oft have we by aid
> Of the impressions which it left behind
> Looked inward on ourselves, and learnd perhaps
> Something of what we are. Nor in those hours
> *By* [?]
> [Did we destroy *del.*]
> Thoriginal impression of delight
> [it *del.*]
> But by such retrospect [it *del.*] was recalled
> *we brought it back*
> To yet a second and a second life
> *While*
> [And *del.*] In this [pleasing *del.*] excitation of the mind
> A vivid pulse of sentiment & thought
> Beat palpably within us and all shades
> Of consciousness were ours.
> (Cf. *PW,* V, 344)

The dating of the Christabel fragments presents serious problems. Their position in the Notebook, surrounded by material related to 1800, suggests a date not much earlier than 1800; see Mark Reed, *Wordsworth: The Chronology of the Middle Years, 1800-1815* (Cambridge: Harvard University Press, 1975), pp. 613-614. However, their style and substance seem closely related to work of 1798 and 1799.

41. See Abrams' exploration of the wind as metaphor for the creative act, "The Correspondent Breeze: A Romantic Metaphor" in *English Romantic Poets: Modern Essays in Criticism,* ed. M. H. Abrams (New York: W. W. Norton, 1960), pp. 37-54.

42. Leaf 4r. Cf. *PW,* V, 413 and *Prelude,* p. 566. Jonathan Wordsworth *(Music of Humanity,* p. 206) points out: "What is advocated is a state of pure receptiveness similar to that in *Expostulation and Reply:*

> Nor less I deem that there are powers,
> Which *of themselves* our minds impress,
> That we can feed this mind of ours,
> In a wise passiveness."

43. Leaf 6r. Like many of the other Alfoxden fragments, these lines appear to be descriptions of the Pedlar. Cf. *PW,* V, 381, ll. 70-74.

Wordsworth frequently associated this passive subject relationship with the child's experience of nature in which nature impresses its image through the intensity of physical and emotional sensation. By the end of March 1798, Wordsworth had written these lines to describe the Pedlar in his eighth year:

> Sensation, soul and form
> All melted into him. They swallowed up
> His animal being: in them did he live
> And by them did he live. They were his life.
> In such access of mind, in such high hour
> Of visitation from the living God,
> He did not feel the God; he felt his works;
> Thought was not. In enjoyment it expired.
> *(PW,* V, 382, ll. 130-137)

44. *Movements of Thought in the Nineteenth Century,* ed. Merrit H. Moore (Chicago: University of Chicago Press, 1936), p. 63.

45. These lines are drafted in MS. RV of *The Prelude; "active"* is italicized by Wordsworth. Cf. Parrish, *The Prelude, 1798-99,* p. 191. In the same manuscript Wordsworth illustrates the working of the alliance:

[Hence my vision oft *del.*]
[Was from within and *del.*] an auxiliar light
Came from my mind which on the setting sun
Bestowed new splendour.
(Cf. Parrish, *The Prelude, 1798-99,* p. 203)

See Michael C. Jaye, "Wordsworth at Work: MS. RV, Book II of *The Prelude,*" *PBSA,* 68 (1974), pp. 259-260.

46. *An Introduction to Metaphysics,* trans. T. E. Hulme (London: Macmillan, 1913), p. 8.

The New Sublimity in "Tintern Abbey"

Carl Woodring

Wordsworth's poems about daisies and cuckoo birds are concerned with the human condition. Both *The Prelude* and *The Excursion* assert, to a degree beyond the assent of Byron and Shelley, the potential and therefore the essential equality of all persons. His conclusion in *The Prelude* that "the inner frame is good" (XII.280) is to be equated with his assertion that, however low of station a person may be, "high service is perform'd within" (XII.226). One of his most famous phrases of concern for our kind occurs in the poem called "Tintern Abbey"—"the still, sad music of humanity." Critics with an ear for English agree that the phrase is justly famous; they quote it as representative of Wordsworth's *ethos;* but they have not made clear how the phrase found its way into "Tintern Abbey." It belongs there, I will suggest, because of a current change, marked by Wordsworth as early as 1798, in attitudes toward the sublime.

The "Lines Composed on Revisiting the Banks of the Wye" begin by confronting a speaker with "a wild secluded scene" of "steep and lofty cliffs," seen again after the passing of five years. When Wordsworth took his vacations from college, and when he composed this poem, rules had been established for the observation of landscape. Books told you where to go, how to stand, how to look, and what to see. William Gilpin had published several editions of accumulated "Observations" and essays on where to stand, how to look, and how to sketch picturesque vistas.[1] For most who wrote concurrently with *Lyrical Ballads,* everything in nature or art was either beautiful or sublime, much as critics who thought they were Freudian used to declare every object in a symbolic poem, a novel by Kafka, or a realistic drama either male or female. Instead of saying male trees and female hills, writers in the age of sensibility and taste said beautiful trees and sublime hills.[2]

In 1756 Edmund Burke had made "A Philosophical Inquiry into the Origin of Our Ideas of the Sublime and Beautiful." With a rough hand, he separated the beautiful sheep from the sublime goats. Beautiful things are small, smooth, gently curved, and delicate. The colors of a beautiful object are clear and bright. To be sublime, a thing must be vast, "rugged and negligent," massive, angular, dark, gloomy, and obscure.

Burke and other writers on the Longinian sublime were trying to explain why certain things give a kind of pleasure even though in some sense they terrify. A beautiful landscape, said Burke, ought to evoke a pleasure akin to love. A sublime landscape ought to evoke awe, terror, a sense of the awful power of divinity. The sublime smacks into your feelings. Soon came those many novels, dramas, and ballads of terror; in Jane Austen's phrase, horrid novels, horrid ballads, horrid plays; in the denigrating phrase of Coleridge, Lamb, and Keats, "the *material* sublime."

In Burke's account, the characteristics of the object determine the reaction of the observer. By this account, transferred to art, one can paint a beautiful picture only of a pretty object; as if to say, one can ignore Sophocles if one sees enough sadness in life itself. In the counterview that we call Romantic, value lies in an interrelationship with the object, in response to it, in an artist's treatment of it, seldom if ever in the artist alone but not in the object itself.

The materials for history are seldom neatly structured. The paintings most admired in Burke's day, and in Wordsworth's youth, were neither merely beautiful nor purely sublime. The landscapes of Poussin and Claude, and of their imitators, were asymmetrical but balanced. Not determinedly "sublime," they were uniformly ideal. They revealed the beauty of repose, but also the mystery of some power beyond: Poussin sought that power, it may be, through reason, Claude through feeling.

A third category began to be talked about, the picturesque, meaning "like a painting." For most, "picturesque" meant like a painting by Poussin; "sublime" meant like a painting by Salvator Rosa. Late in the century, the picturesque took over the intermediate ground unoccupied by the beautiful or the sublime. The space available seemed to be that of intricate variety. Neither smooth nor grand, but varied and intricate. The emergence of a third category helped change critical and popular views of the other two, especially the sublime. The idea of the picturesque was concerned with the composition of a scene. "Tintern Abbey" curls its way toward the word *sublime* and a redefinition of it, but it seems to open with the picturesque. It lays out a scene, intricately various.

To take it as picturesque, even with the double focus of the five-year interval, would be to leave out not only the poet but nearly everything that has made the poem endure. Philosophers after Locke had gone on to say that objects depend on the observer not only for sound and color, taste and smell, but also for any knowable mass and weight and shape, that the human mind can know only its own perceptions, never the object itself. If a person can know only through individual experience, it follows that the mind itself must play a very large part in any awareness of sublimity. Richard Payne Knight, in *An Analytical Inquiry into the Principles of Taste* (1805), went far beyond John Baillie's point in *An Essay on the Sublime* (1747) that an encounter with the sublime expands the mind; rather, Knight explained, the mind creates its own feelings of sublimity by grasping at the sublime. In grasping at infinity, the mind exalts itself until its own feelings become sublime. "Tintern Abbey" had already gone further, to point toward the mind's part in the continuous creation of a sublime universe. Like other major poems to follow, the lines written on the banks of the Wye concern the uses, including the misuse, of mankind's essential sublimity.

When the poem first appeared, argument over the picturesque was nearing its peak. Soon the picturesque could be anything you liked, provided that you resembled everybody else in liking an asymmetrical arrangement of natural forms. Amidst the plethora of talk and the dearth of sublime new poetry, William Lisle Bowles, Byron's "maudlin prince of mournful sonneteers," seemed important and revolutionary. He attached to the picturesque a variety of tender feelings. Allowing for a few exceptions within Wordsworth's family, probably all the first readers of "Tintern Abbey" had read—and fewer than we might think had forgotten—

Bowles's sonnet "At Tynemouth Priory," published in the year of the French Revolution:

As slow I climb the cliff's ascending side,
Much musing on the track of terror past,
When o'er the dark wave rode the howling blast,
Pleased I look back, and view the tranquil tide
That laves the pebbled shore: and now the beam
Of evening smiles on the gray battlement,
And yon forsaken tower that time has rent;
The lifted oar far off with transient gleam
Is touched, and hushed is all the billowy deep!
Soothed by the scene, thus on tired Nature's breast
A stillness slowly steals, and kindred rest,
While sea-sounds lull her, as she sinks to sleep,
Like melodies that mourn upon the lyre,
Waked by the breeze, and, as they mourn, expire.

As in the opening stanza of "Resolution and Independence" and the close of Coleridge's "Dejection: An Ode," storm has been followed by a clearing of the air. But Bowles knows only the terror of the howling blast, not the terror of the divided self. He represents himself as musing in tranquility on a storm just past.

He gives us a picturesque scene, with the sun setting in calm on a ruin of pointed Gothic arches emblematic of an ancient religion eroded by time. He begins with a steep cliff and a recent storm; distance has converted fright into solemnity of response to the sublime. Art enables him, and enabled the readers he used to have, to contemplate the sublimity of a storm without being terrified by actual thunder and lightning.

Coming after Bowles, Wordsworth could be expected to write a poem about the picturesque ruin of Tintern Abbey. The ever-generous David V. Erdman has pointed out to me a precise example of what Wordsworth's poem could be expected to say. In the summer of 1792 Julius Caesar Ibbetson and two other painters journeyed along the Wye for the purpose of making preliminary sketches to be etched and sold to a public hungry for picturesque scenes. The report of Ibbetson, John Laporte, and John Hassell appeared promptly in London the next year as *A Picturesque Guide to Bath, Bristol Hot-Wells, the River Avon, and the Adjacent Country.* In search of the picturesque along the Wye one thanks God, Longinus, and Dr. Syntax that the "awful magnificence" of Tintern Abbey lies ahead: "The Wye, at Monmouth, does not exhibit such romantic scenes as about Chepstow. . . . By land, there is not a single object till we reach Tintern abbey, that deserves notice" (p. 245). The reference to the abbey in Wordsworth's title invites lovers of the picturesque to read on. The various engravings and photographs of Tintern Abbey that have been published with the poem, if collected in this volume, would provide a survey of technological changes in book illustration since 1800, but they have nothing to do with Wordsworth's text. Peter A. Brier has pertinently suggested that the poet designated Tintern Abbey in the title to "reidentify" Tintern with a pantheistically oriented natural religion,[3] but I would propose that the proffered irony is still greater. In "Simon Lee" the poet stops to scold the reader for expecting "Some tale will be related." The title of "Michael: A Pastoral Poem" promises to readjust the reader's conception of pastoral poetry. Aside from designating a particular segment of landscape along the Wye,[4] the force of the words "Tintern Abbey" in the title is to say "You have been misguided by Bowles and such; now let me introduce to you a better picturesque and the true sublime."

Bowles had begun, "As slow I climb the cliff's ascending side." Climbing, for a plump parson, had taken physical effort, the hard work of seeking the picturesque and the sublime in the hinterlands. The poet revisiting the banks of the Wye says, "once again, / Do I behold these steep and lofty cliffs." I *behold.* By contemplation (as the derivation of *behold* implies) I make them mine to keep. By contemplation, I make them *mind.* What I perceive I can thus completely hold. Less objectively than it might seem, "The day is come when I repose here." The opening movement is slow, not to suggest physical effort, but partly to elicit questions from the reader, partly to emphasize the importance of the years passed, "five summers, with the length of five long winters,"[5] and partly because a poem dedicated to the spiritual effort of evaluation is not yet ready to say why this day is momentous.[6]

The first verse paragraph of 22 lines, which keeps some of its rhetorical devices unobtrusive, openly exploits a series of implied contrasts. England is a green and pleasant land, but the western area described in these opening lines is greener than most. The home counties near London are green, snug, and populous. The absent but normal scene that the reader of "Tintern Abbey" visualizes is rolling country, the hills near enough on each side to give neighborly comfort without crowding the traveler. Along the road, again on each side, neatly trimmed hedges sit in rectangles. They do not "run wild." Green, but less green than the banks of the Wye, the small squares are still hedged in as they continue, with occasional squares of beige or yellow, up the slopes toward the domesticated hills.

In this normal farmscape that Wordsworth imagines into the mind's eye of the reader, the English house, of brick or stone, seems to sit in a clearing, with a coach road or driveway, beds of flowers, perhaps raw dirt where the wagon sits. Chimneys on the steep roofs are often capped by ornamented chimney-pots, from which in Wordsworth's day smoke emerged the year round, for cooking and for warmth. From the road, the traveler saw that the family was at home, because smoke curled from the chimney.

In his *Guide through the Lakes,* which in general reverts to Burke's antithesis of the beautiful and the sublime, Wordsworth pays especial attention to chimneys. Here too he makes a contrast with the home counties. Following a "View of the Country as Formed by Nature," which is founded on uniformitarian geology but concentrates on the play of light over surfaces—the human eye experiencing permanence in the transitory—the second section provides a history of human habitation in the district, and the third advances a program for preserving "the joint work of Nature and time," with its blending of cottage life into the mountain scenery, against the intrusion of garish mansions that dispute Nature's primacy. In a way that illuminates the opening of "Tintern Abbey," he praises the cottages made of native stone, extended organically as needed by each generation, "so that these humble dwellings remind the contemplative spectator of a production of nature, and may (using a strong expression) rather be said to have grown than to have been erected;—to have risen, by an instinct of their own, out of the native rock—so little is there in them of formality, such is their wildness and beauty." Then he gets to the chimneys. Some "are of a quadrangular shape, rising one or two feet above the roof; which low square is often surmounted by a tall cylinder, giving to the cottage chimney the most beautiful shape in which it is ever seen. Nor will it be too fanciful or refined to remark, that there is a pleasing harmony between a tall chimney of this circular form, and the living column of smoke, ascending from it through the still air." [7]

Along the Wye, the poet looks down on farms that are not laid out in checks. The plots of cottage-ground are not divided by hedges into rectangles, but by wavering lines of unclipped trees, "little lines of sportive wood run wild." The region looks more like green woods than like populated farms. The farms are like pastures, "Green to the very door." People thrive in this unravished region. Their fathers lived here, and their children will live here; but the trees almost conceal all human activity. Wreaths of smoke are

> Sent up, in silence, from among the trees!
> With some uncertain notice, as might seem
> Of vagrant dwellers in the houseless woods,
> Or of some Hermit's cave, where by his fire
> The Hermit sits alone.

These lines make their point of contrast by negatives and abatements: "hardly hedge-rows," absence of a clearing "to the very door," smoke sent up "in silence" (a sublime deprivation, according to Burke), "vagrant," "houseless," and "alone"—yet not really houseless. In the home counties, the houses would give certain notice of busy lives; here the daily work of these families causes no more disruption to the processes of nature than a hermit would. Chimneys in the Lakes are the most beautiful to be seen (heard melodies are sweet); but chimneys along the Wye, not seen at all, are melodies unheard, sweeter and sublime: the unnoisy melody of human life.

Elsewhere as well Wordsworth commends for our admiration natural places that hide life and power beneath apparent calm, and similarly, the power hidden in cottagers, shepherds, or a nearly inarticulate, eloquent leech-gatherer. In the sea at Calais, and in the child at the poet's side, Nature speaks softly but carries a big stick. In the sleeping city seen from Westminster Bridge, as in the silence of those seemingly houseless woods along the Wye, sounds the unheard music of humanity. People seen seem puny, but those unseen are potent.

At first in "Tintern Abbey" Wordsworth barely hints at the interchange of values between man and Nature in the act of human perception. In sketching the scene along the Wye, he understates the marriage between mind and Nature: The steep and lofty cliffs impress on a wild secluded scene thoughts of more deep seclusion. During the five years since he first saw these groves, draining himself in the muddy flow of existence in rented rooms, he has remembered from the seemingly houseless woods the still sad music of fellow sufferers, all, given such experiences as he has had, capable of little nameless acts of kindness and love. From this day of reaffirmation his companion and dearest friend need have less fear of lonely rooms. Instead of a ruined abbey, a green landscape giving a sense of solitude to gregarious human life becomes emblematic of that life, past, present, and to come.

The visit to the Wye five years earlier, recollected so fervently now, had been an extension of the days on Salisbury Plain, with their visions of savage ancient warfare and their scenes of human dereliction in the present. Indeed, the entire walking tour of 1793 either came hard upon or continued his nightmares

> of despair,
> And tyranny, and implements of death,
> And long orations which in dreams I pleaded
> Before unjust Tribunals, with a voice
> Labouring, a brain confounded, and a sense
> Of treachery and desertion in the place
> The holiest that I knew of, my own soul.
> (*The Prelude,* 1805, X.375-381)

These terrors and torments of experience and conscience, toned down until they became the *Guilt and Sorrow* of 1842, are both recapitulated and purged in "the still, sad music of humanity." These, again, are images that could have been expected had Wordsworth found sublimity in physical prowess. But the poem moves irreversibly toward an "aspect more sublime" (line 37), a "sense sublime of something far more deeply interfused" (lines 95-96), a true sublimity not dependent on physical vastness, roughness, darkness, loudness, or violence.

Burke had included an impression of solitude as a category of sublime deprivation. Kant, not in his *Beobachtungen über das Gefühl des Schönen und Erhabenen* (1764) but in his return to the subject in the *Kritik der Urteilskraft* (1790), emphasized the subjective state of mind put in motion by an object thereby regarded as sublime. In the same year (1790), Archibald Alison's *Essays on the Nature of Taste* shifted attention from the sublime object to the mind that perceives sublimity. Increasing (or recircling) emphasis on the perceiver was coincident with increased emphasis on the godliness of tranquility. Leigh Hunt published his distress at the storm and flames and noise at the end of Mozart's *Don Giovanni.* Assuming, as many critics and stage directors have, that Mozart was trying to achieve the sublime, Hunt thought that quiet should prevail.[8] A true ghost could do without the noise and smoke appropriate to a pretender like Horace Walpole. Hunt quoted 1 Kings 19:11-12, as Ruskin in a similar context did after him:

> . . . A great and strong wind rent the mountains, and brake in pieces the rocks before the Lord; but the Lord was not in the wind: and after the wind an earthquake; but the Lord was not in the earthquake: And after the earthquake a fire; but the Lord was not in the fire: and after the fire a still small voice.

That still small voice, the true sublime, is the divinity within the still sad music of humanity.

Probably much of the new emphasis on the sublimity of silence in solitude came indirectly from Johann Winckelmann's stress, notably in his *Geschichte der Kunst des Altertums* (1764), on the still spirit and tranquil eye reflected in Hellenic art.[9] Both the humanity and the tranquility are present in "Those green-robed senators of mighty woods" (Keats, *Hyperion* I.73); in preparation, the divinely majestic tranquility of "grey-haired Saturn, quiet as a stone, / Still as the silence round about his lair," has given way to awesome deprivation, not waiting for the lines on Saturn's nerveless, listless, unsceptered hand and realmless eyes (I.17-18) but apparent in the sympathetic quiet around him, the stirless air and voiceless stream (8-12). It is "more noble to sit like Jove" than "to fly like Mercury," Keats told Reynolds.[10] The Hellenic sublimity of "silence and slow time" comes immediately to the fore in "Ode on a Grecian Urn." Although the juxtaposition of external and internal sublimity can be seen in Shelley's work as early as the "Hymn to Intellectual Beauty" (1816)—the "awful shadow" is deeper in effect than any "voice from some sublimer world" (lines 1, 25)—the contrast is nowhere more forcefully made than in his notes and letters of 1819 on the gross inferiority of Michelangelo to Phidias, Praxiteles, and other Hellenic masters. The figures of Michelangelo, "rude, external, mechanical," communicate energy, terror, distortion of nature; Hellenic figures "combine the irresistible energy with the sublime & perfect loveliness supposed to have belonged to the divine nature."[11] Strong silence begets awe. Thus far the romantic internalization involves a movement from Hebraic obscurity to Hellenic linearity.

Apart from this movement, "Tintern Abbey" insinuates a similar silence to the ear, "quiet of the sky" to the eye, and to both ear and eye the smoke sent up "in silence" with "uncertain notice." The quiet comes no doubt partly from what Lionel Trilling described as Wordsworth's rabbinical passivity.[12] But the new sublimity is above all epistemological. A poet coming in self-conscious unease after Locke, Berkeley, and Hume (and after Schiller's essay *Uber naive und sentimentalische Dichtung),* if he would speak on human life, had first to find nature in his own consciousness. It is inadequate to describe romantic subjectivity as J. R. Watson does: ". . . the romantics brought to the landscape their own pre-occupations: Coleridge's unhappiness, Byron's pride, Shelley's restlessness, Scott's sense of the past."[13] Albert O. Wlecke comes much nearer in arguing that "the 'sense sublime' refers to an activity of the esemplastic power of the imagination during which consciousness becomes reflexively aware of itself as an interfusing energy dwelling within the phenomena of nature."[14] Wlecke (p. 79) aptly quotes Coleridge: "I meet, I *find* the Beautiful—but I give, contribute, or rather attribute the Sublime."

One preposition in lines 93-102 has never been accounted for:

And I have felt
A presence that disturbs me with the joy
Of elevated thoughts; a sense sublime
Of something far more deeply interfused,
Whose dwelling is the light of setting suns,
And the round ocean and the living air,
And the blue sky, and in the mind of man,
A motion and a spirit, that impels
All thinking things, all objects of all thought,
And rolls through all things.

I have quoted the first edition, which, like Wordsworth's three other editions of *Lyrical Ballads,* has a comma at the end of line 99; from 1815 on, a colon ("the mind of man:") replaces that comma.[15] The punctuation here apparently troubled Wordsworth; the preposition *in* should have troubled the rest of us. How does it function grammatically? The solution, I think, lies in the proleptic appearance here of "spousal verse." Everything after the colon is within the mind, a reflection of the supposedly external world, of objects, and of other minds thinking objects, *in* the mind of the perceiver. To paraphrase Iago, " 'Tis in ourselves, that a thing is thus, or thus: our minds are gardens" in which we must will to replant what is natural, that there may be a correspondence between internal and external creativity and growth. The life abroad is the life within; the sublimity is from within.

Epistemologically, Shelley's "Mont Blanc" and the passage in "Tintern Abbey" could serve for exegesis of each other: "The everlasting universe of things / Flows through the mind . . . ." These are ruminations over the limits to human knowledge, but they are less cries of despair that the world has lost its props than exclamations of awe that the mind half-creates through interfusion with what it had once regarded as external to it. Each is tentative. Shelley's poem moves toward uncertainty; his what-if comes at the close. "Tintern Abbey" begins and ends with the phenomena most certain; the scene before the eye, and the poet's hope for his sister. His if-not and if-vain come deep in the center of the poem.

Yet he would find it still more majestically sublime if the ultimate sense of the one life in this active universe had no need of eye or ear. In remembering the banks of the Wye, he has concluded that we are in such moments "laid asleep in body, and become a living soul."

He makes here still another point against the "mimic rules" of the sublime and the picturesque. It is not the immediate sense of terror, awe, or pleasure that is most important, nor even one's previous associations with that sense, but what one does with the experience of awe or pleasure in later moments of quiet reflection. And what one does *after* reflection. The strength of landscape is realized by a strength of humanity and divinity within. William Empson led his many admirers to ask, "more sublime" than what? Even more sublime, the poem says, than little nameless acts of kindness, which are themselves sublime—as "beauteous forms" without "an eye made quiet" are not.

The philosophical function of that surreptitious preposition *in* is to say that all objects take definition and value only from the human mind. But the ultimate poetic function is to evoke such a direction of thought, rather than to state the thought. In his greatest philosophical passages Wordsworth is metaphysically, and even epistemologically, the most elusive of poets. *Why* he concealed or blurred the academic sources and rational explanations of his thought is debatable; *that* he did so is indisputable. He knows, and sometimes makes clear, what explanations of experience he regards as inadequate. As a poet he declines to be rationally paraphrased. The critic who gives a consistent epistemological interpretation equally to one of Wordsworth's great passages and to each phrase within the passage has invariably falsified some of the phrases and opened the larger interpretation to rebuttal because of the inevitable distortions. One way to begin an explanation is to say that Wordsworth knew poetry to be not only more philosophical than history but also more sublime than philosophy.

On the sublime itself he has left us a fragment in prose, with fewer appeals to Burke's physical categorization than in his *Guide to the Lakes* and fewer withdrawals into eighteenth-century aesthetics generally than in most of his prose and poetry after 1808. He asserts forcefully some of the points I have attributed to the romantics generally:

> To talk of an object as being sublime or beautiful in itself, without references to some subject by whom that sublimity or

> beauty is perceived, is absurd; nor is it of the slightest importance to mankind whether there be any object with which their minds are conversant that Men would universally agree (after having ascertained that the words were used in the same sense) to denominate sublime or beautiful. . . . The true province of the philosopher is not to grope about in the external world &, when he has perceived or detected in an object such or such a quality or power, to set himself to the task of persuading the world that such is a sublime or beautiful object, but to look into his own mind & determine the law by which he is affected.
>
> *(Prose Works,* II, 357)

W. J. B. Owen has written valuably on the identification of sublimity with power in Wordsworth's essay.[16] W. P. Albrecht has written equally well on "the sublime of vision" in the romantic view of tragedy: "The fullness of the imaginative process became more important to the sublime than visible size or the duplication of its emotional impact."[17] Wordsworth's lines on revisiting the Wye were an important force in this change; I do not believe that the phrase "more sublime" appears in the poem by chance. "To this point was Wordsworth come . . . when he wrote 'Tintern Abbey,'" said Keats, "and it seems to me that his Genius is explorative of those dark Passages" *(Letters,* I, 281).

Despite Lessing's *Laokoön* of 1766, Bowles had assumed that a poem is like a painting. The scene in each is to be arranged by the same rules. Wordsworth, like Constable and Turner, is concerned with the value of landscape. Like them, he renders a scene more deeply human by removing the human figures from the foreground yet discovering, far more deeply interfused, the strengths of ordinary human life, with its silent suffering and its quiet joys—in Constable's vernacular, its wet planks. The unleashed, volcanic forces of the French Revolution as well as the unleashed forces of the Gothic villain, had found a worthy successor in the cottager whose emission of smoke was no more obtrusive than a hermit's. According to the Freudian economy advanced by Thomas Weiskel in *The Romantic Sublime,* not only Wordsworth but Burke as well was attempting to get something for nothing—a return without a deposit—but few have gone emotionally bankrupt from Wordsworth's belief in the sublimity of humble human feeling.

NOTES

1. One of Gilpin's most popular books was *Observations on the River Wye and Several Parts of South Wales* (1782). Gilpin appears in *The Cambridge Bibliography of English Literature* (1940) only as a translator; *The New Cambridge Bibliography of English Literature* has caught up with interest in the picturesque for literary studies to the extent of listing the two chief secondary sources: William D. Templeman, *The Life and Work of William Gilpin* (Urbana: University of Illinois Press, 1939); Carl Paul Barbier, *William Gilpin: His Drawings, Teachings, and Theory of the Picturesque* (Oxford: Clarendon Press, 1963).
2. Of many careful studies in this area, the standard works are Samuel H. Monk, *The Sublime: A Study of Critical Theories in XVIII-Century England* (Modern Language Association, 1935; Ann Arbor: University of Michigan Press, 1960); Christopher Hussey, *The Picturesque: Studies in a Point of View* (London: Putnam, 1927); Walter John Hipple, Jr., *The Beautiful, The Sublime, & The Picturesque in Eighteenth-Century British Aesthetic Theory* (Carbondale: Southern Illinois University Press, 1957); Elizabeth Wheeler Manwaring, *Italian Landscape in Eighteenth Century England: A Study Chiefly of the Influence of Claude Lorrain and Salvator Rosa on English Taste 1700-1800* (New York: Oxford, 1925; rpt. London, 1965); Edward Malins, *English Landscapin and Literature 1660-1840* (London: Oxford University Press, 1966); J. R. Watson, *Picturesque Landscape and English Romantic Poetry* (London: Hutchinson, 1970). For a deconstructionist Freudian view, discovering in attention to the sublime the rise of modern anxiety, see Thomas Weiskel, *The Romantic Sublime: Studies in the Structure and Psychology of Transcendence* (New Haven: Yale University Press, 1976).
3. "Reflections on Tintern Abbey," *Wordsworth Circle,* 5 (1974), 6.
4. Hardy appropriately called the poem "Wye above Tintern"—Florence Emily Hardy, *The Early Life of Thomas Hardy* (London: Macmillan, 1928), p. 267. In *Biographia Literaria* Coleridge calls it, *inter alia,* "his lines 'on re-visiting the Wye' " (London, 1817, p. 83). Wordsworth's surviving early references to the poem are few; on 9 December 1803, he called it "the Wye"; on 6 March 1804, he called it *"Tintern Abbey"—The Letters of William and Dorothy Wordsworth: The Early Years 1787-1805,* ed. E. de Selincourt, rev. C. L. Shaver (Oxford: Clarendon Press, 1967), pp. 425, 455.
5. Here Wordsworth exploits what he often defied, Pope's denunciation, "And ten low words oft creep in one dull line" *(An Essay on Criticism* II.147).

6. The interpenetrations of space and time in the poem have been much studied, perceptively but variously by Albert S. Gérard, "Dark Passages: Wordsworth's *Tintern Abbey," English Romantic Poetry: Ethos, Structure, and Symbol in Coleridge, Wordsworth, Shelley, and Keats* (Berkeley: University of California Press, 1968), pp. 89-117; Geoffrey H. Hartman, *Wordsworth's Poetry 1787-1814* (New Haven: Yale University Press, 1964; rpt. 1971), pp. 26-30; Robert M. Maniquis, "Comparison, Intensity, and Time in 'Tintern Abbey,' " *Criticism,* 11 (1969), 358-382.
7. *The Prose Works of William Wordsworth,* ed. W. J. B. Owen and J. W. Smyser, 3 vols. (Oxford: Clarendon Press, 1974), II, 202.
8. *Examiner,* 17 August 1817, rpt. in *Leigh Hunt's Dramatic Criticism,* ed. L. H. and C. W. Houtchens (New York: Columbia University Press, 1949), pp. 146-152.
9. For some of the channels of Winckelmann's influence, see Bernard Herbert Stern, *The Rise of Romantic Hellenism in English Literature 1732-1786* (Menasha, Wisconsin: Banta, 1940), pp. 78-117.
10. *The Letters of John Keats,* ed. H. E. Rollins, 2 vols. (Cambridge: Harvard University Press, 1958), I, 232.
11. *The Letters of Percy Bysshe Shelley,* ed. F. L. Jones, 2 vols. (Oxford: Clarendon Press, 1964), II, 80, 88-89, 112.
12. "Wordsworth and the Iron Time," in *Wordsworth: Centenary Studies . . . ,* ed. G. T. Dunklin (Princeton: Princeton University Press, 1951), pp. 131-152.
13. Watson, p. 196.
14. *Wordsworth and the Sublime* (Berkeley: University of California Press, 1973), p. 8.
15. I am obliged to Professor Stephen Maxfield Parrish for pointing out that a copy of *Lyrical Ballads,* 1805, at Cornell University has no punctuation after "man"; the absence of a comma (or colon) draws "All thinking things, all objects of all thought" more forcefully within the mind of the perceiver, who, in assuming the existence of thought in other minds, assumes also (after Bishop Berkeley) the existence of an impelling unity to account for the similarity between mind and mind.
16. *Wordsworth as Critic* (Toronto: University of Toronto Press, 1969), pp. 203-210.
17. *The Sublime Pleasures of Tragedy: A Study of Critical Theory from Dennis to Keats* (Lawrence: University Press of Kansas, 1975), p. 97.

Wordsworth and Spontaneity

Paul Magnuson

An irony of literary history is that one of the best known and often-quoted definitions of poetry is, at least in its briefest form, most resistant to analysis. Twice in the Preface to *Lyrical Ballads* Wordsworth says that "poetry is the spontaneous overflow of powerful feelings." [1] The word "overflow," as M. H. Abrams pointed out in *The Mirror and the Lamp,* embodies all the implications of an expressionistic aesthetic; the poet expresses his feelings and projects them on the external world. But what does Wordsworth mean by the word "spontaneous"? Abrams and later students of Wordsworth's literary theory assume that it means the natural as opposed to the artificial, the conventional, and the contrived.[2] A spontaneous language and poetry is the language and poetry of feeling and of the heart responding honestly and sincerely to genuine experience, not the stilted and inappropriate response to unfelt, vicarious experience.

Yet there are several other possible definitions of "spontaneous." A first possible definition is "unpremeditated." This meaning recalls Milton's invocation in Book IX of *Paradise Lost* to his "Celestial Patroness, who deigns/Her nightly visitation unimplor'd,/And dictates to me slumb'ring, or inspires/Easy my unpremeditated Verse." [3] A second parallel might be Shelley's skylark, who pours forth its song in "profuse strains of unpremeditated art." [4] But such a definition would involve Wordsworth in a discussion of inspiration, which is simply not in the subject matter of the Preface. His program for literature excludes the fictions with which such theories have been associated.[5] Furthermore, theories of inspiration, whether from Urania or Nature, emphasize passivity, which Wordsworth counters, in spite of the lines in "Expostulation and Reply" on a "wise passiveness," by insisting on the necessity of formative, deliberate thought. One major message of the Preface is that poetry is produced by long meditation: "Poems to which any value can be attached were never produced on any variety of subjects but by a man who, being possessed of more than usual organic sensibility, had also thought long and deeply" *(Prose Works,* I, 127). And when, toward the end of the Preface, he returns to the phrase "the spontaneous overflow of powerful feelings," he adds that poetry "takes its origin from emotion recollected in tranquillity: the emotion is contemplated till, by a species of re-action, the tranquillity gradually disappears, and an emotion, kindred to that which was before the subject of contemplation, is gradually produced, and does itself actually exist in the mind" *(Prose Works,* I, 149). This formulation defines a retrospective and meditative poetry. To explain a poem is to explain its origins and growth, and Wordsworth here offers his clearest explanation of that process. Poetry begins with meditation upon past experiences and emotions that, in the passage of an indefinite time, have subsided into thoughts, which are "the representatives of all our past feelings" *(Prose Works,* I, 127). Contemplation transforms the recollected raw experience into poetry and changes thought into present emotion. Repeated contemplation of significant feelings and thoughts and their relations will, Wordsworth argues, lead to habitual associations and impulses which can be followed blindly by the poet. Yet the impulses of association are automatic and mechanical only after the lengthy discipline of thought and contemplation. Wordsworth's theory does not imply that poetry is unpremeditated and is far from Shelley's statement in the *Defence of Poetry* that "the mind in creation is as a fading coal, which some invisible influence, like an inconstant wind, awakens to transitory brightness," [6] or from Keats's claim in his letter to John Taylor of 27 February 1818 that "if Poetry comes not as naturally as the Leaves to a tree it had better not come at all." [7]

A second, more applicable, definition, and one that reflects Wordsworth's usage, is "voluntary," "without constraint," and "of one's own accord or free will." This meaning, shared by eighteenth-century dictionaries,[8] first appeared in philosophical and biological contexts and emphasized the contrast between the free and voluntary as opposed to the externally constrained. The *OED* records its first occurrence in Hobbes: "That all voluntary actions . . . are called also spontaneous, and said to be done by man's own accord"; similarly, Hume wrote, "Few are capable of distinguishing betwixt the liberty of *spontaneity,* as it is call'd in the schools, and the liberty of *indifference;* betwixt that which is oppos'd to violence, and that which means a negation of necessity and causes."[9] In its philosophical context "spontaneous" indicates freedom, and in its biological context it indicates self-generation. Edward Young wrote that "an original may be said to be of a vegetable nature, it rises spontaneously from the vital root of genius; it grows, it is not made; imitations are often a sort of manufacture wrought up by those mechanics, art and labour, out of pre-existent materials not their own."[10] Wordsworth combines both of these meanings and does not imply a lack of premeditation. The first usage in that sense that the *OED* lists occurs in 1851 for "spontaneous" and in 1826 for "spontaneity." Perhaps the newer definition arose from an interpretation of Wordsworth's famous phrase.[11]

At several crucial points in the Preface, Wordsworth touches upon the self-sufficiency of the poet and his independence from immediate external stimulation. He rejects contemporary sensational literature, the "gaudiness and inane phraseology of many modern writers" *(Prose Works,* I, 123) and the "frantic novels, sickly and stupid German Tragedies, and deluges of idle and extravagant stories in verse" *(Prose Works,* I, 129), because the "mind is capable of being excited without the application of gross and violent stimulants," and observes "that one being is elevated above another, in proportion as he possesses this capability" *(Prose Works,* I, 129). In the eight paragraphs added to the Preface in 1802 he defined the poet as

> a man pleased with his own passions and volitions, and who rejoices more than other men in the spirit of life that is in him; delighting to contemplate similar volitions and passions as manifested in the goings-on of the Universe, and habitually impelled to create them where he does not find them. To these

> qualities he has added a disposition to be affected more than other men by absent things as if they were present; an ability of conjuring up in himself passions, which are indeed far from being the same as those produced by real events, yet (especially in those parts of the general sympathy which are pleasing and delightful) do more nearly resemble the passions produced by real events, than anything which, from the motions of their own minds merely, other men are accustomed to feel in themselves . . . .
>
> (*Prose Works,* I, 138)

Wordsworth implicitly distinguishes between the passions that result directly from events and the passions that the poet conjures up in himself. The poet's passions are not those stimulated by immediate experience but "resemble" those passions more than do the passions of individuals who cannot sympathize with the general feelings of mankind. The passions of real events are significantly distinct from those passions that are conjured up by the poet, and the distinction stands behind much of what Wordsworth says about poetic language in the following paragraphs. He anticipates an objection to his theory from a critic who might maintain that since "it is impossible for the Poet to produce upon all occasions language as exquisitely fitted for the passion as that which the real passion itself suggests" (*Prose Works,* I, 139), why should he not use a poetic language and diction? Why, in other words, should a poet not use the capabilities of a poetic language when he cannot reproduce reality's language exactly? Wordsworth's answer rests upon his rejection of the notion of poetry as a fiction, as an idle, fashionable pleasure, and his insistence that a serious literature must not be based on mere convention but upon reality.

Since the poet habitually creates a poetic emotion that resembles more closely the passion occasioned by real events, "he has acquired a greater readiness and power in expressing what he thinks and feels, and especially those thoughts and feelings which, by his own choice, or from the structure of his own mind, arise in him without immediate external excitement" (*Prose Works,* I, 138). Wordsworth concludes the 1802 addition by saying, "The sum of what was said is, that the Poet is chiefly distinguished from other men by a greater promptness to think and feel without immediate external excitement, and a greater power in expressing such thoughts and feelings as are produced in him in that manner" *(Prose Works,* I, 142). Five years later, explaining to Lady Beaumont the sentiments in his sonnet "With Ships the Sea Was Sprinkled," he said that once his attention is caught, the imagination creates powerful feelings: "The mind once fixed and rouzed, all the rest comes from itself . . . ."[12] And in the "Essay, Supplementary to the Preface" of 1815 he wrote, "To be moved, then, by a passion, is to be excited, often to external, and always to internal, effort . . ." *(Prose Works,* III, 81-82).

Perhaps it is a bit disturbing to find so many declarations of independence from external stimulation from the pen of a poet who, until recently in the history of criticism, has been presented as the archetypal poet of nature, who receives his inspiration from the "language of the sense." And it is perhaps even more surprising to find Wordsworth acknowledging in prose what he seemed unwilling to face directly in his poetry: the independence of his imagination.[13] For instance, at the beginning of Book XII of the 1805 *Prelude,* the book in which Wordsworth recounts the restoration of imagination and taste after the alienations of the French Revolution, he says that emotion originates externally:

> From nature doth emotion come, and moods
> Of calmness equally are nature's gift,
> This is her glory; these two attributes
> Are sister horns that constitute her strength;
> This twofold influence is the sun and shower
> Of all her bounties, both in origin
> And end alike benignant.[14]

W. J. B. Owen, in his notes to the Preface, cites these lines as being relevant to the definition of poetry as "emotion recollected in tranquillity," but adds that while these lines stress nature as the source of emotion, "there is no suggestion of this in *P. L. B.,* for Wordsworth is here concerned with 'the general passions and thoughts and feelings of men' " *(Prose Works,* I, 184). Wordsworth does mention that the emotions which generate poetry may have their origin in external nature, but, first of all, that emotion is changed by the poet, and, when nature is barren, the poet must fill up the vacuity and create moods in objects and situations.

Owen has argued that the 1800 text of the Preface "presents a theory of poetry mainly mimetic" and that the text of 1802, with additions, "presents a poetic almost entirely expressive,"[15] yet the declaration of poetic independence from external stimulation is implicit in Wordsworth's definitions of the origins of poetic creation contained in the 1800 text. The 1800 text emphasizes the imitation of rustic life and the selection of the language really used by men, but, first of all, Wordsworth intends to imitate, not narrative action, but individual feelings. The primary purpose of the poems is to trace "the primary laws of our nature: chiefly, as far as regards the manner in which we associate ideas in a state of excitement" *(Prose Works,* I, 123-124), and the narrative element in the poems takes its significance from the feelings that are embodied in it. Additionally, Wordsworth said that "poetry takes its origin from emotion recollected in tranquillity,"[16] from the contemplation of a former emotion that has subsided into thought. During that recollection a "similar" emotion is produced, the mood which overflows into poetry when the poet begins to write. Wordsworth argues that there are two different emotions, not one, in creation: one is engendered, perhaps by personal experience or nature, and subsides, and a second is stimulated by contemplating the first. The second, the aesthetic emotion, is not a recreation, rediscovery, or recapturing of the first; if it were only a recreation, it would be merely regressive, chasing the phantoms of a departed emotional moment.

Wordsworth changed the word "similar" to "kindred" in the 1802 Preface to describe the relationship between the two emotions, perhaps to emphasize the genesis of the poetic emotion. For example, the two emotions are often, in his poetry, the child's fear and terror and the adult's awe. Illumination comes, not from immediate experience, but from contemplation and writing, a process that transforms the experiences of life into the emotions of poetry. Although Wordsworth usually writes about the relations of childhood to poetic maturity, there is nothing in his theory that would specify that a particular period of time must elapse between the two emotions; it might be a matter of years or days. What is crucial is that the first emotion must subside into thought, become the subject of meditation, and produce a "kindred" emotion. Poetry and its emotions come, thus, not from the experiences of life and its emotions, but from a transformation of life's experiences. Contemplation is the essential ingredient, and while life's experiences may provide the raw material for poetry, they are neither the sole nor primary ingredient. There is nothing in any experience of life that necessarily leads to poetry rather than, say, political action, philandering, or religious musings. Poetry, as Wordsworth conceived of it, is thus spontaneous and autogenous.

In a manuscript apparently intended for Wordsworth's *A Guide Through the District of the Lakes,* which the editors have entitled "The Sublime and the Beautiful," Wordsworth describes two kinds of sublimity, a distinction which parallels that between the two kinds of emotion he discusses in the Preface. Of the several possible reactions to the scenery of mountains and clouds, Wordsworth notes that "Familiarity with these objects tends very much to mitigate & to destroy the power which they have to produce the sensation of sublimity as dependent upon personal fear or upon wonder; a comprehensive awe takes the place of the one, and a religious admiration of the other, & the condition of the mind is exalted accordingly." He distinguishes between a sublime based upon terror and personal fear, which, if continued "beyond a certain point," results in "self-consideration & all its accompanying littleness" and a second, the more exalted sublime, which "rouses us to a sympathetic energy & calls upon the mind to grasp at something towards which it can make approaches but which it is incapable of attaining" *(Prose Works,* II, 353-354). The familiarity with natural objects that mitigates personal fear and transforms it into the more exalted sublime resembles the deliberate process of contemplation (Wordsworth does not specifically call it "imagination" in 1800) which transforms the original emotion into the poetic emotion. The initial emotion, then, is the feeling aroused by an actual event, the raw material of experience; the mood in which writing begins derives from contemplating the earlier emotion but is not that original emotion.

Wordsworth's distinction between the two kinds of emotion may derive from John Dennis' distinction between vulgar, or ordinary, passion and enthusiastic passion. "Vulgar Passion," to Dennis, "is that which is moved by the Objects themselves, or by the Ideas in the ordinary Course of Life," and for example he offers "Admiration or Wonder, (the common Passion, I mean; for there is an Enthusiastick Admiration, as we shall find anon) by the Sight of a strange Object, or the Relation of one." "Enthusiastick Passion, or Enthusiasm," on the other hand, "is a Passion which is moved by the Ideas in Contemplation, or the Meditation of things that belong not to common Life." Dennis argues that "Thoughts in Meditation are naturally attended with some sort and degree of Passion" and those thoughts are, in their most sublime, religious ideas, which produce thoughts quite different from those of common objects: "As for example, the Sun mention'd in ordinary Conversation, gives the Idea of a round flat shining Body, of about two foot diameter. But the Sun occurring to us in Meditation, gives the Idea of a vast and glorious Body, and the top of all the visible Creation, and the brightest material Image of the Divinity."[17] More immediately relevant to Wordsworth's poetic theory and practice is Dennis' distinction between ordinary and enthusiastic terror. Common terror

> is a Disturbance of Mind proceeding from an Apprehension of an approaching Evil, threatning Destruction or very great Trouble either to us or ours. And when the Disturbance comes suddenly with surprize, let us call it Terror; when gradually, Fear. Things then that are powerful, and likely to hurt, are the Causes of common Terror; and the more they are powerful and likely to hurt, the more they become the Causes of Terror; which Terror, the greater it is, the more it is join'd with Wonder, and the nearer it comes to Astonishment.[18]

Enthusiastic terror derives from religious ideas, such as fear of an angry God. Wordsworth used Dennis' distinction in the 1815 Preface, where he distinguished between the "enthusiastic and meditative Imagination," "the prophetic and lyrical parts of the Holy Scriptures, and the works of Milton," and the "human and dramatic Imagination" *(Prose Works,* III, 34). Wordsworth may also have taken a hint from Dennis when he wrote that familiarity tends to change the initial sublime of wonder based on personal fear into the more exalted sublime of religious admiration, for to

Dennis the vulgar passion may come from the sight of a "strange Object." [19]

Dennis is not presenting a theory of poetic creation; he is prescribing generic rules for sublime poetry. Consequently he is little interested in theories of creation and does not concern himself explicitly with the possible genetic relationship between vulgar and enthusiastic passions or with a temporal priority of the ordinary passion. Furthermore, he says that the vulgar passion is one that can be present in dramatic literature, whereas Wordsworth, at least in the Preface, suggests that the initial emotion of experience is completely transformed into another emotion. Yet still within Dennis' criticism is the hint that there might be more of a relationship between the two passions than is suggested by their separate categorizations; he mentions that admiration and wonder belong to both the vulgar and enthusiastic passions. Wordsworth clarifies the relationship.

Wordsworth's theory of autogenous poetry, stated in 1800 and elaborated in 1802, derived from his own experience in writing. "Tintern Abbey" is Wordsworth's first major poem concerned with autogeny and the poet's power to generate poetic emotion from an earlier self. Its immediate source is Coleridge's "Frost at Midnight," written in February 1798. Wordsworth appropriates Coleridge's cyclical form and retrospective mode, and had it not been for "Frost at Midnight," "Tintern Abbey" would not have taken what for Wordsworth was a new form. That Wordsworth would have written a poem inspired by the Wye valley is understandable without Coleridge's influence, but that the poem should take its particular form cannot be accounted for except by the assumption that "Frost at Midnight" provided one. From January to March 1798 Wordsworth was at work on "The Pedlar," an expansion of "The Ruined Cottage," written the previous summer. "The Pedlar" is the first extended portrait of the development of a poetic temperament, but it is objectified in the third person and, beginning with the Pedlar's birth, is strictly chronological.[20] "Frost at Midnight" provided Wordsworth with the retrospective mode and presented him with the alarming possibility that a poet's meditation may become vexed and disturbed, so that imagination is inhibited. Coleridge is a presence in "Tintern Abbey," not because he is an intimidating influence, but because he presents to

Wordsworth the possible weakness of a retrospective mode of poetry: that a poet could not behold what once he was, that he is removed from his former self, and that the autogenous aesthetic, as Wordsworth later defined it, is questioned.

A perplexity that Wordsworth encounters in "Tintern Abbey" is directly related to the theme of spontaneity. A retrospective mode demands the affirmation of a continuity of self. Were the development of his poetic power unproblematic, a steady growth uninterrupted by personal uncertainties such as that of the Pedlar, who felt no "piteous revolutions" and "no wild varieties of joy and grief,"[21] a simple chronology would serve for narrative form. Like Coleridge, Wordsworth was not completely confident about affirming the generative relationship between his early life and poetic power. His doubt is expressed in the motif of seclusion, which recurs throughout the poem. The only thought mentioned in the first verse paragraph, aside from the recollection of the first visit, is seclusion. The "steep and lofty cliffs" that "connect/The landscape with the quiet of the sky" offer as neat an image of romantic unity as any critic could want, yet the cliffs, secluded like the scene, impress "thoughts of more deep seclusion." Wordsworth sees harmony and unity and thinks of seclusion, to which he returns throughout the poem: the hermit before his lonely fire, the city's lonely rooms, his own flight from society, and the fear of future separation from Dorothy.

A fear of society's absence is more typically Coleridgean than Wordsworthian. Wordsworth's affirmation of the landscape's presence in his absence from it hints at a worry over a permanent absence. A greater fear is that of seclusion from his own past and a consequent future decay of his "genial spirits." Those genial spirits are genius and imagination and have their origin in physical energy, one of Wordsworth's more astonishing claims. In order to overcome the fear of seclusion, he glances back toward his life before 1793, the first visit to the Wye. He recalls the passing of the "coarser pleasures of my boyish days,/And their glad animal movements." Often characterized as the period of childhood and sensation, it is, in reality, neither, but an age of adolescence and physical energy, an age of doing, not seeing. Wordsworth simply does not mention the influence of nature on his early childhood.

The later period of 1793 is characterized by both physical energy and the haunted moments of strong feeling. Then he was led to the

Wye by a love of nature and pursued by a personalized fear. He first came "more like a man/ Flying from something that he dreads than one/ Who sought the thing he loved," bringing an emotion to the scene. The dread is not identified explicitly in the poem, but most literally and biographically it was his visit, in the summer of 1793, to the Isle of Wight, where he saw the British fleet preparing for war against the French, and his solitary walk across Salisbury Plain, where he had a vision of the ancient druids rising to execute their horrible sacrifices. Partly, then, his dread was over the return of the specter of war, and this dread complements the fearsome aspects of the "deep and gloomy" wood and the "sounding cataracts." His joy is in his love of visible nature, which to him then was "all in all"; but, since he was flying from an unstated dread, an undefined vacancy, the flight to nature is to the visible which masks the dread. During the first visit nature does not lead beyond itself.

Youth's "aching joys" and "dizzy raptures," exuberant physical action and emotional responses unqualified by thought, constitute the former self and its emotion that he contemplates in 1798. These youthful fears and joys, Wordsworth asserts, have been and continue to be transformed into poetic emotions. Physical energy is subdued, so that he is "laid asleep/ In body" to become a "living soul," but subdued energy is not lost because it becomes creative genius. With the coming of mature thought, the dread of war changes into the "music of humanity," which "chastens and subdues," and into sympathy with his fellow man. The love of nature's colors and forms and the appetite for visual sublimity matures into an ability to "see into the life of things" and to experience "a sense sublime/ Of something far more deeply interfused." He has learned to see nature "not as in the hour/ Of thoughtless youth," when the forms and colors were nature's totality, and has learned to hear in nature an articulate language of a deeper sublimity and majesty not understood before. Wordsworth's eye, earlier completely filled with the visible, is now creative. The present creative love is the poetic emotion as Wordsworth defines it in the Preface, and physical activity, fears, and affections are the contemplated emotions.

The affirmation in "Tintern Abbey" is won in the face of a perplexity about seclusion from a former self, and Wordsworth's hope is that genius will be preserved through the years of deadening life. His assertions of spontaneity assume that poetic emotions derive from personal emotion and that a vigorously exercised autogeny will not fail. Yet, as affirmative as "Tintern Abbey" is, Wordsworth's poetry that immediately followed it is, in part, addressed to the same perplexity over seclusion. The early drafts of *The Prelude* and the lyrics of the Goslar winter of 1798-99 share elegiac themes, a distant youth and a maturity uncertain of its poetic career. Wordsworth's fear of seclusion is a fear that his poetry might be autogenous in a second sense: that it might be the product of only one moment and that imagination is free, not only from nature, but also from his past.

"The Two-Part Prelude," compiled before the writing of the Preface and including many of the drafts written in the late fall of 1798, opens with a question about the relationship between his present and his past. And when the question arises, his past is recalled, not by visible images, but in rhythms and cadences internalized and woven into his childhood dreams, a past of hearing, not seeing:

> Was it for this
> That one, the fairest of all rivers, loved
> To blend his murmurs with my nurse's song,
> And from his alder shades and rocky falls,
> And from his fords and shallows, sent a voice
> That flowed along my dreams? [22]

The antecedent of "this" is not explicit and not included in *The Prelude* manuscripts until 1804, but it clearly refers to a present creative frustration revealed by his use of the image of the creative breeze. Toward the end of a 1798 manuscript Wordsworth sketched the first version:

> a mild creative breeze
> A vital breeze that passes gently on
> Oer things which it hath made and soon becomes
> A tempest a redundant energy
> That sweeps the waters and the [ ] this power
> Creating not but as it may
> disturbing things created [23]

When Wordsworth's creativity is frustrated, he turns to his past in order to overcome frustrations. At the end of Part One he states that he "might fetch/ Reproaches from my former years, whose power/ May spur me on, in manhood now mature,/ To honorable toil." In the 1805 text he gave clearer expression to the generating thought of the whole poem; he hoped to find "Invigorating thoughts from former years" and to "fix the wavering balance" of his mind. Reproaches come from his knowledge that he is a chosen one and that he cannot himself choose; Wordsworth received signs of election from nature's spirits, who "when they would form/ A favor'd being open out the clouds/ As at the touch of lightning/ Seeking him with gentle visitation . . ." *(Prelude,* p. 640). Wordsworth later expanded the rough draft of lines on the "vital Breeze" at the end of the 1798 manuscript. The gentle breeze awakens him with "A tempest, a redundant energy/ Vexing its own creation" *(Prelude,* 1805, I.46-47). He repeats the image, more explicitly borrowing the image from Coleridge, and again uses the image, not to represent creative joy, but to represent creative frustration. "Eolian visitations" arrive, "but the harp/ Was soon defrauded, and the banded host/ Of harmony dispers'd in straggling sounds/ And, lastly, utter silence" *(Prelude,* 1805, I.104-107). Wordsworth attributes the frustration to the eruption of energy without containing form, to imaginative thrust without proper object or bound. His dawn appears but does not ripen "into steady morning." Specifically he lacks an appropriate form or fable, one that "may be singled out with steady choice," and he is left with the distress of his own "unmanageable thoughts." A generating thought which prompted early work on *The Prelude* was his recognition that he had not fulfilled the promise of his past. He chose retrospection to overcome his seclusion from his past and to provide a form for his imaginative energy.

Retrospection leads him to a deeper understanding of the influences of his childhood experiences upon his poetic maturity, and working on the early drafts of *The Prelude* leads him toward a theory of spontaneity. "The Two-Part Prelude," in comparison to later versions, is much leaner in commentary on childhood events. Wordsworth's focus is almost entirely on the child's emotion, and he does not devote much time to describing the poetic emotions that arise from contemplation of earlier ones. The one incident in

Part One that does discuss the poetic emotion is the famous stolen-boat episode. The child's emotions are those of troubled desertion and alienation, a violent separation from the pleasant and familiar sights of nature which is represented literally by blankness and dark vacuity. The child is thrust suddenly into a consciousness of a persistent, inhuman fear. The mature poet, however, transforms the personal fear into a kindred emotion. He gives thanks to the presences in nature:

> from my first dawn
> Of childhood, did ye love to intertwine
> The passions that build up our human soul
> Not with the mean and vulgar works of man,
> But with high objects, with eternal things,
> With life and Nature, purifying thus
> The elements of feeling and of thought,
> And sanctifying by such discipline
> Both pain and fear, until we recognize
> A grandeur in the beatings of the heart.
> (ll. 132-141)

Meditation on the "pain and fear" brings the adult's acknowledgment of the heart's grandeur, the greatness of human emotion. The distinction between the child's emotion and the adult's is signalled by a shift in tense from "did . . . interwine" to "we recognize." The recognition of grandeur is stated in appropriately physical terms, "the beatings of the heart," because its origin is to a large extent a physical event. Personalized terror is transformed into its kindred emotion, the acknowledgment of human grandeur. The transformation is accompanied by a reversal of isolation and desertion into the recognition of presence. Nature's ministry has led him to realize, not her own grandeur (that predominates in childhood), but his own grandeur, his poetic power.

The final lesson of Part One provides the only extended explanation of the way in which recollection feeds imagination and feelings follow feelings. The child's "vulgar joy" and "giddy bliss" pass into the blood and are forgotten, but the accidental associations and scenes that accompany those joys remain:

And if the vulgar joy by its own weight
Wearied itself out of the memory,
The scenes which were a witness of that joy
Remained, in their substantial lineaments
Depicted on the brain, and to the eye
Were visible, a daily sight.
(ll. 425-430)

If anything remains of the vulgar joys and the accidental emotions which accompany early events, they are "obscure feelings representative/Of joys that were forgotten." The mature poet's affection for nature is a result of memory's obscurity combined with repeated fear and joy as well as the familiarity that repeated associations brings to a particular scene. The personalized fear and terror, typical of the child's reaction to nature, is transformed into religious awe and love.

Wordsworth's preparation for writing the Preface was as much his experiences writing poetry as it was reading previous and contemporary criticism. His concern with past moods and present poetic emotions was a natural outgrowth of his meditations embodied in "Tintern Abbey" and the early drafts of *The Prelude.* Although the workings of imagination upon memory remained in other respects mysterious to him, the transformations of emotion that poetry demanded became clearer. Poetry was a result of meditation and discipline which changed life's emotions into essentially different moods, ones which overflow spontaneously into poetry.

NOTES

1. *The Prose Works of William Wordsworth,* ed. W. J. B. Owen and Jane Worthington Smyser (Oxford: Clarendon Press, 1974), I, 127, 149. Subsequent references to Wordsworth's prose are to this edition, abbreviated *Prose Works.*
2. M. H. Abrams, *The Mirror and the Lamp* (New York: Oxford University Press, 1953; W. W. Norton, 1958), pp. 102, 105, 111, and 113. See also James A. W. Heffernan, *Wordsworth's Theory of Poetry* (Ithaca: Cornell University Press, 1969), pp. 49-53 and W. J. B.

Owen, *Wordsworth as Critic* (Toronto: University of Toronto Press, 1969), pp. 37-52, 68-69.

3. *Paradise Lost* IX.21-25 in *John Milton: Complete Poems and Major Prose,* ed. Merritt Y. Hughes (New York: Odyssey Press, 1957).
4. "To a Skylark," 1. 5 in *Shelley: Poetical Works,* ed. Thomas Hutchinson, corrected by G. M. Matthews (London: Oxford University Press, 1970).
5. For a discussion of Wordsworth's attitudes toward fictions in literature, see James Scoggins' "The Preface to *Lyrical Ballads:* A Revolution in Dispute," in *Studies in Criticism and Aesthetics,* ed. Howard Anderson and John Shea (Minneapolis: University of Minnesota Press, 1967).
6. *Complete Works of P. B. Shelley,* ed. Roger Ingpen and Walter Peck (London and New York, 1926-1930; reprinted, London and New York: Gordian Press, 1965), VII, 135.
7. *The Letters of John Keats,* ed. Hyder Rollins (Cambridge: Harvard University Press, 1958), I, 238-239.
8. See John Kersey, *Dictionarium Anglo-Britannicum* (1708), Nathan Bailey, *Dictionarium Britannicum* (1730), Samuel Johnson, *A Dictionary of the English Language* (1755), and William Kenrick, *A New Dictionary of the English Language* (1773).
9. Thomas Hobbes, *The Questions concerning Liberty, Necessity, and Chance* (1656), in *The English Works of Thomas Hobbes,* ed. Sir William Molesworth (London: Bohn, 1841), V, 79. Elsewhere in the same essay Hobbes says that "*spontaneity* is a word not used in common English." David Hume, *A Treatise of Human Nature,* ed. L. A. Selby-Bigge (Oxford: Clarendon Press, 1888), p. 407.
10. Edward Young, *Conjectures on Original Composition,* in *The Complete Works: Poetry and Prose,* ed. James Nichols (London: William Tegg, 1854; reprinted Hildesheim, Germany; Georg Olms, 1968), II, 552.
11. In the *Biographia Literaria* Coleridge traces the "*origin* of metre" in "the balance in the mind effected by that spontaneous effort which strives to hold in check the workings of the passion" *(Biographia Literaria,* ed. John Shawcross [London: Oxford University Press, 1907], II, 49). For Coleridge's discussion of the historical usages of the term, see *BL,* I, 66 ff.
12. *The Letters of William and Dorothy Wordsworth: The Middle Years,* ed. Ernest de Selincourt, 2nd ed.: *Part I: 1806-1811,* rev. Mary Moorman (Oxford: Clarendon Press, 1969), p. 149.
13. See Geoffrey Hartman, *Wordsworth's Poetry: 1787-1814* (New Haven: Yale University Press, 1971), pp. 33-69.
14. William Wordsworth, *The Prelude,* ed. Ernest de Selincourt and Helen Darbishire, 2nd ed. (Oxford: Clarendon Press, 1959). Subsequent parenthetical references to this volume are abbreviated *Prelude.*
15. Owen, *Wordsworth as Critic,* p. 112.

16. The phrase "emotion recollected in tranquillity" may originally have come from Coleridge, who claimed in 1802 that the Preface arose from "the heads of our mutual Conversations &c—& the f[irst pass]ages were indeed partly taken from notes of mine" and that "Wordsworth's Preface is half a child of my own Brain/ & so arose out of Conversations, so frequent, that with a few exceptions we could scarcely either of us perhaps positively say, which first started any particular Thought . . ." *(The Letters of Samuel Taylor Coleridge,* ed. Earl Leslie Griggs [Oxford: Clarendon Press, 1956], II, 811, 830). There is an entry in one of Coleridge's notebooks which, although quite difficult to read, can be read in part: "recalling of passion in tranquillity . . . Metre distinct and artificial—till at length poetry forgot its essence in those forms which were only hieroglyphic of it." Kathleen Coburn believes that "we may be justified in entering for Coleridge a very strong claim (or some would say, blame) for the well-known phrase" *(The Notebooks of Samuel Taylor Coleridge,* ed. Kathleen Coburn [New York: Pantheon Books, 1957], I, 787, 787n). Owen, on the other hand, maintains that "since this passage can neither be read or dated precisely, it is impossible to decide who is quoting whom" *(Prose Works,* I, 185). Coleridge's notebook entry is tantalizingly obscure, teasing scholars to assert more than can be determined beyond any doubt about both attribution and meaning. L. A. Willoughby believes that Coleridge derived the idea from a phrase by Schiller in a review of Bürger's *Gedichte* in the *Jenaische Allgemeine Literatur Zeitung* (1791), "Aus der sanftern und fernenden Erinnerung mag er dichten," but Schiller's statement is a plea for emotional restraint and an idealized universality rather than impassioned individuality, not a theory of the transformation of emotion or the genetic relationship of emotions (L. A. Willoughby, "Wordsworth and Germany," in *German Studies Presented to Professor H. G. Fiedler* [Oxford: Clarendon Press, 1938], p. 444). If entry 787 was written between the fall of 1798, when Coleridge left for Germany, where he might have seen Schiller's review, and the writing of the Preface in 1800, both Coleridge and Wordsworth had been writing retrospective poetry before Coleridge read Schiller.
17. John Dennis, *The Grounds of Criticism in Poetry* (1704), in *The Critical Works of John Dennis,* ed. Edward Niles Hooker (Baltimore: The Johns Hopkins Press, 1939), I, 338-339.
18. Dennis, I, 356.
19. If Wordsworth did not find this idea in Dennis, he might have found it in Priestley: "Great objects please us for the same reason that *new* objects do, viz. by the exercise they give to our faculties" and "Whenever any object, how great soever, becomes familiar to the mind, and its relations to other objects is no longer attended to, the sublime vanishes" *(A Course of Lectures on Oratory and Criticism* [1777;

reprinted Menston, England: The Scolar Press, 1968], p. 151.

20. Transcriptions of the early manuscripts of "The Ruined Cottage" and "The Pedlar" are available in Jonathan Wordsworth, *The Music of Humanity* (London: Thomas Nelson, 1969).
21. "The Pedlar," ll. 272-273 in Jonathan Wordsworth, *The Music of Humanity,* p. 181.
22. "The Two-Part Prelude," in *The Norton Anthology of English Literature,* ed. M. H. Abrams, 3rd ed. (New York: W. W. Norton, 1974).
23. The early drafts of *The Prelude* (MS. JJ), written in the late fall of 1798, are printed in *Prelude,* pp. 633-642.

By Peculiar Grace: Wordsworth in 1802

Irene Tayler

Wordsworth didn't take criticism graciously, as for example in the spring of 1802 when he received a letter from Sara Hutchinson, speaking lightly of a new poem she had just seen in manuscript—"The Leechgatherer," as it was called until Wordsworth gave it the more formal title of "Resolution and Independence." Sara, and her sister Mary, who was to become Wordsworth's wife in a few months, had hazarded the opinion that the Leechgatherer's speeches were tedious, that too much space was devoted to the story of his dead wife and children. So outraged was William's answering letter that his sister Dorothy felt constrained to add a postscript of conciliatory advice:

> Dear Sara
>
> When you happen to be displeased with what you suppose to be the tendency or moral of any poem which William writes, ask yourself whether you have hit upon the real tendency and true moral, and above all never think that he writes for no reason but merely because a thing happened—.

William's own letter springs to defend what he considers the poem's "real tendency"; and his reason for writing it he locates unhesitatingly in his own feelings about the Leechgatherer and in those he expects to arouse:

> A person reading this Poem with feelings like mine will have been awed and controuled. . . . You say and Mary (that is you

> can say no more than that) the Poem is *very well* after the introduction of the old man; this is not true, if it is not more than very well it is very bad, there is no intermediate state. You speak of his speech as tedious: everything is tedious when one does not read with the feelings of the Author—. . . But Good God! Such a figure, in such a place, a pious self-respecting, miserably infirm . . . Old Man telling such a tale!

It is "an affair of whole continents of moral sympathy," he concludes, adding suggestively, "I will talk more with you on this when we meet." [1]

Wordsworth's skin was always thin, but on the subject of his Leechgatherer it seems to have thinned to airy nothing. Mary and Sara had certainly picked the wrong item to find fault with, given the feelings of the Author, though later he apparently reconsidered and found their criticism more just, perhaps assuming that what their sympathies had missed, others would miss as well. At any rate, in subsequent drafts he dropped the account of the dead wife and children, concentrating not on the details of hardship the old man had endured, but rather on the poet-speaker's shocked reverence for the endurance itself. The resulting poem offers the literary biographer an especially complex and subtle index to the development of Wordsworth's feelings in the spring of 1802 and indicates, as I hope to show, a point of crisis in his developing concept of the "true Poet."

Let us begin by retreating a little in time. As we know, Coleridge's grand vision for Wordsworth was that he should write a great philosophical poem to be titled, "The Recluse: or Views of Man, Nature and Society." *The Prelude,* or the "Poem to Coleridge" as it was often called, was seen as Wordsworth's way of defining for himself his competence to write the great philosophical opus. But for years *The Recluse* comprised, in addition to a few snatches of blank verse, only some lines referred to as "The Ruined Cottage," begun according to Wordsworth in 1795 and worked on at Racedown and Alfoxden in 1797 and 1798.[2] These lines relate the story, as told by a Pedlar, of a model marriage that deteriorated under external pressure and ended with the sudden departure of the husband to try to earn a living at sea. Each time the Pedlar passes by their home he finds the good wife Margaret sunk lower as she despairs of seeing her husband again; when she finally abandons herself to grief and dies, the "silent overgrowings" of nature repossess the ruined cottage that had been the family's home.

Wordsworth's stay at Racedown, where he later said this poem was begun, saw his painful recovery from a near breakdown: war with France had cut off communication with Annette Vallon and his natural daughter Caroline, and Wordsworth's own sense of poetic purpose seems to have faltered dangerously. By his later account in *The Prelude,* it was his sister Dorothy who then "maintained for me a saving intercourse/ With my true self" and "preserv'd me still/ A Poet." Critics have of course been quick to point out the analogies between the stories of Margaret of "The Ruined Cottage" and Annette; for although Annette, far from fading in anguish, appears to have behaved with vigor and resourcefulness, still Wordsworth's guilt and lack of communication may have prompted him to imagine the worst. But by 1798 "The Ruined Cottage" had grown to a poem of some nine hundred lines, of which, as Dorothy wrote to Mary Hutchinson in March, "the Pedlar's character now makes a very, certainly the *most,* considerable part of the poem." [3] In other words the story of the abandoned woman was, in effect, itself more or less abandoned as Wordsworth, recovering a sense of vocation, turned his creative attention from Margaret to the figure of the narrating Pedlar and undertook the beginnings of an imaginative "intercourse" with his "true self"; for in his mind the Pedlar was so closely identified with aspects of himself that he was later able to transfer whole passages ostensibly about the Pedlar's youth directly into *The Prelude.*

From Racedown, where Wordsworth's intimacy with Coleridge first began, he and Dorothy moved to Alfoxden to be near Coleridge and spent the marvelous year that culminated in the *Lyrical Ballads;* then brother and sister endured a bitterly cold winter in Goslar, Germany, where they had gone intending to learn the language that they might do translation. Although they learned little German, Wordsworth wrote some extraordinary poetry: important material (now openly about his own childhood) for his newly undertaken autobiographical poem—that is, *The Prelude*—as well as other poems evoking his early youth, and four of the Lucy series. It has been widely thought that at some level the Lucy of these poems was Dorothy. Even if Wordsworth was not, as Bateson has argued, [4] in love with his sister and becoming increasingly aware of it, it does seem clear that she embodied for him a combination of his redemptive past and his poetic salvation. In any case, when William and Dorothy returned from Germany they went straight to Northumberland—the neighborhood of their childhood—to visit the Hutchinson brothers and sisters, dear friends who like the Wordsworth children had been early orphaned. Among these, Mary had been an object of Wordsworth's mild romantic interest on and off for years. Here William and Dorothy stayed for seven months, and William wrote Book II of *The Prelude,* in which some lines from "The Ruined Cottage" are incorporated. It was in these months too that Coleridge, already acutely unhappy in his marriage and, like Wordsworth, eager for the company of his fellow poet, came to visit and fell passionately and (of course) hopelessly in love with Mary's sister, Sara Hutchinson. That family must have seemed to offer sanctuary of many kinds to both displaced young poets. To Dorothy, too, there was surely great appeal in the sight of brothers and sisters so successfully making a home together.

Although this was indeed a return—and after many years—to the places of his youth, Wordsworth wanted to be even more "home," and apparently that meant necessarily to be in the neighboring vale of Grasmere, first known to him as a schoolboy at Hawkshead and ever since then a place of great symbolic significance. So, near the end of the stay in Northumberland, William, his favorite brother John (home from the sea), and Coleridge set off on a kind of pilgrimage in which Coleridge was to be shown the spots so meaningful to Wordsworth. Coleridge was indeed moved by the beauty of the country, and William—triumphantly—found a cottage that he and Dorothy might rent at Town End, Grasmere. In December 1799 they moved to Dove Cottage in time to bring in the new year, 1800, and an important new stage in their own lives: Wordsworth was at last to be the Recluse, "Home at Grasmere," among his family and dearest friends. John stayed with them at their cottage for nine months, after which he went again to sea in the hope of making enough money to build houses of their own in Grasmere for William and himself; the Hutchinsons, especially Mary and Sara, were close by and frequent visitors; and Coleridge brought his family to live in neighboring Keswick the following summer.

That year, 1800, saw of course publication of the second edition of the *Lyrical Ballads,* with Wordsworth's ambitious and controversial Preface, as well as some fine new poems. And some time before the end of 1801 William and Mary Hutchinson became engaged. But a few days before Christmas there came an important turn of events: the new peace negotiations had reopened communications with France, and a letter arrived from there, presumably William's first word from or about Annette in a long time. Their daughter Caroline was by now nine years old.

That same morning, 21 December, Wordsworth had returned after long absence to his manuscript of "The Ruined Cottage," now tellingly referred to as "The Pedlar," apparently with an eye to fresh revisions. Dorothy's Journal records his eagerness: "Wm sate beside me and read the Pedlar, he was in good spirits, and full of hope of what he should do with it." Mary, who had been staying with them for a prolonged visit, was just then returning with the day's mail: Dorothy summarizes without comment: "He went to meet Mary and they brought 4 letters, 2 from Coleridge, one from Sara and one from France."[5] It must have been a disturbing situation for all: such a contact renewed at such a time—to be sure, a chance for "saving intercourse" with his "true self," but in what a confluence of intensities!

From January to March a series of letters was exchanged with Annette, and during the same period Wordsworth's chief poetic energies were occupied in revising "The Pedlar." The work made Wordsworth sick and miserable, maybe partly because the weight of so much retrospection finally began to take its toll, and I would guess partly from the nature of the job itself. Perhaps realizing that the work was by now really two poems, he seems to have been trying to separate the account of Margaret from that of the narrator, to give the latter the autonomy that in fact it never did achieve. But its lines weave most strikingly in and out of Wordsworth's recurrent preoccupations. The Pedlar's boyhood was, as I have said, modeled on Wordsworth's own, though the grown man is less William himself than an idealized projection of what he would like to grow into.

Yet it was the superficially unrelated issue of the language and purpose of poetry that finally became as much Wordsworth's topic as the history and character of the Pedlar; already in an early draft of that poem were couched assumptions and even phrases that the 1800 Preface to *Lyrical Ballads* echoed and amplified. "Much did [this Pedlar] see of men":

> Their passions and their feelings, chiefly those
> Essential and eternal in the heart
> Which 'mid the simpler forms of rural life
> Exist more simple in their elements
> And speak a plainer language.
> (*The Excursion* I.341-347) [6]

This is, in paradigm, the central theme of the Preface. When the third edition of *Lyrical Ballads* appeared in April 1802, it included no new poems, but Wordsworth enlarged the Preface by the addition of more than eight paragraphs on the twin subjects, "What is the Poet, and what the true language of poetry," adding as well a separate Appendix that undertook to explain more fully his special meaning for the term "poetic diction." And in a letter of June 1802 written to the young John Wilson, he may be seen again sifting and grappling with these issues, central to his whole aesthetic:

> But where are we to find the best measure of this [*i.e., human nature*]? I answer, [from with] in; by stripping our own hearts naked, and by looking out of ourselves to[wards me]n who lead the simplest lives most according to nature men who [ha]ve never known false refinements, . . .effeminate habits of thinking and feeling, or who, having known these [t]hings, have outgrown them.[7]

But a great poet ought to do more than "reflect" human nature, Wordsworth continues, in words that sound almost Johnsonian: "he ought, to a certain degree, to rectify" our feelings, "to render [them] more sane pure and permanent. . . ." In short—and this was crucial to Wordsworth—the poet's business is the same in relation to his public as is the Pedlar's and Leechgatherer's in relation to the young poet-speaker in each of these poems. Or, put another way, the poem is meant to *provide* precisely the regenerating experience that it recounts. Hence Wordsworth's dismay at Sara's and Mary's suggestion that "The Leechgatherer" was no more than "very well" after the introduction of the Old Man.

Wordsworth's personal life at this time surely needed regeneration—there was much to trouble and alarm him. Letters and visits from Coleridge had been growing more painful as it became clearer how thoroughly shattered were his health and happiness. It would be hard to overestimate the importance of Coleridge in these years to Wordsworth's sense of his own poetic development. *The Prelude* was "The Poem to Coleridge" not only because in so dedicating it Wordsworth was dedicating himself to Coleridge's view of his great gift and promise, but also because of his love and respect for the man. Coleridge thought Wordsworth the greatest English poet since Milton, and Wordsworth knew how to value that judgment. But "Coleridge's were very melancholy letters," writes Dorothy in December 1801; "We were made very unhappy." And on Christmas day, Coleridge's "letter made us uneasy about him. I was glad I was not by myself when I received it." In late January 1802, "A heart-rending letter from Coleridge—we were sad as we could be." The same months are full of accounts of William's own difficulty with his work—his sleeping badly, his headaches, his being "exhausted" and "unwell."

In this time, too, Dorothy's feelings about William seem more deeply stirred than usual, to judge from her Journal. When, in mid-February, he leaves her for a brief visit to Mary, Dorothy is overwhelmed with loneliness: "Went to bed at about 12 o'clock. I slept in Wm's bed, and I slept badly, for my thoughts were full of William." Two days later: "A fine morning but I had persuaded myself not to expect William, I believe because I was afraid of being disappointed." But he does arrive in the evening—"his mouth and breath were very cold when he kissed me. We spent a sweet evening. He was better—had altered the Pedlar. We went to bed pretty soon and we slept better than we expected and had no bad dreams." A couple of weeks later—the fourth of March—William again leaves for a short trip, this time to see Coleridge, and again Dorothy feels lost: "Now for my walk. I *will* be busy, I *will* look well and be well when he comes back to me. O the Darling! Here is one of his bitten apples! I can hardly find in my heart to throw it into the fire. I must wash myself, then off—" and she takes her walk, stopping to sit down, as she confides in her Journal, "where we always sit. I was full of thoughts about my darling. Blessings on him." That evening she comforts herself by reading the *Lyrical Ballads* and writing to William before going to bed. But the next night the charm works less well: "Read the LB, got into sad thoughts, tried at German but could not go on—Read LB.—Blessings on that Brother of mine!" But she did not sleep well: "I awoke with a bad head ache." And the next night "I could not fall asleep when I went to bed." But the day after that all is well again: ". . . in came William. I did not expect him till tomorrow. How glad I was. . . . We went to bed pretty soon and slept well."

Some ten days after that trip to visit Coleridge, Wordsworth made another trip and this time brought back with him Coleridge, a shockingly sick man. "I was much affected with the sight of him," writes Dorothy; "he seemed half stupefied. . . . Coleridge went to bed late, and Wm and I sate up till 4 o'clock. . . . My spirits were agitated very much." When, two days later, Coleridge left again, it was apparently clear that he was in really desolate condition; even his opium addiction may have been obvious, if that is the inference to be drawn from Dorothy's remark that he seemed "half stupefied."

Disturbance over Coleridge, concern for Annette, plans to marry Mary, certainly some awareness of Dorothy's nervous devotion and perhaps a share of such feelings himself in return—all these were occupying Wordsworth's mind along with his revisions of "The Pedlar" in the first months of 1802, and they may help account for the sore longing one hears behind these revealing lines describing the old Pedlar:

In his steady course,
No piteous revolutions had he felt,
No wild varieties of joy and grief.
Unoccupied by sorrow of its own,
His heart lay open;

. . . . .

for, in himself
Happy, and quiet in his cheerfulness,
He had no painful pressure from within [after 1814 changed
to "without"!]
That made him turn aside from wretchedness
With coward fears. He could *afford* to suffer
With those whom he saw suffer.
(*Excursion* I.358-371)

The suffering chiefly in question in that poem was of course Margaret's, and the progress of the framing device, the exchanges between the Pedlar and the young man he addresses—the "I" of the poem—is the progress of that young man's ability to accept Margaret's suffering, too, without being weakened by what Wordsworth later calls "the impotence of grief" (*Excursion* I.924).

Whether or not Wordsworth felt a connection between Margaret and Annette, he certainly knew by now that in Annette's case grief was not really called for—she was not fading in anguish, though her life had been hard; yet he seems certainly to have been considering how he should best deal with that long unfinished business of his past. During this time, starting with "The Singing Bird" on 11 or 12 March, his poetry began suddenly to blossom like an early spring, with a continuing burst of fine short lyrics in the next weeks. By 22 March, after another letter from France, a personal resolution had been reached; Dorothy records the decision in her Journal: "We resolved to see Annette, and that Wm should go to Mary." It must have been a momentous decision; certainly it meant facing one portion of his youthful past, and in his daughter Wordsworth may even have hoped to see glimpses of his still younger self. It was to be, then, a journey at once backwards and forwards. If the story of Margaret was his nightmare fantasy about Annette, then clearly he had decided to revise the ending—at least in life. Whereas Margaret had "lingered in unquiet widowhood" "nine tedious years," Annette (who, by the way, called herself "veuve Williams," widow Williams) would after nine years see her "husband" return—even if only to settle affairs so that he could marry someone else. Still, the story would have its new ending, Wordsworth would not "turn aside from wretchedness/ With coward fears"; perhaps it could mean for Annette, as for himself, a liberation from the past.

On 26 March he wrote to Annette, presumably explaining his and Dorothy's decision, and that same evening just before bed composed a poem, especially suggestive in the context of the day's events:

> My heart leaps up when I behold
> 　A rainbow in the sky:
> So was it when my life began;
> So is it now I am a man;
> So be it when I shall grow old
> 　Or let me die!
> The Child is father of the Man;
> And I could wish my days to be
> Bound each to each by natural piety.

He is surely in a state of high agitation, for though he might wish his days to be bound each to each, it is clear that he is living in a whirlwind of change. The very next morning—"A divine morning" Dorothy tells us—Wordsworth at breakfast, "wrote part of an ode." This is, by all evidence, the first four stanzas of what was to become the great Intimations Ode. As everyone knows, these stanzas record a deep sense of loss: "The rainbow comes and goes," he admits, possibly alluding to the rainbow of his poem the evening before, "And lovely is the rose"—but "the things which I have seen I now can see no more." Though all of Nature has joined to celebrate the spring,

> To me alone there came a thought of grief:
> A timely utterance gave that thought relief,
> 　And I again am strong.

Many critics feel that the "timely utterance" was the Rainbow poem, but I see no reason to insist on its having been a poem at all; it might even have been the letter to Annette announcing his projected trip. It's hard to speculate meaningfully on the basis of so little information; but the crucial point in any case is that he did avoid "the impotence of grief" and was led back to strength ("I again am strong")—at least for the moment.

The four "Intimations" stanzas written in 1802 end on the note of loss, but they put it as a question:

> Whither is fled the visionary gleam?
> Where is it now, the glory and the dream?

Wordsworth was not to try to answer the question in the context of the Ode itself for another two years: but Coleridge thought he knew the answer, and when he heard the four stanzas a few days later, he offered his answer in a verse-letter addressed to Sara Hutchinson, the first version of "Dejection, an Ode." The verse-letter tells of his own grief, his own loss of "The Passion & the Life, whose Fountains are within!" and contrasts his grief with the happiness he desires for Sara, a happiness that he can share only vicariously, but which, if she partakes in it, will at least partly revivify him. His description of the family gathering seems to borrow directly from plans the Wordsworths were actually developing:

> When thou, & with thee those, whom thou lov'st best,
> Shall dwell together in one happy Home,
> One House, the dear *abiding* Home of All
> I too will crown me with a Coronal—
> Nor shall this Heart in idle Wishes roam
> Morbidly soft!

William, Mary, Dorothy, John, and Sara had not thought of living in a single house—John's wish in going back to sea had been to earn enough so that he could afford to build one house for William and another for himself—but the allusion to the general idea of an "abiding home" is clear; Coleridge seems even to be promising not to begrudge John's coming precedence in Sara's life, for it was now widely assumed that *they* would marry.[8] And he echoes William's "coronal" from the "Intimations" verses to express the satisfaction he will himself experience on behalf of them all.

We recall that when William and Dorothy decided to visit

Annette, it was decided also that "William should go to Mary," presumably to explain to her in person the reasons for their projected trip. Without doubt Mary had long known of William's liaison with Annette—it was not kept a secret among friends—but a plan to visit a former love and her child will still be broached with some tact to a fiancée.

William left to see Mary on 7 April, his thirty-second birthday, and the next morning Dorothy wrote to Mary. On the tenth she received a letter from William, apparently written before he had reached Mary, and then on the twelfth came a letter from William and Mary together, exciting an anxiety that creates a funny little scene described in Dorothy's Journal—funny, that is, in its depiction of her frustration at not being permitted to be alone with her letter. She has gone for mail, and a friend walks her part way back, trying to make conversation—or, in Dorothy's words, "questioning me like a catechizer all the way. Every question was like the snapping of a little thread about my heart I was so full of thoughts about my half-read letter and other things." One of the other things was surely her own relationship to William. Her Journal notes that she "slept ill" that night and kept busy the next day, but when she was told "*William* was come" (her italics), "The surprise shot through me"; she adds elsewhere "I believe I screamed." [9] Oddly she does not mention at this time the Glow-worm poem that William had written for her after parting from Mary, on his trip home, though she often alludes to it later and treasured it greatly. It begins by addressing Dorothy as "my Love" and recalls a tender incident seven years earlier at Racedown, in which he had caught and saved a glowworm to show Dorothy, who had never seen one before. "O joy it was for her and joy for me!" the poem ends.

But the trip was fraught with even more anxiety for William than for Dorothy. He had just been to see Coleridge and possibly heard Coleridge's "Dejection" letter answering his own Ode; he was leaving Dorothy to see Mary (that he knew this was hard for Dorothy, and that it aroused nostalgia in him, seems clear from the Glow-worm poem). And of course he was bearing news to Mary that was likely to disturb her, however fully she might be expected to concur in the decision. Possibly, too, he planned to propose to her the date of their own wedding, as their coming marriage was more openly talked about in May and June.

But to return to William on his trip: he said later that he had experienced an unstable mood of elation followed by depression as he crossed over Barton Fell—the route he was taking for the visit to Mary; [10] this mood, and his concern about its implications for his mental and moral health, bore fruit in the season's greatest finished poem, "Resolution and Independence," that is, "The Leech-gatherer" whose speech Sara and Mary had pronounced "tedious." William and Dorothy had in fact encountered an old leechgatherer in their first year at Dove Cottage, as Dorothy recorded in her Journal at the time. "N.B. When Wm and I returned from accompanying Jones we met an old man almost double. . . ." Her account is detailed and dispassionate, mentioning that his wife and nine of his children were dead, while the tenth, a sailor, had not been heard of for many years. He himself had been "hurt in driving a cart, his leg broke his body driven over his skull fractured." But sensitive as she was, Dorothy records no awareness of anything especially noble or lofty about him, nor even resolute or independent: "His trade was to gather leeches, but now leeches are scarce and he had not strength for it. He lived by begging. . . ."

Wordsworth made, then, a considerable transformation of this figure in his poem of 1802, and the changes show how absolutely right Dorothy was in assuring Sara and Mary that he never "writes . . . merely because a thing happened." Of course the meeting with the real leechgatherer might have come to nothing; or it might have offered material for another "Simon Lee" or "Alice Fell," where the poet-speaker regards hardship with a kind of bitter pity. But in fact Wordsworth was on quite a different track just then, and its direction is pretty clear. Consider these imaginative connections: at the time in 1800 when William and Dorothy had met the actual leechgatherer, William was deeply preoccupied with the theoretical issues raised by his Preface, first published that year, and also—uncomfortably, I think—with John's departure to sea again to earn money for their homes. (John apparently accepted, cheerfully and without question, that his poetic brother was not himself up to the drudgery of moneymaking.) In any case, at about the time of John's departure, Wordsworth began a significant poem about his relationship to John. "When to the attractions of the busy world/ Preferring studious leisure, I had chosen/ A habitation in this peaceful Vale," it begins, and tells how, on arriving at Dove Cottage, William had found a fir-grove nearby that he loved in every way except that he hadn't been able to locate in it a length of open ground for pacing—something he liked to do as he composed. But then one day months later he returned to the grove to discover that *John* (who, recall, was living with them those nine months) had seen there just the sort of spot William himself had sought,

> winding on with such an easy line
> Along a natural opening, that I stood
> Much wondering how I could have sought in vain
> For what was now so obvious.

Quite simply, John "had surveyed" the grove "with a finer eye,/ A heart more wakeful," had seen what William had not, and had worn a path there with his sailor's restless feet. Now how should a mere sailor regard Nature more responsively than he whose whole aesthetic was posited on sensitivity to "the beautiful and permanent forms of nature"? The implication seems clear, and William spells it out in the next lines: through all those years at sea John had carried with him "undying recollections" that made him a poet too:

> Nature there
> Was with thee; she, who loved us both, she still
> Was with thee; and even so didst thou become
> A *silent* Poet.

But there remains an unspoken further implication too; for William, the practicing poet, has had to acknowledge in himself a relative insensitivity in that though living always close to the inspiring sights of nature he had seen no path where the "finer eye" and "heart more wakeful" of his silent-Poet brother had discovered at once a "natural opening." . . . Then John left for the sea again and William left his poem unfinished.

But in the spring of 1802—apparently on the very day of "My Heart Leaps Up," the day before the Intimations stanzas [11]—Wordsworth returned to work on this poem addressed to John and wrote its conclusion. "Back to the joyless Ocean thou art gone" he tells his brother, but the spot in the fir-grove is now named for him and William goes there to admire the view of Silver-How and the lake in the distance and through that view to commune with John in a kind of visionary intimacy. Notice, as Wordsworth describes this moment of communion, how the important words that close the "Intimations" stanzas (to be written the next morning) are already collected here, as if in preparation: "visionary," "gleam," and "dream."

the steep
Of Silver-How, and Grasmere's peaceful lake,
And one green island, gleam between the stems
Of the dark firs, a visionary scene!
And while I gaze upon the spectacle
Of clouded splendour, on this dream-like sight
Of solemn loveliness, I think on thee,
My Brother, and on all which thou hast lost.

John has lost, of course, the literal sight of such scenery, but William will lament the next day his own far greater loss of the ability to see in it "the visionary gleam." Meanwhile in this imagined communion with John in the fir-grove, briefly seeing the "gleam," the "visionary scene," the "dream-like sight," he momentarily recaptures his own waning capacity, and in this mood imagines John, the silent Poet, on shipboard quoting his, William's, poetry, pacing there as William paces here, "for aught I know,/ Timing my steps to thine,"

Mingling most earnest wishes for the day
When we, and others whom we love, shall meet
A second time, in Grasmere's happy Vale.

If John could give him the vision, the poem seems to suggest, he could give John the voice. Could *this* be the "timely utterance" that made him once more "strong"?

This is 26 March; next day came those four stanzas of the "Intimations Ode"; then on 7 April the trip to Mary to explain that he and Dorothy would go to France. And it was on this trip, remember, that he passed over Barton Fell, where he had experienced that unstable mood of elation followed by depression soon to be memorialized in the opening lines of "Resolution and Independence." This mood was surely a most distressing recurrence in himself of those "wild varieties of joy and grief" which the Pedlar, in his "steady course," had been blessedly free of, and which Wordsworth hoped to purge through the process of the poem: as he had insisted to Sara, "A person reading the poem with feelings like mine will have been awed and controuled."

The imaginative connections I suggest we consider come, then, to this: in 1800 the theoretical problem of what it is that makes a true poet and the immediate personal one of William's own perplexingly dependent relationship to John had attached themselves imaginatively to that concurrent meeting with the actual leechgatherer: the re-emergence in 1802 of both the theoretical and the immediate concerns revivified the old leechgatherer as well, but by the same motive transformed him. He is now to show what makes the true poet, indeed to demonstrate the purpose of poetry as Wordsworth defined it in that letter of June 1802 to the young John Wilson—that is, he is to provide an occasion for poet and reader to rectify their feelings (to "awe" and "controul" them) by "stripping" their hearts "naked" and looking out of themselves "towards men who lead the simplest lives . . . men who have never known . . . effeminate habits of thinking and feeling, or who, having known these things, have outgrown them." It should come as no surprise that Wordsworth wrote this letter when he was directly embroiled in the composition of "Resolution and Independence," for clearly the leechgatherer of that poem is just the man towards whom one should look with heart stripped naked; and the young poet-traveller illustrates the rectifying effect of doing so, as he begins in the last lines the process of "outgrowing" his own "effeminate habits of thinking and feeling."

Let us briefly trace the events. The poem opens on a scene of sunshine after a night storm; but, perversely, the poet, "a Traveller then upon the moor," reverses in himself the moods of Nature, sinking suddenly from joy to dejection as "fears and fancies thick upon me came." Although he has always been, he says, "a happy Child of earth"—"Far from the world I walk, and from all care"—he is now suddenly gripped by fear:

> But there may come another day to me—
> Solitude, pain of heart, distress, and poverty.

Back in "Tintern Abbey," envisioning Dorothy's future and the benefit she would later receive from memories of that moment in the Wye valley, Wordsworth had depicted strikingly similar trials for her:

> Oh! then,
> If solitude, or fear, or pain, or grief
> Should be thy portion, with what healing thoughts
> Of tender joy wilt thou remember me,
> And these my exhortations!

In "Resolution and Independence," however, the poet's position is reversed: he is himself the one in need of healing thoughts, and with him other poets, too:

> We Poets in our youth begin in gladness;
> But thereof come in the end despondency and madness.

The cause of this, the poem implies, is that such "poets" are too much tempted to consider themselves children of the earth, to assume—even after youth—that they will be cared for as children are (perhaps even as John is preparing to care for him):

> My whole life have I lived in pleasant thought,
> As if life's business were a summer mood;
> As if all needful things would come unsought
> To genial faith, still rich in genial good;
> But how can He expect that others should
> Build for him, sow for him, and at his call
> Love him, who for himself will take no heed at all?

It is in this context that he thinks of Chatterton, who "perished in his pride," and of Burns who, though he did walk "in glory and in joy," also wrote the "Ode to Despondency," which Wordsworth knew well and said he could never read "without the deepest agitation." Certainly he has Coleridge in mind as well. And, surely, himself.

At the moment of the poet's greatest depression—with the words "thereof come in the end despondency and madness"—the needed exhortation comes:

> Now, whether it were by peculiar grace,
> A leading from above, a something given,
> Yet it befell, that, in this lonely place,
> When I with these untoward thoughts had striven,
> Beside a pool bare to the eye of heaven
> I saw a Man. . . .

I was a child, I saw a man—almost a synopsis of the poem. Like a huge stone, a reposing sea-beast, a motionless cloud, the old man takes on the symbolic significance of steady, solid, quiet perseverance—"a man from some far region sent,/ To give me human strength, by apt admonishment." The "grace" is "peculiar," of course, in the sense that it is special, individual, not general—so the theological meaning of the term. But a theologian might well find it peculiar in another sense, for its source is not God, but poetry. The words that characterize the old leechgatherer—and especially those that characterize his language—are significant: he makes "gentle" answer in "courteous" speech, his words "each in solemn order followed each"—his is "lofty utterance," "choice word," "measured phrase," "stately speech." In short, he speaks the true language of poetry, the permanent and philosophical language of those who—to quote Wordsworth's Preface—"hourly communicate with the best objects from which the best part of language is originally derived." The poet-Traveller recognizes in the resolute dignity and "demeanor kind" of this old man a proper rebuke for his erratic moodiness and the childish assumption that for him all needful things should come unsought. Seeing the apt admonishment for what it is, he makes his judgment:

and when he ended
I could have laughed myself to scorn to find
In that decrepit Man so firm a mind.

In short, the historical leechgatherer-turned-beggar has metamorphosed in Wordsworth's imagination into a variant of the Pedlar, who, like John, is one of the "silent poets" who possess that vision Wordsworth fears to lose; among the lines added to the Pedlar MS after this critical Spring [12] are these:

Oh! many are the Poets that are sown
By Nature; men endowed with highest gifts,
The vision and the faculty divine;
Yet wanting the accomplishment of verse . . .
. . . live out their time,
Husbanding that which they possess within.
(*Excursion* I.77-90)

Though the lines here refer to the Pedlar, they might just as well be said of the leechgatherer or John—all figures with whom Wordsworth identifies himself, whose initial endowment he shares, but whose "human strength" he must emulate if that endowment is to be realized in great poetry. The overall lesson is clear. The true Poet—he whose pure language and rectifying purpose are so passionately recommended in the Preface—need not ever even write "poetry"; moreover, those who call themselves "poets" may not depend on their gift, their talent, to sustain them. To remain poets, they must learn to become balanced, responsible; they must obtain "human strength"—if necessary, by "apt admonishment."

Now clearly what "happened" in the Leechgatherer poem was essentially Wordsworth's invention—his "vision" one might say—a direct outgrowth of what he himself called "the feelings of the Author." Acutely aware of his own dependency, aware of his own "piteous revolutions" of "joy and grief," his "painful pressure from within" (I quote from "The Pedlar"), Wordsworth created once more, and in even starker outline, a figure whose "peculiar grace" it is first to *embody* the qualities of calm humanity, strength, and independence that Wordsworth so ardently sought for himself, and then, by force of encounter, to *infuse* them in the young poet-Traveller, thereby in Wordsworth himself, and finally in his readers. In this way Wordsworth's and our feelings are to be "rectified" and made "sane, pure, and permanent," as Wordsworth had said they should be, in that letter to Wilson written as Wordsworth was composing "Resolution and Independence."

In the *Apology for Smectymnuus* Milton had connected poetry and the poet in terms a dedicated moralist like Wordsworth would not be likely to forget:

> He who would not be frustrate of his hope to write well hereafter in laudable things, ought himself to bee a true Poem, that is, a composition, and patterne of the best and honourablest things.

I think that as Wordsworth considered his unstable mood in crossing over Barton Fell on the way to Mary's, he recognized that if he was to justify himself as a Miltonic "true Poem" his position at the center of so many gathered lives would require a steadying self-control.

> "God," said I, "be my help and stay secure;
> I'll think of the Leech-gatherer on the lonely moor!"

Yet of course it is not really to God that he is turning—but rather to himself, to his own poetic creation built to meet his own needs; the old man embodies what Wordsworth must become, as the poem that gives him life is manifest evidence that its author feels he is on the way to becoming it.

On 9 July William and Dorothy set off on the first stage of their great journey to France—Dorothy speaks movingly of their closeness on the coach ride: "A heavy shower came on, but we buttoned ourselves up, both together in the Guard's coat and we liked the hills and the Rain the better for bringing us so close to one another—I never rode more snugly." They stayed ten days with Mary and Sara on the way, arriving in London 29 July, and on the thirty-first taking the morning coach to Dover, passing over Westminster Bridge on their way. Dorothy records the thrilling view in her Journal, and Wordsworth wrote either then, or on his return (as the title states: Sept. 3), his great sonnet "Earth has not anything to show more fair."

For years Wordsworth had written no sonnets at all, when on 21 May of this same spring of 1802 Dorothy had read aloud to him some sonnets of Milton. Here is Wordsworth's own account of the occasion, offered many years later.

> I had long been acquainted with [Milton's sonnets], but I was particularly struck on that occasion by the dignified simplicity and majestic harmony that runs through most of them. . . . I took fire . . . and produced three sonnets the same afternoon.

He couldn't remember what two of those sonnets were, but the one he did remember is "I grieved for Buonoparté," a study of the relationship between private life and public responsibility: like the Poet, the Governor must be wise and good—in Milton's words "a composition, and patterne of the best and honourablest things." And among these things are

> Books, leisure, perfect freedom, and the talk
> Man holds with week-day man in the hourly walk
> Of the mind's business.

These are Miltonic values, but subsumed under the terms of Wordsworth's own experience. In France, during the quiet month that he and Dorothy finally spent with Annette and Caroline, Wordsworth wrote seven more sonnets, only one concerning the private experience of their visit; that one is the lovely "It is a beauteous evening calm and free." All the rest, and the flood of sonnets that continued after his return to England, he later included quite properly under the rubric "Poems Dedicated to National Independence and Liberty." All ring with a new confidence, a new sense of clarity and power:

> Milton! thou shouldst be living at this hour:
> England hath need of thee . . .
> . . .

Thy soul was like a Star, and dwelt apart;
Thou hadst a voice whose soul was like the sea;
Pure as the naked heavens, majestic, free,
So didst thou travel on life's common way,

In cheerful godliness; and yet thy heart
The lowliest duties on herself did lay.

Not much, maybe, as a description of Milton, but fine as an idealized view of what Wordsworth now wanted for himself. With the momentous spring of 1802 behind him and with the renewed dedication to "true" poetry—the vision that comes of human strength—found in "Resolution and Independence," it's not surprising that he should erupt at the hint from Sara that some part of that poem might be *tedious:* "Good God! Such a figure in such a place!" Whole continents of moral sympathy indeed—for in his view he had done no less than create, and then receive, his own peculiar grace by means of his silent poets, through them outgrowing his "effeminate habits of thinking and feeling." He could now turn his attention outward, to "Man, Nature and Society," as projected in *The Recluse.* Taking Milton as his guide, he could realize the claim that Coleridge has always made for him—of being Milton's true heir and one of England's finest poets. Such were "the feelings of the author" that in the spring of 1802 lay so close to the surface of his ever-thin skin.

NOTES

1. *The Letters of William and Dorothy Wordsworth: The Early Years 1787-1805,* ed. Ernest de Selincourt, 2nd ed., rev. by Chester L. Shaver (Oxford: Clarendon Press, 1967), pp. 366, 367 (hereafter cited as *Early Letters).* This letter is dated 14 June 1802.
2. See Mark Reed, *Wordsworth: The Chronology of the Early Years* (Cambridge: Harvard University Press, 1967), Appendix XIII, "The Date of The Ruined Cottage." Reed discounts Wordsworth's claim to have begun the poem in 1795.
3. *Early Letters,* p. 199.
4. *Wordsworth: A Re-Interpretation* (London: Longmans, 1954); see especially Chapter 5, "Egotistical Sublime."
5. *Journals of Dorothy Wordsworth,* ed. Mary Moorman (London: Oxford

University Press, 1971), pp. 70-71. All further quotations from Journal entries are taken from this edition, in which they may be located by date.

6. These lines appear in MS B, dated January-February 1798 in *The Poetical Works of William Wordsworth,* ed. Ernest de Selincourt and Helen Darbishire (Oxford: Clarendon Press, 1940-1949), V, 386. Quotations from Wordsworth's poetry, identified in the text by title and line number, are from the de Selincourt edition.
7. *Early Letters,* p. 355.
8. By family tradition, John first loved Mary, but then gave way to William and began to shift his own affection to Sara. See Mary Moorman, *William Wordsworth, A Biography: The Early Years* (Oxford: Clarendon Press, 1957), pp. 472-473.
9. For "I believe I screamed," see *Early Letters,* p. 350.
10. See Moorman, *Wordsworth . . . Early Years,* pp. 540, 556.
11. De Selincourt in *The Poetical Works of William Wordsworth,* II, 488-489, points out that the poem, apparently begun in 1800, was by Wordsworth dated 1802 in his 1815 and 1820 editions. Much later (1836 and in the Isabella Fenwick notes, 1843) Wordsworth changed this to 1805, the year of John's death. I would be inclined to credit the earlier recollection as to dating even without the internal evidence that ties the poem to the spring of 1802, and specifically to this point in March. Accordingly, I join those who conjecture that this is the poem Dorothy refers to in her Journal of 26 March 1802, as "his Silver How poem." But see Mark Reed, *Wordsworth: The Chronology of the Middle Years* (Cambridge: Harvard University Press, 1975), p. 156n.
12. These lines first appeared in MS E^2 *(Poetical Works,* V, 10), which, according to de Selincourt, contains "the work done in later February and early March" of 1802 *(Poetical Works,* V, 410). But recently, in "The Chronology of Wordsworth's *The Ruined Cottage* After 1800" *(Studies in Philology,* 74 [January 1977], 89-112), James A. Butler argues persuasively that MS E^2 was once the first gathering of MS M, the manuscript the Wordsworths prepared for Coleridge to take to Malta in early 1804. Butler dates the E^2 portion of that undertaking early March—within days, in fact, of the time Wordsworth is thought to have returned after a two-year hiatus to his work on the "Intimations Ode" (see *Poetical Works,* IV, 465). Indeed, the conjunctions here deserve another study.

Poetry of Familiarity: Wordsworth, Dorothy, and Mary Hutchinson

Donald H. Reiman

In 1954 F. W. Bateson created a minor scandal in the then staid precincts of Wordsworth scholarship by declaring in *Wordsworth: A Re-Interpretation* that much of Wordsworth's best poetry arose directly from the *Sturm und Drang* not only of his love affair with Annette Vallon in 1792 (as well as the guilt consequent on their separation) but also of his unacknowledged love for his sister Dorothy.[1] Bateson's thesis is, in fact, much broader. In his opening chapter, "The Two Voices," and in his conclusion, "The Critical Verdict," he tries to explain all of Wordsworth's poetry by examining the conflict between the poet's stated motive of providing "his readers with moral instruction" which, Bateson believed, underlay the poems in Wordsworth's "Augustan Voice," and the unconscious motivation behind his writing of poems like "Tintern Abbey," the Lucy poems, and *The Prelude,* which exhibit Wordsworth's "Romantic Voice."

Bateson's basic approach to Wordsworth—using the poetry as well as biographical evidence to pinpoint problem areas in the poet's psyche and then reexamining individual poems with these conflicts in mind—has gained wide acceptance.[2] But—though many earlier statements by Ernest de Selincourt in his notes to the Oxford English Text Edition and by Mary Moorman in her later, two-volume *William Wordsworth: A Biography* provide factual material tending to corroborate Bateson's view of the poet—there has been a militant resistance on the part of some Wordsworthians, particularly in Great Britain, to accepting two possibilities: first, that William Wordsworth felt a stronger emotional tie to his sister Dorothy during their years living together at Windy Brow, Racedown, Alfoxden, Germany, and Grasmere (1794-1802) than he ever did to Mary Hutchinson, whom he married in 1802; and, second, that the Lucy poems and several other poems owe their inception to the conflict deep within Wordsworth between his strong feelings for his sister and his fear of the possibly dangerous consequences of their mutual love.

The strength of this resistance, which some of us believed to be dying out, was illustrated in 1970 in Mary Moorman's lecture to the Royal Society of Literature in which, by simplistic paraphrasing, she reduced Bateson's complex argument to this conception: "All the poems addressed to Dorothy, directly or indirectly, are considered to be out-and-out love poems, and on this evidence, and this alone—for there is no other—he based his 'reinterpretation' of Wordsworth."[3] Mrs. Moorman, provoked by Kenneth Clark's equally simplistic account of Wordsworth and Dorothy in his lectures on *Civilization,* attempted to discredit what she termed "crude and insensitive writing about" William and Dorothy (p. 93). In her lecture she brings together much useful information about the history of Wordsworth's relationship with his sister, providing for example (as Helen Darbishire had earlier in the fine edition of *Journals of Dorothy Wordsworth* that bears both scholars' names[4]), a clear account of the history of Dorothy's later physical and mental deterioration. But she overlooks the tone of the many poems Wordsworth wrote to or about Dorothy (and Mary Hutchinson). Sometimes—even in the generally judicious account of Dorothy's health—she identifies superficial causes for reactions that, from the tone of both Dorothy's letters and journals and William's poetry, may well have had deeper psychological roots. For example, she mentions the many "headaches and internal upsets" that Dorothy and William suffered during their years of living alone and then attributes the "great improvement in her health" after William's marriage partly to the fact that "the care of her brother was now shared with Mary" (pp. 92-93). But the psychosomatic effects of conflicts between sexual desire and social taboos had been recognized at least as early as the Biblical account of Amnon, who "was so tormented that he made himself ill because of his sister Tamar" (2 Samuel 13:2). Dorothy's minor illnesses and her later improvement in health cannot be definitely related to William's marriage, but Mrs. Moorman's explanation of the possible relation is patently inadequate.

During a subsequent exchange in the letters column of *TLS*, initiated by Alethea Hayter's contention that Mrs. Moorman's lecture should have "refuted once for all" the "allegation of incest against William and Dorothy Wordsworth," I maintained the position that, while we could never know what exactly went on between William and Dorothy Wordsworth during their years together, several of Wordsworth's poems seem to reflect an emotional struggle to define his feelings toward Dorothy within a socially acceptable context.[5]

While I acknowledge my debt to *Wordsworth: A Re-Interpretation*, it will be clear that I reject a number of Bateson's detailed conclusions.[6] I believe that Wordsworth's great original contribution to English poetry lies in those poems that grew out of his own various psychological turmoils (which I do not regard, however, as ending with his marriage) and that his decline as a poet can be traced directly to the resolution, one by one, of the conflicts within him—one of the strongest of which arose from the mixed feelings of fraternal affection, passion, and guilt toward his sister Dorothy. Thus, though the following pages concentrate on some of the less frequently examined poetry relating to Wordsworth's feelings for his sister and his wife, the discussion should be seen as part of a larger view of Wordsworth's art relevant to all of his poems that evidently resulted from the series of internal conflicts that began to surface soon after his return to England from France in 1792. I do not attempt to trace the origins of these conflicts to possible deeper roots in Wordsworth's childhood, though I think that some suggestions made by Bateson and Onorato are probably relevant here.[7] My central focus, at present, is on the poetry arising directly out of the interactions of William, Dorothy, and Mary Wordsworth.

I.

On 4 October 1802, Mary Hutchinson married William Wordsworth. The emotional relationships among Mary, William, and his sister Dorothy during the months leading up to that union are adequately documented only by Dorothy, who in her *Journals* recorded her feelings about the event in great detail—too great to include here in full. After recounting with warmth and affection her last weeks alone together with William at Dove Cottage, Grasmere, and their departure from it on 9 July 1802, Dorothy describes their journey to see the Hutchinsons at Gallow Hill, where they arrived on Thursday evening, 15 July. Within this account of the week in transit, we find Dorothy and William, who were riding atop the coach, protecting themselves from the rain: "we buttoned ourselves up, both together in the Guard's coat and we liked the hills and the Rain the better for bringing [us] so close to one another—I never rode more snugly." [8] After a brief stay with the Hutchinsons at Gallow Hill, William and Dorothy traveled to London (where they arrived on 29 July) and thence via Dover to Calais (1 August) where they met Annette Vallon and William's natural daughter Caroline. They spent exactly four weeks at Calais, living in lodgings and seeing Annette and Caroline, or Caroline alone, daily. The Wordsworths returned to England on 30 August, having settled financial arrangements with Annette and having had an opportunity to become well acquainted with William's daughter.[9] After remaining in London from 31 August till 22 September, Dorothy and William returned to Gallow Hill on 24 September. Dorothy's account of the wedding day (even those crucial sentences omitted from earlier printed texts) is too well known to quote in full. Dorothy did not attend her brother's wedding, though she had worn the wedding ring the night before it; she lay on her bed in emotional shock during the time the wedding party was gone and pulled herself together to greet the groom (and bride) only at the insistence of Sara Hutchinson; Dorothy writes at the end of her account, perhaps projecting her feelings into Mary Hutchinson Wordsworth: "Poor Mary was much agitated when she parted from her Brothers and Sisters and her home." [10]

William Wordsworth's marriage, no matter how much Dorothy liked Mary Hutchinson, was a turning point in Dorothy's life, leaving her ever after half an outsider in the household that she and William had kept together for seven years. Dorothy's feelings are more than explicable: they are inescapable. William selected a mate who, as one of Dorothy's closest friends, would accept her as a continuing member of the family (beginning with their honeymoon), but even though his choice was itself an act of kindness and love, Dorothy was displaced as William's closest companion.

It was natural that at age thirty-two, seeing ahead the means to meet the responsibility of supporting a wife and children, William Wordsworth—a virile man of exceptional sexual magnetism, if we are to trust Coleridge [11]—should desire to marry. It was natural also that he should want to do so in a way compatible not only with his own needs, but also with those of Dorothy, whom he repeatedly acknowledged to be the person dearest to him throughout the years since his return from France. In those few allusions to Mary Hutchinson in William's surviving early letters there is, on the contrary, no evidence of warmth, passion, or love that was more than brotherly. Perhaps the most striking allusion occurs in a letter Wordsworth wrote to Coleridge from Grasmere on Christmas Eve 1799, five days after he and Dorothy had moved into Dove Cottage. After he and Coleridge had visited Grasmere to select the house, Coleridge had preceded him to Sockburn, Yorkshire, where Dorothy was staying with Mary and Sara Hutchinson and *their* brother Tom. William writes: "I arrived at Sockburn the day after you quitted it . . . . I was sadly disappointed in not finding Dorothy; Mary was a solitary housekeeper and overjoyed to see me. D[orothy] is now sitting beside me racked with the tooth-ache" *(Early Letters,* p. 274). William's disappointment at finding himself alone with Mary Hutchinson may be either genuine or feigned (Dorothy is sitting at his side). In neither case is it the sentiment a lover would express to his closest friend. The most charitable interpretation, and the one that fits best with the other evidence, is that William had no deep romantic feelings for Mary at this date, that Mary was (as the other surviving correspondence suggests) a closer friend of Dorothy's than of William's.

When William and Dorothy settled at Dove Cottage, Grasmere, neither of them apparently thought of marrying or of ever changing their household. For example, on 8 November 1799, a few weeks before the letter I have quoted, Wordsworth and Coleridge wrote a joint letter from Keswick in which William remarks to Dorothy: "C.[oleridge] was much struck with Grasmere and its neighbourhood and I have much to say to you, you will think my plan a mad one, but I have thought of building a house there by the Lake side." He goes on to discuss the cost and financing, mentioning that "a Devonshire gentleman has built a Cottage there which cost a £130 which would exactly suit us every way, but the size of the bedrooms we shall talk of this." He closes his part of the letter by mentioning Dove Cottage as an alternative: "There is a small house at Grasmere empty which perhaps we may take, and purchase furniture but of this we will speak. But I shall write again when I know more on this subject" *(Early Letters,* p. 272). In suggesting they borrow money to buy land and build a cottage suitable to the needs of the two of them, Wordsworth at the end of 1799 envisioned their joint household to be a permanent arrangement. Early in 1799 Dorothy had complained in letters from Goslar, Germany, that they could not afford to enter into German society: "a man travelling alone may do very well, but, if his wife or sister goes with him, he must give entertainments," for *"a man and woman"* were there "considered as a sort of family" *(Early Letters,* pp. 247, 244). Clearly throughout their time of living together since September 1795—first at Racedown with Basil Montagu's young son, then at Alfoxden, then in Germany, Dorothy and William had considered themselves a viable family.

Dorothy's own attitude toward spending a lifetime keeping house for her brother is mirrored interestingly in her letter from Sockburn in April 1795 to her childhood friend Jane Pollard. Dorothy writes:

> You must recollect my friends the Hutchinsons, my sole companions at Penrith, . . . whose company in the absence of my brothers was the only agreeable Variety which Penrith afforded. They are settled at Sockburn—six miles from Darlington *perfectly to their satisfaction,* they are quite independent and *have not a wish ungratified,* very different indeed is their present situation from what it was formerly when we compared grievances and lamented the misfortune of losing our parents at an early age and being thrown upon the mercy of ill-natured and illiberal relations. Their brother has a farm, of about 200 £ a year, and they keep his house; *he is* a very amiable young man, *uncommonly fond of his sisters,* and in short,

> *every thing that they can desire.* (*Early Letters,* pp. 141-142, italics added)

In the pre-Freudian culture, Dorothy's emphasis on how the Hutchinson sisters' life with their brother *satisfied* their every *desire* did not, of course, carry the nuances that the same language would bear today. Rather, it suggested the limits of Dorothy's aspirations for her own life. She does not speak about either marriage (and children) or a separate life with some personal career as a situation more desirable than that of keeping house for one's brother.

Presumably even in a pre-Freudian culture, young women experienced sexual longings and needs, but their psychic and social censors must have been more militant, often preventing them from viewing consciously their needs in this direction. Ellen Moers, in a perceptive article in *The New York Review of Books,* after pointing to certain Gothic elements in the imaginations of Emily Brontë and Christina Rossetti, writes:

> both women grew up in a family of four siblings, male and female, bound together in a closed circle by affection and by imaginative genius, as well as by remoteness from the social norm. . . . Quentin Bell's recent biography of Virginia Stephen, a girl in another family of like-minded sisters and brothers, allows us at least to speculate openly on the sexual drama of the Victorian nursery. (Though Mr. Bell does not . . . settle the question of the fantasy component in Virginia Woolf's memories of fraternal incest, to the reality of the incest fantasy he brings important evidence, if evidence is needed.) . . . to Victorian women the sister-brother relationship seems to have had . . . perhaps greater significance—especially to those women, so commonplace in the intellectual middle class, who in a sexual sense never grew to full maturity. The rough-and-tumble sexuality of the nursery loomed large for sisters: it was the *only* heterosexual world the Victorian literary spinsters were ever freely and physically to explore.[12]

Without speculating as to the specific nature of Dorothy Wordsworth's sexual development, it seems quite clear that her affection for her brothers—especially William and John—satisfied her and that she usually demanded no more sexually fulfilling relationship.[13]

II.

As one would expect from a poet, William Wordsworth recorded his emotions during the months just before his marriage chiefly in his verse, embodying them in a group of poems he wrote at Grasmere in a prolific burst of inspiration from mid-March 1802 until the very day of his wedding, 4 October of the same year. Some of these poems center on the experience of others and many draw upon the past, exemplifying the doctrine of the 1800 Preface by taking their "origin from emotion recollected in tranquillity" that generates "an emotion, kindred to" it and spontaneously overflows into expressions of "powerful feelings." Such are four poems of 11-17 March: "The Sailor's Mother," "Alice Fell; or Poverty," "Beggars," and "The Emigrant Mother."[14] But a large number of the poems of March through May of this year treat specifically and with great warmth and affection incidents in the long relationship between William and Dorothy Wordsworth. On 14 March he wrote "To a Butterfly" ("Stay near me—do not take thy flight!"), a poem recalling,

> Oh! pleasant, pleasant were the days,
> The time, when, in our childish plays,
> My sister Emmeline and I
> Together chased the butterfly!
>
> *(PW,* I, 226)[15]

On 12 April, William wrote the poem later called "The Glow-worm," beginning, "Among all lovely things my Love had been;/ Had noted well the stars, all flowers that grew/ About her home; but she had never seen/ A Glow-worm, never one, and this I knew." The twenty-line poem ends:

> I led my Lucy to the spot, "Look here!"
> Oh! joy it was for her, and joy for me!
>
> *(PW,* II, 466)

Mary E. Burton mentions a transcription by Sara Hutchinson "with the name of Mary where the printed versions use 'Lucy' and 'Emma'."[16] That must have seemed right to the Hutchinson sisters when Dorothy transcribed the poem in a letter to Mary Hutchinson on 16 April 1802: for who else could be addressed as "my Love" by William on that date? But as Wordsworth explained to Coleridge, in his letter of the same day where he transcribed the same poem (using "Emma" instead of "Lucy" for his beloved's name), "The incident of this Poem took place about seven years ago between Dorothy and me" *(Early Letters,* p. 348). Dorothy, not Mary, is the "Emma" or "Lucy" of the poem, which like "To a Butterfly" describes the siblings' appreciation of the minor elements of nature.[17] On 20 April, he wrote another poem "To a Butterfly" (beginning, "I've watched you now a full half-hour,/ Self-poised upon that yellow flower"). The second stanza of this poem is significant for our theme:

> This plot of orchard-ground is ours;
> My trees they are, my Sister's flowers;
>
> * * *
>
> Sit near us on the bough!
> We'll talk of sunshine and of song,
> And summer days, when we were young;
> Sweet childish days, that were as long
> As twenty days are now.
>
> *(PW,* II, 22-23)

The interaction between the Grasmere family—"we"—Dorothy and William—continues in the poems that follow, as Mary Moorman's edition of Dorothy's Journal of the period, containing the texts of the appropriate poems, makes clear. The poems written early in 1802 about the smaller living forms of nature—the daisy, the cuckoo, the green linnet, the robin, the skylark, and the sparrow's nest—derived their imaginative force, as Wordsworth himself tells us in *The Prelude* (XIV. 232-266), from his associations with Dorothy.[18] The chief emotional catalyst to Wordsworth's imagination during the unusual poetic activity early in 1802 was not Coleridge nor pleasurable excitement about his forthcoming marriage to Mary Hutchinson: rather, that imaginative stimulus was his struggle to take the step that would inevitably create an irrevocable psychic barrier between himself and his beloved sister. Wordsworth's regrets about breaking up his happy "Home at Grasmere"[19] are epitomized in a poem that Dorothy, in her Journals, called "his poem on Going for Mary,"[20] which exhibits in almost painful detail the emotional struggle William faced. Though I cannot quote the entire poem here, three of its eight stanzas should illustrate my point:

Farewell, thou little Nook of mountain-ground,
Thou rocky corner of the lowest stair
Of that magnificent temple which doth bound
One side of our whole vale with grandeur rare;
Sweet garden-orchard, eminently fair,
The loveliest spot that man hath ever found,
Farewell!—we leave thee to Heaven's peaceful care,
Thee, and the Cottage which thou dost surround.

* * *

We go for One to whom ye will be dear;
And she will prize this Bower, this Indian shed,
Our own contrivance, Building without peer!
—A gentle Maid, whose heart is lowly bred,
Whose pleasures are in wild fields gatherèd,
With joyousness, and with a thoughtful cheer,
Will come to you; to you herself will wed;
And love the blessed life that we lead here.

* * *

Help us to tell Her tales of years gone by,
And this sweet spring, the best beloved and best;
Joy will be flown in its mortality;
Something must stay to tell us of the rest.
Here, thronged with primroses, the steep rock's breast
Glittered at evening like a starry sky;
And in this bush our sparrow built her nest,
Of which I sang one song that will not die.

William and Dorothy are the "we" into whose garden Mary, the "gentle Maid" with "lowly bred" heart will come and "wed" the garden as she learns its history. He and Dorothy will tell her tales of "this sweet spring, the best beloved and best," though "Joy" will have "flown" with the "mortality" of the season. This poem is, in part surely, a poem about the mortality of the moment, about "Joy, whose hand is ever at his lips,/ Bidding adieu," but it is something more. It is more than merely a poem of solidarity with Dorothy, assuring her that her brother will always love and value her and that the home they have loved together will always be theirs, no matter who else enters its magic garden. The poem is a farewell to an Eden that, as the tone clearly indicates, can never be recaptured, no matter how wide the world of choice that lies before them.

III.

As we have seen, from March through May 1802, while he and Dorothy at Grasmere contemplated the end of their private Eden, many of Wordsworth's poems deal with the relationship of childhood experiences to the poet's adult attitudes. In the first poem "To a Butterfly," the poet says that the creature brings "a solemn image to my heart,/ My father's family! . . . The time, when, in our childish plays,/ My sister Emmeline and I/ Together chased the butterfly!" When he listens "To the Cuckoo," Wordsworth can recall his "schoolboy days"—"till I do beget/ That golden time again" *(PW,* II, 207-208). There is no question that the famous poem beginning "My heart leaps up when I behold/ A rainbow in the sky," written on 26 March 1802, in the midst of these poems associated with Dorothy, also derives from the same inspiration. Wordsworth's greatest earlier assertion of the continuity of past and present, "Lines composed a Few Miles above Tintern Abbey," had also been written (1798) with Dorothy present and it contains an address to her in the final lines.[21] The same is true of another poem in which the poet moves from an experience in his boyhood and relates it to his present state of mind—this on a theme of crucial importance to my argument.

In "Nutting," written in Germany late in 1798 when William and Dorothy were living alone at Goslar, Wordsworth recounts how, while he was a boy at Hawkshead School, he went out one day with his "nutting-crook in hand": "O'er path-less rocks,/

Through . . . tangled thickets,/ Forcing my way, I came to one dear nook/ Unvisited, where . . . hazels rose/ Tall and erect, with tempting clusters hung,/ A virgin scene!—" The poet recalls his reaction thus:

A little while I stood,
Breathing with such suppression of the heart
As joy delights in; and with wise restraint
Voluptuous, fearless of a rival, eyed
The banquet;—or beneath the trees I sate
Among the flowers, and with the flowers I played;
A temper known to those who, after long
And weary expectation, have been blest
With sudden happiness beyond all hope.

* * *

. . . Then up I rose,
And dragged to earth both branch and bough, with crash
And merciless ravage: and the shady nook
Of hazels, and the green and mossy bower,
Deformed and sullied, patiently gave up
Their quiet being: and, unless I now
Confound my present feelings with the past,
Ere from the mutilated bower I turned
Exulting, rich beyond the wealth of kings,
I felt a sense of pain when I beheld
The silent trees, and saw the intruding sky.—

The version of the poem Wordsworth published in 1800 concludes with three lines addressed to Dorothy, urging her, in the manner of the conclusion to "Tintern Abbey," to learn the same lesson William believed he had learned from his earlier experience:

Then, dearest Maiden, move along these shades
In gentleness of heart; with gentle hand
Touch—for there is a spirit in the woods.
(*PW,* II, 211-212)

But in a long manuscript fragment published by de Selincourt in

Poetical Works (II, 504-506) there is another, much longer conclusion, which begins:

> Ah! what a crash was that! with gentle hand
> Touch these fair hazels—My beloved Friend!
> Though 'tis a sight invisible to thee
> From such rude intercourse the woods all shrink
> As at the blowing of Astolpho's horn.
> Thou, Lucy, art a maiden "inland bred"
> And thou hast known "some nurture"; but in truth
> If I had met thee here with that keen look
> Half cruel in its eagerness, those cheeks
> Thus [ ] flushed with a tempestuous bloom,
> I might have almost deem'd that I had pass'd
> A houseless being in a human shape,
> An enemy of nature, hither sent
> From regions far beyond the Indian hills—
> (*PW,* II, 504-505)

Here William chides Dorothy for her almost unnatural "half cruel . . . eagerness" to ravage the hazel trees of a more recent day. And he calls Dorothy, "Lucy," as he later referred to her in the manuscript of "The Glow-worm."

"Nutting," as has been recognized by recent critics, is filled with language of sexual ravishment. It describes, in fact, the rape of "a virgin scene" of Nature. The boy "voluptuous, fearless of a rival," toys with and fondles the secluded nook and then lets himself go in an act of "merciless ravage," leaving the "mossy bower,/ Deformed and sullied." In the published poem, William cautions the "dearest Maiden" against making his mistake; in the manuscript version, he accuses her of having done so. All is expressed in terms of two hazel groves, one of the distant past and the other in the present.

Soon after William addressed these lines to Dorothy as "Lucy," asking her not to exhibit so much "tempestuous bloom" of the kind that he recalled as his own "voluptuous" state of being, he wrote the first versions of two of the five poems now called the "Lucy poems." Two of these poems, now identified by their first lines as "She dwelt among the untrodden ways" and "Strange fits of passion have I known," have their first surviving texts in a letter that William and Dorothy wrote to Coleridge on 14 or 21 December 1798 *(Early Letters,* pp. 236-238).

1

My hope was one, from cities far,
  Nursed on a lonesome heath;
Her lips were red as roses are,
  Her hair a woodbine wreath.

2

She lived among the untrodden ways
  Beside the springs of Dove,
A maid whom there were none to praise,
  And very few to love;

3

A violet by a mossy stone
  Half-hidden from the eye!
Fair as a star when only one
  Is shining in the sky!

4

And she was graceful as the broom
  That flowers by Carron's side;
But slow distemper checked her bloom,
  And on the Heath she died.

5

Long time before her head lay low
  Dead to the world was she:
But now she's in the grave, and Oh!
  The difference to me!

Wordsworth later revised the poem essentially by compression, eliminating its original first and fourth stanzas and rephrasing the first two lines of the final stanza *(PW,* II, 30). But the discarded stanzas cast considerable light on the poem, if only in the reference to "Carron's side": Carron is the name of a river and a lake in Ross and Cromarty county in the Highlands of Scotland, an area that Wordsworth had not visited by this date. Like "the bonny braes of Yarrow," it apparently came to him through his reading of eighteenth-century ballads (in this case "Owen of Carron" by John

Langhorne). Since Wordsworth is attempting a ballad of an idealized sort, the equally arbitrary "springs of Dove" allusion cannot be used to identify—or eliminate—the personal origins or thematic content of the lyric. As de Selincourt observes, "Wordsworth knew a river Dove in Derbyshire, in Yorkshire, and in Westmorland; and it is impossible to say of which he was thinking" *(PW,* II, 472).

The early text of "Strange fits of passion" begins and ends quite differently than does the later, more familiar one:

1
Once, when my love was strong and gay,
And like a rose in June,
I to her cottage bent my way,
Beneath the evening Moon.
* * *
6
Strange are the fancies that will slide
Into a lover's head.
"O mercy" to myself I cried
"If Lucy should be dead!"
7
I told her this; her laughter light
Is ringing in my ears;
And when I think upon that night
My eyes are dim with tears.

This poem—"a favorite of mine," Dorothy writes to Coleridge before copying it—certainly refers to Dorothy as Lucy, as de Selincourt observes. And, as he notes in connection with "She dwelt among the untrodden ways," "If Coleridge is right in saying that 'A slumber did my spirit seal' was written to suggest what W[ordsworth] would have felt on the death of his sister, this poem had probably a similar source." [22] From the last stanza of the version in the letter to Coleridge, we see not only the origin of the poem in Wordsworth's fearful premonition of Dorothy's death, but Dorothy's own reaction of "laughter light." There can be no doubt, I believe, that the five so-called "Lucy poems" were written about the same imagined death of Dorothy, as Wordsworth writes of his own imagined death in "There was a boy." [23] As I have argued elsewhere, another poem beginning " 'Tis said that some have died for love" (written at Grasmere in 1800) is also about Dorothy's imagined death and William's imagined reaction to it.[24]

Most of the poems I have named as being inspired by William's affection for Dorothy are among his best, and the five "Lucy poems" are among the best short lyrics in English. "Tintern Abbey," whatever its structural difficulties, contains some of Wordsworth's finest language as well as his most elevated thoughts. Many of the lyrics on birds and flowers written at Grasmere are among Wordsworth's most characteristic and successful shorter poems. And one quality they convey is shared with Dorothy Wordsworth's *Journals:* deep, spontaneous emotional commitment. The emotional force of the seven-quatrain lyric about Dorothy's death was undoubtedly what moved William to add the stanza that gives it both its name and its categorization as a love poem:

> Strange fits of passion have I known:
> And I will dare to tell,
> But in the Lover's ear alone
> What once to me befell.
> (*PW,* II, 29)

Only a lover, says Wordsworth, can really appreciate this poem. Why? Because it is essentially a *passionate poem* about *true love*—not necessarily about passionate love, but about deeply felt, romantic love.

There has been considerable discussion about the question of Lucy's age. In one of the poems she is represented as dying very young, soon after "her virgin bosom" began to "swell." [25] But this aspect of the poems—a mystery if they are thought to have been associated with an actual lover of Wordsworth—becomes clear in the light of William's recurring emotional association of Dorothy with his own childhood and growth. The ambiguity of tone remains in the poems (though the text itself can be shown to speak in terms of a mature woman rather than a child) because Wordsworth loved "Lucy" as his sister from childhood as well as the helpmate of his adult years. William continually alludes to his childhood associations with Dorothy. William and Dorothy, though siblings, had been separated upon the death of their mother in 1778, when William was nine and Dorothy seven years old. There is no evidence that they so much as saw one another again until 1787, when William was seventeen and Dorothy fifteen years old. For sociological, if not genealogical purposes, they were (like Byron and his half-sister Augusta) not siblings but a boy and a girl of similar backgrounds and sympathetic aspirations meeting at a highly impressionable stage in their maturation.[26] The only surviving evidence [27] of William's feelings for his newly found sister emerges from his poems, in which he repeatedly ties his adult relationship with her to their childish play as siblings. Perhaps he needed constantly to reinforce this sense of kinship with Dorothy, reminding himself (probably subconsciously) that Dorothy was unacceptable as the object of a romantic or sexual attachment.

If I am correct in discerning this tendency in the pattern of William's poems, then the origin—not of the writing of the "Lucy poems" themselves, but of the dream or premonition of Dorothy's death that provided their emotional impact—may lie in William's subconscious struggle to avoid focusing his obviously strong sexual drive on the sister he lived with for seven years.[28] It would also suggest why, in poems like "Strange fits of passion" and "The Glow-worm," Wordsworth would shift his imaginative stance from brother to lover. Because he had, for the most part, successfully repressed his desire for Dorothy in his dreams—which end in her death rather than in their forbidden union—he was free at the conscious level to revise them, fully utilizing their emotional energy by casting them as love poems.

IV.

Having surveyed the emotional interaction between Dorothy and William, let us glance briefly at the much smaller body of poems William wrote to and about Mary Hutchinson. Here one crucial document is, obviously, "She was a phantom of delight," a poem written in 1804 that is usually pointed to as embodying Wordsworth's strong love for his wife. The poem begins, ostensibly, with an impression of Mary as she appeared to William on their first encounter:

She was a Phantom of delight
When first she gleamed upon my sight;
A lovely Apparition, sent
To be a moment's ornament. . . .
(*PW,* II, 213)

But in his talks with Isabella Fenwick, Wordsworth explained the origin of these lines and of the poem: "The germ of this poem was four lines composed as a part of the verses on the Highland Girl. Though beginning in this way, it was written from my heart, as is sufficiently obvious" (*PW,* II, 506). If the first four lines were inspired by an unknown Highland girl seen on the six-week Scottish tour that William, Dorothy, and Coleridge took in 1803 (while Mary remained behind, caring for her first child), we must eliminate the first stanza from serious consideration as being about Mary—for the subsequent lines of that stanza merely elaborate the first four. The third stanza is of little help also, filled as it is with philosophical abstractions in which Mary is called a "machine" and "A Being breathing thoughtful breath,/ "A Traveller between life and death." The remaining stanza reads:

I saw her upon nearer view,
A Spirit, yet a Woman too!
Her household motions light and free,
And steps of virgin-liberty;
A countenance in which did meet
Sweet records, promises as sweet;
A Creature not too bright or good
For human nature's daily food;
For transient sorrows, simple wiles,
Praise, blame, love, kisses, tears, and smiles.

Here, I submit, is the true measure of William's feelings for Mary, articulated about two years after their wedding but referring to the feelings that determined his decision to marry her. He was attracted by her "household motions," her "virgin-liberty," a countenance combining "sweet records" with "promises as sweet," and he was glad that she was a "Woman" "not too bright or good/ For human nature's daily food." The "daily food" image is fundamental to William's conception of Mary, as is evident from his poem "To M.H.," written late in December 1799, soon after he and Dorothy had taken up their residence at Dove Cottage.

> Our walk was far among the ancient trees:
> There was no road, nor any woodman's path;
> But a thick umbrage . . .
> . . . of itself had made
> A track, that brought us to a slip of lawn,
> And a small bed of water in the woods.
> * * *
> The spot was made by Nature for herself;
> The travellers know it not, and 'twill remain
> Unknown to them; but it is beautiful;
> And if a man should plant his cottage near,
> Should sleep beneath the shelter of its trees,
> And blend its waters with his daily meal,
> He would so love it, that in his death-hour
> Its image would survive among his thoughts:
> And therefore, my sweet MARY, this still Nook,
> With all its beeches, we have named for You!
> *(PW,* II, 118)

It should be obvious that William here uses the place as a metaphor for Mary and that he is the "man" who may "plant his cottage" in this "still Nook" and "blend its waters with his *daily meal,"* just as in "A Farewell" he speaks of Mary as "a gentle Maid" who will come to the "little Nook of mountain-ground" at Dove Cottage and to it "herself will wed" *(PW,* II, 23-24). And, for those to whom these two "nooks" recall that other isolated, "virgin bower" in "Nutting," it may be equally clear that I shall suggest that all this "blending" and "daily food" are metaphors for sexual union. If, in "Nutting," Wordsworth recalled with regret his ravage of "one dear nook . . . a virgin scene" to convey to Dorothy during their dangerous isolated proximity at Goslar the perils of excessive passionate license, it is equally clear that Mary provided the proper and acceptable substitute object for those strong passions that were chained within William. She was acceptable to William as a "virgin" at "liberty," with graceful "household motions" and the promise of sweet "daily food" *(PW,* II, 213).

One of the most striking corroborations of this judgment is to be found in two sonnets, the first composed by Wordsworth on the day of his marriage as he, Mary, and Dorothy traveled toward Grasmere. At sunset among the clouds and light "in the western sky, we saw shapes of Castles, Ruins among groves, . . . a minster with its tower unusually distinct, minarets in another quarter, and a round Grecian Temple also" *(Journals,* p. 156). The sonnet, beginning "Dark and more dark the shades of evening fell," describes the scene faithfully as Dorothy records it before concluding: "but we felt the while/ We should forget them; they are of the sky,/ And from our earthly memory fade away" *(PW,* III, 25-26). The second sonnet, written sometime before March 1804, carries further the message that the poet must (regretfully) renounce the sky-castles in favor of the more mundane pleasures:

> Those words were uttered as in pensive mood
> We turned, departing from that solemn sight:
> A contrast and reproach to *gross delight,*
> And life's unspiritual pleasures *daily wooed!*
> But now upon this thought I cannot brood;
> It is unstable as a dream of night;
> Nor will I praise a cloud, however bright,
> Disparaging Man's gifts, and *proper food.*
>
> * * *
>
> The immortal Mind craves objects that endure:
> These cleave to it; from these it cannot roam,
> Nor they from it: their fellowship is secure.
>
> *(PW,* III, 26; italics added)

"Wordsworth is by nature incapable of being in Love," wrote Coleridge to Henry Crabb Robinson in 1811, "tho' no man more tenderly attached—hence he ridicules the existence of any other passion, than a compound of Lust with Esteem & Friendship, confined to one Object, first by accidents of Association, and permanently, by the force of Habit & a sense of Duty. Now this will do very well—it will suffice to make a good Husband—. . . but still it is not *Love*—" [29] So, at least, Wordsworth's feelings for Mary, several years after marriage, appeared to Coleridge (whose own romantic attachment had much greater proportions of both fantasy and impossibility). And however much one discredits

Coleridge, there remain Wordsworth's poems written to and about Mary that invariably stress the habitual and the practical, the "compound of Lust with Esteem & Friendship," and there remains the clear tone of his "poem on going for Mary" and the two sonnets written about the day he got her, saying he had knowingly sacrificed a romantic joy to cleave to "secure fellowship" and Man's "proper food."

Aside from the ambiguity of his own feelings, there was only one obstacle to William's union with Mary, and this was the known—and perhaps declared—affection of his brother John for her. We must assume that Mary had made clear to the younger brother her preference for William, but John's farewell letter, written "when he has returned from a voyage to receive her announcement of her plan to marry, shows," the editor of Mary's letters writes, "much deeper emotion":

> I have been reading your letter over and over again, My dearest Mary, till tears have come into my eyes and I know not how to express myself—Thou art a kind and dear Creature.—But whatever fate Befal me I shall love thee to the last, and bear thy memory with me to the grave.[30]

"John, (who is to be the sailor,) has a most excellent heart," Dorothy had written to Jane Pollard in July 1787, and of the Wordsworth children's inheritance, she added: "John poor fellow! says that . . . two hundred pounds will be enough to fit him out, and he should wish Wm to have the rest for his education . . ." *(Early Letters,* pp. 3-4). Thus William, who began by sharing part of John's inheritance for his education, ended by appropriating John's beloved for his "daily food." And, though I do not intend to pursue this topic, William's resultant naggings of guilt had important consequences for another group of his greatest poems.[31]

V.

Another subject there is no space to pursue here in detail is the large group of Wordsworth's early poems centering on the theme of "Guilt and Sorrow" (which is the ultimate title of one of them). Aside from the ballads and lyrics that derive from his feelings for

Dorothy and for Mary Hutchinson, poems on this theme constitute almost all the poems about romantic love written before 1807. Included are such excellent works as "The Ruined Cottage" (later incorporated into the first book of *The Excursion),* "The Thorn," and "Ruth." In each of these poems, a loving, trusting woman marries or is seduced by a weak or thoughtless or undisciplined young man and is then abandoned with a child or two that she is unable to care for. These poems—which relate thematically to Wordsworth's many early poems and passages on such topics as poor, vagrant women or the abandoned Indian woman—clearly embody Wordsworth's feelings of guilt and sorrow for his own abandonment of Annette Vallon. All these are, in their published versions, rather long narratives, usually filtered through the consciousness of an objective observer (like the Pedlar in *The Excursion* or the curious retired sea captain in "The Thorn") whose presence is clearly intended to mitigate the pain generated by the tale itself.[32] After William and Dorothy visited Annette and Caroline at Calais in 1802, the only further poem on this theme is "Vaudracour and Julia," at one time destined for *The Prelude.* That retrospective, official account of the romance seems finally to have exorcized the demon of guilt and sorrow that had driven Wordsworth to so much of his best early poetry.

Likewise, after William's marriage to Mary in October 1802, there are no more passionate lyrics like the "Lucy poems." Instead, in 1802, Wordsworth, who had earlier written few sonnets that he thought worth preserving,[33] suddenly composed eighteen sonnets—some good, some excellent—most of them during his trip to see Annette and Caroline. As Carl Woodring observes, "His sonnet-writing began, then, in a period of great agitation. He probably had this private agitation much in mind when he wrote the sonnet beginning, 'Nuns fret not at their convent's narrow room'." [34] The emotional force of his visits with Caroline on the beach at Calais and of his love for England in its confrontation with France is shaped into fourteen-line jewels. After this date Wordsworth never published a new volume of poetry without including one or more sonnets.[35] The control that the sonnet form provided for his intense emotions of 1802 was later supplanted by the support it gave to his flagging imagination in such sequences as *The River Duddon, Ecclesiastical Sketches,* and "Sonnets on the Punishment of Death." This complete reversal of the needs of both his psyche and his poetry is epitomized in one of the few important poems that is not a sonnet which he began after 1808. "Laodamia," Wordsworth told Isabella Fenwick, "cost me more trouble than almost anything of equal length I have ever written" *(PW,* II, 519). Why this should be so provides the focus of my final speculative look into the workings of Wordsworth's imagination.

"Laodamia" is based on a classical legend treated by Euripides, Virgil, and Ovid. Laodamia was the wife of Protesilaus, the first Greek to be killed by the Trojans. In her bereavement, as Wordsworth relates the tale, Laodamia prays to Jove to restore her husband to her. When the god grants her request and the shade of Protesilaus joins her for a three-hour visit, she is delighted and suggests they go to bed:

> "No Spectre greets me,—no vain Shadow this;
> Come, blooming Hero, place thee by my side!
> Give, on this well-known couch, one nuptial kiss
> To me, this day, a second time thy bride!"

But at this proposal, "Jove frowned in heaven" and her husband admonishes Laodamia for her light and irreverent thoughts:

> ". . . Earth destroys
> Those raptures duly—Erebus disdains:
> Calm pleasures there abide—majestic pains.
>
> "Be taught, O faithful Consort, to control
> Rebellious passion: for the Gods approve
> The depth, and not the tumult of the soul;
> A fervent, not ungovernable, love."
> *(PW,* II, 269; lines 70-76)
>
> "And Thou, though strong in love, art all too weak
> In reason, in self-government too slow;
> * * *
> Learn, by a mortal yearning, to ascend—
> Seeking a higher object. Love was given,
> Encouraged, sanctioned, chiefly for that end; . . . .
> *(PW,* II, 271; lines 139-140, 145-147)

Laodamia, however, refuses to accept her husband's advice, and when "Hermes reappears" to carry off the shade of Protesilaus, she shrieks, and—anticipating the ending of Keats's *Lamia*—"on the palace-floor a lifeless corse She lay."

The poem's final regular six-line stanza, in which the poet passes judgment on Laodamia, was repeatedly revised during Wordsworth's lifetime, with the severity of the judgment increased dramatically. The first version, published in 1815 and 1820, reads:

> Ah, judge her gently who so deeply loved!
> Her, who, in reason's spite, yet without crime,
> Was in a trance of passion thus removed;
> Delivered from the galling yoke of time
> And these frail elements—to gather flowers
> Of blissful quiet 'mid unfading bowers.

But the final version (1845) is much harsher:

> Thus, all in vain exhorted and reproved,
> She perished; and, as for a wilful crime,
> By the just Gods whom no weak pity moved,
> Was doomed to wear out her appointed time,
> Apart from happy Ghosts, that gather flowers
> Of blissful quiet 'mid unfading bowers.
> (lines 158-163)

The poem concludes with eleven irregularly-rhymed lines that, Wordsworth said, had provided the germ of his poem. They describe "a knot of spiry trees" which grew "for ages" along the Hellespont; whenever they grew tall enough to see the walls of Troy, "the trees' tall summits withered at the sight;/ A constant interchange of growth and blight!"

If Wordsworth wrote the poem simply, as he told Isabella Fenwick, because "the incident of the trees growing and withering put the subject into my thoughts, and I wrote with the hope of giving it a loftier tone than . . . has been given it by any of the Ancients" *(PW,* II, 518), then his numerous revisions of the poem between manuscript and print, in proof in 1815, and during the next thirty years may simply indicate how slowly and intermittently his stream of inspiration flowed after the great years 1797-1808. But close examination of the text of the poem, as it evolved in proofs in 1815 and as Wordsworth revised it, suggests other possible reasons for his having written a moving poem on the theme of withering treetops and the need for a woman to control her passions.

Two of Wordsworth's children died in 1812, four-year-old Catharine in June and six-year-old Thomas late in November. Wordsworth tried to bear the deaths with Christian stoicism. Mary reacted more openly, especially to the death of Catharine. William wrote to his brother Christopher: "I have but a poor account to give of Mary. . . . she is yet little recovered from the deplorable dejection in which I found her. Her health has suffered: but I clearly see that neither thought nor religion nor the endeavours of friends, can at once quiet a heart that has been disturbed by such an affliction."[36] When Thomas died, however, Wordsworth depicted Mary as stronger in meeting their common suffering:

> My Wife bears the loss of her Child with striking fortitude. . . . Miss Hutchinson also supports her sorrow as ought to be done. For myself dear Southey I dare not say in what state of mind I am; I loved the Boy with the utmost love of which my soul is capable, and he is taken from me—yet in the agony of my spirit in surrendering such a treasure I feel a thousand times richer than if I had never possessed it. God comfort and save you and all our friends and us all from a repetition of such trials—O Southey feel for me!
>
> (2 Dec. 1818; *MY,* II, 51)

In January 1813 William began drafting additional lines for Book II and Book III of *The Excursion,* adding to the story of the Solitary, as the chief cause of that man's disillusionment, the deaths of a young son and daughter and the consequent alienation and (ultimately) the death of his beloved wife. De Selincourt was convinced by these additions that Wordsworth "was led to imagine personal bereavement as a leading contributary cause of his [the Solitary's] despondency by his own passionate grief at the loss of his two children" *(PW,* V, 419), but no one has, I believe, commented upon the significance of lines like these about the Solitary's marriage to his "Anna" (which again support the theme of the earlier sections of this paper):

> "To my heart's wish, my tender Mate became
> The thankful captive of maternal bonds;
> * * *
> Her whose submissive spirit was to me
> Rule and restraint—my guardian—shall I say
> That earthly Providence, whose guiding love
> Within a port of rest had lodged me safe;
> Safe from temptation . . . ."
> (Book III. 554-555, 563-567; *PW,* V, 94)

Or these lines, about the aftermath of the bereavement of the Solitary and his wife:

> "Calm as a frozen lake when ruthless winds
> Blow fiercely, agitating earth and sky,
> The Mother now remained. . . .
> * * *
> This second visitation had no power
> To shake; but only to bind up and seal;
> And to establish thankfulness of heart
> In Heaven's determinations, ever just.
> The eminence whereon her spirit stood,
> Mine was unable to attain. Immense
> The space that severed us! . . ."
> (Book III. 650 ff.; *PW,* V, 98-99)

From Dorothy's letter to Catherine Clarkson in January 1813, we learn how the family could not separate their sadness from their locale in the Rectory, Grasmere:

> in spite of all we could do, the very air of the place—the stillness—the occasional sounds, and above all the view of that school, our darling's pride and joy—that church-yard his playground—all oppressed us and do continue to oppress us with unutterable sadness—
>
> (*MY,* II, 60)

And in this letter Dorothy tells of their determination to move to Rydal Mount. On 1 May the family removed to their new home. In a letter to Francis Wrangham on 28 August 1813, Wordsworth speaks briefly of his children's deaths as a subject almost too painful to face. On 28 April 1814, he writes to Thomas Poole of the "heavy affliction" of the deaths and suggests that he has been unable to compose poetry. Later, in November 1814, Wordsworth writes to his brother Christopher that William, his second surviving son, is very ill. Between these last two dates Wordsworth wrote his poem about the need to control passions, deriving it from a myth about how the very trees withered when they viewed the place that had been the cause of two lovers' deaths.

The story of Laodamia centers on the grief of bereavement, but Protesilaus' admonition is directed against misuse of the sexual passion. Is Wordsworth here using a metaphor to strengthen himself and his family in their Christian stoicism? Just as we have seen him use food as a metaphor for sex, we have seen him employ a sexual metaphor for a psychic problem of another nature in "Nutting" and we have seen him turn his fears about his sister's death back into love poems. But, as we have also seen, the conscious use of the sexual metaphor seems, in Wordsworth's case, to have released in a disguised form something otherwise trapped below his consciousness. Thus, when in the first published version of "Laodamia" he uses a highly-charged sexual word in an unusual way and then entirely revises the line in the next edition, we can speculate on two possible reasons for the original choice and the revision. In 1815, the lines finally designated 74-76 read:

> Be taught, O faithful Consort, to control
> Rebellious passion: for the Gods approve
> The depth, and not the tumult of the soul;
> The fervor—not the impotence of love.[37]

In 1820, he revised the fourth line of the stanza to read: "A fervent, not ungovernable, love." Wordsworth's use of "impotence" conforms with *OED* definition #3, "Lack of self-restraint, violent passion." This usage, now obsolete, finds its latest *OED* examples in Milton's *Paradise Lost* (II. 156) and Pope's translation of *The Iliad* (XXIV. 53).[38] With such precedents, Wordsworth may well have included the word for its archaic precision. In this case, his revision is explicable as an attempt to make the line more immediately comprehensible and to avoid suggesting irrelevant meanings, such as *impotence* in its most usual modern meaning: *OED* 2b, "Complete absence of sexual power; usually said of the male." To a student of Shelley, however, who has traced from the letters of Shelley and *his* Mary through the complexities of the maniac's speeches in "Julian and Maddalo" the effect of the deaths of two children within one year into the dim world of *their* marriage bed,[39] it seems more than possible that the unusual diction in line 76 of "Laodamia" may point to another kind of withering in the wake of the Wordsworths' bereavement.

In her January 1813 letter to Catherine Clarkson, Dorothy had described Mary Wordsworth as being "as thin as it is possible to be except when the body is worn out by slow disease" *(MY,* II, 60), suggesting the state of Mary's health to be such as William in *The Excursion* pictures the Solitary's wife Anna, who "fell/ Into a gulf obscure of silent grief," and, wasting away in his arms, "left me, on this earth, disconsolate!" *(PW,* V, 99). Sara Hutchinson's letters throughout 1813, even after the move to Rydal Mount, give evidence that, though at the surface, life in the household had returned to normal, Mary's spirits remained precarious. On 23 June she wrote to Thomas Monkhouse: "We have had abundance of other visitors; I think we have scarcely been one day unengaged for the last month."[40] In the next surviving letter to Mary Monkhouse Hutchinson, Sara writes of her sister Mary: "Her spirits have I think been better—at least in company—and except when in bed she has never been out of it [i.e., "company"] for many weeks" (SH, *Letters,* p. 58). Forced to keep up her spirits in public because of the stream of summer visitors to Rydal Mount, Mary Wordsworth may well have had only one place to vent her true emotions—when she retired to bed. And if the emotional distance that Wordsworth describes coming between the Solitary and his wife after their children's deaths reflects, in part, an emotional distancing in Wordsworth's own marriage (a relationship, Coleridge had described in 1811 as "a compound of Lust with Esteem & Friendship"), one element may have passed out of Wordsworth's feelings for Mary, never to return.

A year later, on 18 July 1814, William, Mary, and Sara

Hutchinson set out on a tour of Scotland. By 3 August 1814, Sara could write to Mrs. Thomas Hutchinson: "dearest Mary is much improved by her journey; she truly enjoys herself; & William is happy that the journey has accomplished this his chief aim" (SH, *Letters,* p. 77). By October 1814, Mary Wordsworth had, by all the available evidence, resumed her accustomed equanimity. At the same time,[41] Wordsworth was composing "Laodamia," suggested by a story of trees that repeatedly wither when confronted by a scene of former anguish, and including both an unusual use of the phrase "impotence of love" and stern admonitions to a woman to control her passions in the presence of a bodily lover who was yet only the ghost of his former self.

The possible inference is complicated further when we read in one of Mary Wordsworth's letters to Dorothy on 29 October 1814: "Poor William's right hand is crippled—the speck which he was examining thru the microscope last Saturday has proved another plaguy boil. It is situated between the thumb and forefinger of his right hand and carries the inflammation in a red line all the way to the arm-pit. I hope it may not be so tedious as his last was . . . but for this he meant to have written to you . . . ."[42] Here we have impotence of yet another kind and definition, a series of boils that incapacitate Wordsworth from writing. Is there a causal relationship among these phenomena that seem to coalesce in the various meanings of a single word? Does the progressively harsher judgment on Laodamia in late editions of the poem suggest that Wordsworth felt increasingly threatened by both conjugal and literary expectations that he was incapable of fulfilling?

These hints and complexities do not yield themselves to certainties. But I hope that my agnostic speculations about some of the possible motive forces behind "Laodamia," added to the somewhat more complete evidence surrounding the poems of 1797-1808, will contribute to the understanding of the kinds of circumstances that drove Wordsworth to produce great poetry. Like most artists, he seems to have had psychic wounds—feelings of guilt and isolation; hidden fears of incestuous passion and equally hidden guilt for dreaming Dorothy's death; guilt concerning his brother's sacrifices; sorrow at the death of loved ones; and, quite possibly, resentment toward his wife for his own feelings of sexual and creative inadequacy. And when these wounds are seen as the source of Wordsworth's poems that we all acknowledge to be great, the most obvious answer to those who ponder the later decline of Wordsworth's powers is that, one by one, the ghosts that haunted the poet's psyche were exorcized either by the march of events or by the transmutation of emotion into poetry.

Wordsworth's greatest poems—those nuggets of gold washed down the stream of time—derive from a massif that on its surface stonily resisted the winds of guilt, self-doubt, and despair. Whereas Coleridge was like a tree whipped, buffeted, and twisted by his fears, doubts, guilt, and sense of isolation, William Wordsworth flung back each blast of life's emotional storm in "an echo and a light unto eternity." Here again, his sister Dorothy knew him best and he himself became her voice, speaking to us of William's sublime egoism, poetically triumphant over circumstance: [43]

> There is an Eminence,—of these our hills
> The last that parleys with the setting sun;
>
> * * *
>
> . . . this Peak, so high
> Above us, and so distant in its height,
> Is visible; and often seems to send
> Its own deep quiet to restore our hearts.
>
> * * *
>
> . . . 'Tis in truth
> The loneliest place we have among the clouds.
> And She who dwells with me, whom I have loved
> With such communion, that no place on earth
> Can ever be a solitude to me,
> Hath to this lonely Summit given my Name.

NOTES

1. I have used the 1963 impression of the second edition, London: Longmans, 1956, hereafter cited as "Bateson." In this edition, while maintaining his thesis, Bateson softened the language in various places. (See his "Preface to the Second Edition.") For a sidelight on Bateson's early differences with the Dove Cottage Trustees, see his letter to *TLS,* 9 April 1976, p. 430.

2. The most ambitious attempts thus far to interpret Wordsworth's poetry in relation to his psychology are Wallace W. Douglas' *Wordsworth: The Construction of a Personality* (Kent, Ohio: Kent State University Press, 1968) and Richard J. Onorato's *The Character of the Poet: Wordsworth in THE PRELUDE* (Princeton: Princeton University Press, 1971). Though I have consulted both books, I have related my argument to the latter, hereafter cited as "Onorato."
3. "William and Dorothy Wordsworth," *Essays by Divers Hands, Being the Transactions of the Royal Society of Literature.* NS, 55 (1972), 75-94.
4. *Journals of Dorothy Wordsworth,* with an Introduction by Helen Darbishire. A New Edition edited by Mary Moorman (London: Oxford University Press, 1971, corrected 1973, 1974). Hereafter cited as *"Journals."*
5. The correspondence, most of it published under the heading "Brothers and Sisters," appeared in *TLS* for 9 August 1974 (p. 859), 23 August (p. 906), 13 September (pp. 979-980), 4 October (pp. 1078-79), 1 November (p. 1231), 8 November (p. 1261), 15 November (p. 1288), 22 November (p. 1317), 27 December 1974 (p. 1464). My contributions appeared on 13 September, 1 November, and 27 December.
6. Among them, his contention that "after the Lucy poems, . . . there was no place for [Dorothy] in the organs of Wordsworth's poetic imagination, and she was cut out like so much decayed tissue" (Bateson, p. 202). As will become clear, I believe that William's feelings for Dorothy remained a vital force in his poetry up to the very day of his wedding (see p. 161) and beyond.
7. Both Bateson (pp. 41-56) and Onorato (pp. 24-25 *et passim)* rightly emphasize, for example, the effect upon the Wordsworth siblings of the early deaths of their mother and father and their unhappy childhood among unloving kinsmen. Onorato sees Wordsworth's repression of his sorrow at his early bereavement as determinative for his later attitude toward Nature.
8. *Journals,* pp. 147-148.
9. William and Dorothy had carried on a regular correspondence with Annette and Caroline that has disappeared. See *The Letters of William and Dorothy Wordsworth,* ed. Ernest de Selincourt, I. *The Early Years: 1787-1805,* 2nd ed., revised by Chester L. Shaver (Oxford: Clarendon Press, 1967), 282 (hereafter cited as *Early Letters).*
10. *Journals,* p. 154.
11. See, for example, Coleridge's frequent references to his jealousy of Wordsworth in relation to Sara Hutchinson. In *The Notebooks of Samuel Taylor Coleridge,* ed. Kathleen Coburn, II (New York: Pantheon Books, 1961), entries 2001n, 2055n, 2975n, 2998 and n, 3148 and n (and others) show that Coleridge imagined that on Saturday, 26 December 1806, in the Queen's Head Inn, Stringston, Wordsworth had gone to bed with Sara Hutchinson, his sister-in-law and

Coleridge's beloved. (Coleridge later accused his imagination of playing tricks on him in this instance.) Bateson (p. 44) quotes Thomas De Quincey, who wrote (in part): "Wordsworth's intellectual passions were fervent and strong: but they rested upon a basis of preternatural animal sensibility diffused through *all* the animal passions (or appetites) . . . ."

12. "Female Gothic: Monsters, Goblins, Freaks," *New York Review of Books,* 21 (14 April 1974), 36-37.
13. Many have surmised Dorothy's interest in Coleridge from 1797, and John E. Jordan presents some evidence to support Malcolm Elwin's speculation that Dorothy at age thirty-eight may have been infatuated with young Thomas De Quincey during his early years in the Lake District. See *De Quincey to Wordsworth: A Biography of a Relationship* (Berkeley: University of California Press, 1962), pp. 228-230. I should add, also, in fairness to Dorothy and her modern admirers who would object to a description of her as a case of arrested sexual development, that a number of readers of the evidence are more willing than I to suggest the occurence of actual physical incest between William and Dorothy. See, for example, pages 51-52 of Rachel Mayer Brownstein's excellent essay, "The Private Life: Dorothy Wordsworth's Journals," *MLQ,* 34 (1973), 48-63.
14. Unless otherwise indicated, Wordsworth's poems and their titles are quoted from *The Poetical Works of William Wordsworth,* ed. Ernest de Selincourt and Helen Darbishire (Oxford English Text Edition), 5 vols. (Oxford: Clarendon Press, 1940-1954); vols. I-III being the Second Editions (hereafter cited as *PW).* The reader will often have to consult the notes and variant readings to reconstruct the earliest texts.
15. Additional information may eventually be forthcoming from a previously unknown manuscript, sold at Sotheby's in London (6 July 1977, lot 405), which contains nine lines apparently intended as an addition to this poem, copied by Dorothy Wordsworth. This addition can be dated (from the contents of a fragmentary letter by Dorothy on the verso) before June 1802. This and other new letters and manuscripts by Wordsworth, Coleridge, and their circle, sold at the same time, are now in the Dove Cottage Library.
16. *The Letters of Mary Wordsworth, 1800-1855* (Oxford: Clarendon Press, 1958), p. xxiv.
17. In *William Wordsworth: A Biography,* Mary Moorman, always scrupulous both in handling facts and in acknowledging the force of William's affection for Dorothy, writes of "The Glow-worm": "It was written in the spring of 1802, when William was riding back to Dorothy after a visit to Mary Hutchinson, with whom he had just completed the arrangements for their wedding. His first and immediate thought even in that hour was for Dorothy, and [Mrs.

Moorman adds by way of interpreting these facts] he speaks as if to reassure her that the communion between them could never be changed" (I [Oxford: Clarendon Press, 1957; corrected 1967], 319-320).

18. See, for example, Dorothy's account of the composition of "Children Gathering Flowers" ("Foresight") *(Journals,* pp. 116-117) and her allusion on 15 April to the flower that, two weeks later, Wordsworth immortalized in two poems "To the Small Celandine" (pp. 109, 118-119).
19. William's exceptionally blissful reaction to the residence that he and Dorothy chose at Town End, Grasmere (the cottage now known as Dove Cottage), has been widely, if not universally acknowledged. See, for example, Karl Kroeber, " 'Home at Grasmere': Ecological Holiness," *PMLA,* 89 (1974), 132-141. For a reading of "Home at Grasmere" involving Wordsworth's possible ambiguous feelings in the period, see Kenneth R. Johnston, " 'Home at Grasmere': Reclusive Song," *SiR,* 14 (1975), 1-28. Johnston and those who see underlying tensions in all parts of "Home at Grasmere" emphasize the poet's recognition that the idyllic situation is necessarily mortal and, therefore, temporary. One necessary cause of the transitory nature of the poet's bliss was, I submit, the instability of the situation involving the cohabitation of a brother and sister who could never fulfill one another's sexual longings without guilt. For the dating of various portions of this poem and Wordsworth's revisions, which gradually removed most of the references to Dorothy and cast the poem into a far less personal form, see Beth Darlington's edition of *Home at Grasmere: Part First, Book First of THE RECLUSE* in the Cornell Wordsworth Series (Ithaca: Cornell University Press, 1978).
20. In the Appendix to *Journals* the poem is titled "Our Departure" (p. 217); when published in 1815 it was titled "A Farewell" *(PW,* II, 23-24).
21. Stephen Parrish reveals in his Cornell Wordsworth edition of *The Prelude, 1798-1799* (Ithaca: Cornell University Press, 1977) that in "the earliest state of *The Prelude,"* found in MS JJ, "where a listener is identified at the close, it seems, as in *Tintern Abbey,* to be the poet's sister" (p. 8).
22. *PW,* II, 472. See, in confirmation of this judgment, Moorman, *William Wordsworth,* I, 318-319.
23. The confirming evidence of the origin of this poem is found in MS JJ, where "my" appears in the place of "his" (see Onorato, p. 196).
24. *TLS,* 13 September 1974, pp. 979-980.
25. "Three years she grew in sun and shower" *(PW,* II, 214-216). Some commentators have (mistakenly) interpreted the poem as referring to the death of a three-year-old child; but see lines 31-33. Frances C. Ferguson, whose essay "The Lucy Poems: Wordsworth's Quest for a Poetic Object" *(ELH,* 40 [1973], 532-548) takes rigidly anti-bio-

graphical analysis of the poems about as far as it can go, argues that "through the course of these poems, Lucy is repeatedly and ever more decisively traced out of existence," and she goes on to assert that "the chief difficulty in talking about these poems lies in our uncertainty about what the name 'Lucy' refers to" (p. 533). Many of the difficulties that Professor Ferguson explores disappear, however, if one recognizes that "Lucy" derives from Wordsworth's conflicting feelings about his sister Dorothy and that the ambiguities in "Lucy's" nature (as well as her eventual disappearance) evolve naturally from Wordsworth's symbolic, externalized resolution of his psychic dilemma.

26. Dorothy's first surviving letter, to Jane Pollard in July 1787, describes her brothers—especially William and John—with deep affection, but conveys no hint of romantic attachment. She clearly looked to her brothers to provide her the stable home that she had lacked since the death of their mother *(Early Letters,* pp. 4-5).

27. One of the nagging difficulties that haunts Wordsworth studies is the absence or mutilation of crucial manuscripts that might have cast light on some of the questions raised here. Dorothy's Alfoxden Journal has disappeared since 1897, and there are erasures and cancellations in the surviving Journals by someone other than Dorothy (see Moorman in *Journals,* p. viii). What must have been numerous letters exchanged by the Wordsworths and Annette Vallon are not to be found, and we know that some references to Annette and Caroline in surviving letters were destroyed by Gordon Graham Wordsworth (see *Early Letters,* p. 282 and n.). No letters at all of Mary Hutchinson Wordsworth or Sara Hutchinson survive from the crucial years 1801-1804, and we have none of their letters to each other until 1811. In short, many important questions that may once have been answered in manuscripts that survived the principals cannot be answered, perhaps because the evidence has been destroyed or mutilated by those responsible for safeguarding the manuscripts for posterity. The emergence of previously unknown letters between Wordsworth, Mary, and Dorothy at the Sotheby sale of 6 July 1977 not only provides new evidence for the questions explored in this essay, but also offers some hope that further documents may ultimately come to light.

28. Here are relevant, I suggest, the headaches and tensions that Dorothy's *Journals* record as afflicting William and her during the years of their life together (see p. 143 above).

29. *Collected Letters of Samuel Taylor Coleridge,* ed. Earl Leslie Griggs, III (Oxford: Clarendon Press, 1959), 305. It may be significant that Wordsworth composed "Yarrow Unvisited," which celebrates the free-play of the visionary imagination, as a result of his Scottish tour with Coleridge and Dorothy in 1803, whereas he wrote "Yarrow Visited," a derivative poem which tells how the poet's loss of his

"waking dream" was mitigated by a fine (though inferior) reality, in September 1814 while touring with Mary and Sara Hutchinson (*PW,* III, 83-85, 106-108).

30. *The Letters of Mary Wordsworth,* p. xxiii. The full text of this letter is to be found in *The Letters of John Wordsworth,* ed. Carl H. Ketcham (Ithaca: Cornell University Press), pp. 125-126.
31. I have not presumed to encroach upon the area of the relations between William and John Wordsworth in 1802 because Irene Tayler has stated the case so well in "By Peculiar Grace: Wordsworth in 1802."
32. A variant of this theme appears in "Michael," which—though partially based on the objective story associated with the sheepfold in Green-head Ghyll—generates much of its emotional force from the failure of Luke to vindicate his tutelage by Nature and the trust placed in him by his parents. Like the other poems on the "guilt and sorrow" theme, the story of Michael and Luke is told by a narrator who centers on the reactions of the betrayed party. Like the Youth who seduces Ruth and like the wayward husband in "The Ruined Cottage," Luke seeks "a hiding-place beyond the seas." The emotional power of this poem derives, I suggest, from Wordsworth's own passionate feelings about his failure to carry out his responsibility toward Annette Vallon, though by 1800 he was able to give his feelings further aesthetic distance through the story of Michael's devotion to his fathers' land and through the poet-narrator's own quest for a different kind of permanence—his desire for the immortality of poetry through which to relate the homely history "For the delight of a few natural hearts/ And . . . for the sake/ Of *youthful Poets, who* among these hills/ *Will be my second self when I am gone"* (*PW,* II, 81; italics added).
33. The sonnet "Written in Very Early Youth" ("Calm is all nature as a resting wheel"; *PW,* I, 3), which de Selincourt dates in its present form ca. 1795-97, but which Wordsworth retrieved and first published in the *Morning Post* on 13 February 1802 is one. On the questionable "Sonnet on Seeing Miss Helen Maria Williams Weep at a Tale of Distress," see Carl Woodring, *Politics in English Romantic Poetry* (Cambridge: Harvard University Press, 1970), p. 339 n. Mark Reed, in *Wordsworth: The Chronology of the Early Years, 1770-1799* (Cambridge: Harvard University Press, 1967), lists also "Sonnet Written by Mr. —— Immediately after the Death of His Wife" (p. 19) and two unpublished sonnets preserved in MSS (pp. 22, 23).
34. *Wordsworth,* corrected ed. (Cambridge: Harvard University Press, 1968), p. 157.
35. I base this assertion on my personal conviction, held since 1963 and expressed at a number of conferences but not yet argued in print, that Wordsworth restructured *The Prelude* from thirteen to fourteen books to give it the form of the Italian sonnet, with the books now

forming natural groupings of four/ four/ three/ three, with the strongest break occuring between the first eight books and the last six.

36. *The Letters of William and Dorothy Wordsworth,* ed. Ernest de Selincourt. *The Middle Years* in two vols. revised by Mary Moorman and Alan G. Hill (Oxford: Clarendon Press, 1969-1970), Part II, 26. Though there may be some confusion (since Parts I and II of *The Middle Years* are also numbered as volumes II and III of *The Letters),* I shall follow the established practice of Wordsworthians in citing these two volumes as *MY* I and *MY* II (plus the page references).
37. Wordsworth's *Poems, including Lyrical Ballads and the Miscellaneous Pieces of the Author, . . . in Two Volumes* (London: Longman, Hurst, Rees, Orme, and Brown, 1815), I, 228.
38. The words "impotence" and "impotent" occur eight times in the texts analyzed in Lane Cooper's *Concordance to the Poems of William Wordsworth* (London: Smith, Elder, 1911). In every instance, the context shows that the meaning intended is either *OED* 1 ("utter inability or weakness; helplessness") or 2a ("Want of physical power; feebleness") for the noun and either 1 ("powerless, helpless; ineffective") or 2a ("Physically weak; . . . decrepit") for the adjective.
39. See Donald H. Reiman, *Shelley and his Circle,* VI (Cambridge: Harvard University Press, 1973), 857-865.
40. *The Letters of Sara Hutchinson from 1800 to 1835,* ed. Kathleen Coburn (London: Routledge & Kegan Paul, 1954), pp. 55-56. (This edition hereafter cited as "SH, *Letters".)*
41. Mark L. Reed in *Wordsworth: The Chronology of the Middle Years, 1800-1815* (Cambridge: Harvard University Press, 1975) dates the composition of the 130-line original version of "Laodamia" as ca. mid-October to 27 October (pp. 53, 580) and that of lines 115-120 ca. early February, "certainly by 5 Feb" (pp. 589, 590).
42. *The Letters of Mary Wordsworth,* pp. 22-23. Mark L. Reed suggests that Mary began this letter on 27 October.
43. "Poems on the Naming of Places," III *(PW,* II, 115), written and published in 1800.

Lamb Recreates a Burney Wedding

Joyce Hemlow

> I do not know when I have been better pleased than at being invited last week to be present at the wedding of a friend's daughter.
>
> (Charles Lamb, "The Wedding," 1825)

A cross between the eighteenth-century man of feeling and the romantic, with his own feelings much to the fore, Charles Lamb not only invested fact with feeling but as an artist modified the facts or cast them into such molds as would best contribute to the predominant feeling or the dominant theme of his piece. The modifications were imaginative, playful, loving, and with respect to strict truth, fact, or reality, recognizable and therefore harmless. But they were more than that; they served a purpose with respect to the work as a whole. The craftsman at work, the interactions between Life and Art, can be observed in "The Wedding," where the facts or realities are known from other accounts, one of them published for the first time here.

The Burney wedding had taken place on Saturday, 14 April 1821, not at St. Mildred's in the Poultry, the church dedicated to the Saxon princess, but at St. Margaret's, Westminster. The "friend" was James Burney (1750-1821), F.R.S., the "Captain Burney" of the warm hospitality and the whist parties, author of a book on whist (1821), who in recognition of his *Voyages of Discovery* and works on navigation and exploration was to be gazetted as of 19 July 1821 Rear-Admiral on the retired list. In the years 1772 and 1773 he had sailed "round the world" with Captain Cook and again accompanied the circumnavigator in his last voyage (1776-1780). Sailing ships in uncharted seas, sighting unknown lands, and botching up the sailing ship itself was the day-to-day work of the "scientific" navigator of the eighteenth century. "One of the greatest geographers of his day," James kept important journals of his voyages and in such studies as his letter to the First Lord of the Admiralty on the causes of the mutinies of 1797 at Spithead and the Nore, he showed a humanity with respect to leaves, discipline, flogging, and the like, far beyond his age. ("I served in a Ship where every one on the maintopmen were stripped and flogged at the gangway for no other cause than that another ship in company got her topgallant yards up first, and not from any wilful negligence. . . .")

Although he repeatedly applied for a ship, James was unemployed during the revolutionary and Napoleonic wars, and "an old post Captain" for these forty years, he had had to make his way, as did most of the Burneys, with his pen. "My dear Admiral!—My noble Admiral! My admirable Admiral," wrote his sister Fanny (Madame d'Arblay) in high jubilation when the promotions were published, delighting to sign herself thenceforth "an Admiral's Sister," though herself the famous Madame d'Arblay and a comtesse by her husband's right.

The Admiral lived to enjoy his honor only four months, dying on 17 November 1821. "I am grieved to the very Soul!" wrote Mme. d'Arblay to her son. "Your excellent Uncle was at the Royal Society on the Thursday Night—& surrounded by heartily congratulating members F.R.S. [Charles] Babbage [first man to invent a mechanical computer], who called here yesterday with enquiries for you, & condolences for me . . . was amongst them." James's sisters had hoped the long-deferred honor would "lengthen as well as sweeten" his days, "but his days were full," wrote his niece Charlotte Barrett, "& he was taken—May God pardon & accept him, for His sake in whom alone the best & the wisest can be accepted."

All this—the wedding, James's promotion, and his death—had occurred within eight months of the year 1821, four years before Lamb set his pen to the first of the events, which is therefore tinged with the sadness of the last. It is not the bride who takes the spotlight at the wedding but the father of the bride. What Lamb divined James must have felt on the occasion and what Lamb himself felt and did are the subjects of the essay. Feeling is its subject. What was felt by the author himself, one of the chief actors of the piece, and what in his imagination the hero must have felt, these are the imaginatively tender subjects of "The Wedding."

After the event—
  This stillness.
    Emptiness.
      Vacancy.
        Absences.

(I. A. Richards)

Lamb had marked James's "growing infirmities," had detected and analyzed the hurt pride of the father whom the bride was deserting for the groom, had stayed on after the breakfast to comfort him. Imaginings, memories, a tender maze of sentiment were shot through with fact. Mme. d'Arblay, with her clear, more objective head, could convey a more unrelieved sense of pain and concern, thus, in a report to her sister:

> Our good James is tolerably well; but alas, my dear Esther, by no means as flourishing as last year: I think him changed, & broken; he is weak, & stoops cruelly; but, at times, he retains all his wonted powers of wit & humour, & his parts & understanding are brighter, I think, than ever. God preserve him!—his Wife & Son & daughter are remarkably well & prosperous.

The Admiral's wife Sarah was a daughter of the bookseller "honest Tom Payne" (1719-1799) of the Mews Gate, Castle Street, Leicester Fields, not far from Newton House, the famous dwelling of the Burneys in St. Martin's Street. The marriage had not always been a happy one. James had been known to pack up and leave and stay away for years. No Burney blamed this on the wife, her sister-in-law Susan alone thinking that Mrs. B. with all her sterling qualities may have lacked warmth. She had, Lamb said, a "fine last-century countenance," and, according to a friend's daughter, she held her own among the handsome women of her set.

> I should tell you that amongst these beauties Mrs. Burney, with her small thin figure and pale face, in black velvet and gold lace, older than all the rest, had an air of dignity, and her little foot was remarkably well supported by an exquisite black satin French slipper.
>
> (Manwaring, p. 283)

She had a good understanding and good principles. She was a fond and indulgent mother. As seen in Lamb's representation of her in "Mrs. Battle's Opinions on Whist," she would not cheat or take unfair or meanly fair advantage. "She sate bolt upright; and neither showed you her cards, nor desired to see yours."

> I never in my life—and I knew Sarah Battle many of the best years of it—saw her take out her snuff-box when it was her turn to play; or snuff a candle in the middle of a game; or ring for a servant, till it was fairly over.

She was not sensual. She took no pleasure, as Lamb did, in the pictures on the cards ("the pretty antic habits," the reds and blacks and verdant greens). Such was her "quaker spirit of unsensualizing" that for her "All these might be dispensed with; and with their naked names upon the drab pasteboard, the game might go on very well, pictureless." Perhaps this alleged starkness of spirit or matter-of-factness may have rubbed off in real life in the game of love. Lamb saw something "genteel in this sort of self-denial." "To have the feeling of gentility, it is not necessary to have been born gentle." Yet these were not the qualities always satisfying perhaps to the warm-hearted, irrational, emotional, and radically-minded James, though in these latter days they lived together, went hand-in-hand across the Green Park to visit Mme. d'Arblay at Bolton Street. She had never seen them so happy. "Their harmony & chearfulness & sociality is such as it NEVER was till now from the even dawn of their Union."

Mrs. Burney was to die in 1832, a loss to all the house of Burney, such had been her kindness, hospitality, and loyalty. Lamb took leave of her in the ruins of Blakesmoor. Everywhere, desolation, demolition, the felling of "solidity with magnificence," the burnt ashes, and in fancy a "haunted room—in which old Mrs. Battle died," thus, in the ruins of grandeur. To Lamb there was something redoubtable even in the memory of Mrs. Battle.

Her daughter Sarah, the bride, was of another sort. Fat and a little hoydenish as a child, she grew up a Burney. "A more improved young person I never saw," observed her aging and multi-experienced aunt d'Arblay. *"Spirituelle,"* and eventually as accomplished as lessons in music, languages, and dancing could make her, she was the delight of her father's heart. For her he had returned in 1803 to his own fireside. "James is miserable without his little girl," explained his half-sister Sarah Harriet Burney (1772-1844), the novelist, with whom he had been living for five years, this being the explanation of the return and the end of that liaison. In that year 1803 he had taken his children on holiday to the Isle of Wight. "There's a little girl he's brought with him," wrote Lamb, "that has cost I don't know what in codlings.—No ordinary orchard would be a jointure for her." Now the matter of the jointure was relevant.

Born on 14 December 1796 and baptized shortly after at the font in St. Margaret's Church, Sarah Burney had all but reached the complement of twenty-four years stipulated by the father of the bride in the fictional wedding. At twenty-five (not nineteen, as Lamb pretended), she was a clever and engaging creature, by all accounts, but still the all but dowerless daughter of an "old post Captain" in limited circumstances. All James had to give the couple, he gave, that is, a house in Mickleham, Surrey, the rents of which he could not have easily spared.

The groom was John Thomas Payne (ca. 1796-1880), the natural son of Thomas Payne, the younger (1752-1831), who having worked for years with his father in the bookshop at the Mews Gate, had moved it in 1806 to premises within Schomberg House, on the south side of Pall Mall. The illegitimate John was therefore a nephew of Mrs. Battle and a cousin of the bride. He was of the firm of antiquarian booksellers, Payne and Foss (nicknamed by Lamb, "Pain and Fuss") of 81 Pall Mall and was therefore a tradesman. To face the social implication of the time squarely, he was "in the trade" or "in trade." And dour were some of the comments on this score.

The dour doubts proved not without some foundation, as the bride's cousin Charlotte Barrett found at Boulogne in 1822 when Mrs. Burney and Sarah joined them, taking lodgings in the same street and adding immeasurably to the pleasure of their evening walks. There they met an old friend of the Burney family, Andrew—now Sir Thomas—Strange, of ancient Scottish lineage, and Lady Strange, who was thought by no means to "admire the connection" and who kept aloof after she heard of it, in spite of Mrs. Burney's efforts to explain its welfare and happiness. Happiness it had provided on all scores. During temporary separations like this on jaunts for health, John continued to send "the tenderest letters full of money," which Sally turned to improvements, such as French silks and lessons every day in Italian, music, and dancing. "She is a clever & delightful creature," Charlotte observed, "& might have made a better marriage if she had wished—but I do think this good generous John will make her happy if he does not spoil her." Charlotte herself had married in 1807 a man old enough to be her father, Henry Barrett (1756-1843), or, as his mother-in-law called him, 'gentleman Barrett,' for, in spite of the failure of his sugar plantations in the West Indies and the urgent needs of a growing family of five, he could (or would) not lower his hand to any kind of work. The set of values held even in 1846, when Charlotte's grandson was discouraged in his ambition to become a bookseller like "Murray" because "it was not *quite* considered a gentleman's profession." "That's a pity," argued the child, "for he must be well educated, or he could not know whether his books were spelt right. He might be a gentleman."

In 1822 Charlotte, half ashamed of being "ashamed" of the connection, let her better sense prevail: "Poor Johnny cannot help it, & is such an excellent fellow that one must love & honour him, as well as make the best of it all to poor Sally, now she has married him." "I cannot but forgive this generous fellow for being a bookseller—& place him henceforward in my best books." Charlotte had heard from the bride on her return from a long honeymoon in Italy.

> She seems to have been much liked & admired abroad, & says that Aunt d'Arblay praised M[r] J Ps manners as being

> gentlemanly & elegant. Poor dear Sall! I hope she will be happy, & she is such a clever & good tempered girl, & has such good sense withal, that I think she will not miss of it.

Still there were social difficulties that it would take all the Burneyean charm and liveliness to overcome. Sarah Harriet Burney, writing from her apartments in Chelsea College or Hospital (a home for aged military men or those maimed in the wars), saw the great probability of her niece "losing cast by the union."

> I am perplexed also as to the class of society to which she will henceforth find herself restricted. Admired & liked as she is, will *her pill* be swallowed in consideration of the sweetener she can administer with it? How will your Richmond folks stand affected on this subject? How, even, will the higher description of her present associates deport and comport themselves on the occasion? The proud militaires here, I grieve to think, will all hold aloof.

At Richmond there lived at this time the bride's Aunt Broome (*née* Charlotte Ann Burney) and her daughter Charlotte Barrett, who later edited Mme. d'Arblay's *Diary and Letters* (7 vols., 1842-1847). Visiting the Broome and Barrett families on the very date of the wedding were Mme. d'Arblay herself and her son the Rev. Alexander d'Arblay. From Richmond Mme. d'Arblay dispatched a joint letter "For the Fair Bride of this Morning, 14th of April, 1821," conveying

> warmest and kindest wishes . . . that you, your happy partner, and your excellent parents, may meet every anniversary of this day by rejoicing in the event with which it will commence.
>
> Most affectionately yours, my dear Girl, ever,
> F. D'Arblay.
> (Manwaring, p. 265).

"In hearty concurrence with this benediction" all members of all three families—d'Arblay, Broome, and Barrett—signed their names, while Alexander, mindful of "the many kindnesses" he had received at his uncle's house, sent "warmest and sincerest wishes" of his own for "present contentment and future happiness."

According to Aunt d'Arblay, Sarah was "as amiable as she [was] cultivated and *spirituelle,*" but gentlemen born came high, usually requiring a portion or a jointure along with the bride. This the aunts knew very well and comfortably they decided, probably in concert, to make no fuss. So, likewise, did honest Tom Payne's daughter, mother of the bride, who, in Lamb's account, betrayed in "prim looks and quiet deportment" an "infinity of full satisfaction."

A member of the immediate family and certainly at the wedding-breakfast, though excluded by the description of the bride as "an only child," was and lived and had his own peculiar being the bride's brother Martin Charles Burney (1788-1852), whom Lamb had known very well these twenty years. No one, according to Hazlitt, was more frequently to be found at Lamb's home than Martin Burney. He was "on the top scale of [the author's] friendship ladder," and to him he had dedicated his *Works* in 1818.

> . . . I have watched thee almost from a child,
> Free from self-seeking, envy, low design,
> I have not found a whiter soul than thine.

He had known him in the summer of 1803 on the Isle of Wight, a fifteen-year-old schoolboy rendering Terence "into canine Latin at Breakfast and other meals, till the eyes of the infatuated Parent let slip water for joy." On other occasions awkwardness and boyish blunders brought down parental wrath. "The time expended in *Martin being scolded* would serve as great a sinner as Judas to repent in."

Educated at the famous school of his uncle Charles Burney at Greenwich and articled ca. 1806-1809 to the philologist, historian, and solicitor, Sharon Turner (1768-1847), he earned the praise of the latter for "great honour and integrity." ("He never told me a lie in his life!") As an attorney or solicitor, Martin had chambers for a time in Cook's Court, Carey Street, Lincoln's Inn Fields, prospered not at all, ran sometimes into debt, but may always be remembered for his reading several volumes of *Clarissa* while standing in the bookstalls. Literate, and not a bad literary critic, he was known to Hazlitt, Crabb Robinson, Leigh Hunt, and all the Lamb circle, and loyal to the last, followed Mary Lamb to her grave in 1847.

No hand for weddings, he was nevertheless married, having made a secret and unacknowledged alliance in 1816. He had married at St. Mary Matfallon, Whitechapel, a maidservant of sixteen or seventeen years of age, one Rebecca Norton (ca. 1799-1868), who outlived him. An "odd joker," he was blurred out of the dream wedding, though certainly there in the flesh at his sister's wedding at 26 James Street on 14 April 1821. An artist cannot put all things into a picture at once, not if he is to create a dominant impression, in this case, the yawning impact of vacancy left when the high-spirited girl had departed. Martin would have understood the literary expediencies of his literary friend, not to say, his tricks and hoaxes, and would not have minded, let us hope, his literary oblivion.

Officiating at the wedding in St. Margaret's Church was the bride's cousin the Rev. Charles Parr Burney (1785-1864), a Doctor of Divinity (Oxon., 1822), who had succeeded his father the Greek scholar as head of the well-known school, that which Martin had attended, at Greenwich. That in real life Lamb had been overcome by mirth in the course of the solemn rites, Sarah Harriet Burney, for one, could readily have believed. "What a singular, and I must say, melancholy combination of the truest & warmest piety, with the most extraordinary & irreverent profaneness! I cannot understand the union of two such opposites." Neither perhaps could Charles Parr, who, replete with excellent qualities, though not particularly blessed with humor, may well, if grins there were, have failed to see the joke, and the practiced and quelling eye of the schoolmaster, the future Archdeacon of St. Albans, was the original, perhaps, of "the awful eye" of the fictional vicar in the Poultry. Generous, genial, and social, Charles Parr must have attended, all things being equal, the *déjeuner* in James Street.

The bridesmaids "habited all in green" and styled the three Foresters, who were not "so blest as to have a mother living," Manwaring has identified as Ann, Maria, and Elizabeth Ward Tomlinson, whose mother lived till 1839. Their father was an old shipmate of the father of the bride—one Nicholas Tomlinson

(1765-1847), Rear-Admiral (1830), Vice-Admiral (1841), who in 1782-1783 had sailed with Captain Burney on the *Bristol,* a man-of-war convoying a fleet of fourteen sail to the East Indies, but who, unlike James, had since pursued an active career on the sea, capped with highly successful enterprises as a privateer (see *DNB*). But Lamb was not writing a documentary; in literary pieces like his one must attend to the unities and especially a unity of feeling. It augments the prevailing sense of grief and loss to have the bridesmaids motherless and to doom them, all three, to virginity, though clad in fertile green. Such was not the fate of the figure shining in white, Sarah Burney. She was not to be sacrificed a virgin handmaiden to an old man of the sea. The sacrifice was to be a very un-Greek one on the part of the father. "She [was] the delight of the very soul of our dear James." And the pathos of the piece is presently to settle on him.

Among the "elderly ladies present" or, perhaps more accurately, the *married* ladies present would have been intimate friends of the house, including, one can be almost sure, Susannah Rickman, aged fifty, the wife of John Rickman (1771-1840), statistician, F.R.S., and Secretary to the Speaker in the House of Commons, whom the Burneys often visited in their country place near Epsom. Mrs. Rickman was able to obtain "good seats" for herself and her friend at the magnificent coronation of George IV on 19 July coming, and she was to keep Mrs. B. for long visits, offering comfort and hospitality in the years of her widowhood.

The Turner ladies were probably there in full force. Bright and beauteous, and wearing possibly her turban of "gold tissue," as "beautiful, accomplished, and agreeable" as she appears in contemporary accounts (and even in the *DNB*), Mrs. Sharon Turner (d. 1843), wife of the historian-cum-attorney, may have made part of "the morning's pageant" as did her daughters "the handsome Miss T——s," with whom Lamb got into conversation about his black wedding suit. The third daughter Mary (d. 1870) was to marry in 1825 the economist William Ellis (1800-1881) and also to make the *DNB,* as did many of the guests at that Burney wedding—Charles and Mary Lamb, the Rickmans, the Turners, the Tomlinsons, the Paynes, the Phillipses, and others, like the Ayrtons, whom one could well conjecture to have been there.

Certainly there and to be added to the list of guests by her own testimony was the bride's cousin Fanny Raper (1782-1860), who, in addition to Lamb, left a written account of the breakfast, a *pièce de resistance,* an informative analogue. Fanny was the daughter of James's sister Susanna Elizabeth (1755-1800), who in 1782 had married a gallant Irishman Molesworth Phillips (1755-1832), Captain of the Marines. Like James, he had sailed with Captain Cook on his last voyage and, striking down the savage who had killed the circumnavigator, was remembered until his death as the hero of the expedition *(DNB).* The couple lived happily at Mickleham, Surrey, for some twelve years, when for reasons unknown the gay and ingenious Captain became the "cruel Major." For pecuniary reasons he moved his family in 1796 to the farmstead, Belcotton, County Louth, Ireland, where Susan's health rapidly failed. No persuasion could induce the Major to bring her home to be nursed, and her death at Parkgate on 6 January 1800, when the Burneys thought her at last within reach, was the hardest blow they had had yet to bear. Charles, the Greek scholar, had gone with a warm carriage to Holyhead, then to Parkgate (for so had the winds blown the yacht) to meet her. Mme. d'Arblay, waiting at West Humble, heard the news with anguish. As for Molesworth Phillips, she hoped never to see his baleful visage more. "I try to revive," she wrote to Charles, some ten months later,

> but Oh God keep me from the sight of that baleful being who NOW can have the heart—the hard black Heart—to visit all the Friends of the Angel he wasted into her Tomb by keeping from them!— If he comes hither, we are determined never to admit him. So as we solicited! so humbly—& in such anguish his return!—& THEN—he could assert his leaving Ireland would be irreparably injurious! yet keep alive expectation, just sufficiently to prevent my going to her——
>
> (M. Burney-Cumming, 11 Nov. 1800)

This she resolved in 1800. In 1821 and indeed to the end of her life Mme. d'Arblay saw no reason to temper her aversion. "Revolting while Memory holds her seat" was Phillips' presence in James Street or intrusion in Burney matters. "Not one MOMENTS penitence has ever appeared to soften off his crime, or plead for its forgiveness. THEREFORE is it I hold against him my inalterable horrour."

> He has never been presented to me in any light of appeasement—a 2[d]. wife deserted—Children by a 2[d]. Bed abandoned—a mistress openly kept——& the possession of spirits triumphant in boldness!——oh my dear Esther—was That the lot of the most delicate, as well as purest & most excellent of human beings?—

Nevertheless Phillips apparently came and went at will in James's household. There, through the obliging stupidity of a servant in identifying him, a sheriff succeeded in serving him with a warrant, and were it not for the generosity of shipmate James, who paid the bill, he would have landed in debtor's prison, as he did in any case, it was said, for still another debt. There in the days following James's death, he arranged for the death mask and the bust of the Admiral, as well as his own burial in James's grave, and he may have been at the wedding as well. The mere possibility was enough to keep Mme. d'Arblay far away, and it is not unlikely that for this reason she planned her visit to her sister Broome in this particular week of April.

We would do better, however, to follow Lamb's example of selectiveness and focus upon Susan's daughter Fanny Phillips (for in due course she will speak of the wedding). In 1807 she had married Charles Chamier Raper (ca. 1777-1845), Clerk in the Foreign Office. They lived in Field Cottage, King's Parade, Chelsea, and often visited Aunt d'Arblay in Bolton Street. *She,* Fanny, was in her late thirties, "still a Hebe of freshness & beauty, *he* ever more her adorer, & therefore happy." They had one child, Minette, aged fourteen, and Fanny with her husband or her daughter (or both) attended "Sarah's Breakfast and met there beaucoup de monde—" So she reported to her cousin Charlotte Barrett. "Martin said there is only one thing wanting here, that is one Person & that is M[rs] Barrett and his opinion was unanimously echoed."

> Sarah looked particularly well She was very nicely dressed had a beautiful Bonet of transparent figured thicke gauze with

> a plume of white feathers a Gros de Naples Spencer and a nosegay of Myrtle and Roses— She was (I hear) a good deal affected by the Ceremony but recovered her spirits and paid particular attention to all her guests—after breakfast she put on a purple silk Gown and Spencer and Bonnet and took leave separately of all present Uncle James handed her into the carriage and John Payne followed, they smiled out of the Window and drove off a very happy couple the people looked a little blank for a minute or two and Miss Lamb and two little Girls cried a little but they all soon began to chirp and chatter and in about half an hour we all dispersed.——

The chatter, James said, followed the receding focus of interest. Could the couple reach Sittingbourne before nightfall?

The blankness of the moment Lamb described in blank verse handily found in Shakespeare.

> As in a theatre, the eyes of men,
> After a well-graced actor leaves the stage,
> Are idly bent on him that enters next,
> Thinking his prattle to be tedious.
> *(King Richard II,* V. ii. 23)

Shakespeare's clause about the prattle and its tediousness, however, our author judiciously omitted, presumably as ill consorting with the success of the prattle he was himself presently to introduce with such excellent effect, as he thought. "I must do justice to a foolish talent of mine,"

> I mean a power . . . of giving vent to all manner of strange nonsense. In this awkward dilemma I found it sovereign. I rattled off some of my most excellent absurdities. All were willing to be relieved, at any expense of reason, from the pressure of the intolerable vacuum which had succeeded to the morning bustle.

The emptiness that the delightful girl had left behind her, Lamb tried to fill with a game of whist that lasted till midnight and sent the Captain to bed, he hoped, "with comparatively easy spirits." "Martin kept Lamb and his sister the rest of the day with us,"

James confirmed in a letter to his son-in-law, "which with my having made free with the pampering pipe has been rather much for me." The therapy (including tobacco as well as whist) had proved of doubtful value. It had been a long day.

The emptiness remained. "We all miss a junior presence." Who now will fill the pampering pipes? The father of the bride, hero of Lamb's essay, tries to bear up, but his puns and "flashes of wild wit" are less ready than formerly they were. "His sea-songs seldomer escape him." Only at times, Mme. d'Arblay noted as well, were his "wit & humour" what they were. His life was coming to an end.

He lived to see the bridal couple return in September from their long honeymoon in Italy and to see them established in quarters of their own in Stratton Street. "I trust you will not be *sharp* upon a Bride for wanting a Cooing shed with her love," wrote Mme. d'Arblay with some concern for "the Bridal first year" ("Don't shorten its Charm.") and with some understanding of her brother, for James, of course, wished his daughter back in 26 James Street. He lived to visit the couple in their own apartments, and fortunately they were in James Street the night of the apoplectic fit that ended the Admiral's life. The medical men declared, however, that "it was *not* Apoplexy. They say that [wrote Fanny Raper] by the constant & too great working of his Brain he has produced an ossification of part of it, and, in Age, this becomes brittle; & similar effects have been known before." The closing words also may be given to Fanny Raper, who with "so much reason to love & honour & regret" her uncle, had asked to see him "in the Parlour" where he lay. "My poor dear Uncle is very little altered, has a very sweet, calm, & benignant expression on his countenance, & looks as if he only slept."

"What fun has whist now?" Lamb asked, "what matters it what you lead, if you can no longer fancy him looking over you?"

After the event——
  This stillness.
    Emptiness.

That loss ("There's Captain Burney gone"), James's loss of his daughter, loss in general, the depth of Lamb's insight and feeling and his sensitive sympathy emerge in his essay "The Wedding," a piece artistically molded and shaded in defiance of factual details to convey what he considered and felt the essence of the event. His deference was not to the "streaks on the tulip" but to his artistic purpose.

This documentary or purview of the copy Lamb actually had in hand in real life at the real wedding of 14 April 1821 may serve to show the artist at work, his selectivity with respect to details, and as well, the subjectivity of the romantic imagination.

SOURCES

Charles Lamb, *The Letters of . . .*, ed. E. V. Lucas (London: J. M. Dent and Methuen, 1935), I, 357; II, 315, 319; and passim. "The Wedding," "Mrs. Battle's Opinions on Whist," "Blakesmoor in H——shire," and "Detached Thoughts on Books and Reading," *The Works of Charles and Mary Lamb,* ed. E. V. Lucas, II (London: Methuen, 1903).

G. E. Manwaring, *My Friend the Admiral . . .* (London: Routledge, 1931), especially chap. xiii, "The Admiral's Son."

Phyllis G. Mann, "A New Gloss of '*The Wedding,*' " *The C. L. S. Bulletin,* 170 (March 1963), 402-3.

James Burney, *With Captain James Cook in the Antarctic and Pacific. The Private Journal of James Burney* (Canberra: the National Library of Australia, 1975), with an Introduction by Beverley Hooper. *A Chronological History of North-Eastern Voyages of Discovery; and of the Early Navigations of the Russians* (London: Payne & Foss, 1819). "James Burney's Opinions on the Naval Mutinies of 1797," ed. with introduction by Hugh Sproule, *The Mariner's Mirror,* 46 (February 1960), 61-62.

Fanny Burney (Mme. d'Arblay), *The Journals and Letters of Fanny Burney (Madame d'Arblay), 1791-1840,* ed. Joyce Hemlow (Oxford: Clarendon Press, 1972–), IV, 204-205 and *passim.* Letters concerning James Burney, the originals of which are in the Henry W. and Albert A. Berg Collection of the New York Public Library, will be published in forthcoming volumes of the above series as Nos. 1233, 1238, 1270, 1272, 1276, 1287, 1296; as well as letters from Mme. d'Arblay to her sister Esther Burney, [3 Aug.], 28 Nov. 1820; 30 July, 21 Oct.–Nov., 23 Nov. 1821; 7 May, 11-24 Dec. 1822; and a letter to her son Alexander d'Arblay, [18 Dec. 1821].

For permission to print quotations from the above letters (and also from those in the Berg Collection cited below), the writer is deeply indebted to the curators and trustees of the Henry W. and Albert A. Berg Collection, the New York Public Library, Astor, Lenox and Tilden Foundations.

The writer is also indebted to the curators of the Pierpont Morgan Library for permission to quote from Mme. d'Arblay's letters to her brother James Burney, [*post* 14 Aug.], [*ca.* 25 Aug.], 4 Sept. 1821 (to be printed as Nos. 1257, 1260, and 1265 in the edition above).

Mme. d'Arblay's letter of 11 Nov. 1800 to her brother Charles Burney is in the possession of Mr. M. Burney-Cumming, who is kindly allowing it to be printed as No. 394B in an Appendix to the edition above and to be quoted here.

Fanny Raper *née* Phillips, Letter (Henry W. and Albert A. Berg Collection) to her cousin Charlotte Barrett, 21 Apr. [1821]; also a letter copied in part by Mme. d'Arblay in her letter of 23 Aug. 1821 (see above).

Sarah Harriet Burney,	Letter (Henry W. and Albert A. Berg Collection) to Charlotte Barrett, 12 May 1803; also a letter (Dr. Williams's Library, London) to Crabb Robinson, 27 Feb. 1821, printed by Edith J. Morley, "Sarah Harriet Burney," *Modern Philology,* 39 (Nov. 1941), 148-150.
Charlotte Barrett *née* Francis,	Letters written at Boulogne, her copies of which are preserved in the "Pink Letter Book" (British Library, Barrett Collection of Burney Papers, Eg. 3705D).
Julia C. Maitland,	Letter (British Library, Barrett Collection of Burney Papers, Eg. 3704B, ff. 163-164b) to Charlotte Barrett, 14 Dec. 1846.

Mary Wollstonecraft in Federalist America: 1791-1802

Marcelle Thiébaux

"I had thoughts of America. I fancy I can write, and Americans, one hears, are gentle to women." So in a moment of wild hope speaks Diana Warwick in *Diana of the Crossways,* when, like many an Englishwoman before her, she finds herself thrown upon the resources of her pen for a livelihood. Had Mary Wollstonecraft ever had thoughts of writing profitably for Americans? If so she might eventually have concluded that Americans need be no more gentle than the rest of the world toward literary women. One is curious to know to what extent Mary Wollstonecraft realized that her works did have a readership, and a mixed one, on our shores. It may well be that she had not, in fact, established contacts with the American publishers who were printing and circulating her works. One hears nothing of her being paid for her efforts, or of her having any knowledge of her critical reception here. The pirating of English books by American publishers was a common practice. Whether published legitimately or not—from Philadelphia to Boston, from Wilmington to New York to Providence, books by Mary Wollstonecraft were printed, excerpted, sold, read, reviewed, talked about, admired, and ungently detested.[1]

We may trace the literary fortunes of Mary Wollstonecraft in Federalist America during the eleven or twelve year period from the first appearance in Philadelphia of one of her translations, to the reviews and lampoons that appeared after the American publication of Godwin's *Memoirs.* Americans knew chiefly *A Vindication of the Rights of Woman,* although they record an occasional response to some of her other books as well. Even before the first American edition of *A Vindication,* the American press showed that it had heard of the rights of woman. *The New-York Magazine* for December 1791 reprinted a satirical piece from the *St. James Chronicle,* [2] under the persona of JENNY SARCASM.

> . . .—rights of a fiddlestick!—rights of *men,* indeed! I should not have thought of the *he* creatures talking so much about their rights, while the *rights* of *women* lie neglected—. . . . Have not *we* RIGHTS, Mr. Baldwin, rights indisputable, natural, abstract, and social, and civil, and municipal? Are not "all women equal?"

Women do already possess many rights, pursues the article, those of visiting, scolding, falling into fits, and, the highest of all rights, that of ruling their husbands. Mention is made of "the answerers of Burke (I am told they are all *bachelors* or *old maids*)." Wollstonecraft was known in America as an answerer of Burke; one of her Philadelphia publishers claimed world renown for her as such.

The humorous appeal of "rights of a fiddlestick" was enduring, for the piece was reprinted in two other American periodicals. *The Columbian Centinel* of Boston ran it on 1 February 1792. The *Centinel's* [3] editor, Benjamin Russell, was highly critical of the "rights of woman" doctrines of Wollstonecraft, which he identified with political excesses and French ideas. He was to wage a virulent battle against her, lasting even after her death. The reviews and correspondence concerning her that appeared in his paper will be discussed here further. Once again the Jenny Sarcasm essay appeared in *The Philadelphia Monthly* for February 1798, substituting "Mr. Printer" for "Mr. Baldwin." [4]

Actually, Wollstonecraft's first publication in America was her translation of Necker's *Of the Importance of Religious Opinions.* The book was advertised for sale at Mathew Carey's Philadelphia bookstore for four-fifths of a dollar. Mathew Carey, whose firm was known after 1787 as Carey, Stewart & Co., was pre-eminent among American publishers. A deeply religious man, founder of the Sunday school system in America, and a Catholic, Carey published a number of religious books. In 1790 he was engaged in publishing the first quarto of the English Bible, and in 1791 he brought out a document of major concern to the Catholic Church in America.[5] Perhaps his interest in publishing Necker's volume in 1791 was stimulated by his other enterprises in this same period. We cannot say if American readers ever associated Wollstonecraft with the work, since neither this nor a later edition by another house bore her name.

When in 1792 *A Vindication of the Rights of Woman* did appear, its reception was not generally adverse. American journals often "reviewed" English books by reprinting extracts, with a minimum of comment. Both the Philadelphia and the Boston editions of *A Vindication of the Rights of Woman* were advertised through pre-publication extracts in the magazines put out by the respective American publishers of the work. In Philadelphia, the September 1792 issue of Gibbons' *Lady's Magazine and Repository of Entertaining Knowledge* [6] printed a portion of Wollstonecraft's prefatory letter to Talleyrand. The editors' introduction reads: *"This lady is known to the world, by her answer to Mr. Burke, and we now behold her employing her pen in behalf of her own sex."* Extracts from the rest of the book follow. At the end of the November issue of the same magazine Gibbons places his advertisement: "IN THE PRESS, and speedily will be PUBLISHED, *that much admired and truly Elegant Performance,* called A VINDICATION of the RIGHTS of WOMAN. (By MARY WOOLSTONECRAFT)."

Similarly, her Boston publishers Isaiah Thomas and Ebenezer T. Andrews printed a few extracts in their important journal, *The Massachusetts Magazine,* announcing that "This valuable work is now in the Press, and will be published in a few weeks." [7] Like other periodicals of its time, *The Massachusetts Magazine* printed many a column containing essays on old maids, hints to the ladies, advice to the fair sex, and lectures on widows. Despite the patronizing tone of such articles, *The Massachusetts Magazine* nonetheless provided the outlet for the feminist author Judith Sargent Murray. Her column, "The Gleaner," appeared regularly, and in 1798, Thomas and Andrews printed her three-volume collection under that title.

Mrs. Murray ardently spoke out in support of women's equality. In a voice of optimism that proved sadly premature, Mrs. Murray congratulates American women "on the happy revolution which the few past years has made in their favour," rejoicing that needlework is now no longer so necessary to their wellbeing and that, with female academies springing up everywhere, women may devote their time to "studies of a more elevated and elevating nature." "Yes," continues Mrs. Murray, "in this younger world, 'the Rights of Women' begin to be understood; we seem, at length, determined to do justice to THE SEX; and, improving on the opinions of a Wollstonecraft, we are ready to contend for the *quantity,* as well as *quality,* of mind. . . . *The idea of the incapability* of women, is, we conceive, in this *enlightened age,* totally *inadmissible* . . . ." Her rhetoric becomes identifiably Wollstonecraftian in her assertion that women everywhere "have successfully opposed themselves to tyranny and the galling yoke of oppression!" Mrs. Murray's faith in education and in the growing independence of women in making their own livings reflects her glowing hopes based upon Wollstonecraft's precepts.[8]

The Massachusetts Magazine of October 1792 and February 1793 cautiously excerpted passages from *A Vindication of the Rights of Woman* both before and after the publication of the American editions. But these excerpts are disingenuous and misleading. Not only is there no allusion to "the rights of woman," but the word "woman" itself is nowhere mentioned beyond the title. Both eschew the inflammatory rhetoric of tyranny, slavery, despotism. The first is a disjointed collection of sayings that belies the character of the work: e.g., "Friendship is a serious affection: the most sublime of all affections, because it is founded on principle and cemented by time." Or, "A modest man is steady, an humble man timid, and a vain one presumptuous." In February 1793, a section was reprinted under the heading *"Politicks.* Remarks on Kings, Nobles, Standing Armies, &c." [9] The selection picks its way daintily about the first, third, and ninth chapters, skipping all the heady statements on women's rights. The same issue reviews the entire volume in a short ambivalent notice, just following a favorable estimate of Helen Maria Williams' *Letters on the French Revolution.*[10] Williams' reviewer, interestingly enough, praises her for her philanthropy and love of liberty: "Greatly superiour to every local prejudice, she dares to contemplate even the African as a member of the general family. . . ."

The review of Wollstonecraft, on the contrary, pays measured tribute to her work. It begins by querying the relevance of this transatlantic publication to the healthy state of America, where women were not apt to suffer degradation as they are in royalty-infested Europe. Next, Wollstonecraft's criticisms of contemporary authors receive approval. The review concludes:

> It is true, we cannot commend every sentence which has fallen from the pen of this animated writer; nor do we conceive that all her schemes are practicable, or if practicable, beneficial. But among a few thinly scattered weeds, there are many durable trees, which unite the beauties of Flora, with the firmness of the elm. Argonistick [sic] feelings, maddened at the supposed inferiority of her sex, and correspondent energies of expression, are the characteristicks of Mrs. Woolstonecraft, as a woman and a writer.

While journals warily judged and excerpted *A Vindication of the Rights of Woman,* especially those journals published by firms that were also publishing and selling the book, private readers plunged ahead and read to the end. In the same year that the reviewer for *The Massachusetts Magazine* wonders whether American women really needed Wollstonecraft, a notable American recorded his vigorous opinion that they did. Aaron Burr wrote to his wife on 8 February 1793 expressing distaste over the "cursed effects of fashionable education! of which both sexes are the advocates, and yours eminently the victims." His concern was for his daughter Theodosia, anxious lest she develop into an idle, vapid woman of fashion. Burr acknowledged in a letter of 15 February that education, prejudice, and habit were responsible for the rarity with which women manifested signs of genius. A day later, on 16 February, he took up the question with fresh interest:

> You have heard me speak of a Miss Woolstonecraft, who has written something on the French revolution; she has also written a book entitled *"Vindication of the rights of Woman."* I had heard it spoken of with a coldness little calculated to excite attention; but as I read with avidity and prepossession every thing written by a lady, I made haste to procure it, and spent the last night, almost the whole of it, in reading it. Be assured that your sex has in *her* an able advocate. It is, in my

> opinion, a work of genius. She has successfully adopted the style of Rousseau's Emilius; and her comment on that work, especially what relates to female education, contains more good sense than all the other criticisms upon him which I have seen put together. I promise myself much pleasure in reading it to you.
>
> Is it owing to ignorance or prejudice that I have not yet met a single person who had discovered or would allow the merit of this work? [11]

If private opinion as expressed among Burr's acquaintance was conservative, the public opinion reflected by editors and journalists tended to be even more so.

The influential *New-York Magazine,* however, took a bolder stand than many, and throughout its history, until December 1797, remained relatively supportive of Wollstonecraft. The February 1793 issue prefaced its reprinting of the entire introduction [12] of *A Vindication of the Rights of Woman* with this notice:

> *While thousands are shedding their Blood in asserting the* Rights of Man, *a Female has lately wielded her Pen, and we think with great success, in vindicating the* Rights of Woman. *As the Chapters of this Work are too lengthy for insertion in this Magazine, we have selected the Introduction to it, which will give our Readers a Sketch of the Author's Plan, and also a Specimen of her Stile.*

Although no magazine was entirely free of those patronizing addresses to the fair sex that *The Massachusetts Magazine* affected, *The New-York Magazine* offered fewer, and usually expressed an enlightened view of woman's education. In September 1794, the magazine printed an essay, "On Female Education," by "G. U.," a woman student from a Seminary in Beekman Street, New York. The essay reinforced a Wollstonecraft position in Wollstonecraft language of slavery and tyranny.

> . . . I am struck with amazement to observe the material difference in the education of the sexes: Whilst the male are rising and shining in all the branches of literature, fitting to be useful members of civil society, an honour to their parents and

> a blessing to the world, the poor females are excluded in some obscure corner, contented with the admiration and flattery of the gentlemen, (even the most despicable of all flatterers) who praise only their beauty, elevate their vanity, and glory in their ignorance.

Why, continues the author, should not women, like men, "establish our rights, and trample on the despised flattery of those who wish to keep us in the base chains of ignorance?" [13]

Over the years, *The New-York Magazine* continued its fidelity to the teachings of Wollstonecraft. With crotchety humor, a "Letter from an Old Bachelor" in the August 1795 issue voices the writer's aversion to the marriage market in which beautiful women make "cattle of themselves, . . . being disposed of to the highest bidder." [14] But he confesses that the "attachment to the ostentatious exteriors of life" is not the fault of women.

> They receive the bent of their ambition, their education and character, from the other sex; and it is in their unmanly vanities, and short-sighted puerile admiration, that we shall find the germ of the evil. But I will refer for a most profound and philosophical investigation of this subject to the ninth chapter of Mrs. Wollstonecraft's Rights of Woman.

By 1795, another translation of Mary Wollstonecraft appeared in America, this one acknowledged to be her work. Salzmann's *Elements of Morality* went through four editions, as many as *A Vindication of the Rights of Woman.* It appeared in Providence, Philadelphia, Wilmington, and Baltimore between 1795 and 1811. Carter and Wilkinson of Providence, the first publishers of *Elements,* advertised this work in their newspaper, *The Providence Gazette,* and repeatedly included the "Rights of Women" [sic] and the "History of the French Revolution," in their list of books "just received" or "new publications." [15] In the 28 February 1795 issue of the paper Mrs. Rowson's *Charlotte: A Tale of Truth,* and Bunyan's *Holy War* were each offered at 75 cents, while the "Rights of Women" was for sale at "1 Dollar." On the date of publication, 22 August 1795, *The Elements of Morality* was conspicuously advertised in a notice of a size (2¼ × 2½ inches) to be equalled only by the advertisement for sale of Pope's *Essay on Man* the following week.[16] The same notice of Wollstonecraft's book ran in two subsequent issues of *The Providence Gazette,* and the title appeared in the customary book lists as well.

Meanwhile, however, hostile attention was catching up with Wollstonecraft in America in the form of Thomas Taylor's *A Vindication of the Rights of Brutes,* republished in Boston in 1795 from the London edition of 1792. Its satire is directed at "those wonderful productions of Mr. PAINE and Mrs. WOLLSTONECRAFT." The first chapter reminds the reader of how Mrs. Wollstonecraft has argued for the equality of women and men in mental as well as in bodily ability. Now is the time to prove that brutes are equal to humans. Once this equality has been understood and accepted, Taylor proposed, animals will have the right to be the lovers of women. The elephant, for example, is "a beast by nature very amorous; and from his prodigious size, very well calculated to become the darlings of our modern virgins . . . who are seldom intimidated by anything large." Classical scholars, he points out, are already acquainted with such practices in antiquity: the Alexandrian elephant, for instance, who delightedly used to caress his mistress's breasts with his proboscis, or the dragon who embraced his naked lady by night, and when displeased with her, lashed her legs with his tail, "expressing by this means gentle and loving anger." Taylor continues:

> And here I cannot refrain from mentioning a most singular advantage, which would arise from an association with dogs, when their language is perfectly understood by us; the advantage I allude to, respects a thing of no less importance than the instruction of youth in one of the most interesting particulars belonging to juvenile tuition. Everyone knows how universally prevalent the practice of self-pollution is become amongst children; and how dreadful its consequences are in debilitating the constitution, and corrupting the morals of the unhappy youths who are the votaries of this detestable vice. Now that extraordinary genius, Mrs. Wollstonecraft, proposes the following remedy for this pernicious practice . . . .

The remedy referred to is "to speak to children of the organs of generation as freely as we speak of the other parts of the body."

Taylor regards this plan as "a most striking proof of her uncommon capacity, and the truth of her grand theory, *the equality of the female nature with the male . . . .* "[17]

Taylor's book does not appear to have occasioned comment in Boston.

In Philadelphia, between 21 February 1795 and 7 July 1798, a magazine flourished that was meant to appeal to a female audience. *The Philadelphia Minerva* presented a tireless round of poems, letters, and essays, rehearsing old maid's prayers and soliloquies, bachelor's replies, remarks on conjugal felicity, lyrics sung three weeks after marriage, lines on the lounging housewife, a tale of two husbands to one wife, and the like. Two acknowledgments of Mary Wollstonecraft are to be found in this periodical, both of an approving sort. On 17 October 1795, a poem is printed called *The Rights of Woman* [By a Lady], to be sung to the tune of "God Save America." It opens:

God save each Female's right
Show to her ravish'd sight
Woman is Free.
Let Freedom's voice prevail,
And draw aside the vail,
Supreme Effulgence hail,
Sweet Liberty.
Man boasts the noble cause,
Nor yields supine to laws
Tyrants ordain;
Let woman have a share,
Nor yield to slavish fear.
Her equal rights declare,
And well maintain.

The ninth, and penultimate stanza reads:

Woman aloud rejoice,
Exult thy feeble voice
In chearful strain;
See Wolstonecraft, a friend
Your injur'd rights defend
Wisdom her steps attend,
This cause maintain.[18]

The familiar Wollstonecraft vocabulary rings clear: the "iron bands," the "cruel chain," the "tyranny," and the "slavery," the exhortations to woman to hide her talents no longer, no longer to cower in awe of "man, your tyrant lord." Seven months later, a short piece "On Modesty" was attributed to Mrs. Wollstonecraft, beginning "Modesty! Sacred offspring of sensibility and reason! true delicacy of mind!" [19] The piece consists of the first, the last, and a middle paragraph ("It is the pale moonbeam . . . .") selected from Chapter VII of *A Vindication of the Rights of Woman.* The closest resemblance between these carefully chosen passages and the revolutionary character of the whole work lies in Wollstonecraft's statement that true modesty "is incompatible with ignorance." Once again, Wollstonecraft has been edited so as to sit comfortably on the page of a journal that also printed the effusions of a Mrs. Griffith, whose treacly "Advice to young women (whether single or married)" is liberally poured in issue after issue of *The Philadelphia Minerva.*

The New-York Magazine meanwhile did not abandon its admiration of Wollstonecraft and continued its flattering practice of printing harmless passages of her work. The December 1795 issue carried a short essay entitled "A Picture of Connubial Felicity [by Mary Wollstonecraft]" lifted from the much quoted ninth chapter.[20] The passage touches on the sentimental scene of the husband's delights at seeing his child suckled and his joy at coming home weary in the evening to find "smiling babes and a clean hearth."

Wollstonecraft's *Letters Written during A Short Residence in Sweden, Norway, and Denmark* had been published in Wilmington in 1796; *The New-York Magazine* ran passages from this work in three consecutive issues: December 1796, January 1797, and February 1797.[21] The first carries the running head, "Beautiful Specimen of Sensibility." It is a description of Tonnberg. The editors write: "The following extract from this work affords a beautiful specimen of her lively fancy and tender sensibility." The next two selections are entitled "Account of the Peasantry of Norway" and "Remarks on the Fate of the unfortunate Matilda, Queen of Denmark." In November of that same year, under "Foreign Deaths," *The New-York Magazine* reported "In England, Mrs. Godwin, formerly Miss Wollstonecraft, the celebrated authoress of the Rights of Woman."

The magazine ceased publication after December 1797.

Glancing tributes were sometimes paid to Wollstonecraft by echoing her words, even where her name was not mentioned. An anthology appeared in 1797 called *The American Spectator, or Matrimonial Preceptor.*[22] It contained essays by divers hands from Valerius Maximus to Mrs. Thrale, and beyond. The editor seemed to feel that American society was ready for egalitarianism where women were concerned, even if other societies were not. Here, "the female mind is . . . generally cultivated, and adorned with that knowledge and sentiment, which qualify for the conjugal, and parental relations. The RIGHTS OF WOMEN, as well as OF MEN, are acknowledged." And the first chapter is entitled "The Female Sex vindicated, or the comparative Estimate of the two Sexes considered." Deliberate differences in education tend to trivialize women, observes the author, who urges a "favorable opinion of their moral and mental accomplishments."

In the lull before the appearance of Godwin's jarring memoirs of his wife, the recognition accorded Wollstonecraft was still relatively kindly. In 1798 Charles Brockden Brown published his *Alcuin,* happily inspired by a woman of learning. Thomas and James Swords, one of the earliest publishers of importance in New York, published the first parts of this dialogue on the rights of woman.[23] The work was printed serially in a somewhat different form in *The Weekly Magazine of Philadelphia.* When Alcuin, the schoolmaster, mouths such benighted sentiments as "women are most eloquent on a fan or a tea-cup," or "women are generally superficial and ignorant, because they are generally cooks and sempstresses," "seldom or never metaphysicians, chemists, or lawgivers," he is corrected by his blue-stocking companion Mrs. Carter—shades of Eliza Carter and Mary Wollstonecraft, with a temperament reminiscent of the heroine of *Original Stories,* Mrs. Mason. Mrs. Carter asserts that "of all forms of injustice, that is the most egregious which makes the circumstance of sex a reason for excluding one half of mankind from all those paths which lead to usefulness and honour." She complains of women's being barred from the professions which would give them, like men, "the means of subsistence and independence." When Alcuin demurs that women, released from professional toil, enjoy the purer, more delicate roles, Mrs. Carter pursues her point. The liberal professions require the greatest mental energy and the "most commerce with books and with enlightened society." These ought to be open to women.

On speaking of the relations between the sexes, Mrs. Carter observes: "Nothing has been more injurious than the separation of the sexes. . . . All intercourse between them is fettered and embarrassed. On the one side, all is reserve and artifice. On the other, adulation and affected humility." On marriage, Mrs. Carter, like Wollstonecraft, suggests the harms that may grow out of this institution:

> The will of her husband is the criterion of all her duties. All merit is comprised in unlimited obedience. She must not expostulate or rebel. In all contests with him, she must hope to prevail by blandishments and tears; not by appeals to justice and addresses to reason. She will be most applauded when she smiles with most perseverence on her oppressor, and when, with the undistinguishing attachment of a dog, no caprice or cruelty shall be able to estrange her affection.

The schoolmaster has finally to admit that women have indeed been injuriously treated by social institutions.

The second part of the dialogue raises the question of women's being permitted to vote. Mrs. Carter expresses her view: "I shall ever consider it as a gross abuse that we are hindered from sharing with you in the power of chusing our rulers, and of making those laws to which we equally with yourselves are subject." [24]

The year 1798 saw other tributes to Wollstonecraft. Mrs. Murray's *The Gleaner* essays were reprinted in a three-volume collection by Wollstonecraft's publishers who also produced *The Massachusetts Magazine,* Isaiah Thomas and Ebenezer T. Andrews. Robert Southey's *The Triumph of Woman,* dedicated to Wollstonecraft, was published in Philadelphia by John Ormrod. The first American edition of his *Poems* came out the following year in Boston, printed by Manning & Loring for Joseph Nancrede, with *The Triumph of Woman* as the first poem in the collection.

With the appearance of Godwin's *Memoirs,*[25] published first in 1799, and later in 1802 and 1804, the critical tide began to turn. Charles Brockden Brown's character Alcuin had become converted to Wollstonecraft's doctrines through the good offices of Mrs.

Carter. But in Brown's journal, *The Monthly Magazine and American Review,*[26] an overwhelmed reviewer, "L.M.," indulges in his "Reflections on the Character of MARY WOLLSTONECRAFT GODWIN" for nearly six stunned pages. It is a long lament over the reviewer's loss of illusion about Wollstonecraft.

> She appeared to me like one whom religion and philosophy had raised above the common elements of life . . . . Her views seemed not to be bounded by this world. The passions which animated her seemed all exalted into a pure ethereal fire . . . . In her *travels* . . . I saw her . . . the child of nature and the sport of feeling; yet like a lovely infant smiling through its tears, changing alternately from anguish to delight; for in the midst of gloom her exquisite genius darted ever and anew, like sunshine on her mind, through the crevices of the clouds which hung upon it.

However, the reviewer now realizes that Wollstonecraft was even then beginning to lose her faith: "she had, by this time, discarded all faith in christianity, and belief in the immediate superintendance [sic] of providence . . . ." Worse, "she suffered [her] mind to be occupied by private interests, and engrossed by an overweening solicitude about selfish enjoyments . . . ." In short, "In the memoirs of her life, and her Wrongs of Woman, I felt shocked, and even disgusted, at the licence she seems to allow to the unrestrained indulgence of the feelings . . . ." The author alludes to the liaison with Imlay, not by name, but as the "monster of insensibility, who deceived and abandoned her." "Could she not have sufficient reliance on the object of her choice, at once to give up her independence, and tie herself to him by indissoluble bonds?" What had hurtled her to her brink of ruin, "L.M." decides, was her "wild and visionary scheme of uniting, in her own experience, the blissful confidence, and tranquil joys of connubial life, with those inestimable privileges, and that perfect independence alone compatible with nothing but a single state."

The author rises to rhetorical heights:

> I stand aghast at the dismal spectacle!—my soul shudders at the terrific ruin!—a creature so noble!—a genius so towering! . . . Oh! Mary, thou who couldst speak with such sublime

> emotion of the God who formed thee, couldst thou think thou hadst a right to destroy his workmanship? . . . What mist obscured thy judgment?—What demon chained thy prudence, and palsied thy activity?—Where slept thy reason, whither wandered thy philosophy at this momentous crisis?

Abandoning the apostrophic mode, the author reflects, "Personal and mental independence was her darling object: she could not submit to have even her thoughts shackled by prejudices— . . ." But "schemes of independence have produced dangerous experiments. . . ."

Some good may come from her sufferings, the author concludes. We may anticipate a greater equality in "the condition and privileges of the sexes," not by returning to a "savage s[t]ate of lawless liberty" but by letting the "clear stream of reason and rapid torrents of eloquence . . . gush with their most impetuous force upon the world."

Before lapsing into complete silence on the subject of Wollstonecraft, Brown's *Monthly Magazine and American Review* for September 1800 introduced her name in a playful round of sparring involving a "malicious" married man, a young unmarried man, and two young women named Maria and Lucy.[27] The column, called the "Speculatist," reports on how the writer has passed the previous evening in that company. The main topic of conversation was the "celebrated authoress, who has, at least, shown some ingenuity in vindicating her sexes' dignity."

> "Lucy," says our married man, "did you ever read Miss Woolstonecraft's *Rights of Women?*" Being answered in the affirmative, he next inquired what was her opinion.

The question has made Lucy nervous, and the "Speculatist" tells us that her "powers were by no means adequate to an accurate decision on a question of some importance." The young man very readily prompts her:

> "Your critical taste, madam, may doubtless perceive imperfections and inelegancies in the style—you may censure her abruptness and want of method, but surely you must be

> charmed with the intrepid spirit of our authoress in stepping forth the champion of her sexes' rights—in combating a thousand prejudices long held sacred—in opposing reason to the force and number of her antagonists, and pointing the way to the luminous regions of truth and science."

Lucy, clearly not up to matching such a flow of eloquence, is left to acquiesce, "Yes, I am very much charmed with it." This is the wrong answer, however, for the married man hastens to point out that Miss Wollstonecraft "has not treated her subject with so much delicacy as is requisite; that is, she talks about things which you ladies are not accustomed to mention, and calls them by their names without ceremony. What say you, Maria, to our female philosopher?" Maria is agonized lest she reveal her indelicacy of mind to the scrutiny of these critics, even though "she thinks that the volume contains a display of genius which adds lustre to the female character; [and] her whole soul assents to the justness and force of Miss Woolstonecraft's eloquence." So she tergiversates, protesting that

> she had never read, but merely glanced it over. "Yet," she said, "she had seen enough to deter her from reading more; that Miss Woolstonecraft's mode of treating her subject was incomprehensible to her; but that she should never qualify herself to judge correctly of so coarse a performance."

Whether American parlors at the turn of the century were really buzzing with conversations like this, we can only conjecture. A popular novel by Mrs. Sarah Wood, called *Dorval: or the Speculator,* records a hotter denunciation of Wollstonecraft, in mixed company, by a gentleman who does not even stop to ask for other opinions. In a conversation about an absent young woman of haughty demeanor, this Mr. Stewart is made to exclaim:

> "And here . . . is a subject at once for pity and aversion, a disciple of Mrs. Wolstonecraft, a masculine woman, a pupil and follower of that British female, who, in her rights of women, has endeavored to shake the foundation of female happiness; who wishes to rob them of their honor, probity,

> and integrity; who would teach them to trample upon duty and virtue, and dismiss those soft and feminine graces, which were given them as ornaments by their creater; who laughs at the institution of marriage, and would deprive the mother, as she has the wife, of her best and sweetest employment. The duties of the nursery must, according to her creed, devolve upon some creature of an inferior capacity; and the parent devote herself to the reform of the nation. The misery in which this system, if pursued, must involve her sex, fills my mind with the highest indignation. I know you will forgive me; but really I consider Mrs. Wolstonecraft's Rights of Women as injurious to female happiness as Tom Paine's Age of Reason is to the cause of religion." [28]

This tirade would seem to call for comment, but abruptly a gentleman from New Haven appears on the scene, leaving the others free of the necessity of formulating an immediate reply to Mr. Stewart.

If an occasional novelistic harangue such as Mr. Stewart's might fall flat, the subject of women's so-called rights could afford the journalist limitless opportunities for merriment. *The Columbian Phenix and Boston Review* for February 1800 printed a piece under the heading of the "Wanderer." [29] May not, queries the author, the state of female manners be divided into the ages of Gold, Silver, Iron and Brass? The author proceeds to amplify, although he changes the order of the ages. Granted, years ago in the Iron Age of Duty, "despotic man lorded it over the suffering sex." Women were kept in childlike ignorance: "A lady knew of an admirable receipt to make Marmalade, but perhaps could not spell the words of which it was composed." During the Silver Age of Pleasure, things improved. Weary of being dolls or slaves, women might take up the theater, walking, or meeting lovers. Today, however, the world was well into the Brazen Age, or the Age of Rights.

> . . . now, on a sudden, a formidable fair has started up, and professed to teach her sex their *Rights.* The Rights of Man had already been tried with considerable success among the refuse of male society, and she who professed to teach the Rights of Woman, was sure of finding an audience equally numerous

> and select among her own sex. The hint ran like wildfire through the nation; complimentary verses and mellifluous sonnets dropped from the pens of the minor poets, girls quitted their samplers, housemaids threw aside the untwirled mop, and nothing resounded from shore to shore but Mary and the Rights of Woman.
>
> This third sect, I am sorry to observe, daily increases in the number of its partizans; the higher ranks teem with these independent amazons . . . .

The upshot is that the author hopes the situation has grown as evil as it can and that the world may look forward soon to a Golden Age of Virtue.

At the turn of the nineteenth century, and thereafter, works began to appear in America that perpetuated a legend of Wollstonecraft. Some of these were British books of a year or two before, which enjoyed a fresh incarnation in New York or Boston and revived some of the talk about the Godwins. Two of these, for example, were George Walker's *The Vagabond: Or Practical Infidelity* (London, 1799) and Richard Polwhele's *The Unsex'd Females* (London, 1798). Both were published in America in 1800.

The Vagabond made its appearance in Boston. Walker's concern was to satirize the "new philosophy"—in grim anticipation of the day when ploughmen might read the *Rights of Man,* and books of law and religion would be destroyed. Wollstonecraft's ideas are freely paraphrased and attributed to the Mary of the story, who first becomes the narrator's mistress, then leaves him for another man. Of the story's Mary, it is said that "she was disgusted with her slavery, and wanted only an opportunity to exert the inborn freedom of her sex." She complains that not being represented in the senate, the bar, and the army is "an outrage against the Rights of Women." "What a glorious thing it would be if the whole female sex would emancipate themselves from those tyrants the men." There is a good deal more allusion of this sort, and in fact Mary Wollstonecraft is given credit in several footnotes. The result of all this is that Mary's husband ends in Bedlam hospital and her children are sent to the workhouse. The Philadelphia *Port-Folio*'s "Literary Intelligence" of 25 April 1801 welcomed the American edition, since its "object is to expose the moral deformity of modern philosophers." The review mentions "the shallow and presumptuous Godwin," but, interestingly, not Wollstonecraft, despite her conspicuous role in the novel.

Also in 1800 William Cobbett, at that date a conservative publisher in New York, reprinted *The Unsex'd Females.* This was a lengthy satire by a British clergyman of the established church, "a classical scholar and an English gentleman of loyalty and honor," the Reverend Richard Polwhele. The poem assailed women writers who had apparently been incited to activity by Mary Wollstonecraft. These "literary ladies, in Great Britain," states the Preface to the American Edition, "had thrown aside that modesty, which is the best characteristic and the most brilliant ornament of their sex, and . . . with unblushing front, had adopted the sentiments and the manners of the impious amazons of republican France . . . ." The Preface exhorts American readers to heed Polwhele's "fearful example in Mary Wollstonecraft, from the contemplation of whose disgraceful life and whose melancholy end he [Polwhele] leads them to the chearing society of another group of Females, who are sufficiently characterized by placing at their head the incomparable Miss Hannah More." Fathers and mothers are warned against "the female productions, which they introduce into their families; for the approaches of vice are never so dangerous as when it is introduced by the pen of a sprightly and profligate woman."

Some of Wollstonecraft's followers are identified in the poem itself: "veteran Barbauld," Charlotte Smith, Helen Williams, "flippant Hays," and Angelica Kauffman depicting Priapus. All together these make up an "amazonian band—the female Quixotes of the new philosophy." The poem urges the reader:

> Survey with me what ne'er our fathers saw,
> A female band despising NATURE's law,
> As proud defiance flashes from their arms
> And vengeance smothers all their softer charms.
>
> . . .
>
> See Wolstonecraft, whom no decorum checks,
> Arise, the intrepid champion of her sex;
> O'er humbled man assert the sovereign claim
> And slight the timid blush of virgin fame.

A further sample of Polwhele's verse may be had in his purple response to Wollstonecraft's recommendation that the study of botany be pursued by the young of both sexes. Polwhele considers how these young women botanists pluck, pant, point, dissect, and gaze. They,

> With bliss botanic as their bosoms heave,
> Still pluck forbidden fruit, with mother Eve,
> For puberty in sighing florets pant,
> Or point the prostitution of a plant;
> Dissect its organ of unhallow'd lust,
> And fondly gaze the titillating dust.
> (pp. 10-11)

The front page review of Polwhele's work that appeared in the 21 June 1800 issue of the Boston *Columbian Centinel and Massachusetts Federalist* [30] occasioned a spirited correspondence over Wollstonecraft. Benjamin Russell, who had reprinted the Jenny Sarcasm piece nine years before, was still the editor. The review (extracted from yet another paper) began by praising Polwhele's satire against

> the moral deformity of those arrogant and audacious, literary, political, philosophical courtezans, who emulous of the fame of MRS. WOOLSTONECRAFT, have striven to divest the sex of their ancient character; to banish shamefacedness, and softness, and delicacy, the retired virtues, and the domestic attainment; and to invite women to become amazons and states*men,* and directors, and harlots, upon philosophical principles.

Enumerating the so-called Wollstonecraft followers, the reviewer terms the whole troupe "those women, who had chosen of late to become naked prize-fighters in the public arena." Following are several dozen lines of Polwhele, and the conclusion that his work will serve as a staunch defense against the new "subtle philosophy."

On the following Saturday,[31] a satiric letter signed OPHELIA

GYMNIC address itself in a style reminiscent of Jenny Sarcasm to "The Unsex'd Females" of Boston. Pretending to attack Polwhele and defend Wollstonecraft, the letter affectedly proceeds:

> I must confess, my dears, that on the first perusal of the review of this Poem, I felt exceedingly alarmed, agitated and confused—and was almost *overtaken by a blush*—but a moment's reflection recovered my reason . . . .

The author claims she will refuse to pardon Polwhele's "attempt to vilify the divine *Wolstonecraft*—that *bright example of Virtue* which we all strove to imitate—that paragon of "Unsex'd Females," that noble champion of the *"Rights of Women,"* that martyr to the baseness of man." The article concludes:

> Let us be firm, steady, and resolute my dears in the pursuits of our object—Let us conduct ourselves with proper dignity and spirit upon this and every future occasion—and teach the tyrant man that *we have rights*—and are determined to support them—that we are their equals *and will be treated as such.* Let us show the world that nothing can resist *the progress of reason*—that we are determined "to banish shamefacedness—and softness, and delicacy, the retired virtues, and the domestic attainment," as our angelic *Mary* did before us, and by her recommendation and invitation we intend "to become amazons, and states*men,* and directors, and patriots upon philosophical principles"—and that we will educate our daughters in such principles—as the only *reasonable and sure path* which will lead them to happiness.

A sober rejoinder to the *Centinel* appears on 9 July 1800. The editor, Benjamin Russell, thinks the letter must be from the pen of a lady, for it protests the calumnies against Wollstonecraft. He prints the piece with the warning to his readers against the "loose principles, delusive visions and false philosophy of the GODWINS and WOOLSTONECRAFTS of the present day." With it, he closes the exchange. The letter writer freely discusses the relationships with Imlay and Godwin, asserting:

> ... though I am far from justifying some parts of her [Wollstonecraft's] conduct, yet I was surprised to find principles ascribed to her, which she expressly condemns. It is easy to call names, and bestow epithets; but the difficulty is in proving them to be true ... I shall not contend for the wisdom of her conduct; let it however be remembered that she was one of those enthusiasts, who supposed a better order of things about to take place; when men would observe an engagement, which honour and honesty forbid them to violate .... I would remind those, who have so meanly indulged themselves in invectives against her, of the example of the great author of our religion, who commanded him without fault, to cast the first stone; and as the principal crime laid to her charge is one, which men allow themselves to commit with impunity, they should according to this divine rule abstain from such severe censures.

As an apologist for Wollstonecraft, the writer interprets *A Vindication of the Rights of Woman* for the *Centinel*'s readers. Far from claiming sovereignty over men, Wollstonecraft favors "giving women an education that would enable them to discharge the duties of life with more propriety; and free them from the perpetual charges of weakness brought against them by the men ...." Wollstonecraft "endeavours to impress on the mind of females the propriety of possessing virtues, rather than their semblance, and cautions them against practising pitiful worldly shifts, and slight of hand tricks, to gain the applause of tasteless fools ...." People who enjoy feminine weakness and artifice, however, need not worry that the Wollstonecraft system will take hold, for, the article concludes, "the common herd of females are as inveterate against her" as are her male detractors.

Such were among the public responses that the literary imports of Walker and Polwhele provoked. Meanwhile, two native men of letters, John Blair Linn and Benjamin Silliman, were making their own use of the Wollstonecraft legend. Linn, a youthful and consumptive writer of prodigious output, composed a massy poem called *The Powers of Genius.*[32] The author was twenty-two. The work was heralded before its appearance in 1801 and extensively reviewed for several years afterward. Amidst a pantheon of geniuses such as Shakespeare, Milton, Burns, Ossian, Ariosto, Rousseau, and, in the female department (since "enchanting woman bears an equal claim" to genius), Zenobia, Sappho, Mary Queen of Scots, Montague, and Barbauld, he allots Wollstonecraft her place:

> In Woolstonecraft's strong lines behold confest,
> The fatal errors of the female breast.

Located not far away in this scheme is Mrs. Hannah More, whose destiny it seems was ever to provide a foil for the fallen star of Mary Wollstonecraft. (When, for example, Mrs. More's complete works were published in 1801, the *Port-Folio* reviewer for 23 May 1801 pointed out that this edition would be happily received by all "who are not in the gall of philosophic bitterness, nor in the bonds of Gallic iniquity.")

Another youthful work, this one from the pen of Yale tutor and future president, the twenty-two year old Benjamin Silliman, was vituperative on the subject of Mary Wollstonecraft. *The Letters of Shahcoolen* purported to be a correspondence from a Hindu philosopher describing American manners and mores to a friend in Delhi. The *Letters* were first published on 5 October 1801 in the New York *Commercial Advertiser* (originally Noah Webster's *American Minerva). The Columbian Centinel* later that year printed the four letters that contained the most material on Wollstonecraft.[33] In 1801 the collection came out in book form in Boston.[34]

Shahcoolen loses no time in introducing the female philosopher who threatens to play upon the credulity of American women everywhere and, through her *Vindication of the Rights of Woman,* to "renovate" their sex. Among the statements contained in "Letter Second" were the following:

> She discards all that sexual tenderness, delicacy and modesty, which constitute the female loveliness; boldly pronounces them equal to the rougher sex in everything but bodily strength, and even imputes their deficiency, in this particular, principally to a falsely refined education. She asserts that a

> husband is a *paltry* bauble, compared with *the attainments of reason.*
>
> Not satisfied with masculine ideas, and masculine habits, Mary Wolstonecraft wished, as the consummation of female independence, to introduce the sex into the Camp, the Rostrum and the Cabinet.
>
> As a necessary preparative for the support of bodily fatigue, the female philosopher recommends an early initiation of females into the athletic sports, and gymnastic exercises of boys and young men.
>
> She would have them run, leap, box, wrestle, fence and fight, that the united exertion of bodily and mental energy may produce, by mysterious cooperation, that amazing force of character, of which she supposes her sex to be capable.[35]

The "Letter Third" informs the reader that Wollstonecraft "writes with the most disgusting coarseness, upon subjects, which are studiously excluded from modest societies, and reserved by common consent, for the investigation of men of science." Wollstonecraft, furthermore, attends "anatomical, chirurgical and obstetrick lectures, conversations and experiments, where the various parts of the human body have been dissected, and their uses descanted upon." She calmly discusses polygamy and "is extremely anxious to establish the idea, that seduced and dishonored females are still entitled to the regard of society."

Moreover, Miss Wollstonecraft is seriously altering the conduct and dress of American women, according to the Fourth Letter. Some of these "vainly emulate a firm step and a manly port." Others affect male dress and swear abominably. One fair girl was heard to "*curse* her fate at the card table, *damn* the soul of her partner for his inattention to the game, *swear* that this was the most unlucky incident of her life . . . ." American girls are taking up sport: one has lately learned to vault into the saddle, and in Salem there is a lady who initiates young virgins into the exercise of ice skating–a "most slippery diversion." Some young women are exposing their persons in such a way as to "excite passion, but to extinguish respect." Shahcoolen had assumed that these must be very depraved, and even mistook them for "courtezans."

> Often, when reclining on a sofa, by the side of *a fair American,* I have thought, that her white bosom, scarcely veiled at all from my sight, and her finely proportioned limbs, which the extreme thinness and narrowness of her apparel rendered quite evident to the eye, would have excited impure emotions in any heart, less subject to reason than that of a *Hindu Philosopher.*

A reviewer in *The Monthly Anthology and Boston Review* [36] found Silliman's production puerile, marked by "a looseness and inaccuracy of expression, inexcusable even in private epistles." Without positively defending Wollstonecraft, he scorns Silliman's remarks on her. Chiefly he appears to be angered at the imputation against the New England woman. "The publications of Miss Wollstonecraft have had little effect, comparatively, with the author's statement. In some of the *warmer* southern states she may have found votaries to whom her notions were congenial, but in the *temperate regions of the north* passion has not yet overturned the empire of reason. It is a gross and indecorous charge . . . ." [37] Another way of dealing with the Wollstonecraft threat was to ignore her entirely. A friendlier review of *The Letters of Shahcoolen* in the *American Review and Literary Journal* suggests that "some of [the author's] pictures of American manners are painted in rather false and exaggerated colours." [38] Despite the heavy preponderance of attention given to Wollstonecraft in Silliman's *Letters,* the reviewer blandly overlooks her and discourses on other matters.

Several newspapers in this period seemed to think that copy about Wollstonecraft provided good front-page reading. One of those is *The Columbian Centinel,* whose editor Benjamin Russell had found Wollstonecraft newsworthy ever since he had reprinted the letter of Jenny Sarcasm; another was *The Mercury and New England Palladium.* [39] We may examine first the *Centinel* for 1801. Material from two of the *Centinel*'s issues, including scurrilous verses on Godwin and Mary, has been quoted by Patricia Jewell McAlexander.[40] On 24 January 1801, Mr. Russell printed a letter from A

FRIEND TO THE SEX who, while deploring Wollstonecraft's revolutionary eccentricities, cannot however conceal some admiration:

> It must be allowed, that in her principal work the *"Rights of Women"* many just principles are advocated, many good improvements in female education are suggested, many pertinent observations may be found, and many shrewd remarks on the writings of others on the same subject, catch the attention, and interest the feelings. Hence it is doubly dangerous.

The author of the letter warns against the enticing ideas of female freedom that emerge from *Maria* (Philadelphia, 1799), the novel which also "forcibly represents the hardships of matrimonial bonds." The letter then makes two interesting points, not quite consistent with each other: one, that there is no reason for American women to be discontent since "in no country, on the surface of the globe, are women in a more happy condition than in these United States"; the other, that Wollstonecraft's doctrines may really wield a dangerous influence here. Revolutionary mania is so rampant, complains the writer, that women are now feeling themselves to be "wronged and oppressed." "The minds of some women, have at length, caught the infection, and they seem ardently to wish for a revolution in their present situation."

The issue of 14 February 1801 contains further evidence of discontent. A scandalized FRIEND TO HER SEX reports to the columnist called the "Latitudinarian" that "There is a society of Young Ladies residing not more than *twenty miles* from *Boston,* who throwing aside all *that delicacy* which is *so natural and essential* to the female character, have presumed to come forth in defiance of order and authority and boldly assume what *they stile* the *'rights of women'*. . . . They dress out vice in the most alluring colours." They use *"satanic arts"* to contaminate others. "They think that every girl who is not furnished with ideas from *Mary Wolstonecraft* is wanting in understanding." In fact, being so furnished is a requirement for joining their society, which goes by the appellation of the "Moschetto (i.e., mosquito) Fleet." Could not the "Latitudinarian" recommend to the group readings instead from Miss Hannah

More? That columnist's terse editorial afterword is simply to express hope that the *"abberators"* will get back on the right path. These remarks elicited a furious response from a gentleman correspondent, who protested the "bold, daring, and outrageous attack which was made on the characters of certain young ladies, descended from among the most respectable families of one of the most respectable towns of the commonwealth." Several weeks' worth of irate name-calling passed between the "Latitudinarian" and this correspondent before the whole thing trailed off into silence.

The "Latitudinarian" for Wednesday 25 February 1801 cautions readers against giving credence to words of praise mouthed by just anyone. *"The pupil of Mary Wolstonecraft,* will tell you with the *smile of fascination* that her dear friend and companion possesses all the *finer feelings of the heart.*" But, continues the columnist, so will a courtesan highly rate her *"female inmate."* Immediately following the "Latitudinarian" is a letter from a woman correspondent who is worried about a friend of hers, one Camilla. This Camilla has been reading Rousseau, Godwin, and Wollstonecraft, and now goes about asserting her rights and vindicating her wrongs. In fact, Camilla accuses her, the writer, of being weak, nerveless, and mean-spirited. Considering the life Wollstonecraft led, the writer now fears the worst may be in store for the misled Camilla. The letter includes a further lament over the formation of the notorious "muschetto fleets."

Was there real cause for alarm? Was Wollstonecraft being taken seriously by young ladies forming reading societies and asserting themselves? Or are the columns of the *Centinel* shot through with Mr. Russell's fantasies? [41] Another newspaper, *The Mercury and New England Palladium* anchors its position firmly with a no-nonsense approach in the 4 September 1801 issue. The columnist called the "Restorator" begins:

> Since the writings of MARY WOLSTONECRAFT, many errors have been propagated and embraced respecting the *rights of woman.* Infinite pains have been taken to convince the ladies, that they are formed by nature equal to our sex, and that their general inferiority of talents can reasonably be attributed solely to their inferiority of education.

> What can be the object of the superficial philosophists, who disseminate such absurdities . . .[?] The prostitution of MARY herself, of HELEN MARIA WILLIAMS, and other disciples of the new school, affords the best commentary on the principles and writings of those learned ladies.

The rest is a sermon on woman's lesser ability and place. On 8 September a correspondent, ANTI-MOHAMMED, defends learning among women, citing "the Mores and the Barbaulds," though not the Wollstonecrafts. The "Restorator" on 15 September 1801 continues in his earlier vein, denouncing "the monstrous doctrine of the *Rights of Woman,*" doctrine which would have been spurned by the great women of antiquity.[42] Pointedly, the "Restorator" notes that "These *Rights of Woman,* if practised agreeably to the theory, would become the *wrongs of man* . . . ."

These stiff threats give way to something new in the paper. A breezy series by the columnist "Morpheus" opens on 24 November 1801.[43] In it the comical fellow Morpheus pays a visit to the Land of Nod. This turns out to be the next world. When he discovers Mary Wollstonecraft Godwin she is holding forth from the philosophical chair:

> Women (began the Female Philosopher) are entitled to all the rights, and are capable of all the energies, of men. I do not mean merely mental energies . . . . I intend bodily energies. They can naturally run as fast, leap as high, and as far, and wrestle, scuffle and box, with as much success.
>
> That is a mistake (said an old man just before her.)
>
> It is no mistake (said the Female Philosopher.) . . .
>
> My boys were always stronger than my girls (rejoined the old man) and frequently beat them.
>
> They would not have beat *me* (said MARY) I could have vanquished them all in wrestling, leaping—
>
> You would have shown your stockings, (said a wag on the right hand of the chair.)
>
> I should not have regarded it, if I had, (said MARY.)
>
> Why then (said the senior again) are women always feebler than men?
>
> Because (said MARY) they are educated to be feeble; and

> by indulgence merely, and false philosophy, are made poor, puny, baby-faced dolls; instead of the *manly women,* they ought to be.
>
> *Manly women!* (cried the wag) Wheu! a manly woman is a hoydon, a non descript.
>
> Am I a hoydon? (interrupted MARY, with spirit.)
>
> You used to be a strumpet, unless your husband, who wrote an account of your life, is a liar.
>
> You are a boor and a brute (tartly retorted MARY, reddening.)
>
> Not so much of a brute as your ladyship—thinks, perhaps.
>
> Put your words nearer together, Impudence.

The wag continues to heckle and lecture the philosopher:

> When women leave their character, and claim the character, and rights, of men, they relinquish their own rights, and are to be regarded, and treated, as men.

The old man admonishes the wag:

> You ought to remember that she is a woman.
>
> *She* ought to remember it (said the young man).
>
> [*To be continued*]

In the next installment, a matron in the crowd brings up Mr. Imlay and Mr. Godwin, severely reminding the philosopher that chastity is woman's first virtue:

> You never were loved nor esteemed by any body, because you never deserved to be loved or esteemed. . . . Hence you were driven to find pleasure in the empty hope of fame. You wrote, therefore, and became extensively known, not by the worth, or good sense, of your writings, but by their oddity and impiety, merely.

The philosopher manages to change the subject by initiating a gymnastic session among the girls present:

> Who opens the ring with wrestling?
>
> I, (said a rosy looking girl of sixteen, whose name I found was NELLY.)
>
> *And* I, (said another, rather slender and pale faced) if mamma will let me.
>
> You may try, if you have a mind to, JANE, (said her mother.)
>
> By this time the two combattants had begun their strife, and as the young men, who wrestle, say, taken hold. The business of tripping and twitching was, I believe, quite new to them; for they appeared rather awkward. Instead of wrestling they pulled, and twisted, and hauled, and shoved, until, finally, the slender girl was fairly laid in the dirt. As she fell she displayed her feet a little, but her stockings were clean. La! NELLY, said she, you hurt me. You need not throw me down so hard. She then got up, and brushed off the dirt, as well as she could. It will make you hardy (said her mother.) 'Twill make a *manly woman* of you.
>
> Yes, (said the merry fellow,) and it may make her, one day, a sentimental lover.

Nelly, now the winner of the first round, receives a challenge from a second sturdy girl named Nancy. They wrestle, amid shouts from the onlookers:

> As she began to pull her antagonist violently, she cried out, There, now, you have torn my new muslin shawl.
>
> Never mind the shawl, NELLY, (said the wag,) down with her.
>
> NELLY, strengthened in the bodily energies by her resentment, gave her antagonist a sudden twitch, and flung her fairly into a puddle. Miss rose with her face, and hands, and clothes, all besmeared with mud. La! NANCY (said an elderly woman, at my right hand,) what a fright you are! This all comes of your whim to wrestle. I wish Mrs. Philosopher had staid in her own country and wrestled with her pigs. She'll make pigs of all our girls.

Nelly takes on a third girl:

> The combattants scuffled for some time with great vigour; when NELLY, happening to take hold of the skirt of her companion's gown, a thin sheer muslin, fairly tore off the skirt at a single pull. Her adversary at the same time seizing her cap, stripped it off, and a sandy coloured wig, which was under it and left poor NELLY without any covering to her head but her own thin hair. NELLY's resentment kindled. She seized her fellow by the cheek, and with her nails drew several streams of blood from it. Her antagonist was a girl of spirit; and, after tearing the muslin from her neck, gave her a violent blow on the side of the head, and laid NELLY sprawling.

The mothers get involved, friends take sides, and join in a free-for-all:

> Homer . . . would have seen, not one, but a score of Amazon queens. Caps, bonnets, sandy coloured wigs, cravats, puddings, feathers, &c. all flew in the air, and covered the field of battle.

The high point of this knock-down-drag-out is the female philosopher's being pushed into a puddle.

The concluding episode shows Mary expostulating with the crowd, who eventually succeed in reducing her to red-faced silence. Throughout the three installments, Morpheus regales the reader with accounts of how the philosopher "coloured with vexation," "shrieked with indignation," "bit her lips," and wrathfully said "Hoity, toity!" Wollstonecraft had at last been immortalized in the pop world of the Federal comic strip.

One is tempted to speculate that Wollstonecraft's worst critics were those writing for the public readership of newspapers and magazines. Feeling themselves to be responsible to their readers as custodians of public morality, editors were free to reinforce their own ideas by printing chiefly those readers' replies that most agreed with their position. The press, moreover, gave space to writers who found that fashionable satires upon Wollstonecraft were highly saleable. A surprising exception to this general position is the reprinting of an English review, unearthed from the *London*

Monthly Visitor of 1787, of *Thoughts on the Education of Daughters,* which the *Boston Weekly Magazine* ran in 1802. For the most part, however, the press showed its hostility, and only occasionally does a favorable reader's opinion make its way into print.

It is interesting to look at private diaries and letters to find defenses of Wollstonecraft, not, however, unmixed with caution. Elizabeth Sandwith Drinker, despite her many domestic responsibilities, managed to read much and note down her impressions. In April 1796 when she was sixty-two, she wrote: "I have read a large octavo volume entitled *The Rights of Women* by Mary Wollstonecraft. In many of her sentiments she, as some of our friends say, 'speaks my mind.' In some others, I do not altogether coincide with her. I am not for quite so much independence."[44] Martha Laurens Ramsay, a woman born in South Carolina in the same year as Mary Wollstonecraft, was said to have read her work. Perhaps she imbibed some of the new ideas, since she nursed all eleven children, and devoted herself to the study of Greek and Latin, together with French and English grammar, so as to be able to preside over their education. She studied her husband's medical books to become informed on the diseases of women and children. She read botany and "most of the modern works of genius, taste, and imagination," including Locke, Rousseau, Young's *Night Thoughts* (which she had nearly by heart), and Watts's *Logic,* his *Improvement of the Mind,* and *Philosophical Essays.* Her own writing was, however, deeply pious and in this she differed from Wollstonecraft. As her husband wrote after her death, "Such were the principles and conduct of a wife who had read Mary Wollstonecraft's Rights of Women but studied her Bible with care and attention." Her husband declares that even though she had read "the plausible reasonings of modern theorists, who contend for the equality of the sexes . . . she yielded all pretensions on this score" in accordance with the scriptural exhortations to wives to submit to husbands.[45] Despite this claim, one cannot know what Martha Ramsay thought of Wollstonecraft. She was obviously an unusual and energetic woman whose life illustrated many of the precepts of her contemporary.

An explicit response to Wollstonecraft, one full of conflicts, may be descried in the letters of a young New England woman, Eliza Southgate. We have her exchange of letters at the beginning of the nineteenth century with her cousin Moses Porter. The words of Wollstonecraft have impressed her, and yet, there is an uncomfortable feeling that she ought not espouse the daring philosophy of so fallen a woman. Eliza Southgate,[46] now seventeen, recounts first her development as a younger girl at school, where, incidentally, she was taught by Susanna Rowson, "one of the blessings of creation": "I found the mind of a female, if such a thing existed, was thought not worth cultivating, I disliked the trouble of thinking for myself and therefore adopted the sentiments of others." She then had cared little for the mind and only for adornment and accomplishments. She found that when she left school she had a "few patchwork opinions,—they are now almost worn threadbare, and as I am about quilting a few more, I beg you will send me any spare ideas you may chance to have . . . ."[47] Presumably her cousin took up the subject, for shortly thereafter Eliza pursues her thinking along the same lines. Forlornly, she points out that women's mental qualities, endowed by nature, "are left to moulder in ruin. In this dormant state they become enervated and impaired, and at last die for *want of exercise.*"

"Why, my dear Cousin, were we furnished with such powers, unless the improvement of them would conduce to the happiness of society?" But the letter reveals her divided mind. She fears she may be accused of insubordination, or of attempting to infringe upon male prerogatives. Just after avowing passionately in words of Wollstonecraft that she could not "live a slave to the despotic will of another," she retracts them:

> I am aware of the censure that will ever await the female that attempts the vindication of her sex, yet I dare to brave that censure that I know to be undeserved. It does not follow (O what a pen!) that every female who vindicates the capacity of the sex is a disciple of Mary Wolstoncraft. Though I allow her to have said many things which I cannot but approve, yet the very foundation on which she builds her work will be apt to prejudice us so against her that we will not allow her the merit she really deserves,—yet, prejudice set aside, I confess I admire many of her sentiments, notwithstanding I believe should any one adopt her principles, they would conduct in

> the same manner, and upon the whole her life is the best comment on her writings. Her style is nervous and commanding, her sentiments appear to carry conviction along with them, but they will not bear analyzing.[48]

Responses such as these, recorded for private exchange rather than for publication, may be indicative of a more thoughtful reception of Wollstonecraft among American readers. The public indignation is readily discoverable. One has to gather inferences about reading societies from the allegations of outraged journalists and correspondents against young women growing restless about their rights. One has to imagine the Camillas and the "mosquito fleets" who read and praised Wollstonecraft within earshot of Boston. Mary Wollstonecraft's work did not receive a truly critical response in Federalist America. The intellectual content of her work was not seriously explored. Early publishers, by careful editing, had succeeded in tricking her forth as a sentimental and sententious author. When the truth was known, she caused rashes and reactions: words like "pestilence," "infection," "contamination," and "slow poison" appear in journalists' essays about her. Often her worst detractors forced themselves to admit the validity of some of her positions. For this reason she was held to be all the more dangerous. Some critics express fear lest the plausible philosopher corrupt the impressionable young. For artists of wit and genteel scurrility, she afforded bountiful subject matter. Another way of dealing with Wollstonecraft was to denounce her as a whore, a courtesan, a prostitute, and to attempt to provoke disgust for her "lechery." Once in a while a former admirer will engage in emotional elegiacs over her fall. Or, she simply became unmentionable; writers ignored her, especially where to omit her name was glaring. One professional writer, Judith Sargent Murray, gave unreserved support. Such was the sum of opinion concerning Wollstonecraft in the first dozen years of her American fame.

Some twenty years and more after Wollstonecraft's death the attitudes about her had changed little. Thomas G. Fessenden, in 1818, found that Wollstonecraft was still a topic for didactic humor in his *Ladies' Monitor.*[49] And Hannah Mather Crocker in the same year published a tempered approbation in her *Observations on the Real Rights of Women, With Their Appropriate Duties Agreeable to Scripture, Reason and Common Sense:*

> Mary Wolstonecraft was a woman of great energy and a very independent mind; her Rights of Women are replete with fine sentiments, though we do not coincide with her opinion respecting the total independence of the female sex. We must be allowed to say, her theory is unfit for practice, though some of her sentiments and distinctions would do honour to the pen, even of a man.[50]

Mrs. Crocker's evaluation recalls the cautious praise of some of Wollstonecraft's first reviewers. For a more complete, more personal sympathy, Wollstonecraft would have to wait until the mid-century, with the rise of the new feminists. Then Margaret Fuller could declare that Mary Wollstonecraft "was a woman whose existence better proved the need of some new interpretation of Woman's Rights than anything she wrote." [51] In the earlier period we have surveyed here, perhaps what is most remarkable is not the objurgation of her but the notion that she was superfluous, that America had no need of Wollstonecraft's doctrines, for here were no inequalities that abased women, here women's privileges were far greater than they could appreciate.

NOTES

1. The following works have been particularly useful in locating the material for this paper: Frank Luther Mott, *A History of American Magazines,* I (1741-1850), (Cambridge: Harvard University Press, 1930); Marthe Severn Storr, *Mary Wollstonecraft et le mouvement féministe dans la littérature anglaise* (Paris: Presses Universitaire Française, 1932); Ralph M. Wardle, *Mary Wollstonecraft: A Critical Biography* (Lincoln: University of Nebraska Press, 1951); Sidney Ditzion, *Marriage, Morals, and Sex in America: A History of Ideas,* (1953; rpt. and expanded edition, New York: Octagon Books, 1969); Frank Luther Mott, *American Journalism: A History: 1690-1960,* 3rd ed. (New York: Macmillan, 1965); Mary S. Benson, *Women in Eighteenth-Century America: A Study of Opinion and Social Usage* (New York: Columbia University Press, 1935; rpt. Kennikat, 1966); Henri Petter, *The Early*

American Novel (Columbus: Ohio State University Press, 1971); Patricia Jewell McAlexander, "The Creation of the American Eve: The Cultural Dialogue on the Nature and Role of Women in Late Eighteenth Century America," *Early American Literature,* 9 (1975), 251-266. The Appendix, which follows these Notes, lists early American editions of Mary Wollstonecraft's works, together with editions of Godwin's *Memoirs.*

2. *The New-York Magazine: or, Literary Repository,* 2 (December 1791), 713-714.
3. *The Massachusetts Centinel and the Republican Journal* shed its regionality in 1790, becoming *The Columbian Centinel and Massachusetts Federalist.* See Frank Luther Mott, *American Journalism: A History: 1690-1960,* 3rd ed. (New York: Macmillan, 1962), p. 132.
4. *The Philadelphia Monthly, or Universal Repository of Knowledge and Entertainment,* 1 (February 1798), 82-83.
5. John Tebbel, *A History of Book Publishing in the United States,* 2 vols. (New York: R. R. Bowker, 1972), I, 116, 182, 189.
6. *The Lady's Magazine: and Repository of Entertaining Knowledge,* 1 (September 1792), 189-198.
7. *The Massachusetts Magazine or, Monthly Museum of Knowledge and Rational Entertainment,* 4 (October 1792), 598-599.
8. Judith Sargent Murray, *The Gleaner. A Miscellaneous Production In Three Volumes* (Boston, 1798), III, 188, 191, 192.
9. *The Massachusetts Magazine,* 5 (February 1793), 104-105.
10. *The Massachusetts Magazine,* 5 (February 1793), 111-112.
11. Matthew L. Davis, ed., *Memoirs of Aaron Burr with Miscellaneous Selections from His Correspondence,* 2 vols. (1836-1837; rpt. New York: Da Capo Press, 1971), I, 361-363.
12. *The New-York Magazine; or, Literary Repository,* 4 (February 1793), 77-81.
13. *The New-York Magazine,* 5 (September 1794), 569-570.
14. *The New-York Magazine,* 6 (August 1795), 483-486.
15. Wollstonecraft's book on the French Revolution was published the same year in Philadelphia. The annotations of John Adams in his copy of her book have been discussed by Elisabeth Luther Cary, "John Adams and Mary Wollstonecraft," *The Lamp: A Review and Record of Current Literature,* 26 (February 1903), 35-40; selections are given in "John Adams' Comments on Mary Wollstonecraft's French Revolution," *Bulletin of the Public Library of the City of Boston,* 4th series, 5 (1923), 4-13. Facing the preface of his copy, Adams wrote:

> This is a Lady of a masculine masterly Understanding. Her Style is nervous and clear often elegant; though sometimes too verbose. With a little Experience in Public Affairs and the Reading and Reflection which would result from it, She would have produced a History without the Defects and Blemishes

> pointed out with too much Severity perhaps and too little Gallantry in the Notes.

The dates attached to Adams' notes are 1796 and 1812.

16. Tebbel (I, 146) observes that Pope was "the most popular published poet of the century in America."
17. Thomas Taylor, *A Vindication of the Rights of Brutes* (1792), ed. L. S. Boas (Gainesville: Scholars' Facsimiles and Reprints, 1966), pp. 75-79, 80-82.
18. *The Philadelphia Minerva,* 17 October 1795.
19. *The Philadelphia Minerva,* 14 May 1796.
20. *The New-York Magazine,* 6 (December 1795), 710-711.
21. *The New-York Magazine,* NS 1 (December 1796), 648 f.; NS 2 (January 1797), 23 f.; NS 2 (February 1797), 68 f.
22. *The American Spectator, or Matrimonial Preceptor. A Collection of Essays, (with Additions and Variations) Epistles, Precepts and Examples, Relating to the Married State . . . Adapted to the State of Society in the American Republic* (Boston, 1797), pp. vi, 13-16.
23. Charles Brockden Brown, *Alcuin: A Dialogue* (New York, 1798).
24. Passages are quoted from pp. 17, 23-24, 28, 34, 41, 42, and 66.
25. When Godwin's *Memoirs of Mary Wollstonecraft Godwin* appeared in Philadelphia in 1802, the volume contained a four-page "Preface to the American Edition." In it the editor states that the work is "without exception the most impudent and profligate performance in the English language," but trusts that "our fair country women will feel, on perusing these memoirs, that virtuous indignation, which her perversion of talents and profligacy of sentiment must inspire, and that they will turn with horror from a detestable philosophy, which would degrade the sex to the lowest infamy . . . ."
26. *The Monthly Magazine and American Review,* 1 (August 1799), 330-335.
27. *The Monthly Magazine and American Review,* 3 (September 1800), 161-163.
28. Mrs. Sarah Wood, *Dorval: or The Speculator* (Portsmouth, New Hampshire: Printed at the Ledger Press, by Nutting & Whitelock for the Author, 1801), pp. 46-47.
29. *The Columbian Phenix and Boston Review, containing useful information on Literature, Religion, Morality, Politics and Philosophy; with many interesting particulars in History and Biography, forming a compendium of the Present State of Society.* Boston, 1 (February 1800), 110-113.
30. The same review is printed in *The Columbian Phenix and Boston Review* for June 1800, pp. 367-369.
31. 28 June 1800.
32. See the study of Linn by Lewis Leary, *William and Mary Quarterly,* 3rd ser., 4 (1947), 148-176.

33. *The Columbian Centinel* for 4, 7, and 21 November 1801.
34. Benjamin Silliman, *The Letters of Shahcoolen* (1802), ed. Ben Harris McClary (Gainesville: Scholars' Facsimiles and Reprints, 1962).
35. *Letters of Shahcoolen,* pp. 22, 24, 26-27.
36. *The Monthly Anthology and Boston Review,* 2 (February 1805), 85-88.
37. *The Monthly Anthology and Boston Review,* pp. 85-86.
38. *American Review and Literary Journal,* 2, no. 2 (for April, May, and June 1802), 209-212.
39. I am indebted to Janet M. Todd's *Bibliography of Mary Wollstonecraft* for references to the latter newspaper. Dr. Todd kindly permitted me to consult her *Bibliography* shortly before its publication by the Garland Press in 1976.
40. See her article, "The Creation of the American Eve: The Cultural Dialogue on the Nature and Role of Women in Late Eighteenth-Century America," *Early American Literature,* 9 (1975), 263, 266, n. 52, 53, 54.
41. Perhaps we may attribute to him the satirical Creed of PETRONIUS: "I believe in the Age of Reason, the Rights of Woman, and Godwin's Political Justice, and all books which tend to disorder and confusion . . . Amen." (26 August 1801).
42. The issues of 18 September 1801 and 9 October 1801 continue the argument against "women of masculine minds;" and against the reading of novels by such authors as Wollstonecraft. The 25 September 1801 issue carries a long letter from a lady named PRUDENTIA, generally agreeing with the "Restorator."
43. The series continues on 27 November, when Godwin is introduced, and appears on 8, 11, and 15 December 1801. Morpheus then makes a comeback on 2, 5, and 9 March 1802, with Mary Wollstonecraft.
44. Quoted from Elizabeth Drinker's diary, in Elizabeth Evans, *Weathering the Storm: Women of the American Revolution* (New York: Charles Scribner's Sons, 1975), p. 183.
45. David Ramsay, M.D., *Memoirs of the Life of Martha Laurens Ramsay, who died in Charleston, S.C. on the 10th of June, 1811, in the 52nd year of her Age. (Boston, 1812), pp. 45n., 43.*
46. Clarence Cook, ed., *A Girl's Life Eighty Years Ago: Selections from the Letters of Eliza Southgate Bowne* (New York: Charles Scribner's Sons, 1887).
47. *A Girl's Life,* letter of May 1801.
48. *A Girl's Life,* pp. 59, 61-62, letter of 1 June 1801.
49. A young woman named Narcissa attempts to formulate a Wollstonecraftian defense to her Mentor:

Our Powers and Duties you have dwelt upon,
And given us rules to regulate the ton,
But we have *rights,* of which you know a draught,
Was sketch'd by one Miss Mary Wolstonecraft,
And which, I take it, as a lady's friend,
Your worship's etching ought to comprehend.
Since you esteem our sex so good and great,
Why not hold offices in Church and State?
Some female warriors have been found as famous
As any heroes history can name us,
In private life, each day's experience teaches,
We cannot be surpass'd in making speeches,
And none can doubt but lady-legislators
Would make at least most capital debaters.

Her wily Mentor, however, wittily dissuades her from this position, beginning:

Dame Nature tells us Mary's rights are wrong,
Her female freedom is a syren-Song.

Thomas G. Fessenden, *The Ladies' Monitor, A Poem* (Bellows Falls, Vermont, 1818) pp. 58-59.

50. Reprinted in *Sex and Equality: Women in America from Colonial Times to the Twentieth Century* (New York: Arno Press, 1974), p. 41.
51. Margaret Fuller, *Woman in the Nineteenth Century* (Boston, 1855; rpt. New York: W. W. Norton, 1971), p. 75.

APPENDIX

MARY WOLLSTONECRAFT: EARLY AMERICAN EDITIONS

1791. Of the Importance of Religious Opinions. Translated from the French of Mr. Necker. Philadelphia: From the Press of Carey, Stewart & Co. MDCCXCI.

The translator's name does not appear in the volume.

1792. A Vindication of the Rights of Woman: With strictures on Moral and Political Subjects. By Mary Woolstonecraft. Philadephia:—Printed and sold by William Gibbons, N° 144, North Third Street.

1792. A Vindication of the Rights of Woman: With Strictures on Moral and Political Subjects. By Mary Wollstonecraft. Printed at Boston, by Peter Edes for Thomas and Andrews. Faust's Statue, No. 45, Newbury-Street. MDCCXCII.

1794. Vindication of the Rights of Woman, With Strictures on Political and Moral Subjects. By Mary Wollstonecraft. Philadelphia: Printed for Mathew Carey, No. 118, Market-Street. 1794.

1794. Vindication of the Rights of Woman, With Strictures on Political and Moral Subjects. By Mary Wollstonecraft. Philadelphia: Printed for M. Carey.

1795. An Historical and Moral View of the Origin and Progress of the French Revolution: and The Effect It has Produced in Europe. By Mary Wollstonecraft. Volume I. Philadelphia, Printed by Thomas Dobson, at the Stone-House, South Second-Street. MDCCXCV.

1795. Elements of Morality for the Use of Children; With an Introductory Address to Parents. Translated from the German of the Rev. C. G. Salzmann. The First American Edition. Printed at Providence (R. Island) By Carter and Wilkinson, and sold at their Book and Stationary Store, opposite the Market. MDCCXCV.

The name MARY WOLLSTONECRAFT appears on p. v, at the end of the Advertisement.

1796. Elements of Morality for the Use of Children; With an Introductory Address to Parents. Translated from the German of the Rev. C. G. Salzmann. Illustrated with Twenty Copper-Plates. In Two Volumes. Philadelphia: Printed by J. Hoff & H. Kammerer, Jun. MDCCXCVI.

The name MARY WOLLSTONECRAFT appears on p. viii, at the end of the Advertisement.

1796. Elements of Morality for the Use of Children; With an Introductory Address to Parents. Translated from the German of the Rev. C. G. Salzmann. The Third American Edition. Wilmington: Printed by Joseph Johnson Market-Street Opposite the Bank. 1796.

The name MARY WOLLSTONECRAFT appears on p. iv, at the end of the Advertisement.

1796. Letters Written during a Short Residence in Sweden, Norway, and Denmark. By Mary Wollstonecraft. First American Edition. Printed for, & sold by J. Wilson, & J. Johnson, Booksellers, Wilmington, (Del.) 1796.

1796. Of the Importance of Religious Opinions. Translated from the French of Mr. Necker. Boston: From the Press of Thomas Hall; Sold by Thomas and Andrews, William P. Blake, David West, and John West, 1796.

1799. Memoirs of Mary Wollstonecraft Godwin, Author of "A Vindication of the Rights of Woman." Philadelphia: Printed by James Carey, N°. 16, Chesnut-Street. 1799.

1799. Maria: Or The Wrongs of Woman. A Post-humous Fragment. By Mary Wollstonecraft Godwin. Author of A Vindication of the Rights of Woman. Philadelphia: Printed by James Carey, N°. 16 Chesnut-Street. 1799.

1802. Memoirs of Mary Wollstonecraft Godwin, Author of "A Vindication of the Rights of Woman." Printed in 1802. [Philadelphia]: 1802.

1804. Memoirs of Mary Wollstonecraft Godwin, Author of A Vindication of the Rights of Woman. Philadelphia: Printed by Samuel Akerman, N°. 159, Race-street. 1804.

1811. Elements of Morality, For the Use of Children. With an Introductory Address to Parents. Translated from the

German of the Rev. C. G. Saltzman. First Baltimore Edition, Revised and corrected. Printed and Published by Joseph Robinson, Baltimore 1811.

The name MARY WOLLSTONECRAFT appears on p. iv, at the end of the Advertisement.

Whose Little Footsteps? Three Shelley Pieces Re-Addressed

G. M. Matthews

Shelley's personal life was very complicated, and we may be wrongly interpreting some of his shorter poems, even familiar ones, by mistaking their human context. This essay proposes that three compositions—one well-known lyric, one well-known fragment, and one oddity—have been misunderstood in this way. Although some of the arguments urged here may be at issue with those of Kenneth Neill Cameron in *The Esdaile Notebook* and the volumes of *Shelley and his Circle,* the nature of their debt to his approach, his learning, his method, and his cloud-dispersing brilliance, must be obvious. The reason for their shortcomings will of course be equally obvious.

Quotations referred in the text to "Hutchinson" are to the *Complete Poetical Works,* ed. Thomas Hutchinson, corrected by G. M. Matthews (London: Oxford University Press, 1970).

Near the end of the "Esdaile notebook" are two poems in Harriet Shelley's handwriting, consecutive but separated by one blank page. They read, unedited:

(a) To Harriett

Thy look of love has power to calm
The stormiest passion of my Soul
Thy gentle words are drops of balm
In lifes too bitter bowl
No grief is mine but that alone
These choicest blessings I have known

Harriett! if all who long to live
In the warm sunshine of thine eye
That price beyond all pain must give
Beneath thy scorn to die
Then hear thy chosen own too late
His heart most worthy of thy hate

Be thou then one among mankind
Whose heart is harder not for state
Thou only virtuous gentle kind
Amid a world of hate
And by a slight endurance seal
A fellow beings lasting weal

Cook's Hotel

For pale with anguish is his cheek
His breath comes fast his eyes are dim
Thy name is struggling ere he speak
Weak is each trembling limb
In mercy let him not endure
The misery of a fatal cure

O trust for once no erring guide
Bid the remorseless feeling flee
Tis malice tis revenge tis pride
Tis any thing but thee
O deign a nobler pride to prove
And pity if thou canst not love
May 1814

(b) fraught
Full many a mind with radiant genius
Is taught the dark scowl of misery to bear
How many a great soul has often sought
To stem the sad torrent of wild despair

T'would not be Earths laws were given
To stand between Man God & Heaven
To teach him where to seek and truly find
That lasting comfort peace of mind
Stanmore. 1815

I.

Despite their physical separation, these two poems may have been placed consecutively because they share a common subject. For chronological reasons, however, the second piece (b) will be discussed first, although its elucidation involves much more guesswork and is offered with less confidence.

The last four of the five additions made in Harriet Shelley's hand to the Esdaile notebook are very imperfect. Two which are there identified as "to Harriet" (although to different Harriets) would be hard to reject from the canon, but readers have been less willing to accept the other two, those beginning "Full many a mind . . ." and "Late was the night . . ." as Shelley's work. Richard Garnett scribbled in Dowden's transcript of the notebook: "I can scarcely believe that this and the following poem [i.e., "Full many a mind . . ." and "Oh Harriet love like mine . . ."] are Shelley's at all." [1] Later editors have inclined to attribute the worst of these verses to Harriet Shelley. Neville Rogers relegates "Full many a mind . . ." and "Late was the night . . ." to an appendix, adding his belief that Harriet wrote them both.[2] Kenneth Neill Cameron says forthrightly of "Full many a mind . . .":

> We are unable to identify the lines. The verse, however, is so poor and the sentiment in the second stanza so unShelleyan that they are certainly not by Shelley.
>
> It is possible that the stanzas represent two poems and not one and that they have been copied from some book of verse. The probability, however, seems to be that they were by Harriet herself and were intended to form one poem: the irregularity of the meter and other crudities indicate an amateur poet. . . .[3]

It might be urged, on the contrary, that their distinctive kind of crudity is just what puts Harriet's authorship of these two poems out of the question. Their badness is nothing like that of an educated amateur poet. Harriet was an accomplished and tidy-minded young lady, "exceedingly well instructed" at school, according to Hogg, "a credit to the establishment." [4] Hogg's praises hide a sneer, to be sure, but a sneer at qualities it cannot dispute. Harriet translated *Claire d'Albe* "exactly and correctly, and wrote the whole out fairly, without blot or blemish . . . . She read remarkably well, very correctly, and with a clear, distinct, agreeable voice . . . . She was always pretty . . . not a hair out of its place." [5] The less frustrated Peacock's account is identical: "She was well educated. She read agreeably and intelligently. She wrote only letters, but she wrote them well." [6] Is it conceivable that a girl who prompts such expressions as *exceedingly well instructed, well educated, very correctly, clear, distinct, not a hair out of its place,* should compose, and copy into a valued gift-book, an utterance like this?—

That stream so swift that rushes along
Has oft been dyed by the murderes song
It oft has heard the exulting wave
Of one who oft the murderes braved

—or like this?—

T'would not be Earths laws were given
To stand between Man God & Heaven

Of course Shelley is the author: every line, every word, probably every letter of verse in the Esdaile notebook derives from something very similar in Shelley's handwriting. Harriet could only have written such stuff in a state of mental derangement.[7] But the lines could easily have been puzzled out of one of Shelley's rough drafts. Jefferson Hogg, who knew his hand well, was defeated by two lines even in a fair copy, and printed:

To know in dissolution's void
    That mortals baubles sunk decay,[8]

and examples could be multiplied. Mary Shelley, with far more experience than Harriet, mistook as "No, Music, thou art not the God of Love" a draft line that should have ended "food of Love." [9] The probability is that, after the entries made by Shelley himself, Harriet added to the Esdaile notebook whatever poetry by Shelley she found among the papers he left with her, whether fair copy or foul. The blank page of f. 93^{v} marks the division between complete poems and lines she did her best to salvage, preserving a tidy verse form if possible while carefully imitating the letters he seemed to have written. The well-taught schoolgirl would never have misspelled *walls* as *wals,* but *wals* could be a scrupulous misreading (a Swiss word, perhaps?) of Shelley's *vale.*[10] Similarly, in "To stand between Man God & Heaven", *Man God* may well have been *Mankind* (compare Mary Shelley's mistake over *God* and *food*). As for these lines from "Full many a mind . . ." seeming unShelleyan, the sentiment involved is not necessarily Shelley's own; but even so, both sentiment and phrasing are echoed in *The Triumph of Life* (288-289):

> And Gregory, and John, and men divine,
> Who rose like shadows between Man and God

That Shelley broke with Hogg in the autumn of 1811 because the latter had made sexual advances to Harriet during her husband's absence is well known, and further details, besides more accurate texts, are now available in the third volume of *Shelley and his Circle.* Shelley's disclosure of the affair, however, is still easily misunderstood. "You know . . . the exalted thoughts I entertained of his excellence," he told Elizabeth Hitchener. "Can you then conceive that he would have attempted to *seduce my wife . . . ?*" [11] Amusement has been caused by this evidence that despite Shelley's theorizing his reaction at such a crisis was so "normal." But it was the conventionality of Hogg's behavior that shocked Shelley: he used and underlined the cliché in order to stress his amazement that so enlightened a being should adopt the bourgeois tactic of seduction, furtively and selfishly, like any "everyday villain who parades St. James' Street." [12] Openly solicited and returned love would have been a different matter. "If it merely relates to me, my friend, you were welcome to even this, the dearest—but we must not sport with the feelings of others."[13] Harriet disliked Hogg. So, for a period always intended to be temporary, Shelley removed her from Hogg's company. The separation was agreed after a harrowing explanation, probably on the morning of the third or fourth of November; but while Hogg was absent the Shelleys jumped the gun and set off for the Lake District, leaving a note to say they were going to spend the night at Richmond, Yorkshire. Richmond was a good "blind," as both sides recognized. Eighteen miles northwest of York, Shelley's party would have joined the main London-Carlisle-Glasgow coach route at Boroughbridge, and would only have left it at Penrith, the same distance from Keswick.[14] If Hogg had followed the trail to Richmond he would have taken the wrong coach at Boroughbridge; and any letters addressed to Shelley in that town would have been neither delivered nor forwarded. The likelihood is, therefore, that "Prince Prudent," suspecting the "blind," kept his letters unposted until he had been given a firm address to send them to: that is, until after receiving Shelley's letter of 6 November. If so, Shelley's undated letter beginning "Your letters are arrived—you did right in conjecturing that Richmond was a blind"[15] can hardly have been written before the eleventh.[16] Shelley's letter to Elizabeth Hitchener, written probably on 11 November, shows no sign that Shelley had yet heard from Hogg since the departure from York; and the short gap in Shelley's correspondence with Hogg is much more likely to have occurred between the announcement of his own arrival in Keswick on 6 November and the receipt of Hogg's first letters on the eleventh, than between 7-8 and 10-12 November, *after* communications had been restored.

However this may be, the Shelleys' road to the Lakes took them over the Pennine ridge, and the point at which this road crosses from Yorkshire into Westmorland lies in an impressively desolate region known as Stanmore. The spelling, now regularized to Stainmore, varied a good deal in Georgian times. Nicholas Carlisle's *Topographical Dictionary of England* (London: Longman, 1808, vol. II) spells the nearby township "STAINMORE, or STANEMORE," while Dugdale's *New British Traveller; or, Modern Panorama of England and Wales* (London, 1819) prints "Stanemore" in the text (IV, 433) but "Stainmoor" on the map (IV, facing p. 424). Rees's *Cyclopaedia* (London, 1819; art. "Westmorland") gives

"Brough-under-Stanmore" and "Stanemore." But Walter Scott in *Rokeby* (an estate at Greta Bridge, itself a stage on Shelley's coach route) consistently used the spelling "Stanmore" both in the text and in the notes, and this poem was one of Harriet's favorite books after its publication on 12 January 1813: she "read it aloud more than once throughout" [17] as part of her defensive precautions against the resurgent Hogg; so she had the strongest reasons to remember Stanmore—the locality itself, its associations, and its spelling.[18] If Shelley wrote any lines during their flight to the Lakes, this might well be the name she would record underneath them. Indeed, for a half a century at least there had been an inn on the top of Stanmore, just at the county border, and, although the season was November, it is not impossible that the small party spent a night in it.[19] When Shelley told Hogg that he had arrived in Keswick "after some days incessant travelling, which has left me no leisure to write to you," [20] he was plainly equivocating in order to excuse his silence. Either the traveling was not "incessant" (i.e., nonstop), or else it had not occupied "some days." The distance from York to Keswick was 113 miles, and daily coaches performed this journey in under twenty-four hours, at an average speed (including stops for meals) of just over five miles per hour.[21] When the Shelleys really undertook "incessant" traveling, as they did in returning to Dublin from Killarney in March 1813, they covered more than twice this distance, on Irish roads, in two days and two nights.[22] As they left York in the afternoon, therefore, they probably spent two nights at inns, or went sightseeing on the way, or both. The fragmentariness of "Full many a mind . . . ," and Harriet's apparently accidental retrieval of it in 1815, suggests that it may have been scribbled on an innkeeper's bill, or something similar. Mary Shelley rescued a comparable scrap of verse from a night spent at an inn while crossing the Apennines on 4-5 May 1818, though in this case the lines were scribbled in a notebook, and—no doubt as Harriet did—Mary tried to tidy up the lines she actually found.[23]

The transcript is too slight and unreliable for close analysis, but it makes more sense when "Stanmore" connects it with the Hogg-Harriet situation. Shelley had grossly overvalued Hogg's powers of mind ("that reason I *once* almost fancied omnipotent" [24]), and the apostasy of such a Lucifer disturbed him profoundly. Shelley's subsequent letters continually urge him to live up to the ideal imagined of him, to master his passions and endure his misery with a courage proportioned to his true mental stature. "Never could you conceive," he lamented to Elizabeth Hitchener, "the illumination of that countenance on which I have sometimes gazed till I fancied the world could be reformed by gazing too." But alas, "High powers appear but to present opportunities for occasioning superior misery." [25] In the words of the poem:

> Full many a mind with radiant genius fraught
> Is taught the dark scowl of misery to bear
> How many a great soul has often sought
> To stem the sad torrent of wild despair

The phrasing of these lines echoes, perhaps consciously, the opening of Beattie's *The Minstrel; or, the Progress of Genius* (1771):

> Ah! who can tell how many a soul sublime
> Has felt the influence of malignant star,
> And waged with Fortune an eternal war!
> (3-5)

The expression in line 4, "To stem the sad torrent of wild despair", is ambiguous, and may simply repeat the sense of line 2, "to bear misery," [26] but the notion of suicide would not exaggerate Hogg's state of mind. He more than once threatened suicide in the Keswick letters, and had apparently told Shelley in York that he had thought of suicide when first tempted to assail Harriet's virtue, for in one of his later replies Shelley wrote:

> if they [your passions] could have urged you [at that time] to the dismaying brink of *suicide* . . . what *then* wd. be your feelings [i.e., if you came back to us and found yourself *again* tempted?] [27]

The second stanza could equally be expressing Hogg's or Shelley's sentiments, as on this issue they coincided. The marriage laws of convention should not be permitted to stand between man and happiness, nor should they pretend to be the means of ensuring man's peace of mind. Or the stanza may still be concerned with suicide: a man driven to destroy himself will not admit the right of earthly laws to block his way to "Heaven" and lasting rest. The curious initial letters of line 5 may even indicate that there were quotation marks in the original. But at this point guesswork becomes counter-productive. Shelley's authorship of the fragment, and its connection with Hogg and the flight to Keswick in November 1811, are the issues that matter.

II.

"To Harriett" was first published by Dowden,[28] who had been given permission to print in his *Life of Shelley* those poems in the Esdaile notebook which were of biographical interest, and this one has been quoted or paraphrased in practically every subsequent account of Shelley's life as unique evidence of his emotional relations with Harriet at the date she appended to her transcript, "May 1814".

May 1814 is an otherwise obscure month in the poet's life-story, transitional between his two principal loyalties, to Harriet and to Mary Godwin. No personal letters by either Shelley or Harriet have survived between their return from Scotland early in December, and mid-March 1814—a period of three and a half months. Things had evidently been going wrong during this interval, much of which Shelley had spent in company with Mrs. de Boinville and her daughter Cornelia at Bracknell. When Shelley eventually broke silence to Hogg, on 16 March, he had been unable, he said, "even to write a common letter," having "sunk into a premature old age of exhaustion, which renders me dead to everything, but the unenviable capacity of indulging the vanity of hope, and a terrible susceptibility to objects of disgust and hatred"[29]—one of these being Harriet's unfortunate sister Eliza. The letter ended with the stanza beginning "Thy dewy looks sink in my breast," addressed either to Cornelia de Boinville or (less probably) to her mother. By the end of April Shelley had consciously recognized the failure of his marriage, as he told Hogg five months later:

> In the beginning of spring, I spent two months at Mrs. Boinville's without my wife. If I except the succeeding period these two months were probably the happiest of my life . . . I suddenly perceived that the entire devotion with which I had resigned all prospects of utility or happiness to the single purpose of cultivating Harriet was a gross & despicable superstition. . . . I believed that one revolting duty yet remained, to continue to deceive my wife.— [30]

He went on to describe a daydream evoked by this recognition, "a train of visionary events," wherein he met a more suitable partner than Harriet, culminating in the composition of an imaginary letter to Harriet announcing his "passion for another." His reluctance to return to Harriet at the end of April produced the well-known "Stanzas: April, 1814," beginning "Away! the moor is dark beneath the moon."

Shortly afterwards, back in London, he did indeed meet the female who was destined to be his; on 26 June he and Mary Godwin became declared lovers, and he wrote her the poem "To Mary W— G—: June 1814," beginning "Mine eyes are dim with tears unshed." A month later they eloped together.

Hitherto, "To Harriett" has seemed to fit logically and helpfully between those other two poems dated by the writer himself: the "Stanzas: April, 1814," and "To Mary W— G—: June 1814." The pattern emerging was of estrangement, attraction elsewhere, desperate appeal to Harriet, and (the appeal having been disregarded) union with Mary Godwin; some blame for this outcome was thus thrown on Harriet, who either from policy or spite had failed to respond to her husband's obviously sincere overture of reconcilement. This may have been why Harriet's grandson withdrew his permission to reprint the poems used in Dowden's *Life,* on the ground that his mother, Ianthe, would not have wished them to appear.[31]

W. M. Rossetti at once saw the biographical significance of the new poem, and urged Dowden to make the fullest use of it:

> I have always thought that [the separation] was precipitated, if not mainly occasioned, by an indifference on Harriet's part,

> perhaps real, but more probably assumed as a means of winning Shelley's affections back. Your interesting discovery of the verses addressed to her renders this nearly a certainty.[32]

And again, in a memorandum meant primarily for Sir Percy and Lady Shelley:

> By far the strongest evidence in vindication of Shelley is afforded by the lines addressed to Harriet etc. in May, discovered by Professor Dowden, read in connection with those addressed to Mary Godwin at a somewhat later period. They show how earnestly he struggled to act in accordance with what must have seemed to him a severe view of his duty: and I cannot doubt that their nominal union might have lasted a long time had Harriet met him in the same spirit. Instead of that she went to Bath. She was a foolish woman, who cared little for him at any time, and now, probably by her sister's bad advice, adopted the line of conduct best adapted to drive him from her. No wonder that a passion for Mary should spring up in his heart: the point to be kept steadily in view is that the (virtual) separation caused the passion, not *vice versa.*[33]

To these representations Dowden replied: "I adopt precisely your views."[34] His treatment of the evidence, in the ninth chapter of the *Life of Shelley,* includes a full paraphrase of the crucial poem:

> In this piteous appeal Shelley declares that he has now no grief but one—the grief of having known and lost his wife's love; if it is the fate of all who would live in the sunshine of her affection to endure her scorn, then let him be scorned above the rest, for he most of all has desired that sunshine; let not the world and the pride of life harden her heart; it is better that she should be kind and gentle; if she has something to endure, it is not much, and all her husband's weal hangs upon her loving endurance; for, see, how pale and wildered anguish has made him; oh! in mercy do not cure his malady by the fatal way of condemning him to exile beyond all hope or further fear; oh! trust no erring guide, no unwise counsellor,

> no false pride; rather learn that a nobler pride may find its satisfaction in and through love; or if love be for ever dead, at least let pity survive in its room.[35]

He summarizes: "It is evident that in May, 1814, Harriet had assumed an attitude of hard alienation towards her husband, who pleaded with almost despairing hope for the restoration of her love."

Dowden nowhere commits himself as to the particular occasion of this "piteous appeal," and later biographers have been equally noncommittal. According to a recent one, for instance, "The slight endurance, for which he asks her, is of his recent preoccupation with the Boinvilles, or of his intolerance of Eliza, or both."[36] Little enough cause, one might think, for panting breath and trembling knees. The hesitance reflects an uncertainty over the progress of Shelley's entanglement with Mary Godwin. Dowden knew, from Godwin's journal, that Shelley had been visiting Godwin from 5 May onwards (Mary having returned to the household at the end of March), but he suggests no link between the visits and the poem, presumably because other considerations led him to see June as the critical month in Shelley's relationship with Mary. But if the substance of Shelley's retrospective letter to Hogg of 4 October is to be credited, he was already estranged and in a susceptible state when he first saw Mary again. Moreover, there are some public signs that 5 May was noticed by both parties as a special private date. On the first anniversary, 5 May 1815, Mary's journal records: "Go to the Tomb"—that is, the tomb of her mother in St. Pancras churchyard which had been the lovers' rendezvous and was the symbol of their union. Mary's journal for May 1816 is missing, and in May 1817 there were guests at Marlow; but on the eve of the fifth, 1818, Shelley began to write a poem for Mary[37] ("Listen, listen, Mary mine"—Hutchinson, pp. 552-53), and Mary's journal entry for the following day begins: "Our day is passed in passing the mountains." At any rate, it was Cameron who first associated "Thy look of love" directly with Mary Godwin. Having quoted Dowden's paraphrase in full, he continued:

> There is doubtless truth in this interpretation, but it seems to miss the main point. What was it that stirred Shelley to write

> it? . . . Why the obvious suffering and moral conflict? . . . The answer must be that he had begun to feel an attraction to Mary and was torn between this and his duty to Harriet . . . Seen in this light, "To Harriett" is a very different poem from what it appeared to Dowden and other commentators. Shelley, frightened by the intensity of his feeling for Mary, is trying to move back to Harriet and urges her, for this reason, finally to get rid of Eliza (the "erring guide" is obviously Eliza). Clearly Harriet still has more attraction for him than he admitted in his letter to Hogg in the fall in which he represented the charms of Mary as instantly overwhelming. At the time of writing this poem—probably late in May—he has by no means decided that his way out must lie with Mary; he is, in fact, in turmoil, caught up by "the stormiest passage of my soul." [38]

Shelley—the argument now runs—has been seeing Mary through most of May; he feels himself falling and appeals to his wife's understanding; the response is presumably negative, and this decides him. The further step in interpretation is attractive. Nevertheless, there are strong reasons for thinking it mistaken and that it increases rather than lessens the difficulty of the poem, which does not seem to have anything to do with Shelley's love for Mary, or his alienation from Harriet either, or indeed to be concerned primarily with Shelley himself at all.

The chief objection to the accepted readings lies in the wording of the poem itself. Dowden's paraphrase makes sense as a whole, but only by skating fast and lightly over fatal syntactical weaknesses, especially in the last two lines of the first stanza. Here the manuscript reads:

> No grief is mine but that alone
> These choicest blessings I have known

Dowden glosses: "Shelley declares that he has now no grief but one—the grief of having known and lost his wife's love." This is not the natural prose meaning of the lines, but a translation inspired by the human circumstances that the lines are posited as trying (clumsily) to express. Koszul's tactful French version exposes the strain on Shelley's English even more clearly:

> —Et je n'ai point d'autre malheur
> Que d'avoir connu ces bienfaits.[39]

The word *that* must be a demonstrative, anticipating *These . . . blessings,* and the semantic content of the line must depend on words that were not written but have to be mentally supplied by the reader: "I have no grief but that single grief: [namely, that] I have known these blessings [in the past and now no longer do so]." The entire force of the couplet (and so the whole case for presuming Shelley's loss of his wife's love) is concentrated into the last six words—which are not in the poem.

Louise Schutz Boas, plainly worried by the obscurity, explains the ellipses as follows:

> The first two stanzas are not immediately clear, and have been subject to misconstruction. Shelley was giving voice to a fear of having lost her love; alone, he grieves that the blessings of her love *have been* his; it is the Horatian use of the perfect tense, expressing a cessation—in this case of Harriet's calming "look of love", her "gentle words".[40]

The reading "alone, he grieves" will require yet more composition on the reader's part: "No grief is mine but that [left] alone [as I now am] . . ."—or else drastic punctuation:

> No grief is mine but that—alone—
> These choicest blessings I have known

Some grammatical support might possibly be claimed from "Stanzas in Dejection near Naples," ll. 41-42. But the Horatian perfect seems to be invoked solely to make the poem mean the opposite of what it says, and the sense remains intractable. "I haven't a care, except that I am solitary through having lost my wife's love, which is what I most care about." The insuperable difficulty is with *but that alone.* If *that* were only *this,* the line could then—with the help of Horace—be made to mean: "I have no grief but this, that . . ." If the word was correctly transcribed, however, what Shelley actually *says* in these lines (putting aside what he ought to be saying in the circumstances) is, simply: "My sole regret is that I have been the only one to enjoy the blessings of your look of love and gentle words."

There are other serious problems. The required timing of the poem's composition is delicately critical. Shelley's feeling for Mary has to be already so intense as to bring him near to physical collapse ("Weak is each trembling limb", etc.), yet still superficial enough, after all, for "a slight endurance" on his wife's part to set him up again ("seal/A fellow beings lasting weal"). Such a precarious moment, wildly overdramatized, may be just thinkable. But is it easy to see Shelley, seriously attracted to another girl, in a posture of such passive supplication and yet appealing, not as lover or husband, but only as "a fellow being"? Can he really be saying that even if Harriet does not love him any more, her pity alone would be enough to keep him from Mary Godwin? The same man who said in the autumn that the happiest time of his life was when, "in the beginning of spring, I spent two months . . . without my wife"? [41]

The circumstantial evidence for dating the poem is inconclusive, but not unhelpful. In her transcript, Harriet wrote *Cook's Hotel* at the bottom of the first page; that is, in the middle of the poem. She wrote *May 1814* at the end of the poem, on the opposite page. So far as is known, neither Shelley nor Harriet had any connection with Cooke's Hotel in May 1814, but it is true that Shelley was in London for much of that month, using accommodation addresses; and even if it were not written there, the address might have been added to remind Harriet of their mutual associations during the previous year. But this poem is not a draft, it is a finished whole, and Harriet could scarcely have found the words *Cook's Hotel* interpolated between stanzas 3 and 4 of the original from which she was copying. Nor were the words at the foot of that original, or there would have been no reason to copy them until they were reached. The first three stanzas of Harriet's transcript occupy one notebook page. So the likeliest supposition is that, having copied those first three stanzas, she thought momentarily that she had copied it all—perhaps because the same three stanzas filled a page in the original—and added *Cook's Hotel* on her own initiative because for her the poem was memorably associated with that place.

Although Shelley might conceivably have written *Cook's Hotel* underneath "To Harriett", he is less likely to have dated the poem before giving or sending it. "To Harriett" is an impulsive personal appeal of *some* sort. It is easy *now* to see the date as a crucial one in Shelley's biography, but the writer himself is unlikely to have thrust it so presciently under his wife's eye, unless it recorded the particular day as well as merely the month. Evidently the date was added later, and by the recipient, not the writer. So it may well be the date on which the poem was copied into the book, not that of composition. The dates attached to poems in the Esdaile notebook constitute a problem in themselves; but of the four poems dated at the bottom, only one—the anniversary sonnet on Harriet's birthday [42] in Shelley's own hand—demonstrably belongs to the date attached. The other three poems are in Harriet's hand, and the date following two of these, "1815", is after Shelley had left her and cannot be the date of composition if he composed them. It therefore seems very possible that the dates at the foot of all three of the poems in Harriet's hand, including the date at the foot of this first of them, are transcription dates. If so, the date below this poem would mean that the poem was copied out while Harriet was much alone, before the crisis over Mary Godwin but when relations with her husband were already cool. That she copied it at this time may even reflect her bitter consciousness of the change a year had made in Shelley's love for her.

The fact is that all difficulties, circumstantial and semantic, vanish without need of elaborate argument if "To Harriett" was written in May 1813, and not May 1814. All ten of Shelley's known letters addressed from Cooke's Hotel belong to 1813, and in F.L. Jones's arrangement all are assigned to dates between 18 May and 9 July in that year. After returning from Dublin on 5 April 1813, the young couple certainly lived for an indeterminate time at Cooke's [43] keeping at least the use of a room there until their move to Bracknell towards the end of July. Mrs. Boas, following Medwin, thinks that Ianthe Shelley was born at Cooke's Hotel on 23 June,[44] although it seems more probable, as Cameron has argued, that the Shelleys' lodgings at 41 Half-Moon Street or in

Pimlico were taken in anticipation of that event.[45] But in either case Harriet's memory of months and localities at this period is certain to have been accurate.

In May 1813 she was in her eighth month of pregnancy, harassed by hotel life and awaiting a hoped-for reconciliation with her husband's family. Shelley had called on Hogg the previous November,[46] to repair a year's estrangement, and had persuaded his womenfolk to make it up with his disgraced friend. Hogg's own account reveals how uncomfortable the greeting was, by Eliza Westbrook "who smiled faintly upon me in silence, and Harriet, who received me cordially and with much shaking of hands."[47] Harriet, to please her husband, was clearly making a great effort to be civil. "It really seemed as if we were never to meet more!" The Shelleys were living in Wales, which made matters easier, and by February 1813 Harriet had undertaken to write to Hogg, although hoping to avoid personalities by doing so in Latin.[48] The March visit Hogg had been invited to make, however, was twice frustrated, first by the scare at Tan-yr-Allt and then by Shelley's impulsive trip to Killarney. So it was not until the Shelleys had moved into Cooke's Hotel in London some time in April that closer relations were possible, and then, very quickly, Hogg's blandishments became insupportable once more—a note to Harriet of 9 May ends: "àdieu—au grand Dieu quoique tu n'es qu'une petite dèesse"[49] —and the concord broke down. Shelley, hurt and distracted, continued to meet Hogg, but the women evidently forbade him the house, so that, in the end, Hogg had no idea where or when Harriet's baby was born and never even saw the child.[50]

An undated note of this period reads:

> I send this by the Servant that there may be no delay.
>
> ---
>
> My dearest friend.
>
> I have felt myself extremely hurt by Harriets conduct towards you. [*this line deleted, either by Shelley or Hogg*] She writes in this. I only desire that she were as anxious to confer on you all possible happiness as I am. She tells you that she invites

you this evening. It will be better than our l[on]esome and melancholy interview

Your very affectionate
P.B. Shelley

Cooke's Hotel
Wednesday Mor.

I am very sure that Harriet will be as kind as ever. I could see when I spoke to her (if my eyes are not blinded by love) that it was an [mis *deleted*] error not of the feelings but of reason. I entreat you to come this evening [51]

In processing this note in 1858 for his *Life of Shelley,* Hogg roughly dated it "June, 1813" (II, 390), and consequently Cameron assigns it to 2, 9, or 16 June. One of these Wednesdays may be correct, but the note might equally well belong to 19 or 26 May. The situation implied in it is very close to that implied in the poem "To Harriett." Shelley is doing his level best to coax Harriet into being nice to Hogg ("I only desire that she were as anxious to confer on you all possible happiness as I am"), who has been ignominiously banished. Shelley admits her hostility, but persuades himself ("if my eyes are not blinded by love") that her heart is in the right place. If it is assumed that this letter and "To Harriett" are nearly contemporary, every verbal and circumstantial detail of the poem becomes clear, immediately and without strain. A brief paraphrase of the stanzas—although they no longer need one—might go like this:

1. To *me,* your love is tranquillizing and consoling; and I have no regret except that I have been the only one to enjoy these privileges.
2. If all who desire your company deserve to be rejected, then I, your husband, deserve rejection more than anyone.
3. Be one of the few humane and generous people in the world, then; and by making this small concession ensure another human being's happiness,
4. for, truly he is desperately in love with you—don't be so cruel as to destroy him by a summary rejection.

5. Don't listen to Eliza; this ill-natured attitude isn't the real *you.* Show your self-respect in a more admirable way, and treat him with compassion even if you can't return his love.

The argument in the first stanza is that as Harriet's affection has been a calming influence on Shelley, it would probably have the same effect on Hogg. It is Hogg, then, dim-eyed with adoration, who is languishing under Harriet's scorn, and Hogg, not Shelley, who will be lost if she does not pity him.

Strong support for this conclusion can be found in Polidori's diary entry for 18 June [1816], which evidently derives from confidences volunteered by Shelley himself at Geneva: "—He married; and, a friend of his liking his wife, he tried all he could to induce her to love him in turn." [52] Newman Ivey White's generally unchallenged assumption *(Shelley,* I, 401) that the reference must be to Hogg's relationship with Mary Godwin in the early months of 1815 cannot possibly be correct: Mary was not Shelley's wife in 1815, and Polidori well knew that she was not his wife at the time of the diary entry; nor, in fact, had Mary needed any inducement to make her respond to Hogg's liking, as her letters prove.[53] Harriet was obviously the wife whom Shelley "tried all he could" to persuade into overcoming her objections to his friend.[54]

This reading does not disturb what is already known of Shelley's character and principles; he is seen in the familiar role of peacemaker in a conflict which seems to him unamiable, irrational, and unnecessary. But biographically, the blank weeks of the transition in 1814 between his loyalty to Harriet and his love for Mary become blanker still. There was no last-minute approach, on trembling legs, to an unsympathetic wife, to secure her protection against the charms of a rival. It is Harriet's image that is changed, and very much to her advantage; for Harriet did *not,* either through pride or policy or bad advice, choose to ignore a husband's "piteous appeal" on his own behalf. Few will blame her, perhaps, if she chose to ignore this poem.

III.

The box in the Bodleian Library catalogued as MS Shelley adds. c.4 contains at f. 68 (Folder 7) a document of unhappy associations. This is the thin single leaf which carries the fragmentary verses now entitled "On Fanny Godwin," beginning "Her voice did quiver as we parted" (Hutchinson, p. 546), together with those now entitled "To William Shelley," beginning "Thy little footsteps on the sands" (Hutchinson, p. 581). Of these there are now full and excellent transcriptions by Irving Massey,[55] but it will be helpful to have the lines (differing only in detail from Massey's versions) available for reference, with a brief account of their context. Cancellations are in square brackets.

(a) [Friend had I known thy secret grief
  Should we have parted so]
Her voice did quiver as we parted—
  Yet knew I not [that] the heart was broken
From which it came—& I departed
  Heeding not the words then spoken—
Misery—oh misery
This world is all too wide for thee!

Some secret [griefs] woes had been mine own—
  And they had taught me that, the good
The free

And that for [those] who are lone & weary
The road of life is long & dreary

[Yet] [I heeded] Some hopes were buried in my [heart] heart
[Soul]
Whose spectres haunted me with sadness
D one
There was a

(In line 11, "free", with one stroke too many, could be "pure", with one stroke too few.)

(b) Thy little footsteps on the sands
  Of [some] a remote & lonely [sea] shore—
[Thy] The twinkling of thine infant hands
  [Upon thy] Where [even] now the worm will feed no more.

[The laugh] of mingled love & glee
Thy look [of love, thy laugh of glee]
  When [as] *one* returned to gaze on thiee [*sic*]

[I knew that]
  [The pain] All
[And she] These footsteps on the sands are fled
Thine eyes are dark—thy hands are sill
                                                  cold
And she is dead—& thou art dead—
  [And we remain to know how old]
  And the

(In line 14, "remain" is doubtful, and "old" conjectural.)

These two verse fragments are both written on the recto. Draft (a), "Her voice did quiver", occupies the middle of the page, a little toward the left-hand margin, while draft (b), "Thy little footsteps", in darker ink, begins on the upper right and extends halfway down the page. Thus the last seven lines of draft (b) are written to the right of the first six lines of draft (a), giving a strong impression that (b) was crowded into this upper corner because the other draft already occupied most of the page. To the left of draft (b), heavily cancelled, is what might have been a heading: "In sympathy" (Massey reads "No sympathy", which may be correct). Following draft (b), on the right-hand side of the page, is a sketch of a tree with "mont" (and just possibly "Blanc") written in small letters among the leafage at its base. The verso carries a large central sketch, in a style unusual for Shelley, of what appears to be a flight of steps in a formal garden, with three double urns containing plants standing along its left-hand edge, and a young tree at its head at the far end. What I have called a flight of steps was identified by Roger Ingpen in *Verse and Prose from the Manuscripts of Percy Bysshe Shelley* (London: Privately Printed, 1934, p. 72) as "a sketch of a grave," and the implication is not wholly impossible. That they *are* steps is clear from the profile of their edges on the left (and unmistakable steps are also drawn in the top right-hand corner of the sheet). However, they seem to be inset in a raised surround, and the tree blocking the way at the top suggests that they are steps for going *down* rather than up—so perhaps to an unseen vault. Above the urns, on the left-hand side of the page, Shelley has written vertically: "These cannot be forgotten—years / May flow", and to the right of the tree: "Breaking thine indissoluble sleep", with the word "miserable" just below. Lower still, Shelley has written: "It is not my fault—it is not to be attributed to me—", and "When said I so? " (written with different ink or a different quill) directly above, a downstroke on the "W" suggesting a link between the two sentences. At the foot of the page is a row of downward-gazing flowers, the middle one in a flowerpot on which is written: "I drew this flower pot in October 1816 and now it is 1817". Peacock wrote confidently in 1858: "I know the circumstances to which the fragment refers. The initials of the lady's name were F. G., and the date assigned to the fragment, 1817, was strictly correct" [56] ("strictly correct," that is, as opposed to Medwin's guess that the initials belonged to Harriet Grove and the lines to 1810). But are the little footsteps really those of William Shelley? William died, aged three and a half, on 7 June 1819, so the lines were first assigned to that year by Rossetti (Mary Shelley did not date them [57]), and if the reference is right, they obviously cannot be earlier. But for lines 3-4 to make sense the fragment must be *later* than 1819. Even allowing for the climate of Italy and the writer's bitterness, Shelley cannot have written "Where now the worm will feed no more" of hands committed to the earth less than a year earlier—and hardly then. Yet there is no other evidence that Shelley added to this mournful sheet so late in his life. *Two* different years are already vouched for by his inscription on the flowerpot, and the simplest *a priori* assumption would have been that "Her voice did quiver" was written when the flowerpot was drawn, and "Thy little footsteps" (which is in different ink) when the inscription was added.

Why should Shelley's most tenacious memory of William, a year at least after his death in Rome, be of the child's *footsteps on the sands?* What sands? Perhaps these questions have not been asked because of the fragment's superficial likeness to another poem indisputably addressed to William Shelley which begins "The billows on the beach are leaping around it" (Hutchinson, pp. 544-545), but that poem, composed at Marlow in July or August 1817 when Mary was pregnant with Clara (lines 18-19), describes an imaginary Channel crossing. William only learned to walk in April 1817,[58] and did not know any English seashore. Shelley might have associated him with the Lido at Venice, where his sister was buried in September 1818, or with the beach at Naples the same winter, lonely enough for Shelley in the "Stanzas written in Dejection." But why should Shelley first refer to the Adriatic or the Mediterranean as *some remote* sea? And who was the special *one* who returned to gaze at William?

The phrasing suggests a locality unknown to Shelley himself, and there is a relevant one in Mary Wollstonecraft's *Letters written during a Short Residence in Sweden, Norway and Denmark* (London: J. Johnson, 1796) and in her letters to Imlay published in *Posthumous Works of the Author of a Vindication of the Rights of Woman* (London: J. Johnson, 1798), both of which Shelley had read in the autumn of 1814 and no doubt later also.[59] As part of the mission she had undertaken for Gilbert Imlay, Mary Wollstonecraft had set out from Gothenberg in Sweden for Tönsberg, Norway, on about 10 July 1795, leaving their daughter Fanny behind in the care of a nursemaid.[60] She was very unhappy, and the six weeks' separation from Fanny, then fourteen months old and probably just learning to walk, was especially hard to bear. On the way she wrote:

> Light slumbers produced dreams, where Paradise was before me. My little cherub was again hiding her face in my bosom. I heard her sweet cooing beat on my heart from the cliffs, and saw her tiny footsteps on the sands. New-born hopes seemed, like the rainbow, to appear in the clouds of sorrow . . .[61]

Imlay had avoided joining his family, despite Mary's pleas. Even before crossing the North Sea, Mary had written to him: "my little darling is calling papa, and adding her parrot word—Come, Come! And will you not come . . . ?" [62] He did not come. Nine weeks later, now on her way back alone to Gothenberg and Fanny, Mary noticed a father going home with his children:

> My eyes followed them to the cottage, and an involuntary sigh whispered to my heart, that I envied the mother . . . I was returning to my babe, who may never experience a father's care or tenderness.[63]

There was only one parent to be reunited with their daughter:

> I arrived here last night, and with the most exquisite delight, once more pressed my babe to my heart. We shall part no more. You perhaps cannot conceive the pleasure it gave me, to see her run about, and play alone.[64]

Other parts of Shelley's fragment derive from Mary Wollstonecraft's fiction, not her letters, but from fiction based transparently on her own experience with Fanny and understood by Shelley in that sense. At the time of her death, Mary Wollstonecraft had been writing "The Wrongs of Woman; or, Maria" (also published in her *Posthumous Works),* which opens with a picture of a young woman who had been imprisoned by a callously self-interested husband and deprived of her baby daughter:

> Her infant's image was continually floating on Maria's sight, and the first smile of intelligence remembered, as none but a mother, an unhappy mother, can conceive. She heard her half speaking half cooing, and felt the little twinkling fingers on her burning bosom—a bosom bursting with the nutriment for which this cherished child might now be pining in vain.[65]

The third line of Shelley's fragment, "The twinkling of thine infant hands", was evidently suggested by this scene, which at the same time eliminates the need to repeat the question Hamlet asked the gravedigger: Shelley's following line, "Where now the worm will feed no more", refers not to the child's hands but to the bosom they were touching (he first wrote: "The twinkling of thine infant hands / [Upon thy] . . ."). Mary Wollstonecraft had been buried in St. Pancras churchyard for twenty years, since 15 September 1797.

So the little footsteps are Fanny Godwin's after all, and the lines are a direct sequel to "Her voice did quiver", written, three months or more later, in the same meter. They evoked, with bitter regret, the infancy of the girl for whom Mary Wollstonecraft had prayed: "God preserve this poor child, and render her happier than her mother!",[66] yet whose suicide note anticipated "an end to the existence of a being whose birth was unfortunate, and whose life has only been a series of pain to those persons who have hurt their health in endeavouring to promote her welfare."[67] Now Wollstonecraft was dead, and Fanny was dead. It was not Shelley's fault—and yet, when had he been capable of saying such a thing? After his own daughter's death, on or very near the second anniversary of Fanny's, he associated his loss with suffering "on the beach of a northern sea" in his "Lines written among the Euganean Hills," where again the imagery, of storm-beaten mariner, and lonely beach, and "Norway woodman," is drawn from Mary Wollstonecraft's life experience. But to trace such footsteps any further would outgo the limits of this study.

NOTES

1. MS. Trinity College, Dublin; Dowden Papers R. 4. 38, p. 126.
2. *The Esdaile Poems* (London: Oxford University Press, 1966), pp. 117-118, 131.
3. *The Esdaile Notebook* (New York: Knopf, 1964), p. 300.
4. T.J. Hogg, *The Life of Percy Bysshe Shelley* (London: Edward Moxon, 1858), II, 7; I, 457.
5. Ibid., I, 456, 458-459.
6. *The Works of Thomas Love Peacock,* ed. H. F. B. Brett-Smith and C. E. Jones (London: Constable, 1924-1934), VIII, 95.
7. Archibald Constable quoted to Dowden a letter written after a meeting in 1872 with Cornelia Turner, which says: "Also that poor Mrs Shelley went wrong, morally at least—if not mentally (but Mrs T does not think she was more than very foolish)—and put an end to her life when she was about to be confined of an illegitimate child" (MS. Trinity College, Dublin; Dowden Correspondence No. 534). This is the only hint I have found of Harriet's mental instability after the separation.
8. Hogg, *Life,* I, 198. The intended second line was presumably "That mortals' bubbles sank away." See *Shelley and his Circle,* ed. Kenneth N. Cameron, II (Cambridge: Harvard University Press, 1961), 642-643.
9. *The Poetical Works of Percy Bysshe Shelley,* ed. M. W. Shelley (London: Edward Moxon, 1839), III, 69.
10. In the poem "Late was the night. . . ," line 2, *Shelley and his Circle,* IV (1970), 1060.
11. ?8 November 1811; *The Letters of Percy Bysshe Shelley,* ed. Frederick L. Jones (Oxford: Clarendon Press, 1964), I, 168.
12. *Letters,* I, 208.

13. *Letters,* I, 174-175.
14. The route can be followed in John Cary's *New Itinerary: or, an Accurate Delineation of the Great Roads . . . throughout England and Wales,* 4th ed. (London: J. Cary, 1810), Itinerary 343-360; or in Daniel Paterson, *A New & Accurate Description of all the Direct & Principal Cross Roads in England and Wales,* 15th ed. (London: Longman, 1811), pp. 178-186.
15. *Letters,* I, 171. This letter, which carries no postmark, is dated c.10 November by Jones and 7-8 November by Cameron (*Shelley and his Circle,* III, 1970, 41-45).
16. Cameron reasons *(Shelley and his Circle,* III, 28) that Hogg wrote promptly to Richmond (presumably directed "Poste Restante") on finding Shelley's note, that his letters were forwarded by arrangement from Richmond to Keswick, and that Shelley's acknowledgment of these was therefore probably written on 7 November. But if the object of the Richmond "blind" had been to cover the trail in case Hogg followed in person, Shelley would hardly have undone the stratagem by sending a forwarding address to Richmond (he was almost certainly never in Richmond himself). F. L. Jones assumes a later date, but thinks Hogg did write to Richmond and had his letters returned *(Letters,* I, 171n). It is unlikely, however, that uncollected letters would be sent back so quickly from an accommodation address.
17. Hogg, *Life,* II, 312.
18. The most eligible "Stanmore" is, of course, the north-London suburb that is now an Underground terminus of the Bakerloo line. Cameron concludes *(Esdaile Notebook,* pp. 300-301; *Shelley and his Circle,* IV, 775) that Harriet must have written the lines herself while staying there in 1815, but no connection has ever been shown to exist either between Harriet Shelley and this Stanmore, or between this Stanmore and the poem.
19. "This rugged Part of the Country is called *Stanmore-hills,* which are desolate and solitary, excepting one Inn, for the Entertainment of such as may be hardy enough to go among them"—*A Tour Thro' the Whole Island of Great Britain,* by a Gentleman [D. Defoe] (London: D. Browne et al., 1762), III, 152.

    "*Rere-Cross on Stanmore.*— . . . This is a fragment of an old cross . . . upon the very summit of the waste ridge of Stanmore, near a small house of entertainment called the Spittal." (Scott's note xxxv to *Rokeby* [Edinburgh: J. Ballantyne, 1813].)
20. *Letters,* I, 167.
21. Road-books, op. cit. Southey describes the stages of a journey in the opposite direction (Carlisle to York) in *Letters from England* (1807), ed. J. Simmons (London: Cresset Press, 1951), pp. 256-262. The distance from Carlisle to Boroughbridge (ninety-five miles) was accomplished in a single day, from 6 A.M. to midnight. Boroughbridge is eighteen miles from York, a journey of about three and a half hours.

22. *Letters,* I, 364.
23. Bod. MS. Shelley adds. e. 4, f. 41ᵛ; *Poetical Works* (1839), III, 142.
24. *Letters,* I, 178.
25. *Letters,* I, 168-169.
26. *Letters,* I, 171: "Have I not known you the best, the noblest of men . . . I did esteem you as a superior being. I took you for one who was to give laws to us poor beings who grovel beneath . . . —Become yourself—Bear pain—"
27. *Letters,* I, 175.
28. *Life of Percy Bysshe Shelley* (London: Kegan Paul, Trench, 1886), I, 413-414.
29. *Letters,* I, 384; 383.
30. 4 October 1814; *Letters,* I, 401-402.
31. *The Poetical Works of Percy Bysshe Shelley,* ed. E. Dowden (London: Macmillan, 1891), p. xxxvi.
32. *Letters About Shelley,* ed. R. S. Garnett (London: Hodder & Stoughton, 1917), p. 112.
33. Ibid., pp. 125-126.
34. Ibid., p. 113.
35. *Life of Shelley,* I, 413-414.
36. Jean Overton Fuller, *Shelley: A Biography* (London: J. Cape, 1968), p. 143.
37. "Listen, listen, Mary mine," dated by Mrs. Shelley in her edition of 1839 (III, 142).
38. *The Esdaile Notebook,* pp. 298-299.
39. A. H. Koszul, *La Jeunesse de Shelley* (Paris: Bloud, 1910), p. 207.
40. Louise Schutz Boas, *Harriet Shelley: Five Long Years* (London: Oxford University Press, 1962), pp. 145-146.
41. *Letters,* I, 401.
42. "Evening—To Harriet," on f. 92ʳ, immediately before this poem.
43. Hogg, *Life,* II, 265-270, 389.
44. *Harriet Shelley,* pp. 128-129.
45. *Shelley and his Circle,* III, 180-182; *The Esdaile Notebook,* pp. 287-288.
46. Hogg, *Life,* II, 165-166.
47. Hogg, *Life,* II, 169.
48. *Letters,* I, 353.
49. *Shelley and his Circle,* III, 141-142.
50. Hogg, *Life,* II, 460-462.
51. Text from *Shelley and his Circle,* IV, 822-823. The commentary is very perceptive.
52. *Diary of Dr. John William Polidori, 1816, relating to Byron, Shelley, etc.,* ed. W. M. Rossetti (London: E. Mathews, 1911), p. 128.
53. *Shelley and his Circle,* III, 423-441.
54. "She is prejudiced; . . . tho I hope she will not always be so—" (Shelley to Hogg, 17-18 November 1811, *Shelley and his Circle,* III, 57).

55. *Posthumous Poems of Shelley* (Montreal: McGill-Queen's University Press, 1969), pp. 283; 282.
56. *The Works of Thomas Love Peacock,* VIII, 60.
57. *The Poetical Works of Percy Bysshe Shelley* (London: E. Moxon, 1870), II, 321.
58. *Letters,* I, 541-543.
59. *Mary Shelley's Journal,* ed. F. L. Jones (Norman: University of Oklahoma Press, 1947), pp. 13, 32.
60. Ralph M. Wardle, *Mary Wollstonecraft: A Critical Biography* (Lawrence: University of Kansas Press, 1951), pp. 233-234.
61. *Letters written during a Short Residence* . . . , Letter X (2nd ed., 1802), p. 127.
62. *Posthumous Works,* III, 135.
63. *Letters written during a Short Residence* . . . , Letter XVI, p. 188.
64. *Posthumous Works,* III, 183.
65. *Posthumous Works,* I, 2-3.
66. *Posthumous Works,* III, 102.
67. Quoted in White, *Shelley* (New York: Knopf, 1940), I, 470.

Shelley's Pythagorean Daemons

John J. Lavelle

On 24 December 1812 Shelley wrote to Thomas "Clio" Rickman from Wales asking for a number of books. The letter included a list of classical writers whose works Shelley wanted in editions that combined the original with a translation. The name of Pythagoras is included.[1] Frederick L. Jones takes note of this request in his edition of the *Letters,* adding the observation that "Pythagoras left no writings." [2] That is true enough, of course, and both Shelley and Rickman were doubtless aware of it. But the teachings of Pythagoras and his followers exerted considerable influence in the ancient world, and they were cited or described by writers such as Plato, Plutarch, and Iamblichus. The precepts of Pythagoras are outlined in the so-called "Golden Verses" of Pythagoras, best known in the Greek version recorded in the fifth century, together with commentary, by Hierocles of Alexandria. Even the earliest editors of these verses were not convinced they had actually been written by Pythagoras, but for want of any other verifiable author the titles *The Golden Verses of Pythagoras* or . . . *of the Pythagoreans* were used interchangeably.[3] It was probably the "Golden Verses" that Shelley sent for in 1812. Moreover, it is reasonably certain that Shelley eventually acquired, and was particularly influenced by, the French translation of the "Golden Verses" by Antoine Fabre d'Olivet, published in 1813 together with Fabre d'Olivet's "Explanations" and a discourse on poetry.[4]

The clearest evidence of the influence of Pythagorean moral philosophy on Shelley can be seen in his interest in vegetarianism. Hogg tells us that "It was not until the spring of the year 1813 that he entered upon a full and exact course of vegetable diet." This he refers to as Shelley's "Pythagorean, or Brahminical, existence."[5] Shelley was no doubt encouraged in his vegetarianism by the example of John Frank Newton and his family and by his reading in Plutarch (both the *Moralia* and the *Lives),* but by 26 November, in a letter to Hogg, he demonstrated his knowledge that Plutarch was drawing upon an even more venerable source:

> I have translated the two essays of Plutarch, . . . [On the Eating of Flesh], which we read together. They are very excellent. I intend to comment upon them, and to reason in my preface concerning the Orphic and Pythagoric system of diet. . . .[6]

It seems logical to suppose that Shelley, having encountered the philosophical arguments in support of vegetarianism presented by Plutarch, and, recognizing that they drew upon an older tradition, sent for "Pythagoras" at the end of 1812, in the form of the "Golden Verses," in order to investigate what purported to be the purest survival of the Pythagorean precepts.

For Shelley, Pythagoreanism evidently represented a very ancient authority for moral and philosophical principles which he found attractive. These precepts, including vegetarianism, could be regarded as both fundamental and "uncorrupted," proceeding as they did from a time before the rise of the institutionalized revealed religions that he rejected. Moreover, they had acquired an aura of universality because of the supposition that the wisdom of Pythagoras (who was purportedly the first of the ancient mentors to call himself a *philosopher:* "lover of wisdom," rather than *sophist:* "a wise man") constituted a compendium of the most profound and arcane knowledge he had garnered from the masters of many ancient systems:

> And farther still, it is said, that he was the author of a compound divine philosophy and worship of the Gods; having learnt indeed some things from the followers of Orpheus, but others from the Egyptian priests; some from the Chaldæans and Magi; some from the mysteries performed in Eleusis, in Imbrus, Samothracia, and Delos; and some also from those which are performed by the Celtæ, and in Iberia.[7]

Stuart Curran is clearly right when he says Shelley's conception of "a great work, embodying the discoveries of all ages, & harmonizing the contending creeds by which mankind have been ruled" is consistent with "the massive thrust of contemporary scholarship in syncretic mythology," and when he asserts that this principle is pervasive in Shelley's poetry.[8] Pythagoreanism afforded such a syncretic system that had the merit of authority, by virtue of its antiquity, and did not suffer from the gratuitous surmises and linguistic contortions so evident in the works of Faber, Bryant, Davies, and others among the contemporary mythographers. The Pythagoreans were traditionally concerned with profound truths rather than particular religious observances, and they made no secret of the fact that their master had learned vegetarianism from Orpheus and the concept of metempsychosis from the Egyptians. The assumption was that there existed an ancient body of knowledge that was the common heritage of wise men everywhere, that variations were not fundamentally significant, and that no sect could claim exclusive revelation or authority. James Rieger acutely observes that "Hogg later garbled the printed texts of his dead friend's letters in order to disguise Shelley's anticlericalism and his own youthful atheism. But when he substituted 'Intolerance' for 'Christianity' as the name of the poet's archenemy, he did not so much distort as reveal the essence of the category."[9] One can imagine, then, how congenial Shelley would have found Fabre d'Olivet's observations on Pythagorean tolerance:

> The Christian Religion, exclusive and severe, has changed all our ideas . . . by admitting only one sole doctrine in one unique church, this religion has necessarily confused tolerance with indifference or coldness, and reserve with heresy or hypocrisy; but in the spirit of polytheism these same things take on another colour. A Christian philosopher could not, without perjuring himself and commiting a frightful impiety, bend the knee in China before *Kong-Tse,* nor offer incense to *Chang-Ty* nor to *Tien;* he could neither render, in India, homage to *Krishna,* nor present himself at Benares as a worshipper of *Vishnu;* he could not even, although recognizing the same God as the Jews and Mussulmans, take part in their ceremonies, or what is still more, worship this God with the

> Arians, the Lutherans, or Calvinists, if he were a Catholic. This belongs to the very essence of his cult. A Pythagorean philosopher did not recognize in the least these formidable barriers, which hem in the nations, as it were, isolate them, and make them worse than enemies. The gods of the people were in his eyes the same gods, and his cosmopolitan dogmas condemned no one to eternal damnation.[10]

Fabre d'Olivet, who considered himself a latter-day disciple of Pythagoras rather than a classicist or historian, assumed that the "cosmopolitan dogmas" of the Pythagoreans encompassed much of the lore of the ancient world. His "Examinations" include long excursions into the doctrines of the Zoroastrians, the Hindus, and the Chinese (among others) in which he claims that these are not materially different from the doctrines of Pythagoras. Indeed he goes so far as to assert, quite casually, that Moses was "instructed in the same school as Pythagoras." [11]

Though it seems clear that Shelley was influenced by the "explanations" of Fabre d'Olivet, there was enough in the "Golden Verses" themselves and in the commentary of Hierocles to furnish him with significant ideas that emerge in his works. First, there was the notion that there were "divine" beings other than the "celestial" gods who deserved veneration:

> *Rends aux Dieux immortels le cult consacré;*
> *Garde ensuite ta foi: Révère la mémoire*
> *Des Héros bienfaiteurs, des Esprits demi-Dieux.*[12]

Hierocles refers to these beings as the "Immortal Gods," the "Illustrious Heroes," and the "Demons of the Earth Doing Right Things," observing that "all the intelligent part of the creation bears the image of their maker, God. . . . And of these three sorts of beings, the first takes in those which the verse calls immortal Gods, the middle the illustrious Heroes, and the last the Daemons of the earth . . . ." [13] The "immortal Gods" are reflections of their maker, "the supreme and best God," and so one should not "extoll their dignity above measure." [14] In accordance with this exceedingly neoplatonic theory, there is a "middle" order of "illustrious heroes": "Sometimes we make a threefold division of this middle kind, calling those which constantly inhabit the heavens, angels; those of the earth, heroes; and those which are at equal distance from both, demons . . . ." [15] Shelley's Prometheus clearly belongs to this middle order, of which Hierocles says "they sublimate and raise up our minds from the animal to the divine life." [16] He was an earth-dwelling hero whose transgression against the gods consisted of giving man the wherewithal to better himself (fire, language, etc.).

Perhaps the most interesting category comprises "those men which excell others in virtue," who are "The Demons of the Earth Doing Right Things." Hierocles comments that "By demons here, which signifies knowing and learned, he [Pythagoras] means the souls of men adorn'd with truth and virtue . . . they which are rank'd among the divine beings, such as resemble demons, angels and illustrious heroes." In order to render these individuals the honor due to them, we are obliged "To do right things, . . . that is, to obey the precepts which they have left to us, to esteem their sentences as authentick as laws, and to follow the same course of life, the participation of which they were so far from envying us, that they carefully made it their endeavour to preserve the elements of virtue and rules of truth in lasting monuments, as an immortal and fatherly legacy for the common good of posterity." [17]

Pythagoras was clearly assumed by his followers to belong to this category. According to Iamblichus, "Such . . . was their reverence for Pythagoras, that they numbered him with the Gods, as a certain beneficent and most philanthropic daemon." [18] Unlike Hierocles, Iamblichus made no distinction between "Illustrious Heroes" and "Demons of the Earth" in his outline of Pythagorean cosmology, and he notes that:

> some indeed celebrated him as the Pythian, but others as the Hyperborean Apollo. Some again considered him as Paeon, but others as one of the daemons that inhabit the moon; and others celebrated him as one of the Olympian Gods, who, in order to benefit and correct the mortal life, appeared to the men of those times in a human form, in order that he might extend to them the salutary light of felicity and philosophy.[19]

This was a little too much for Thomas Taylor, who pointed out in a note that Pythagoras "was a *terrestrial hero* belonging to the series of Apollo," and compared him with "Esculapius" (Asklepios) and with "Hercules, Theseus, . . . Plato, &c."[20] The company is still rather impressive, and we can see that if the distinction of Hierocles were imposed upon it we would have Pythagoras and Plato, the historical figures, as "Demons of the Earth," and the rest would fall into the "middle" order (to which Prometheus, Orpheus, and others might be added). In any case, the commentators on Pythagorean doctrine were agreed that there were some mortals who had special insight into fundamental truths by virtue of an inferior sort of divinity, and that these men demonstrated their "daemonic" quality by the example of their lives and their teachings.

That Shelley aspired to be one of those who "preserve the elements of virtue and rules of truth . . . for the common good of posterity" is clear from his remark to Godwin that "I will publish nothing that shall not conduce to virtue, and therefore my publications so far as they do influence shall influence to good."[21] Shelley was chastened by Godwin's dismissal of this determination as youthful hubris, but there was consolation to be found in Fabre d'Olivet.[22] In his "Discourse upon the Essence and Form of Poetry Among the Principal Peoples of the Earth," Fabre d'Olivet asserted that poets were uniquely qualified to exert an improving influence upon humanity:

> Poetry was not at all in its origin what it became later, a simple accomplishment, regarded by those who profess to be savants as even rather frivolous; it was the language of the gods, *par excellence,* that of the prophets, the ministers of the altars, the preceptors and the legislators of the world.[23]

Shelley echoes this latter observation in his own *Defence of Poetry* when he observes that "Poets, according to the circumstances of the age and nation in which they appeared, were called, in the earlier epochs of the world, legislators or prophets . . . ." Of course his conclusion that "Poets are the unacknowledged legislators of the world" assumes that any supposed deterioration had affected the perceptions of the auditors, and not, necessarily, the language of the poet.[24]

In the face of adverse criticism of his poems on the grounds of obscurity, Shelley could take comfort from Fabre d'Olivet's assertion that a poet-preceptor such as the author of "The Golden Verses" did not employ allegory (or "symbols," in the case of Pythagoras) merely to keep esoteric truths from becoming the common property of the uninitiated:

> the poetic inspiration being once received by the poet and his soul finding itself transported to the intelligible world, all the ideas which then come to him are universal and in consequence allegorical.[25]

But Fabre d'Olivet lamented that such a style, in which universals take precedence over accidentals as a matter of course, had fallen prey to a passion for realism and historical precision. He offered the example of ancient "allegorical history":

> This history, confined to the memory of men or preserved among the sacerdotal archives of the temples in detached fragments of poetry, considered things only from the moral side, was never occupied with individuals, but saw only the masses; that is to say, peoples, corporations, sects, doctrines, even arts and sciences, as so many particular beings that it designated by a generic name. . . . The adventures of all were accumulated upon the head of one alone. It was the moral thing whose course was examined, whose birth, progress, or downfall was described. . . . The moderns would mock that allegorical manner of the ancients, if they could believe it possible . . . . How approve of what is unknown? Man approves of only what he likes; he always believes he knows all that he ought to like.[26]

The "Demons of the Earth Doing Right Things," including Pythagoras, were responsible to truths that are timeless and universal, according to Fabre d'Olivet, and their teachings were embodied in allegory dictated by a special sort of insight. If Shelley saw himself as one of them, he would have to be prepared for criticism from those who expected unambiguous poetry that was clearly relevant to contemporary circumstances.

In addition to his speculations on the character of the terrestrial daemons, Fabre d'Olivet imparted some significant reflections on the source of the threefold emanation. He noted that attempts to characterize the several "attributes" and "faculties" of the "Universal Being" had resulted in a multiplicity of deities. But he also gave a great deal of attention to the inscrutable nature of the "Supreme God":

> Before Moses, none of the theocratic legislators had thought it well to present for the adoration of the people, the Supreme God, unique and uncreated in His unfathomable universality. The Indian Brahmans . . . never permit themselves, even in this day . . . to utter the name of God, principle of All. They are content to meditate upon its essence in silence and to offer sacrifices to its sublimest emanations. The Chinese sages act the same with regard to the Primal Cause, that must be neither named nor defined; the followers of Zoroaster, who believe that the two universal principles of good and evil, Ormuzd and Ahriman, emanate from this ineffable Cause, are content to designate it under the name of Eternity.[27]

The same, he says, was true of the Egyptians and of "Orpheus, their disciple." He goes on to observe that "the principal tenets of the mysteries, those upon which reposed all others, were the Unity of God and the homogeneity of Nature.":

> Now the unity of God resides in His essence so that the vulgar can never in any way either conceive or understand. His infinity consists in His perfections, His faculties, His attributes, of which the vulgar can, according to the measure of their understanding, grasp some feeble emanations, and draw nearer to Him by detaching them from the universality—that is, by particularizing and personifying them.[28]

In his own works, Shelley was obviously caught between the allegorizing instinct of the poet and a desire to elucidate fundamental truths without debasing them. If he chose to follow the example of the most venerable custodians of those truths, he could not reasonably ignore the primal creative force, nor could he avoid assigning identities of some sort to its several manifestations. But he had no wish to reduce ineffable forces to domestic familiarity by the "vulgar" device of assigning them conventional names. Hence the references such as that in "Mont Blanc" to the "Power" that "dwells apart in its tranquillity, / Remote, serene, and inaccessible" (ll. 96-97), or in the *Prologue to Hellas* to a Destiny who is "mailed in the omnipotence / Of Him who sends thee forth . . ." (ll. 134-135). Of course the clearest example of the compromise is in *Prometheus Unbound.* When Asia entreats Demogorgon to identify the primal creative power and "Utter his name," Demogorgon will only reply "He reigns" (II.iv.29, 31). When asked his identity by Jupiter, Demogorgon replies: "Eternity. Demand no direr name." (III.i.52). This is the term Fabre d'Olivet says the Zoroastrians applied to the "ineffable Cause"; Shelley uses it to identify the daemonic force that represents its power. When Asia asks whom Demogorgon has initially referred to as "God" and then refused to name, he explains that "I spoke but as ye speak, / For Jove is the supreme of living things." (II.iv.112-113). Demogorgon had offered to answer any questions put to him, and he had tried to convey the supremacy of the ultimate power of which he is a daemonic emanation by using the most appropriate conventional term. But even that is not adequate, for universals can never be satisfactorily represented by terms generated in the world of time and circumstance. When Demogorgon asserts that "the deep truth is imageless," he may be replying like a Pythagorean and not, as Pulos says, "like a sceptic." [29]

Obviously not all of Shelley's allegorical devices were deliberately inscrutable. Shelley's Prometheus and Jupiter are essentially the Prometheus and Zeus of Aeschylus, except that they have become more abstract representations of humanity and tyranny respectively. But to pursue the case of Demogorgon, we can see that Shelley has deliberately chosen the name for its atmosphere of inscrutability and obscurity. Peacock's note on a line in Canto VI of *Rhododaphne* summarizes the qualities associated with the name:

> He was the Genius of the Earth, and the Sovereign Power of the Terrestrial Daemons. . . . This awful Power was so sacred among the Arcadians, that it was held impious to pronounce his name. . . . The silence of mythologists concerning him, can only be attributed to their veneration for his "dreaded name" . . . .[30]

To identify Demogorgon and understand Shelley's choice of the name, we have only to look further in the "Golden Verses."

The condition of man depicted in the "Golden Verses" is almost precisely that represented by Prometheus in *Prometheus Unbound:*

> Man, wretched man, thou shalt be taught to know,
> Who hears within himself the inborn cause of woe.
> Unhappy race! that never yet could tell
> How near their good and happiness they dwell.
> Depriv'd of sense, they neither hear nor see;
> Fetter'd in vice, they seek not to be free,
> But stupid to their own sad fate agree.
> Like pond'rous rolling stones, oppress'd with ill,
> The weight that loads 'em makes 'em roll on still,
> Bereft of choice, and freedom of the will.[31]

This statement depicts mankind as shackled by Blake's "mind-forged manacles," and it is followed by an injunction that both points to the course that will liberate Shelley's Prometheus and characterizes his Demogorgon:

> For native strife in every bosom reigns,
> And secretly an impious war maintains;
> Provoke not this, but let the combat cease,
> And ev'ry yielding passion sue for peace.
> Would'st thou, great Jove, thou father of mankind,
> Reveal the Daemon for that task assign'd,
> The wretched race an end of woes would find.[32]

Demogorgon would appear to be the "Daemon" whose appointed task it is to liberate mankind, as represented by Prometheus, from the circumstances so aptly described by these lines from the "Golden Verses." Moreover, it would seem that Shelley's "Daemon of the World" shares these characteristics with Demogorgon, and that, as Cameron says, "Demogorgon and the Daemon of the world, in short, are the same," though it does not follow that "the Daemon is clearly necessity." [33]

According to Fabre d'Olivet, the Pythagoreans considered the accidental circumstances of a person's birth and social environment "the consequences of an anterior order, severe and irresistible, called Fortune or Necessity." To this he adds a second ingredient:

> Pythagoras opposed to this restrained nature, a free Nature, which, acting upon forced things as upon brute matter, modifies them and draws as it wills, good or bad results. This second nature was called Power or Will: it is this which rules the life of man, and which directs his conduct according to the elements furnished him by the first. Necessity and Power are, according to Pythagoras, the two opposed motives of the sublunary world where man is relegated. These two motives draw their force from a superior cause that the ancients named *Nemesis,* the fundamental decree, that we name *Providence. . . .*[34]

Fabre d'Olivet goes on to distinguish between Necessity, or "Destiny" (effect) and Providence (cause), and complains that these have been confounded. It could be that Shelley confounded them as well. But it might also be that Shelley meant to depict both Necessity ("the mightiest daemon") and Demogorgon / The Daemon of the World as independent agencies, the first superior to the second, both of which are subordinate to some greater determinant. That ultimate determining force, "the deep truth," is inscrutable. But there are various "daemonic" forces, which are simply devices for characterizing certain aspects of the operation of the supreme power at the material level. The daemons would thus resemble Platonic ideals, with innumerable accidental manifestations in the real world.

The greatest of the daemons would be Necessity, a collective term for the manifestations (effects) of the inexorable process of change and development initiated by the primary creative power. But this daemon would be affected by the operations of another, representing "Power" or "Will," for human volition was by no means irrelevant in the Pythagorean system. (It might be added that the Pythagorean Necessity need not exclude that of Holbach, for, as I have noted, the Pythagoreans were eminent syncretists.) Moreover, it need not be assumed that because Necessity and Power are two "opposed motives," according to Fabre d'Olivet, it follows that Power (or "Will") can indefinitely contravene the operation of Necessity upon human affairs. One could assume, as Shelley did, that tyranny was inevitably destined to be replaced with a more enlightened dispensation governed by love, and that the transition could be impeded or accelerated, but not precluded, by the exercise of will.

The agency representing human power or will could not be called daemonic in the same sense as Necessity, for it characterizes activity originating on the material plane. According to the "Golden Verses," it is intelligence or "reason" that acts in conjunction with Necessity to produce enlightenment and progress. But that is only possible when reason is employed productively under the proper guidance; otherwise: "Deprived of sense, they neither hear nor see; / Fetter'd in vice, they seek not to be free, . . ." Guidance for the proper use of reason is precisely what is furnished in the gnomic exhortations of the "Golden Verses," even at the level of dietary regulations:

> Abstain, I warn, from meats unclean and foul,
> So keep thy body pure, so free thy soul;
> So rightly judge; thy reason, so maintain; }
> Reason which heav'n did for thy guide ordain, }
> Let that best reason ever hold the rein.[35] }

In Hierocles' commentary on this passage, which renders the original Greek somewhat differently, we may find a clue to Shelley's representation of reason in his own gnomic works. (The lines, followed by the gloss, are given in the version of Dacier as translated by Rowe):

> Abstain moreover with judgment from those meats which we have spoken of in the lustrations and solution of the soul. And consider all things, setting reason the best charioteer in the uppermost place.
>
> . . . He adds moreover to this performance, the judgment of reason, which is able to bestow such care upon the lucid body as is suitable to the purity of the soul, wherefore he calls it reason the charioteer, as that which was naturally framed for the regular guidance of the vehicle . . . .[36]

It seems reasonable to surmise that Shelley's charioteers represent either reason or else direction that is rational in terms of human understanding, depending upon the context. But it is not necessary to assume, as Cameron does, that Shelley is being as consistent as we would like him to be when he refers to the charioteer in *Hellas* and in *The Triumph of Life.*[37] In *Hellas,* Destiny is referred to as "The world's eyeless charioteer," (l. 711) and in *The Revolt of Islam* Shelley alludes to Necessity's "sightless strength" (l. 3708). Each of these appears to be a metaphorical assertion that Destiny and Necessity (its daemonic manifestation) do not operate in a pattern that is compatible with human rationality. In *The Triumph of Life,* however, the charioteer seems to be an allegorical representation of reason that borrows from the concept expressed in the "Golden Verses." According to Hierocles, reason is "the best charioteer" for the mortal conveyance of that "lucid body" which is the aspiring human soul. It is logical that Shelley should provide him with four faces, for circumspection was one of the most important qualities stressed in the Pythagorean precepts. Retrospection was enjoined in that one should evaluate one's actions after the fact, even to the point of not retiring without reviewing "ev'ry action of the former day." [38] Introspection and prudence are likewise prescribed, which would add two faces to the charioteer that look sideways into present time. All of these kinds of vision are necessary in order for one to see the proper road to a future spiritual growth with any clarity. Of course if all of the charioteer's four sets of eyes are "banded," as Shelley represents them, then men will proceed aimlessly:

> Like pond'rous rolling stones, oppress'd with ill,
> The weight that loads 'em makes 'em roll on still,
> Bereft of choice, and freedom of the will.[39]

Power and Will are exercised through reason or intelligence, and when reason is disabled the inclinations of Necessity cannot be modified by acts of will.

Shelley's Daemon of the World is the power that enlightens and uplifts man when his spirit has been cleansed of folly and vice. Commentators on the "Golden Verses" emphasize that assigning a name to the daemon whose task it is to emancipate mankind, or invoking a name elicited somehow from the supreme power, would be of little use in itself. The daemon's power can only be brought into play once man has accomplished his own purification. He does manifest himself to individuals, but collective purification is hardly to be hoped for. As Hierocles puts it:

> God is always disposed to give what is good, but . . . we then only receive it when we attend upon the divine bounty. For 'tis inconsistent with the liberty of our wills, that good should be obtruded upon us whether we will or no. . . .
>
> The prayer also desires . . . that we may see the dignity of our own essence, for this he means by the phrase what demon they are, which is the soul. . . .
>
> The prayer therefore proceeds on a supposition, that if all did but know who they are, and what demon they use, they would all be free from evil. But this will never be. . . .[40]

It might be said that the daemon is a representation of the consequences of the soul's transformation. We should also note that the daemon manifests himself individually, and perhaps idiosyncratically, according to the way in which an individual comes to understand his own nature:

> Now if we are at all interested in the society of divine men, we shall shew it by applying our selves to honest actions and intellectual disciplines, by which alone the soul of man is heal'd, freed from terrestrial labours, and translated into the divine order. . . .
>
> This being so, let us suppose that all would be freed from evil if their maker did shew to all the knowledge of his own nature, and what demon they themselves use. But we find that all are not at once deliver'd from evil, it follows therefore that he does not make this discovery to all, but to those only who of their own accord, endeavour to free themselves from evil, and voluntarily fix their eye upon what is shewn by the intention of contemplation. . . .[41]

I think it is entirely possible that "Intellectual Beauty" represented Shelley's personal manifestation of the "Daemon of the World." Shelley feels that the cultivation of intellect at the expense of the passions has enabled him to perceive the beauty of creation:

> Love, Hope, and Self-esteem, like clouds depart
> And come, for some uncertain moments lent.
> Man were immortal, and omnipotent,
> Didst thou, unknown and awful as thou art,
> Keep with thy glorious train firm state within his heart.
> (ll. 37-41)

Cultivation of intellect enables him to conquer "Doubt, chance, and mutability" and perceive the "harmonies of evening" and the "harmony" of autumn to which he refers in the "Hymn to Intellectual Beauty." The harmony of creation is, of course, one of the principal doctrines of the Pythagoreans.[42]

In "The Daemon of the World," Shelley presents a dream-vision in which a mortal is vouchsafed a sample of the daemon's influence, his power to transport one to a realm of transcendent perception. But he is careful to note that the vision is a great "boon" usually reserved for the "terrestrial heroes" ("wisest poets"). The dream furnishes a perfect example of the vision that actual spiritual purification might provide:

> For thou hast earned a mighty boon
> The truths which wisest poets see
> Dimly, thy mind may make to own,
> Rewarding its own majesty,
> Entranced in some diviner mood
> Of self-oblivious solitude.
> Custom, and Faith, and Power thou spurnest;
> From hate and awe thy heart is free;
> Ardent and pure as day thou burnest,
> For dark and cold mortality
> A living light, to cheer it long,
> The watch-fires of the world among. (I, 84-95)

In *Prometheus Unbound,* Demogorgon represents the inexorable consequence of Prometheus' "knowledge of his own nature," whereby he embraces eternal love and accepts his role as "The savior and strength of suffering man" (I.817). Demogorgon is the child of Jupiter as much as of Prometheus, for he is a representation of the ultimate fate of those who embrace either tyranny or love. Shelley represented his own liberating daemon as a function of intellect, but he represented that of Prometheus as a function of love and self-sacrifice, activities which are not beyond the scope of even the least "intellectual" segment of humanity. The Spirit of the Hour (the hour when mankind, represented by Prometheus, espouses love instead of hatred and egocentricity) provides a vision of the earth after Demogorgon, the daemon of emancipation, has done his work (III.iv.99-204). It is a vision of social perfection that is as euphoric, in its way, as the transcendental vision experienced by the dreaming Ianthe in "The Daemon of the World."

If Prometheus could be regarded as an "illustrious hero" of the middle daemonic order, both allegorically representing mankind and, traditionally, assisting man, Shelley aspired to be a "Demon of the Earth Doing Right Things," in the company of Pythagoras and Plato. He sought, like Prometheus, to be "The saviour and the strength of suffering man," even in the face of adverse criticism and the sorrowful skepticism of sympathetic friends. His method was the timeless one of the ancient adepts as outlined by Fabre d'Olivet:

> It is well known that all of the eminent men, as many among the ancients as among the moderns, all the savants commendable for their labours or their learning, are agreed in regarding the precepts of Pythagoras as symbolical, that is, as containing figuratively, a very different meaning from that which they would seem to offer literally.[43]

By these methods, Shelley attempted to transmit the precepts of the ancient sages to his contemporaries, and he furnished them with glimpses of the social and spiritual emancipation that could be achieved by following those precepts. The reward promised in the "Golden Verses" is very much like the vision provided in "The Daemon of the World":

Then if this mortal body thou forsake,
And thy glad flight to the pure aether take,
Among the gods exalted thou shalt shine,
Immortal, incorruptible, divine:
The tyrant death securely shalt thou brave,
And scorn the dark dominion of the grave.[44]

As Fabre d'Olivet says:

> It is necessary that this soul be raised to the knowledge of universal truths, and that it should have found, as far as it is possible for it, the Principle and the end of all things. Then having attained to this high degree of perfection, being drawn into this immutable region whose ethereal element is no more subjected to the descending movement of generation, it can be united by its knowledge to the Universal All, and reflect in all its being the ineffable light with which the Being of beings, God Himself, fills unceasingly the Immensity.[45]

NOTES

1. *The Letters of Percy Bysshe Shelley,* ed. Frederick L. Jones (Oxford: Clarendon Press, 1964), I, 343-344 (hereafter cited as *Letters).*
2. *Letters,* II, 482.
3. In the entry on Pythagoras in his *Classical Dictionary,* Lempriere says "There is now extant a poetical composition ascribed to the philosopher, and called the *golden verses of Pythagoras,* which contain the greatest part of his doctrines, and moral precepts; but many support, that it is a suppositious composition, and that the true name of the writer was Lysis." Lysis was a follower of Pythagoras, and only one of the possible authors, but this observation shows that attribution of the verses to Pythagoras was common enough (albeit probably not among classicists). See J. Lempriere, *A Classical Dictionary* . . ., ed. Rev. T. Smith (London: T. Allman, 1831), p. 583; the work was originally published in 1788 and is still in print. Fabre d'Olivet says "The ancients had the habit of comparing with gold all that they deemed without defects and pre-eminently beautiful: thus, by . . . the *Golden Verses,* [they meant] the verses wherein was concealed the most pure doctrine. They constantly attributed these verses to Pythagoras, not that they believed that this philosopher had

himself composed them, but because they knew that his disciple, whose work they were, had revealed the exact doctrine of his master and had based them all upon maxims issued from his mouth. This disciple . . . was called Lysis." See *The Golden Verses of Pythagoras Explained and Translated into French* . . ., tr. Nayán Louise Redfield (New York: G. P. Putnam's Sons, 1917), p. 125.

4. Rickman probably sent Shelley an edition of "The Golden Verses" early in 1813, but he might have had trouble finding the "Original and translation . . . united—" if the translation was to be in English. S. K. Heninger, Jr., notes that the *Carmina aurea* were popular schoolbook exercises during the Renaissance, and that they were, of course, frequently printed and translated in conjunction with Hierocles' "Commentary." He cites the existence of at least 237 texts of the *Carmina aurea* "in various languages, printed between 1474 and 1700," including translations by such noted humanists as Ficino (Latin) and Jean Antoine de Baïf (French). But these would hardly have been available on demand in 1813, except by a happy coincidence. The same could be said of the early English translations by Thomas Stanley (1651, 1660), John Hall (1657), and John Norris (1682), the latter two with Hierocles' *Upon the Golden Verses.* The best solution would have been the "revised Greek text" of Hierocles, with translation, by Peter Needham (Cambridge, 1709). But there were also editions of the *Carmina aurea* by Johann Adam Schier (Leipzig, 1750) and Adamantios Koraës, a Greek scholar living in Paris, in 1812. There was an edition of Hierocles in 1742 by Richard Warren, and Nicholas Rowe produced an English version of André Dacier's French translation of 1706 in the following year, adding his own translation of the verses themselves from the original Greek. Rowe's translation was reprinted several times during the eighteenth century. Shelley's request for "Pythagoras" could have been satisfied by one or more of these volumes, but however Rickman responded it seems clear that Shelley eventually became acquainted with Fabre d'Olivet's *Les Vers dorés de Pythagore, expliqués, et traduits pour la première fois en vers eumolpiques français* . . . (Paris, 1813). See S. K. Heninger, Jr., *Touches of Sweet Harmony: Pythagorean Cosmology and Renaissance Poetics* (San Marino, Calif.: The Huntington Library, 1974), pp. 63-65 (notes 41 and 42); John Edwin Sandys, *A History of Classical Scholarship* (1903-08; rpt. New York: Hafner Publishing Co., 1958), III, 362, 502.

5. Thomas Jefferson Hogg, *The Life of Percy Bysshe Shelley* (London: Edward Moxon, 1858), II, 414.

6. *Letters,* I, 250. As Jones notes, this "commentary" was never produced. Catherine Nugent associated Shelley's vegetarianism with Pythagoreanism when she first met the Shelleys in March of 1812, and it follows that Shelley would have been conscious of the

connection then as well. See Kenneth N. Cameron, *The Young Shelley: Genesis of a Radical* (New York: Macmillan, 1950), p. 374.

7. *Iamblichus' Life of Pythagoras or Pythagoric Life,* Translated from the Greek by Thomas Taylor (London: A. J. Valpy, 1818), p. 110. Herein cited as *Iamblichus.*
8. Stuart Curran, *Shelley's Annus Mirabilis: The Maturing of an Epic Vision* (San Marino, Calif.: Huntington Library, 1975), pp. 43-44.
9. James Rieger, *The Mutiny Within: The Heresies of Percy Bysshe Shelley* (New York: George Braziller, 1967), p. 32.
10. Fabre d'Olivet, *The Golden Verses of Pythagoras Explained and Translated into French and Preceded by a Discourse upon the Essence and Form of Poetry Among the Principal Peoples of the Earth,* trans. Nayán Louise Redfield (New York: G. P. Putnam's Sons, 1917), pp. 128-129. This is a translation of *Les Vers dorés de Pythagore, expliqués, et traduits pour la première fois en vers eumolpiques français; précédés d'un discours sur l'essence et la forme de la poésie, chez les principaux peuples de la terre* . . . (Paris: Treuttel et Würtz, 1813). A modern reprint of this work was produced in 1971 in the *"Collection Delphica": Editions de la Tête de Feuilles* (Paris: Bernard Laville). A reprint of the translation, excluding the "Discourse upon the Essence and Form of Poetry," is also available, with an introduction and a "biographical sketch" by Ehud C. Sperling (New York: Samuel Weiser, Inc., 1975). Subsequent references to Fabre d'Olivet's "Examinations" will be taken from the 1917 translation, which appears to be faithful to the original French.
11. Fabre d'Olivet, p. 141. By 1810, Fabre d'Olivet had completed a work called *The Hebraic Tongue Restored,* which he could not get published until 1815. It purported to correct the modern notion of ancient Hebrew by showing that the language of Moses was actually based on that of the ancient Egyptians, and it included the *Cosmogony of Moses.* This version of Genesis assumed Moses' obligation to the Egyptian "mysteries" rather than divine revelation.
12. Ibid., pp. 114-115. This is Fabre d'Olivet's translation of the "Golden Verses," lines 1-3.
13. *Hierocles Upon the Golden Verses of the Pythagoreans* (Glasgow: Rob. & And. Foulis, 1756), p. 58. This is Nicholas Rowe's version of Dacier's French translation from the Greek, hereafter referred to as "Rowe." It is interesting that, though *"daimones"* clearly appears in the Greek, Fabre d'Olivet does not use it in his translation (see Fabre d'Olivet, p. 134, for his rationale), and Rowe likewise omits it in his own rendering of the original into (rather inflated) English:

> The heroes next demand thy just regard,
> Renown'd on earth, and to the stars preferr'd,
> To light and endless life their virtue's sure reward.
> (p. 39)

The spellings "daemon" and "demon" are used without distinction in this edition.

14. Ibid., p. 54.
15. Ibid., p. 77.
16. Ibid., p. 79.
17. Ibid., pp. 79-82.
18. *Iamblichus,* p. 18. This is a repetition of a statement made concerning the disciples at Samos (p. 7) applied here to those in southern Italy.
19. Ibid., pp. 18-19.
20. Ibid., pp. 4-5, 19.
21. *Letters,* I, 259 (24 February 1812).
22. *Letters,* I, 261, 266.
23. Fabre d'Olivet, pp. 30-31.
24. *The Complete Works of Percy Bysshe Shelley,* ed. Roger Ingpen and Walter E. Peck (1926-1930; rpt. New York: Gordian Press, 1965), VII, 112, 140. All references to Shelley's works, including line numbers for poems, are taken from this edition, hereafter referred to as *Works.*
25. Fabre d'Olivet, p. 39.
26. Ibid., p. 20.
27. Ibid., pp. 129-130.
28. Ibid., pp. 130-131.
29. C. E. Pulos, *The Deep Truth: A Study of Shelley's Scepticism* (Lincoln: University of Nebraska Press, 1962), p. 61.
30. *The Halliford Edition of the Works of Thomas Love Peacock,* ed. H. F. B. Brett-Smith and C. E. Jones (1924-1934; rpt. New York: AMS Press, Inc., 1967), VII, 94.
31. Rowe, p. 44.
32. Ibid.
33. Kenneth Neill Cameron, *Shelley: The Golden Years* (Cambridge, Mass.: Harvard University Press, 1974), p. 514. But Cameron is probably right when he asserts that "In *The Daemon of the World* the temple is described as 'The temple of the mightiest daemon' (208), namely, necessity." Ibid., p. 320.
34. Fabre d'Olivet, p. 143.
35. Rowe, p. 44.
36. Ibid., pp. 274, 284. Fabre d'Olivet explains that the soul is confined in a "gloomy body" of matter, but that it develops a "luminous body" as it becomes purified. Hierocles, he says, "called this body the subtle chariot of the soul, and said that the mortal body is only the gross exterior." See Fabre d'Olivet, p. 277.
37. *Shelley: The Golden Years,* pp. 453-454.
38. Rowe, p. 42.
39. Rowe, p. 44.
40. Rowe, pp. 264-265.
41. Rowe, pp. 266, 270-271.

42. Shelley alludes to "Necessity's unchanging harmony" again in *The Daemon of the World* (l. 291).
43. Fabre d'Olivet, p. 275.
44. Rowe, p. 45.
45. Fabre d'Olivet, pp. 277-278.

"Childe Harold's Monitor": The Strange Friendship of Byron and Francis Hodgson

Leslie A. Marchand

One of Byron's outstanding characteristics was his ability to have close friendly relationships with men (and women) of varied personalities, social backgrounds, and intellectual viewpoints. With all his aristocratic pride and prejudices, there was little of the snob in his nature. The fact that he could be on terms of intimacy with and have genuine liking for such disparate characters as "Gentleman Jackson," the pugilist, Trelawny, the "Pirate," the idealist Shelley and the pragmatic Hobhouse, Thomas Moore and Scrope Davies, the pious Dallas and the atheistic Charles Skinner Matthews, may help to explain his strange friendship with Francis Hodgson.

Moore, who was something of a snob and a great "name-dropper," thought Byron's early friends unworthy of him and roused Hobhouse's indignation by referring to them as "coffee house companions."[1] In truth, Byron's most intimate friends, those with whom he could be most relaxed and free in conversation and confidences, were generally not those of exalted birth or high society. In the aristocratic houses where he was lionized during his years of fame in England, he seemed always on his guard and felt constrained to act the Lord and the gentleman. Even when he was most frank with Lady Melbourne he seemed conscious of certain aristocratic formalities. With Lady Jersey and Lord Holland he was warmly friendly but formal. But his boredom with that society is to be seen in many entries in his 1813 journal.

His friendship with men of lesser social station seemed somehow easier for him to establish and to maintain, perhaps the more so because there was nothing of condescension in his manner, in correspondence or in conversation. Difficult as it was at times to placate the sensitive ego of Leigh Hunt, he succeeded to a remarkable degree until Hunt's dependent situation in Italy made it impossible. He never lorded it over Moore, which he might have done had he been truly obsessed with his own aristocratic birth, for Moore was an Irish grocer's son. On the contrary, he looked up to the other poet with genuine deference and admiration. Yet he was not unaware, as he told Hunt, that "Tommy loves a Lord!"

When Byron first met Francis Hodgson is not clearly established. It was probably in the autumn of 1807 during his last term at Cambridge. Hodgson was appointed resident tutor at King's College in October but was still a master at Eton and did not take his new post until December when Byron left. Nevertheless Hodgson had many friends in Cambridge and visited them often. Byron's growing friendship with Henry Drury, a master at Harrow, was another link, for Drury and Hodgson had been at Eton together and were very close, and Hodgson later married Drury's sister-in-law Matilda Tayler. Younger contemporaries of Hodgson at Eton were Scrope Davies and Charles Skinner Matthews, who were also Byron's friends. They were all older than the young Lord. Hodgson was born 16 November 1781 and was therefore more than six years his senior; Drury was ten years older.

Hodgson had entered Eton in 1794 and King's College, Cambridge, as an Eton scholar in 1799 and won a fellowship in 1802. When Byron met him, he was hesitating between literature and the bar. He had just published his *Translation of Juvenal* (one of Byron's favorite Latin authors), which was roughly handled in the *Edinburgh Review* as was Byron's *Hours of Idleness* shortly after they met, and both were preparing replies in verse. Byron's satire eventually became *English Bards and Scotch Reviewers,* published in 1809. Hodgson's *Gentle Alterative Prepared for the Reviewers* was published with his *Lady Jane Grey, a Tale, and Other Poems,* also in 1809. Hodgson rhymed with great facility, almost as easily as Byron, and many of his letters are verse epistles. Their common interest in satire and poetry, in Juvenal and Pope, drew them together. But there was another strong tie. Byron was an admirer of William Gifford, who in his eyes was a modern-day Pope, who had struck effective satiric blows at the Della Cruscans and other "little wits" of his time in the *Anti-Jacobin* and in his satires the *Baviad* (1794) and *Maeviad* (1795), Byron's chief inspiration and models for *English Bards.* His respect grew almost to awe when he learned that Hodgson's father James Hodgson, a vicar at Croyden, was frequently visited by his schoolfellow William Gifford and that Francis himself knew the great man.

All these common interests contributed to the cementing of the friendship. In addition, Hodgson was a sound Latinist, who was able to correct Byron's imperfect quotations and allusions, and he was a congenial companion. In 1808, when their first correspondence appears, they were already on intimate personal terms. Byron's first extant letter, of 3 November 1808, confided his chagrin and awkward silences when he dined with Mary Chaworth-Musters and her husband, and it was to Hodgson, not Hobhouse, that he showed his sentimental melancholy verses on the occasion. In fact he sent the first draft of these verses in a letter of 27 November 1808, in which he said: "You are the first reader. Hobhouse hates everything of the kind, therefore I do not show them to him." [2] In this draft the poem ends:

> For while I linger near to thee [Mary]
>   I sigh for all I knew before.—
> In flight I shall be surely wise
>   Escaping from Temptation's Snare;
> I cannot view my *Paradise*
>   Without a wish to *enter there.*[3]

In the margin of the manuscript he wrote, "You perceive the last lines are a little too much on the 'Double Entendre' for English poesy." [4]

It was to Hodgson again that Byron wrote to bare his feelings on the death of Boatswain, his favorite Newfoundland dog. "I have lost every thing except Old Murray [the old Newstead servant]." [5] He invited Hodgson to bring Drury and spend Christmas with him at the Abbey, but neither could come.

One measure of their closeness at this time is that not only did Byron confide to Hodgson some aspects of his emotional life, which he was careful not to divulge to the less sentimental Hobhouse, but he suffered criticism of his poems by this friend without rancor or hurt in a way that he did not easily brook or much encourage in others. When Dallas offered a title of his own or amendments to the lines of *English Bards and Scotch Reviewers,* Byron politely snubbed him. And he never showed his verses before publication to Hobhouse. Few of his friends addressed him so frankly about his lapses in style. Hodgson wrote of *English Bards:* "You have written a manly and vigorous composition." But he added:

> To mention now what I conceive to be your faults (and I think I see your face on the occasion—particularly if Hobhouse is with you) you are occasionally careless in your choice of epithets, & sometimes fall into Repetitions . . . your attack on his Lordship [Lord Carlisle] is terrific—but doubtless you had strong & late provocation. The insinuation that most women are selfish I can allow nothing to excuse. You see I have used the liberty of a friend. . . .

In the same letter he added this anecdote for Byron's amusement: "Drury has been translating fragments of Marmion into Latin, & sending them to Scott, & accusing him of plagiarism from some Latinist of the middle ages." [6]

But another letter from Hodgson must have pleased Byron more. He had seen a letter praising Byron's poems and he wrote: "I fancy Gifford is the author . . . . The stile & the handwriting are his." [7] Byron eagerly asked Hodgson to find out if Gifford was really the author, and in his next letter he repeated the request: "You do not tell me if Gifford is really my commentator. It is too good to be true, for I know nothing could gratify my vanity so much as the reality; even the idea is too precious to part with." [8] After *English Bards* was published, Hodgson reported with satisfaction: "I saw Gifford after you had left Town, and he expressed himself highly pleased with the Satire & personally obliged by your commendation. He told me you were generally known to be the author . . . ." [9]

When Byron left for his voyage to the East in 1809, it was to Hodgson that he sent his exuberant farewell letter in verse from Falmouth:

Huzza! Hodgson, we are going,
  Our embargo's off at last

The tone of it suggests the kind of playful high spirits which characterized his association with Hodgson. There was little of the rougher man-of-the-world cynicism that appeared in his correspondence with Charles Skinner Matthews or Hobhouse or Henry Drury. It was a gentler mocking facetiousness. Any misanthropic overtones Hodgson chose to ignore. Byron always modified his letters subtly to accord to his correspondent's sensitivities, though he sometimes delighted in shocking him a little. Byron wrote again to Hodgson from Lisbon, his first letter to any friend in England. He kept up the light facetious tone.

> I am very happy here, because I loves oranges, and talk bad Latin to the monks, who understand it, as it is like their own,—and I goes into society (with my pocket pistols), and I swims in the Tagus all across at once, and I rides on an ass or a mule, and swears Portuguese, and have got a diarrhœa and bites from the mosquitoes. But what of that? Comfort must not be expected by folks that go a pleasuring.[10]

His first letter from Gibraltar was also to Hodgson. This time he wrote more soberly, giving a summary of his travels thus far and extolling the beauties of Seville and Cadiz, and of the Spanish women. "I shall return to Spain before I see England, for I am enamoured of the country." [11]

That Hodgson wrote frequently we have evidence from his own and Byron's letters, but mail was slow moving to the East. Letters forwarded often required from three to six months to reach their destination. There are only three extant letters of Hodgson to Byron during the whole two years of the latter's absence. The first, dated 2 October, tells him that he was delighted with the verses written at Falmouth. The second was dated from Cambridge, 25 March 1810. Before it reached him, Byron wrote again from the Salsette Frigate in the Dardanelles off Abydos on 5 May 1810, telling of his exploit in swimming the Hellespont two days before. He had already written about it to Henry Drury, adding some ribaldry about the Turks. To Hodgson he wrote: "Nobody, save yourself has written to me since I left England . . . ." And in this letter he turned semi-serious, though he kept the light touch that was his wont with all his intimate friends in England: "we have now been very nearly one year abroad. –I should wish to gaze away another at least in these evergreen climates . . . ." But business might cause him to return:

> If so, you shall have due notice. I hope you will find me an altered personage, I do not mean in body, but in manner, for I begin to find out that nothing but virtue will do in this damned world. I am tolerably sick of vice which I have tried in its agreeable varieties, and mean on my return to cut all my dissolute acquaintance, leave off wine and "carnal company", and betake myself to politics and Decorum— [12]

It was not until 6 June that Hodgson's letter of 25 March reached Byron in Constantinople. It was a disturbing letter. Hodgson wrote that the second edition of his satire was sold out and Cawthorn was preparing to print a third, but the publisher had sent to Hodgson a letter addressed to Byron from Ireland. "I have not judged it expedient (from the circumstances & the direction) to send it you. It probably is a challenge—& will keep till you return to England—unless you *wish* me to send it—I shall preserve the seal (which is a very absurd one) unbroken till we meet." [13] This was the letter Thomas Moore had sent to Byron after the second edition of *English Bards* came out with his name on the title page. It asked him to explain or answer for his jesting reference to Moore's "leadless pistol" in his uncompleted duel with Francis Jeffrey. In another part of Hodgson's letter (since cut away) he gave Byron some even more disturbing news. Hobhouse tells the substance of it in his diary of 6 June: "messenger arrived from England—bringing a letter from Hodgson to B.—tales spread—the *Edleston* is accused of indecency." [14] This revelation about the Cambridge choirboy for whom Byron had formed an attachment which he later referred to as "a violent, though *pure,* love and passion," must have shaken him more than he let anyone know.

His next extant letter to Hodgson was dated 4 July 1810, written just before he left Constantinople to return to Greece. He boasted again of his swimming the Hellespont and jested about Hobhouse's "Missellingany" *(Miscellany).* He gave an account of his visit to Ali Pasha, repeating what he had told his mother, that the Pasha said he knew him to be a man of birth because of his "small ears and curling hair." [15]

Hobhouse was on his way home, and Byron, after his return to Athens and during his two trips to the Peloponnesus, had written him frequently, giving amusing details of his encounters with the Greek boy Eustathius Georgiou, with his "ambrosial curls" and his parasol to protect his complexion. "Our *parting* was vastly pathetic, as many kisses as would have sufficed for a boarding school, and embraces enough to have ruined the character of a county in England . . . ." [16] In another letter he told of his visit to Veli Pasha at Tripolitza, who gave him a fine horse. "He honoured me with the appellations of his *friend* and *brother,* and hoped that we should be on good terms not for a few days but for life.— All this is very well, but he has an awkward manner of throwing his arm round one's waist, and squeezing one's hand in *public,* which is a high compliment, but very much embarrasses *'ingenuous youth.'* " [17]

It is significant that Byron did not mention these episodes in writing to Hodgson. His next letter to him was from Patras, where on his second tour he had almost died of a fever. He had already told Hobhouse of his near escape from Dr. Romanelli, who "prescribes a puke" and a "Glyster pipe." [18] Somewhat less crudely he wrote to Hodgson:

> As I have just escaped from a physician and a fever which confined me five days to bed, you won't expect much "allegrezza" in the ensuing letter. . . . Here be also two physicians, one of whom trusts to his Genius (never having studied) the other to a campaign of eighteen months against the sick of Otranto, which he made in his youth with great effect.—When I was seized with my disorder, I protested against both these assassins, but what can a helpless, feverish, toasted and watered poor wretch do? in spite of my teeth & tongue, the English Consul, my Tartar, Albanians, Dragoman forced a physician upon me, and in three days vomited and glystered me to the last gasp.—In this state I made my epitaph, take it,

> Youth, Nature, and relenting Jove
> To keep my *lamp in* strongly strove,
> But *Romanelli* was so stout
> He beat all three—and *blew* it *out.*—
>
> But Nature and Jove being piqued at my doubts, did in fact beat Romanelli . . . . you are my only correspondent [he had not heard from Hobhouse since his return to England]. . . . I have really no friends in the world, though all my old school companions are gone forth into the world, and walk about in monstrous disguises, in the garb of Guardsmen, lawyers, parsons, fine gentlemen, and such other masquerade dresses. . . . I look forward to meeting you at Newstead and renewing our old Champagne evenings with all the Glee of anticipation.—I have written by every opportunity, and expect responses as regular as those of the liturgy, and somewhat longer.— [19]

Although he was tender of Hodgson's moral scruples, he knew that his friend was something of a wine-bibber and was not shocked by accounts of drinking. Hence his free account on another occasion: "The day before yesterday, the Waywode (or Governor of Athens) with the Mufti of Thebes (a sort of Musselman Bishop) supped here and made themselves beastly with raw Rum, and the Padrè of the convent being as drunk as *we,* my *Attic* feast went off with great eclât." [20]

In general Byron wrote to Hodgson when he was in high spirits, and when he wasn't he covered up his mood with facetiae that were the common stock of his correspondence with his intimate friends in England. He wrote to Hodgson because he knew him to be a willing and appreciative listener to such banter and because he had a genuine liking for him without having perfect rapport in all things. In January 1811, he was enjoying a boisterous life with Nicolo Giraud and other boys in the Capuchin monastery in Athens, seeing a good deal of other Englishmen and intelligent foreigners then in the city, and doing enough studying, reading, and writing to occupy his active mind. He wrote with great gusto:

> I am studying modern Greek with a Master, and my current tongue is Levant Italian [Nicolas Giraud was his tutor], which

> I gabble perforce, my late dragoman spoke bad Latin, but having dismissed him, I am left to my resources which consist in tolerably fluent Lingua Franca, middling Romaic (Modern Greek) and some variety of Ottoman oaths of great service with a stumbling horse or a stupid servant. . . . I am living in the Capuchin Convent, Hymettus before me, the Acropolis behind, the temple of Jove to my right, the Stadium in front, the town to the left, eh, Sir, there's a situation, there's your picturesque! nothing like that, Sir, in Lunnun, no not even the Mansion House. And I feed upon Woodcocks & red Mullet every day. . . .[21]

He did not write to Hodgson again until he was nearing England on the Volage Frigate at the end of June. His mood was sober and melancholy. Even the prospect of seeing old friends could not give him much cheer. "I am returning *home,* without a hope, & almost without a desire," he wrote. "In short I am sick, & sorry, & when I have a little repaired my irreparable affairs, away I shall march, either to campaign in Spain, or back again to the East, where I can at least have cloudless skies, & a cessation from impertinence." But he added, "I trust to meet, or see you in town, or at Newstead whenever you can make it Convenient. I suppose you are in Love, & in Poetry, as usual." [22] And he apparently told Hodgson the same story of his ailments that he wrote to Henry Drury a few days later, for he started out in much the same language about Surgeon Tucker, but two lines in the manuscript have been heavily crossed out. Byron wrote to Drury: "The enclosed letter is from a friend of yours Surgeon Tucker whom I met with in Greece, & so on to Malta, where he administered to me for three complaints viz. a *Gonorrhea* a *Tertian* fever, & the *Hemorrhoides,* all of which I literally had at once. . . ." [23]

A few days after Byron's arrival in London on 14 July, Hodgson came down from Cambridge, full of worshipping enthusiasm and good advice. He had written several poems to Byron during his absence, and now he wrote another verse-epistle.

> My dear B—We were interrupted this morning in our interview; I wish to prolong it, so con-*verse* with me again.

Alone, my Byron, at Harrovian springs
Yet not alone—thy joyous Hodgson sings;
The welcome image of his friend's return
Fills his reviving heart, and bids it cease to mourn.
[Then he goes on to admonish Byron gently to exert his moral influence in Parliament.]
First let thy country's foes severely feel
Thy *caustic ardour* for the general weal.[24]

What Byron thought of this sentimental moralizing is not recorded. He probably good-naturedly accepted it as part of Hodgson's amiable character. He knew he had in him an eager and sympathetic listener to his tales of travel, for he kept Hodgson up most of the night not long after in conversation.[25]

Then came the death of Byron's mother and soon after the news of the death of Matthews, who drowned in the Cam where he and Byron used to swim, and on top of that the death of young Wingfield, one of his favorites at Harrow. He was desolated and stunned. Hobhouse, grieving for his friend Matthews, was not very consoling. Scrope Davies had been to see Byron but had gone back to Cambridge. "His gaiety (death cannot mar it) has done me service; but, after all, ours was a hollow laughter," he wrote to Hodgson on 22 August. "Indeed the blows followed each other so rapidly that I am yet stupid from the shock, and though I do eat and drink and talk, and even laugh, at times, yet I can hardly persuade myself that I am awake, did not every morning convince me mournfully to the contrary.—I shall now wave the subject—the dead are at rest, and none but the dead can be so." And he invited Hodgson to come to Newstead where he would find "beef and a sea-coal fire" and "not ungenerous wine." [26]

But Hodgson was not willing to "wave the subject." He offered his sympathy, but he was more interested in something else. He took the opportunity to confront Byron's skeptical beliefs:

> Did we need any proofs from reason of the soul's immortality, surely that obvious inference from the shortness of our visible life would be convincing . . . . [to] you, who, believing that there is a God, must (I think) also believe that the soul of man is immortal. But I once heard you drop a doubt as to future

> individuality . . . I conjecture that you have been smitten with the Platonic fancy of our final absorption in the Divine Intellect. For the refutation of this notion, where can you refer better than to the plain assertions of the New Testament & that you may be assured those assertions are of divine origin, do suffer me to entreat you to read . . . Addison's little tract on the Christian Religion—Locke's Reasonableness, or Paley's Evidences of Christianity. I will not apologize to you for this "Sermon before Orders", as I am persuaded you know the motive of it. So God bless you with it.[27]

In another mood Byron might have passed this off with a shrug. He was well aware of Hodgson's conventional religious views, and he knew that his friend was preparing to take orders in the established church. But observation and reflection in the past two years had strengthened the unorthodox trend of his thinking since his early reading in Hume and other rationalist philosophers. He replied with a skeptical broadside.

> I will have nothing to do with your immortality; we are miserable enough in this life, without the absurdity of speculating upon another. If men are to live, why die at all? and if they die, why disturb the sweet and sound sleep that "knows no waking"? . . .
>
> I am no Platonist, I am nothing at all, but I would sooner be a Paulician, Manichean, Spinozist, Gentile, Pyrrhonian, Zoroastrian, than one of the seventy two villainous sects who are tearing each other to pieces for the love of the Lord and hatred of each other. Talk of Galileeism? Show me the effects—are you better, wiser, kinder by your precepts? I will bring you ten Musselmans shall shame you in all good will towards men, prayer to God, and duty to their neighbours. . . . But I will say no more on this endless theme; let me live, well if possible, and die without pain.

But at the end of his letter he added: "I shall rejoice to see you."[28]

Hodgson continued to plead with him. "Crede Byron! from my soul I repeat to you, Crede Byron! words which chance has ordered should often meet your eyes [it was the motto on the Byron coat of arms]; but which I trust my sense of them, you yet design to lay to heart. My friend—what wild arguments you have advanced?" [29] And he ended by urging Byron to read Butler's *Analogy,* a defense of the Christian religion against the Deists.

Before Byron received this reply he wrote amicably to Hodgson: "I have been a good deal in your company lately, for I have been reading Juvenal [Hodgson's translation] and Lady Jane & ca. [*Lady Jane Grey, a Tale, and Other Poems,* published by Hodgson in 1809] for the first time since my return—The 10th. Sat[ir]e has always been my favourite as I suppose indeed of every body's, it is the finest recipe for making one miserable with this life, & content to walk out of it, in any language." [30] On receiving Hodgson's letter, he replied:

> I won't dispute with you on the arcana of your new calling. . . . As to miracles, I agree with Hume that it is more probable men should *lie* or be *deceived,* than that things out of the course of nature should so happen. . . .
>
> I do not believe in any revealed religion, because no religion is revealed. . . . I will neither read *pro* or *con.* God would have made His will known without books, considering how very few could read when Jesus of Nazareth lived . . . . As to your immortality, if people are to live, why die? And our carcases, which are to rise again, are they worth raising? I hope, if mine is, that I shall have a better *pair of legs* than I have moved on these two-and-twenty years, or I shall be sadly behind in the squeeze into Paradise. . . . I do not wish to shock your prejudices by saying all I do think. Let us make the most of life, and leave dreams to Emanuel Swedenborg.

Referring to his proposed trip to Cambridge, he added: "I should certes like to see you there before you are dubbed a deacon." [31]

Hodgson was indeed shocked. He replied in desperation: "your last painful letter will recur to my thoughts—let me make one other effort—You mentioned an opinion of Hume's about miracles—for God's sake hear me Byron—For God's sake—examine Paley's answer to that opinion—examine the whole of Paley's Evidences—the two volumes may be read carefully in less than a week—Let me for the last time by our friendship implore you to read them."[32] A few days later he wrote again.

> Your last letter has unfeignedly grieved me. Believing, as I do from my heart, that you would be better & happier by thoroughly examining the evidence for Christianity, how can I hear you say, you *will not* read any book on the subject, without being pained? But God bless you under all circumstances. I will say no more. Only do not talk of "shocking my prejudices," and of "wishing to see me *before* I am a deacon"—I wish to see you at all times, & as to our different opinions we can easily keep them to ourselves. Adieu to the subject! with this sincere prayer—May God teach you so to live that you may die full of hope, & be forever happy in a better world— [33]

Byron was willing to accept that, and in his next letter he did not refer to the subject again, though he perhaps took a little pleasure in displaying his libertine attitudes in a way calculated to shock the moral senses of a soon-to-be parson. "I am plucking up my spirits, and have begun to gather my little sensual comforts together. Lucy [the maid who had borne him a son before he left England] is extracted from Warwickshire; some very bad faces have been warned off the premises, and more promising substituted in their stead . . . . Lucinda to be commander . . . of all the makers and unmakers of beds in the household." [34]

Then on the tenth of October the news came of the death of Edleston the previous May while Byron was abroad. It was to Hodgson that he first wrote about it, though he did not reveal the name. "I heard of a death the other day that shocked me more than any of the preceding, of one whom I once loved more than I ever loved a living thing, & one who I believe loved me to the last, yet I had not a tear left for an event which five years ago would have bowed me to the dust; still it sits heavy on my heart & calls back what I wish to forget, in many a feverish dream." [35]

In the meantime Hodgson had some serious problems of his own, somewhat apart from theology. He confessed his sins to Byron in a maudlin letter: "I am very anxious that *you* & a few others should know how far I *have offended against my own sense of honour,* for that is my worst offence—Hear me then for five minutes, and forgive, if you can—if not, tell me so. B[land] [36] at his departure from England, introduced me to his mistress . . . then . . . he earnestly requested me to call on her & administer all the comfort in my power. I obeyed too faithfully . . . ." [37] In fact, he fell in love with the girl, but she turned him down, and now that Bland was back she would have nothing to do with either of them. Byron tried to help and reported his findings to Hobhouse:

> Bland (the *revd.*) has been *challenging* an officer of Dragoons, about a *whore,* and my assistance being required, I interfered in time to prevent him from losing his *life* or his *Living.*—The man is mad, Sir, mad, frightful as a Mandrake, & lean as a rutting Stag, & all about a bitch not worth a bank token—She is a common Strumpet as his antagonist assured me, yet he means to marry her, Hodgson meant to marry her, the officer meant to marry her, her first seducer (seventeen years ago) meant to marry her, and all this is owing to the *Comet!*—During Bland's absence, Hodgson was her dragon, & left his own Oyster wench to offer his hand, which she *refused.*—Bland comes home in hysterics, finds her in keeping (not by H[odgso]n however) & loses his wits.—Hodgson gets drunk & cries, & he and Bland (who have been berhyming each other as you know these six past Olympiads) are now the antipodes of each other—I saw this *wonder,* & set her down at seven shillings worth.[38]

But Byron overlooked Hodgson's weaknesses and visited him in Cambridge toward the end of November and then invited him and William Harness, one of his former favorites at Harrow, to Newstead. There in December, when they came together for conversation in the evenings, Hodgson could not hold to his promise to say nothing more of religion. The young Harness sided with Hodgson but was no match for Byron. He listened with rapt attention and sympathy while the learned Hodgson "with judicious zeal and affectionate earnestness (often speaking with tears in his eyes)" tried ot convert Byron to right thinking.[39]

Byron, however, had other interests in the Abbey. He had fallen foolishly in love with one of the maids, a pretty Welsh girl named

Susan Vaughan. His guests had observed the progress of the affair, one of them with some cynicism, the other with sentimental approval. When Byron confessed that after he left for London at the beginning of 1812 she was unfaithful to him, Hodgson was filled with the deepest sympathy. Byron told him the whole story of how it had affected him. To Moore and to Hobhouse he spoke nonchalantly of the affair. He told Moore, "I am in a state of ludicrous tribulation." [40] And to Hobhouse he wrote, "I have dismissed my Seraglio for squabbles and infidelities."[41] But he revealed the full depth of his despair to Hodgson. "I do not blame her," he wrote, "but my own vanity in fancying that such a thing as I could ever be beloved . . . ." [42] And referring to a kidney ailment from which he had just recovered, he said, "If the stone had got into my heart instead of my kidneys, it would have been all the better." [43] Hodgson wrote:

> Ah, my dear Byron, how every year takes away something from our good opinion of women—In spite of a few little suspicions instilled into me by the conjecture of that extraordinarily observing young man, Harness, I could have staked my life on Susan's love for you—But Susan! . . . What a thoroughly bad heart she must have had! Do you know, I cannot bear these things—your letter made me burst into tears—but I am pleased indeed with your mildness—Bad woman! she did not deserve it. . . .[44]

Byron continued on confidential terms with Hodgson. On 21 February he asked him to review a book of travels by John Galt, whom he had met abroad, in the *Monthly Review,* to which Hodgson was a frequent contributor.[45] And at Hodgon's urging, Byron agreed to write some reviews for the journal himself. Again it was to Hodgson that he gave the most personal and egotistical report of his maiden speech in the House of Lords. "Lds Holland & Grenville, particularly the latter paid some high compts. in the course of their speeches as you may have seen in the papers . . . . I have had many marvelous eulogies repeated to me since in person & by proxy from divers persons *ministerial—yea ministerial!* as well as oppositionists, of them I shall only mention Sir F[rancis] Burdetts—

He says it is the best speech by a *Lord* since the 'Lord knows when'."[46]

Then *Childe Harold* was published (10 March 1812), and Byron was swept into fame and a fashionable world of which he had before known very little. His brief infatuation with Lady Caroline Lamb fully occupied him during the summer, and when that broke up, he easily succumbed to the "autumnal charms" of Lady Oxford. There is an interregnum in his correspondence with Hodgson, though he may have seen him from time to time in London. But there is no evidence that Byron cut his old friends on achieving fame and being lionized in Whig society. On the contrary, he tried to get Hodgson accepted in his new circles, with Rogers, at Holland House, and elsewhere. But his absorbing amours gave him little time or inclination for correspondence with his naïve and sentimental friend.

On 16 November Hodgson sent Byron some verses celebrating his (Hodgson's) birthday along with a complaining letter: "I have been vexed at your not answering my letter of two months ago, sent to Cheltenham." Then he came to the purpose of his letter. His father had died in 1810, leaving heavy debts, which he had resolved to repay. Now creditors were pressing him. "What I wish is this . . . I have a tutorship of King's College, which is worth 100£ pr. annum . . . . On that engagement for annual repayment of 100£ can you lend me for five years five hundred pounds?" [47] He spoke of an "old debt," so Byron must already have given him some money. To this letter he got no reply. Byron was at Eywood with Lady Oxford and in great financial difficulties because Claughton, who had contracted to purchase Newstead, had failed to make his payments.

On 10 December Hodgson tried again: "It is no common cause which would make me trouble you with another letter on the same subject, *after my three last.*" He again asked for a loan of £500, and urged Byron to continue *Childe Harold* but "Be intent at all events on religious principles & associations—or (would to God I could hope it) speak more according to the general direction of our nature." [48] Finally on 21 December he received a letter from Byron (this one has disappeared). Hodgson replied that he was sorry to have troubled him "when you are so vexed with your own affairs," but he seized upon Byron's offer to lend his credit if Hodgson could find a lender. "Unluckily I have not a single friend able to advance such a sum," and he asked Byron to give "real" security for his bond. Referring to Byron's situation at Eywood, he ended with a quotation from Tasso's *Jerusalem Delivered* about Rinaldo and Armida which may have suggested to Byron the comparison of his enchantment with Lady Oxford with that of Rinaldo under the spell of the sorceress Armida.[49]

Byron replied genially, saying that he would join him in the bond, but did not know whether in the present state of his finances he had any real property to pledge. He confessed his pleasure in the company of Lady Oxford and pronounced the "last two months as worthy of the gods in *Lucretius.*" He invited Hodgson to visit him at Kinsham, a house of Lord Oxford which he was planning to lease. "Lady Oxford has heard me talk much of you . . . and desires me to say she would be happy to have the pleasure of your acquaintance."[50]

There the correspondence on Byron's part lapsed for several months. But Hodgson continued to write. On 16 March he sent a verse-letter reverting to the argument about Christianity and Deism. On 17 April, having heard that Byron was going abroad with the Oxfords, he wrote in desperation: "After three fruitless epistles, & half a hundred enquiries, I am making one last & desperate effort to learn some tidings of you before your departure from England. . . . Do at least give me a line to show that the Lethe of Love has not absolutely erased every friend from your memory." He had received an early proof copy of the *Giaour* from Murray. " 'There are some very pretty lines, *very pretty* lines,' said a man to me," but "I wish you had taken the trouble to connect the story."[51] One may assume that Byron's long pauses in his correspondence with Hodgson were chiefly due to the complications of his life and loves. But one might also suppose that he was growing slightly bored with his old friend, though he would never let it appear when he did write, and hardly admitted it to himself.

When in September he was searching for a ship to take him and his sister abroad, he called on Hodgson, who wrote to a friend to inquire about a store-ship. During the autumn Byron recommended him with warm enthusiasm to Dr. Samuel Butler of

Shrewsbury, who was translating Lucian Buonaparte's poem *Charlemagne* and who was considering Hodgson as a collaborator (Hodgson translated the second half).

In the meantime Hodgson had fallen in love with Matilda Tayler, sister of Henry Drury's wife, but her mother would not consent to their marriage because of Hodgson's debts. When Byron learned of the difficulty, he with Henry Drury and Hodgson traveled all night in a post-chaise to see Mrs. Tayler (then in Oxford) and plead his friend's cause,[52] assuring her that Hodgson would soon be free of debt. On their return to London, Byron took him to Hammersley's bank and there transferred to Hodgson's account £1000. Hodgson wanted to give his bond for it, but Byron refused it, knowing that Hodgson would never repay and considering it a gift. Hodgson wrote: "Thanks, generous friend! New life is mine .... How happy you will be to hear that Mrs. Tayler has written to Mrs. Drury a letter quite favourable to my claims, & that all . . . is likely to be settled by or before Christmas—" [53] Byron merely laughed at Hodgson's acknowledgment of the debt, and was much annoyed when, through Hodgson's own confessions to friends, his generosity became known.

In return, Hodgson sent Byron his criticism of *The Bride of Abydos,* which he saw before it was published: "this poem is certainly the most correct of your writings, I am very anxious that every blemish which *your haste* allows you to detect should be removed." [54]

Hodgson continued to be Byron's "Monitor." He read *The Corsair* and preferred Medora to Gulnare. "I . . . now only hope you will continue Childe Harolde [sic] & make him good & happy ever afterwards, or find the Corsair & give him a Bible out of the wreck of a vessel thrown upon his Desolate Island." [55] He returned to a more detailed criticism a few weeks later.

> The first stanza is glorious—so is the second. . . . The allusion at the end of the third is too Scriptural to please me in poetry ["She walks the waters like a thing of life"—*Corsair,* I, 93] . . . The fifth has some obscurity . . . I don't like the Stanza about Charles. It is satirical rather than sublime & too like Juvenal thoroughly to please me.[56]

Byron seemingly took this criticism with remarkable good will, or at least he never let Hodgson know what he thought of it.

When he decided in July to take Augusta and her children to the seashore for a holiday, he wrote to Hodgson at Hastings to ask him to find a house for him. Hodgson was delighted. He replied: "Your letter has given me very great pleasure indeed . . . here we shall be able to talk fully, freely, and as we once were accustomed—your promised visit to Hastings is the 'comble de mon bonheur'."[57] He recommended Hastings House, with a garden, isolated and near the sea, where the Taylers had lived.

Byron and Augusta arrived about the twentieth of July. He enjoyed the retired house and the sea bathing, but he was not as solitary as he might have wished. In addition to Hodgson, there was Byron's cousin, George Anson Byron, young John Cowell (whom he had first met at Brighton in 1808), and a son of Lord Erskine. He was in a ferment. His correspondence with Annabella Milbanke had reached a peak of misunderstandings and fine phrases. Augusta was urging him to get married and was trying to make a match with her friend Lady Charlotte Leveson Gower. Byron wrote to Moore: "I have been swimming and eating turbot, and smuggling neat brandies and silk handkerchiefs,—and listening to my friend Hodgson's raptures about a pretty wife-elect of his,—and walking on cliffs, and tumbling down hills and making the most of the *dolce far niente* for the last fortnight." [58]

Byron had shown Hodgson Annabella's latest letter, so full of pieties and abstractions that he couldn't understand it. Hodgson immediately wrote an enthusiastic eight-page letter extolling the virtues of Miss Milbanke and urging him not to lose the opportunity of being happy. "I am convinced," he wrote, "(as far as one can be convinced about futurity)" that *"this* is the person to call out all the better parts of your character & to assist you in subduing the worse." He begged Byron to write *"such* a letter as you said you would last night—but be quite collected before you do it & be as full and explicit as your heart dictates, for you have to deal with a woman of the highest honour & feeling who will only take one advantage of what you say, namely to use it as she sweetly says, 'for your own peace.' " [59]

What Byron told Hodgson he would write we do not know, but

what he did write was: "Pray then, write to me openly and *harshly* if you please—if there is anything you wish to know or to say—I am ready to answer or to listen . . . you are the last person I would wish to misunderstand." Then he added a postscript: "I have read your letter once more—and it appears to me that I must have said something which makes you apprehend a misunderstanding on my part of your sentiments . . . . and my memory is still retentive enough not to require the repetition that you are attached to another." [60] This letter was successful in getting her to confess, not that she had deceived him (which was true), but that she had deceived herself, and that she was not attached to someone else.

How much Hodgson influenced Byron in his suit of Annabella it is hard to say. Perhaps not at all. But he was persistent in urging him not to lose her. On 28 August he wrote that he was anxious to hear about Newstead (he wanted Byron to keep the Abbey after Claughton defaulted) and about Annabella. "For God's sake embrace both opportunities of recovering all the hope & all the happiness of Existence." [61]

Hodgson continued his frank and detailed criticism of Byron's poems as they appeared. When *Lara* was published in the summer of 1814, he reported that "Merivale & all I have heard from . . . like Lara prodigiously; but it is contended, & I think with justice, that the poor dear Corsair, who was mildness & goodness itself, is metamorphosed into a most ferocious miscreant indeed." [62] He ended his letter with a request that Mrs. Leigh send him a pupil. He must have one or two and a house before he could marry. Byron went to some trouble to persuade his solicitor John Hanson to send his son Newton to Hodgson for tutoring, and it was finally arranged. He also tried to get a domestic chaplaincy for him with Hanson's son-in-law Lord Portsmouth, but nothing came of it because of the lunacy trial of Portsmouth.

It may seem strange that Hodgson was one of the last of Byron's close friends to learn of his engagement to Annabella Milbanke. He got the news from Henry Drury to whom Byron wrote: "I am going to be married—and have been engaged this month . . . . I hope Hodgson is in a fair way on the same voyage—I saw him & his idol at Hastings . . . . I have not yet apprized him of this—he makes such a serious matter of these things—and is so 'melancholy & gentlemanlike' that it is quite overcoming to us choice spirits."[63] Byron's apprehension was justified. Two days later Hodgson wrote:

> My dearest friend—As I have always told you next to my own marriage with my dear M[atilda] from my soul I rejoice at hearing of your intended happiness—for happiness it will be, believe me, beyond all you ever dreamt of—Good God! what a favoured being you are & Crown'd with every object of poetical ambition, restored to the seat of your ancestors, and now blest with one of the first women in England for your wife! For the love of God return thanks to that God for that love—I shall drink to your health today more heartily than I can express. . . . Do pray remember . . . . that there *was* a person who *always* encouraged you to persevere in this noble pursuit, who told you, *throughout,* she alone was the being to call out all that was good in your mind, & throw the contrary into the &c., nay to expel it utterly.[64]

On his return from his first visit to his fiancée at Seaham, Byron stopped at Cambridge and there ran into Hodgson and showed him some of Miss Milbanke's letters. Hodgson was again effusive: "I assure you most unfeignedly that from the whole of Miss M's conduct in this affair, from the first letter you showed me to that glorious and openhearted offering of female affection which I saw last night, I have formed the most *exalted* idea of her I ever did of any woman in my life."[65] Byron left it to Hodgson to write Annabella about the applause that burst from the students when he walked into the Senate to vote for Dr. William Clark for Professor of Anatomy.

But after Byron's marriage any close association with Hodgson ended and the correspondence dropped off. Toward the end of April Byron dictated to his sister a letter to tell Hodgson about his new pupil, Newton Hanson. Augusta added a postscript: "B. desires me to add, Ly. B[yron]—is in the Family Way—& that Ld. Wentworth has left all to her mother & then to Ly B. & children—but B. is *(he says)* a 'very miserable Dog' for all that."[66]

As the miseries and financial embarrassments of his year of marriage increased, he was not inclined to seek consolation from the ever friendly but too romantic and moralizing Hodgson, who from time to time complained that he had news only from Augusta, and wondered at Byron's "unfriendly silence." [67] And when the blow of the separation came, he was even less moved to share his perplexities with the man who had urged upon him this ideal match. There are no more direct letters before Byron went abroad. But a furious correspondence sprang up between Hodgson and Augusta during the separation proceedings and continued afterward when she had turned repentant and pious.[68] First of all, she thought Hodgson might effect a reconciliation by writing to Lady Byron. On Augusta's invitation he had come to London and had a long conversation with Byron, and he wrote to Lady Byron: "I am convinced that the deep and rooted feeling of his heart is regret and sorrow for the occurrences which have so deeply wounded you; and the most unmixed admiration of your conduct in all particulars, and the warmest affection." [69] And he added his fear that Byron was in such a state that he might destroy himself. But the implacable wife was not moved.

After Byron went abroad in 1816, his letters to Hodgson dropped off entirely for several years. In the autumn of 1815 Hodgson had been ordained and held a curacy at Braddon in Northamptonshire, which enabled him at last to marry. In less than a year, through the influence of his kinsman D'Ewer Coke, he was presented with the living of Bakewell in Derbyshire by the Duke of Rutland. Byron wrote to Moore on 5 December 1816, from Venice:

> I hear that H[odgso]n is your neighbor, having a living in Derbyshire. You will find him an excellent-hearted fellow, as well as one of the cleverest: a little, perhaps, too much japanned by preferment in the church and the tuition of youth, as well as inoculated with the disease of domestic felicity, besides being over-run with fine feelings about women and *constancy* (that small change of Love, which people exact so rigidly, receive in such counterfeit coin, and repay in baser metal); but, otherwise, a very worthy man, who has lately got a pretty wife, and (I suppose) a child by this time. Pray remember me to him, and say I know not which to envy most—his neighborhood, him, or you.[70]

Byron did not write to Hodgson because he had little to say that would interest him or that he would approve. He was already immersed in the Venetian gaieties and in his love for Marianna Segati, wife of a "Merchant of Venice." On 4 June 1817 he wrote to John Murray, "I have had a letter from Mr. Hodgson—maudlin & fine-feeling—he is very happy—has got a living—but not a child—if he had stuck to a Curacy—babes would have come of course because he could not have maintained them." [71]

How far his life in Italy had carried him from any genuine rapport with the "excellent-hearted fellow" is indicated in a postscript to a letter to Murray in May 1819:

> I have read Parson Hodgson's Friends [*The Friends: a Poem,* by the Rev. Francis Hodgson, published by Murray in 1818] in which he seems to display his knowledge of the Subject by a covert Attack or two on Some of his own. He probably wants another Living—at least I judge so by the prominence of his Piety—although he was always pious—even when he was kept by a Washerwoman on the New Road. I have seen him cry over her picture which he generally wore under his left Armpit.—But he is a good man—and I have no doubt does his duties by his Parish.— [72]

When Byron finally wrote to Hodgson, it was at the request of Augusta, who had been in constant correspondence with her brother's old friend. His letter was that of one who was trying to be cordial but could not say what was really on his mind. He was searching for subjects that would be agreeable, but it was an effort. He never mentioned the Countess Guiccioli, nor the revolution that was brewing, nor his recent writing (he had just sent the fifth canto of *Don Juan* to Murray), subjects which filled his letters to Murray and Hobhouse and Kinnaird and Moore. "My sister tells me that you desire to hear from me. I have not written to you since I left England, nearly five years ago. I have no excuse for this silence except laziness, which is none." Then he filled up the letter with inoffensive generalities and questions about their friends in England. He even found a word of praise for *The Friends,* which he thought "very good and classical." [73]

Hodgson was touchingly delighted: "out of my own family I have *no* pleasure equal to hearing from you—" He was ambivalent about Hobhouse's radical politics—he operates "under a wrong bias." He was glad Byron was taking the side of "Pope, Poetry, Sense and Genius." And he spoke of "those delightful days of our intercourse which no chance or change will efface from my Memory. . . . God bless you! Do not forget me—while I look round at all my comforts, how can I forget you?" [74]

Hodgson was emboldened to send Byron his two poems, *Childe Harold's Monitor* and *Saeculo Mastix, or the Lash of the Age we live in.* The first, published in 1818, contained some severe strictures not only on *Childe Harold* but on *Manfred* and *Beppo.* The third canto of *Childe Harold,* he says in a note, is disfigured "with violations of the true tone of poetic diction" and "rambling metaphysical sentences of broken prose borrowed from the most worthless of his contemporaries." [75] Byron was not willing to pick a quarrel with him, and answered in perfect mildness and good humor. "At length your two poems have been sent. I have read them over (with the notes) with great pleasure. I receive your compliments kindly and your censures temperately, which I suppose is all that can be expected among poets." [76]

There so far as Byron was concerned the correspondence ended. He occasionally mentioned Hodgson, sometimes cuttingly, in letters to other friends but never wrote to him again. One may wonder whether he would ever have been drawn to such a person in his later sophisticated years. And yet he did form cordial relations with characters even more distant from him in their moral and intellectual outlook. One has only to think of Dr. James Kennedy in Cephalonia and Col. Stanhope and Parry in Missolonghi. And he had a loyalty to early friendships even when he had to admit to himself that they bored him. Hodgson had more to recommend him both in amiability of character and in literary interests than many of Byron's early school friends, whom he did drop by the wayside when he was faced with them in his maturity. After his return from his first voyage to the East he had invited his young Harrow friend John Claridge, one of those "juniors and favourites" whom he had "spoilt by indulgence," to visit him at Newstead. But he was soon writing to Hobhouse:

> now here is a good man, a handsome man, an honourable man, a most inoffensive man, a well informed man, and a *dull* man, & this last damned epithet undoes all the rest; there is S[crope] B[erdmore] D[avies] with perhaps no better intellects, & certes not half his sterling qualities, is the life & soul of me, & everybody else; but my old friend with the soul of honour & the zeal of friendship & a vast variety of insipid virtues, can't keep me or himself awake.[77]

Hodgson lived on and prospered and never forgot nor ceased to be grateful to his "Dearest Friend." When the executors tried to collect Byron's "loan" to him, he wrote to Hanson that "my very kind friend the late Lord Byron did not consider me his debtor and that I am not so either legally or morally." [78] And there the matter rested. But he was not ashamed to admit that Byron had given him in all £1600. Hodgson became in 1836 Archdeacon of Derby and in 1840 Provost of Eton, where he died on 29 December 1852. His reverend son edited his *Memoir* in two volumes, including many of Byron's letters, genteelly expurgated. Fortunately a number of the manuscripts have survived.

NOTES

1. Thomas Moore, *Prose and Verse* (London, 1878), p. 425.
2. *Byron's Letters and Journals,* ed. Leslie A. Marchand (London: John Murray, 1973 ff.), I, 179. (Hereafter referred to as *B's L and J.)*
3. Changed in later printings to the less suggestive "Without the wish of dwelling there."
4. From the MS. in the Milton S. Eisenhower Library, The Johns Hopkins University. Quoted by permission.
5. 18 November 1808; *B's L and J,* I, 176.
6. 21 March 1809; Murray MSS. Byron might not have been amused so much at the practical joke on Scott at a later time when he had met and liked the man. But Hodgson was aware that in *English Bards* Byron wrote stingingly of *Marmion.* All Murray manuscripts are quoted by permission of Mr. John Murray.
7. 16 November 1808; Murray MSS.
8. 27 November 1808; *B's L and J,* I, 179.
9. 21 April 1809; Murray MSS.
10. 16 July 1809; *B's L and J,* I, 215.

11. 6 August 1809; *B's L and J,* I, 216-217.
12. *B's L and J,* I, 241.
13. Murray MSS.
14. Leslie A. Marchand, *Byron: A Biography* (New York: Alfred A. Knopf, 1957), I, 245.
15. *B's L and J,* I, 253-254.
16. 29 July 1810; *B's L and J,* II, 6.
17. 16 August 1810; *B's L and J,* II, 10.
18. 25 September 1810; *B's L and J,* II, 15.
19. 4 October 1810; *B's L and J,* II, 18-20.
20. 14 November 1810; *B's L and J,* II, 27.
21. 20 January 1811; *B's L and J,* II, 37.
22. Volage Frigate at Sea, 29 June 1811; *B's L and J,* II, 54.
23. 7 July 1811; *B's L and J,* II, 58.
24. *Memoir of the Rev. Francis Hodgson, B. D.,* By his son, the Rev. James T. Hodgson, 2 vols. (London, 1878), I, 180.
25. Hodgson, *Memoir,* I, 181.
26. *B's L and J,* II, 77.
27. 31 August 1811; Murray MSS.
28. 3 September 1811; *B's L and J,* II, 89.
29. 10 September 1811; Murray MSS.
30. 9 September 1811; *B's L and J,* II, 95.
31. 13 September 1811; *B's L and J,* II, 97-98.
32. [September 1811]; Murray MSS.
33. 18 September 1811; Murray MSS.
34. 25 September 1811; *B's L and J,* II, 105-106.
35. 10 October 1811; *B's L and J,* II, 110.
36. His friend Robert Bland, who had taken a post as chaplain in Holland, had now returned to England.
37. 17 November 1811; Murray MSS.
38. 16 November 1811; *B's L and J,* II, 129-130.
39. The Rev. A. C. L'Estrange, *The Literary Life of the Reverend William Harness* (London, 1871), pp. 12-13.
40. 29 January 1812; *B's L and J,* II, 159.
41. 10 February 1812; *B's L and J,* II, 162.
42. [28 January 1812]; *B's L and J,* II, 159.
43. 16 February 1812; *B's L and J,* II, 163.
44. 31 January 1812; Murray MSS.
45. *B's L and J,* II, 164.
46. 5 March 1812; *B's L and J,* II, 167.
47. Murray MSS.
48. Murray MSS.
49. Murray MSS. On Byron's affair with Lady Oxford, see David V. Erdman, "Lord Byron as Rinaldo," *PMLA,* 67 (March 1942), 189-231.
50. 3 [January] 1813; *B's L and J,* III, 7.

51. Murray MSS.
52. Hodgson, *Memoir,* I, 272. Byron wrote to Henry Drury on 18 Oct. 1814, recalling that journey to Oxford: "do you recollect our ribaldry?" *(B's L and J,* IV, 214.)
53. [October-November?] 1813; Murray MSS.
54. 15 November 1813; Murray MSS.
55. 2 March 1814; Murray MSS.
56. 22 April 1814; Murray MSS.
57. 10 July 1814; Murray MSS.
58. 3 August 1814; *B's L and J,* IV, 151-152.
59. 1 August 1814; Murray MSS.
60. 1 August 1814; *B's L and J,* IV, 148-149.
61. Murray MSS.
62. 6 September 1814; Murray MSS.
63. 18 October 1814; *B's L and J,* IV, 214.
64. 20 October 1814; Murray MSS. One may wonder what would have happened if Annabella had married Francis Hodgson.
65. 19 November 1814; Murray MSS.
66. 29 April [1815]; *B's L and J,* IV, 291.
67. 19 February 1815, 3 April 1815; Murray MSS.
68. Augusta and Hodgson commiserated with each other on Byron's impious and shocking later poems. She wrote to Hodgson on 17 April 1819 about *Don Juan:* "This new poem, if persisted in, will be the ruin of him, from what I can learn." *The Works of Lord Byron: Letters and Journals,* ed. Rowland E. Prothero (London: John Murray, 1900), IV, 276. (This edition is hereafter cited as *LJ.)*
69. [12? February 1816]; Hodgson, *Memoir,* II, 25.
70. *B's L and J,* V, 131.
71. *B's L and J,* V, 235.
72. 18 May 1819; *B's L and J,* VI, 134. Byron's acerbity may have arisen from the fact that Hodgson's dedication was to the Duke of Rutland, a son-in-law of Lord Carlisle.
73. 22 December 1820; *B's L and J,* VII, 252-253.
74. 11 February 1821; Murray MSS.
75. *LJ,* V, 282.
76. 12 May 1821; Hodgson, *Memoir,* II, 76. Two days before, Byron wrote to Murray: "Why don't you republish Hodgson's Childe Harold's Monitor?"
77. 20 September 1811; *B's L and J,* II, 102-103.
78. 15 September 1824; Murray MSS.

"That Last Infirmity of Noble Mind": Keats and the Idea of Fame

Aileen Ward

In October 1818 Keats wrote to Richard Woodhouse in some embarrassment to retract a rash statement he had made the month before, at the time the first blast against *Endymion* had appeared in *Blackwood's.* After thanking Woodhouse for his kind letter in response to the recent *Quarterly* attack, Keats reassured him that he had no real intention of giving up poetry, as he had announced in a despondent moment in September, then added, "The faint conception I have of poems to come brings the blood frequently into my forehead." Thanks to Christopher Ricks, we have become alert to all the fine shades of embarrassment in Keats's work—blushing and glowing and burning, warming and mantling and reddening. This admission to Woodhouse is a special case, however—an example not of blushing but of flushing, not with embarrassment but with honorable aspiration.[1] The embarrassment is rather on our side. We blush for Keats at the naïve confessions of ambition strewn through his early poems and letters—his artless longing for "posterity's award," "the laurel wreath on high suspended, / That is to crown our name when life is ended," or his fantasied quest for "Wings to find out an immortality." We catch an obsessive note in his recurrent mention of the pantheon of poets to which he aspires—"the laurell'd peers" he imagined looking down on him from the clouds of sunset. To Henry Stephens, his medical-school roommate in 1815-1816, Keats let it be known that poetry was "the only thing worthy the attention of superior minds"; poets were "the greatest men in the world," he informed Stephens, and to rank among them was "the chief object of his ambition." His "thirst for glory" became so extreme at this time that he reportedly told his brothers that if he did not succeed he would kill himself.[2] Even after the publication of his first volume of poems, when success came to seem within his grasp, his ambition was not yet slaked. "How great a thing it is [to be a Poet]," he exclaimed to Hunt as he began writing *Endymion,* "how great things are to be gained by it,—What a thing to be in the mouth of Fame!" Somehow we feel these remarks must be explained away—perhaps as the brashness common to upwardly mobile young men of talent, or as the overassertions of unselfconfident adolescence, or, in more Keatsian terms, as the expressions of a very young man who will soon have the fine point taken off his soul. We prefer to recall his modesty, his realism, his irony: the Keats who, on hearing that he was to be invited to a literary party to celebrate Shakespeare's birthday, remarked "Shakespeare would stare to see me there"; the Keats who once suggested that his friends honor his memory by drinking a dozen of claret upon his tomb.

If young writers today think about being among the English poets after their death, they do not talk about it, much less write poems about it. Indeed the word "greatness" seems to have disappeared from the critical vocabulary in the last fifty years, ever since Eliot stated that the critic's proper task is "not to assign rank, but to discriminate quality." Yet our discomfort with the idea of greatness—to say nothing of the notion of immortality—may be a sign of loss as much as of gain: the dimming of that "habitual vision of greatness" which, Whitehead once said, is essential to education, perhaps even to civilization itself. Keats's unabashed resolve to "be among the greatest" may seem less of an embarrassment when viewed in the context of certain cultural assumptions with which we have lost touch. In his own time, or certainly within the century preceding it, such striving for fame would not be regarded ironically or defensively, as today, but as the necessary concomitant to any real achievement. The desire for the esteem of one's contemporaries, or what is now termed "approbativeness," was viewed by the Enlightenment as the driving force behind culture, even though rooted in human pride rather than reason. As Pope put it,

> Virtue's ends from vanity can raise,
> Which seeks no int'rest, no reward but praise.[3]

From La Rochefoucauld, with his anatomizing of *l'amour propre* and *la gloire,* through Mandeville with his view of pride as the origin of virtue, to Immanuel Kant, who saw the desire for esteem as the instrument of man's moral evolution, the pursuit of individual glory was justified as socially valuable.[4] Indeed it was widely held in the later seventeenth and the eighteenth century that approbativeness was the only motive in social conduct—"ingeniously implanted in man by his Creator as a substitute for Reason and Virtue, which he does not possess," according to Sir Richard Blackmore, and thus "necessary for the good order of society and the progress of mankind."[5] The idea then modulated into the nineteenth-century novel with Stendhal and Balzac and their myth of the young man winning his way up the ladder of worldly power, to fade in our time into the debased lingo of "making it."

Throughout the eighteenth century, of course, this view of human motivation had its opponents, and the countervailing ideal of disinterestedness found one of its last and staunchest supporters in Keats's mentor William Hazlitt. With Hazlitt, if not before, the possibility of disinterested action became linked with the imagination as its ethical goal, thereby transforming the imagination from one of the faculties into "the great instrument of moral good," as Shelley described it in *The Defence of Poetry.* In his *Treatise on Morals* Shelley attempted to rescue the pursuit of glory from its supposed root in pride and to claim it for the cause of the disinterested imagination. Citing the examples of three legendary heroes of Roman history who endured torture and death for their city's sake, he insisted that even if they had sought posthumous fame they were not moved by considerations of "private interest": some of the greatest heroes, he pointed out, "have even defied infamy for the sake of good." "There is a great error in the world with respect to the selfishness of fame," Shelley continued.

> It is certainly possible that a person should seek distinction as a medium of personal gratification. But the love of fame is frequently no more than a desire that the feelings of others should confirm, illustrate, and sympathize with our own. In

> this respect it is allied with all that draws us out of ourselves. It is the "last infirmity of noble minds." [6]

The phrase from *Lycidas* leads us back to the point just before the notion of fame became embroiled in the controversy over the necessary interestedness of all human action. Milton, for all his humanistic faith in man's ethical nature, gave only qualified approval to the approbative impulse:

> Fame is the spur that the clear spirit doth raise
> That last infirmity of noble mind
> To scorn delights, and live laborious days.

When the desire for praise is uprooted from the "mortal soil" of this world and translated to "fame in heaven," it is fully justified; but in this life it remains a kind of honorable weakness. Yet in viewing it as an infirmity of the noble mind in particular, Milton looks back to an earlier tradition which more readily ascribed virtue to worldly fame, the Renaissance concept of the glory to which the poet may aspire: an idea derived from the Horatian assurance that the society whose values the poet proclaims will reward him with a fame more lasting than that of other men. Horace's boast that the greatest heroes of a nation are dependent on the poet to transmit their renown is a theme on which the Elizabethan poets were to play countless variations. In Shakespeare's Sonnets, for instance, it swells from the reassurance to his beloved that his beauty will never die—

> So long as men can breathe, or eyes can see,
> So long lives this, and this gives life to thee. . . .

to the proud assertion *(Exegi monumentum aere perennis)* of his own immortality:

> Not marble, nor the gilded monuments
> Of princes, shall outlive this powerful rhyme. . . .

But this vision of poetic greatness includes more than the self-assurances of triumphant artistry: it rises to the belief, perhaps more Christian than classical,[7] but even more remote to us today, that the great poet is such not by his special skill or insight alone but by nobility of character as well. As Milton stated in the *Apology for Smectymnuus,* the man who hopes to write well of "laudable things" ought "himself to be a true poem." By this definition the great poet has a triple responsibility—not only to delight and to instruct but also to persuade, to move men to wise and noble action not merely by presenting just examples of characters for imitation but by manifesting justice in his own character, by being himself (as Milton said) "a pattern of the best and honorablest things."

For almost any young poet this view of greatness must raise it—as Keats wrote to Hunt in the spring of 1817—"monstrously beyond [his] seeming power of attainment": and poetry since Milton has been one long descent from such a level of aspiration. W. J. Bate has shown how acutely, among writers of his own time, Keats was aware of the burden of the past. Yet we might also recall that Keats—who seems from his letters to have done weight lifting as a form of exercise ("using dumb bells on a rainy day")—once described his study of philosophy as "trying myself at lifting mental weights." If the example of the past was a burden, it was also a challenge, and Keats may be counted fortunate as one of the last heirs of the Renaissance idea of greatness. From the start of his career, Keats veered back and forth between a sense of humility before true greatness—"a cowering under the wings of the great poets," as he once put it, or "awe at [his] own strange pretense" in daring to follow in their footsteps—and a confident squaring up to the example they set him. The writing of the four thousand lines of *Endymion* was one such test—"Did our great Poets ever write short Pieces?"—which he counted on to take him a certain number of paces "towards the Temple of Fame." At first his steps were "all uncertain": "The high Idea I have of poetical fame," he wrote to George Keats, "makes me think I see it towering to high above me." Yet the anxiety he felt at the start of this endeavor was not only generated by his attempt to measure himself against the greatest models but also partly assuaged by them. On the day he finally began writing *Endymion* he opened his copy of Spenser and found a good omen in the first lines his eyes lighted on:

"The noble Heart that harbors vertuous thought,
And is with Child of glorious great intent,
Can never rest, until it forth have brought
Th' eternal Brood of Glory excellent—"

A few weeks later, his work had gone well enough that he let himself fancy Shakespeare as a good genius presiding over him, and he started a confident letter to Haydon telling him of his progress by invoking Shakespeare's own defense of "the pursuit of Honor":

Let Fame, which all hunt after in their Lives,
Live register'd upon our brazen tombs,
And so grace us in the disgrace of death:
When spite of cormorant devouring time
The endeavor of this present breath may buy
That Honor which shall bate his Scythe's keen edge
And make us heirs of all eternity.

Yet in setting "honor" as his "prime object" Keats was not engaging in a kind of Homeric *aristeia* or struggle to be first in the race. Rather he hoped only to "be among the greatest," "among the English poets": and from the start his longing for recognition was joined with a characteristically generous acknowledgment of the achievement of others. "The genius-loving heart" of the Epistle "To George Felton Mathew" spoke of the pleasures of their "brotherhood in song" and invoked their favorite poets in a spirit of "reverence." The memory of great men, Keats remarked several years later, is the only thing to which he will humble himself—along with "the Eternal Being [and] the Principle of Beauty." Throughout his early poems Keats's boyish hero-worship echoes in the recurrent roll calls of "great spirits," not only poets but political figures—from Brutus and Alfred to Kosciusko, from Homer to Wordsworth and Leigh Hunt. He prophesies the victory of Hunt's "immortal spirit" over the "wretched crew" of his jailers in the unsullied fame which he will enjoy long after their deaths. In a letter to Haydon of May 1817 he wrote that the thought of his friend's fame "will be a chief Pleasure to me all my life." Indeed fame is such a certain good to Keats at this stage that he will not begrudge it even to a man whose politics he deplores, the Duke of Wellington: "A Man ought to have the Fame he deserves." But even more characteristic is the twist he gives to the idea of fame in his first sonnet to Haydon of November 1816. The "glorious affection for the cause / Of stedfast genius" shown by the "unnumber'd souls" breathing out "their still applause" for Haydon bespeaks a "highmindedness" in the public which Keats himself applauds. Bestowing fame is thus seen as benefiting those who give it as well as those who receive it.

This easy confidence that a man not only should but indeed will have "the Fame he deserves" must have been somewhat shaken by the faint praise his *Poems* received in the spring and summer of 1817. It was seriously jarred that autumn with the opening of *Blackwood's* campaign against the Cockney Poets, which threatened to lampoon Keats through his association with Hunt months after he had withdrawn from that discipleship. For the first time Keats became aware of the force of literary politics intervening in the ideal relationship between poet and audience in which he had previously trusted. Still more depressing was the onset of Tom's illness that winter, bearing with it the possibility of his own. As it suddenly appeared that the ambitious program he had announced in "Sleep and Poetry" might be cut short years before he fulfilled it, his dreams of fame sank "to nothingness." In such a mood, he told Bailey, he would "refuse a petrarcal coronation": and as Tom grew worse the very thought of fame began to seem "a crime." But it was his dissatisfaction with *Endymion* while revising it in the spring of 1818, and his anxiety over the treatment it seemed likely to receive from the Tory critics, that finally extinguished his hope for immediate recognition. Now the public came to seem "an Enemy": a "thousand jabberers about Pictures and Books" loomed up between him and the readers he had sought, the men "who look with a zealous eye to the honour of English literature." This mingled attitude of bitterness and scorn for "that most vulgar of all crowds, the literary" was to intensify in the months ahead, at times driving him into "a qui bono temper" when there seemed no point to "writing poems and hanging them up to be flyblown on the Reviewshambles," at other times stirring up a "Pride and Obstinacy" with which he felt he could "refuse the poisonous suffrage of a public" even while it was in his power to win it. "Just as much as I am hu[m]bled by the genius above my grasp," he wrote his publisher John Taylor in August 1819, "am I exalted and look with hate and contempt upon the literary world."

Some such disillusionment awaits every young writer, of course. Yet it is striking to note the loss of the sense of a literary community, in which the serious writer could identify more or less readily with his contemporary audience, in the forty or fifty years since Johnson had expressed his willingness to concur with the common reader and defer to the general suffrage. Keats's feeling of hate and contempt for the literary world, conjoined with his respect for his imagined readers, is a curious echo of Wordsworth's distinction between the Public and the People at the end of his 1815 *Essay Supplementary to the Preface* (which Keats undoubtedly had read). With the hostile reception of his own work at the back of his mind, Wordsworth assailed the local and transitory acclamation and "factitious influence" of the Public, which cries up the extravagant and superficial, in contrast to "that Vox Populi which the Deity inspires," the more lasting judgment of the People, through whose wisdom alone great poetry survives.[8] The *Essay* may also have opened Keats's eyes to the fact that both Shakespeare and Milton found far fewer readers in the seventeenth century than a score of far lesser poets. It soon became clear to Keats, once he surmounted his disappointment with *Endymion,* not only that fame in his own time was not the inevitable reward of the great poet but that it could be an irrelevance or worse—"a cloying treacle on the wings of independence." Partly this was the result of his growing independence and maturity of judgment: "Praise or blame," he wrote to Hessey after the worst of the reviews of *Endymion* had appeared, "has but a momentary effect on the man whose love of beauty in the abstract makes him a severe critic on his own works." And in some part this insight may have been sharpened by the experience of his pilgrimage to Burns's birthplace in the summer of 1818, where he was appalled by the cant and "flummery" commemorating a poet who had been miserably undervalued in his lifetime. "O smile among the shades," he exclaimed in his sonnet to Burns, "for this is fame!"

But the dissociation of the ideas of fame and greatness must also be related to Keats's ongoing effort to define the true nature of genius, a project to which he was apparently impelled by his first disillusionment with Haydon in the autumn of 1817. Keats had already sensed the factitiousness of Leigh Hunt's claim to poetic stature—perhaps as a result of Hunt's unfortunate insistence one evening that spring that they actually crown each other with laurel "after the fashion of the elder Bards" and write sonnets on their sensations. "There is no greater Sin after the 7 deadly," Keats wrote Haydon afterward, "than to flatter oneself into the idea of being a great Poet." But it was his growing insight into Haydon's own egotism that precipitated the distinction he made in November 1817 between Men of Genius, who "are great as certain ethereal Chemicals operating on the Mass of neutral intellect—[but] have not any individuality, any determined Character," and Men of Power, who "have a proper self." This distinction—an interesting anticipation of Hazlitt's characterization of Shakespeare in his *Lectures on the English Poets*—was to generate Keats's contrast between Shakespeare and Coleridge on which he based his definition of Negative Capability in December 1817; it was then to be elaborated in his later description to Woodhouse of the poetical character ("that sort of which, if I am any thing, I am a Member") as "every thing and nothing," having "no character," "no self" of its own, but "continually infor[ming] and filling some other Body"—in contrast to "the wordsworthian or egotistical sublime, which is a thing per se and stands alone." Wordsworth as well as Haydon, Keats had discovered in the interim, was given to displays of power, imposing his "proper self" not only on his audience but on his creations, "bullying" his reader and "peacocking" over his speculations till he had stamped them with his own image "in a false coinage." But true poetry—Shakespeare's Sonnets, for instance—is "unobtrusive" in its greatness: it enters the reader's soul and startles it "not with itself but with its subject," as the true poet analogously disappears into the creatures of his imagination. Hazlitt's description of Shakespeare in his February 1818 lecture as "nothing in himself, but . . . all that others partly were, or could become" touched a chord that echoed in Keats's letters for months afterward; he must also have been struck by Hazlitt's statement, in the same lecture, that Shakespeare "had no love of fame." Thus the "humility and capability of submission," the ability to "annul self" in order to take part in the existence of others which Keats was beginning to identify as the source of his own poetic strength, was increasingly linked in his mind with the abjuration of fame. His valediction was announced in two sonnets "On Fame" in April 1819, where he describes Fame as a wayward girl to be repaid "scorn for scorn," or as a ripe plum fingering its own misty bloom; a temptation to the poet to "rob his fair name of its maidenhood" or, still worse, to "spoil his salvation for a fierce miscreed."

So Keats came to realize that to aim at immediate recognition from the public was to lose all chance "to be among the greatest," and that the true poet must learn to endure uncertainty and neglect, even ridicule, in his lifetime. The vision of the "godlike hardship" of great art that had overcome him on first seeing the Elgin Marbles in March 1817 grew in his mind from the "turmoil and anxiety" that must accompany any great plan brought to its conclusion—as he learned in working on *Endymion*—to "the dark passages" which the great poet must explore as the price of his insight into the human condition. So his view of Shakespeare—as always his touchstone—changed gradually from the poet living in gusto, delighting equally in Iago and Imogen, to the "miserable and mighty Poet of the human Heart," who had been "trampled aside into the bye paths of life and seen the festerings of Society." "The english have produced the finest writers in the world," he explained to Mary-Ann Jeffery[9] in June 1819, because "the English world has ill-treated them during their lives and foster'd them after their deaths." Some such understanding of the cost of ultimate recognition—as well as the calm assurance that *Hyperion,* which he had recently begun, would win it—was in his mind in October 1818 when he dismissed the *Quarterly*'s devastating review of *Endymion* as "a mere matter of the moment" and added, "I think I shall be among the English Poets after my death."

This relinquishment of immediate fame for ultimate immortality may appear to be the final transformation of Keats's early ambition, one that links him firmly with those "heirs of all eternity" who had given him heart at the outset of his career. Keats held to the hope of writing a work that would make his friends proud of his memory and (in Fanny Brawne's words) "rescue his name from the obloquy heaped upon it," till the last despairing months of his illness.[10] Still this longing for ultimate renown betrays the approbative impulse. It is at best the secular equivalent of Milton's "fame in heaven," analogous to the secular scheme of salvation through soul-making: not a vindication of his work by the ultimate Critic, but admission into the ranks of "the laurell'd peers" Keats had dreamed of at the start of his career. Although "the living pleasures of the bard" he envisaged in the Epistle "To My Brother George" had proved an illusion, his faith in "posterity's award" sustained him till almost the end. Yet at the same time there are hints scattered through his poems and letters of 1818 and 1819 that Keats was working toward a more profound conception of poetic greatness uniquely his own, one going beyond both Shakespeare and Milton, transcending personal glory in the quest of disinterested achievement. This is not to imply that he reached any final "resting place and seeming sure point" in his thinking on the subject, a clear-cut synthesis of previous antinomies. With his distrust of "consequitive reasoning," his belief that the mind should be a thoroughfare for all ideas, Keats resists being boxed into a neat dialectical progression. Nevertheless, we can trace in his speculations on the nature of greatness a gradual shift of attention away from the poet himself to the poem, or to society at large, or (in a crucial narrowing of focus) to the reader.

Keats's first reaction to the *Quarterly*'s attack on *Endymion* was to withdraw—like Shakespeare's snail shrinking back "into his shelly cave with pain"—into a kind of aesthetic isolation, in which the creation of the poem itself becomes the sole locus of value. This state of "solitary indifference to applause even from the finest spirits" was the most constructive defense he could mount against criticism: in this state, as he wrote Woodhouse in October 1818, he felt assured he would continue to write "from the mere yearning and fondness I have for the Beautiful even if my night's labours should be burnt every morning and no eye ever shine upon them." Such total self-sufficiency strikes a new (and, as it turned out, temporary) note in Keats's poetic, though dedication to the principle of beauty is of course a recurrent theme. The previous summer, his first response to the English Lakes had been a resolve that now more than ever his writing would endeavor "to add a mite to that mass of beauty which is harvested from these grand materials, by the finest spirits, and put into etherial existence for the relish of one's fellows." A similar sense of fellowship with his audience in the self-justifying creation of beauty appears in the ode "To Maia," composed the previous month, in which in effect he put behind him the disappointment and apprehension with which he had sent *Endymion* off to the press. Those Greek bards who died content, "Leaving great verse unto a little clan," would, he hoped, teach him their contentment to be "Rich in the simple worship of a day." But in the autumn of 1818, as his imagined audience narrowed from "few ears" to "no eyes," he found a sublimity in solitude itself: as his imagination strengthened, he wrote George, he felt he lived "not in this world alone but in a thousand worlds." Or, as he put it to Reynolds in August 1819, "The Soul is a world of itself and has enough to do in its own home." Yet the idea of "great verse" as an end in itself, of beauty as a self-sufficient good, raised an almost immediate doubt of its own validity in Keats's mind. This ranged from the mild scepticism he expressed to Bailey in March 1818 of thinking poetry "a mere Jack a lanthern to amuse whoever may chance to be struck with its brilliance," to his scathing self-indictment in a letter to Haydon a year and a half later: "I have done nothing—except for the amusement of a few people who refine upon their feelings till anything in the ununderstandable way will go down with them." The all-consuming dedication to poetry of the previous extraordinarily productive summer—"Poetry is all I care for, all I live for"—came to seem "an idle-minded, vicious way of life" in the fall of 1819.

It is not simply that what Lionel Trilling once described as the "genial" side of Keats's nature could not long be satisfied with such solitude, however creative. There was a deeper demand to be met, one reaching to the bedrock of Keats's character: the need to be of service to others, if not through art then through action of some kind. This pervasive impulse appears as early as his Epistle "To My Brother George," in which he suggests that by renouncing his "mad ambition" in poetry—presumably to continue in his medical career—he would be "Happier, and dearer to society." A year and a half later, at the height of his admiration for Haydon and Wordsworth, Keats could condemn it as a kind of vanity in himself to speak of works of genius as "the first things in the world." Rather, he insisted, the "probity and disinterestedness" with which he still credited his friend Bailey held "the tip top of any spiritual honors"—just as, in the summer of 1819, he qualified his extravagant admiration for *Paradise Lost* by stating that fine writing took second place to fine doing as "the top thing in the world." Pushed to the choice, he wished to be praised "not for verses, but for conduct." Part of his dissatisfaction with *Endymion* in the spring of 1818, we can surmise, sprang from the reawakening of the motive toward disinterested service to others in nursing Tom through the early stages of his illness. It is at this point that the theme of what Keats repeatedly called "ambition" begins to be sounded in his work: an ambition very different from his earlier preoccupation with literary fame. "I find there is no worthy pursuit but the idea of doing some good for the world," he wrote Taylor, a statement echoed the following autumn in his letter to Woodhouse: "I am ambitious of doing the world some good." This ambition was never clearly defined except as an alternative to poetry: sometimes it seems to have been writing on philosophical or political topics—"the road lies through application study and thought"; sometimes, it appears, serving actively in the continuing struggle for freedom after Waterloo. Keats remarked jokingly to Reynolds in the spring of 1818 that he would "jump down Aetna for any great Public good"; more soberly he spoke to Bailey of "placing my ultimate in the glory of dying for a great human purpose."

We catch the note here of Keats's earlier acclamation of the martyrs for human freedom such as Sidney, Russell, and Vane; but the exemplar he had clearly in mind at this time was Milton—"an active friend to Man all his Life"—who for over a year was to replace Shakespeare as his chief model for emulation. Keats had already begun his close study of *Paradise Lost* in preparation for *Hyperion,* and was apparently reading Milton's "delectable prose," as he ironically described it to James Rice—impelled, perhaps, by Hazlitt's quotation in his February lecture of a long and eloquent passage from *The Reason of Church Government.* Milton's ambition to prove himself "anything worth to [his] country" finds an echo in Keats's mention, in the summer of 1818, of "the glory of making by any means a country happier." Certainly there is a strong sense of identification with Milton in one of the notes Keats penned into his copy of *Paradise Lost* at about this time: that Milton would have been content in cultivating his "exquisite passion for poetical Luxury . . . if he could, so doing, have preserved his self-respect and feel of duty performed." In the performance of that duty Milton had interrupted his career in poetry to serve as Cromwell's Latin Secretary—perhaps an example of what Keats had in mind when he remarked, in comparing Milton and Wordsworth, that "a mighty providence subdues the mightiest minds to the service of the time being." And perhaps the thought of Milton was also in Keats's mind when in September 1819 he announced his own intention of giving up poetry to "write on the liberal side of the question." This project soon proved abortive, yet it was not uncharacteristic: Keats had evidently entertained at least a passing thought some months before of joining Lord Cochrane's expedition to South America to fight for Chilean independence.[11] It is also characteristic that Keats could see the temptation to vanity in such heroics. "There are many Madmen," he remarked in his October 1818 journal to George, "who would like to be beheaded on tower Hill merely for the sake of eclat, . . . but there are none prepared to suffer in obscurity for their Country." The quest of a truly disinterested "human purpose" remained elusive—"the work of maturer years," as he described it to Woodhouse at this time: in the interval he would "assay to reach to as high a summit in Poetry as the nerve bestowed upon me will suffer." The most enviable happiness, he thought, would be to fuse these impulses, "the yearning Passion I have for the beautiful, connected and made one with the ambition of my intellect."

This was also the need to bring into focus his two conceptions of the *raison d'être* of poetry, to work out in his mind what "great human purpose" could be served by the poet in his specific function—not so much as a man speaking to men within their shared social context, in "the service of the time being," but more particularly as poet speaking to reader across boundaries of time and space. Milton had been an active friend to man all his life, Keats wrote to Rice, but also "since his death": *Paradise Lost* might stand as the supreme example of what Keats called "the Benefit done by great Works to the 'Spirit and pulse of good' by their mere passive existence." Not a great name, then, but an enduring influence is what the poet should hope to achieve. The nature of the good to be done through "great Works" is suggested by the animizing imagery in which Keats speaks not only of the poet but of the poem, the work of art, as "a friend to man"—one "to soothe the cares and lift the thoughts of man," as he put it in "Sleep and

Poetry." The poem is thus no mere artifact, "a thing of beauty," but possesses a kind of human identity, is indeed a "soul" which the dead poet leaves behind on earth. This idea of the poem as a living and speaking presence articulates the possibility of that "direct communication of spirit" which is the closest Keats could come to a belief in "immortality of some nature or other." So, after Tom's death, he suggested to George in America that they each read a passage of Shakespeare every Sunday at ten o'clock and thus "be as near each other as blind bodies can be in the same room." In the ode on "the double immortality of poets" which he wrote at this time, Keats declares that the poets' "earth-born souls still speak / To mortals of their little week," and thus may "teach us every day / Wisdom though fled far away." Even the silent form of the Grecian urn, by a more complicated process of stirring up questions within the viewer and "teasing" him into an answer, can "say" a message "to the spirit."

Yet Keats was rightly distrustful of poetry "with a palpable design upon us," which "if we do not agree, seems to put its hand in its breeches pocket": and the manner in which the poem teaches was crucial. In "Sleep and Poetry" he resolved not to "insult" the spirit of his reader by telling him "what he sees from native merit." Just as "Man should not dispute or assert but whisper results to his neighbor," the poem with a similar trust and tact should provide a series of "ethereal finger-pointings" for the reader by which he may be led to create within his own mind the imaginative experience which the poem is in essence. As Keats wrote Taylor in February 1818, poetry "should strike the Reader as a wording of his own highest thoughts, and appear almost a Remembrance." Poetry is thus no one-way process running from poet to reader but a transaction, in which the poet in Socratic fashion calls forth some poetic potential within the reader himself. We may count Keats fortunate, among other things, in the progressive schooling he received: at least the Clarkes' most famous pupil took with him an idea of education as a drawing out of knowledge, not a flogging in. "Many have original Minds who do not think it," he wrote Reynolds in his beautiful letter of 19 February 1818; and poetry should foster this originality in the manner suggested by his image of an old man and a child talking together as they walked, with "the old Man led on his Path, and the child left thinking." The metaphorical density of Keats's letters, which often requires as much imaginative activity on the reader's part as that of his poems, may be viewed as another expression of the requirement that the reader collaborate in the poetic process: so Keats concluded another letter to Reynolds, "If you think for five minutes after having read this you will find it a long letter." Thus the reader of the great poet who seeks to "understand [him] to his depths," as Keats did Shakespeare, will in a kind of reflexive action enter into the soul of the poet and be rewarded with a sense of communion with him, as Keats was with Shakespeare his Presider.

The "self-annulling" character of the poet as teacher, or of poetry which startles the reader "not with itself but with its subject," is implicit in the catalytic image of his earlier definition of Men of Genius as "certain ethereal Chemicals operating on the Mass of neutral intellect": in this view the poet transforms his audience while remaining invisible, "nothing in himself" as Hazlitt said. The nature of this transformation is suggested more clearly, however, in another strain of imagery recurrent in Keats's writing, in which he speaks of the poet not as remaining catalytically unchanged in the process but as ingested and assimilated by his readers as they draw nourishment from his work. In an early sonnet he himself describes his favorite poets as "the food / Of my delighted fancy," and in April 1818 he wrote Reynolds of his longing "to feast upon old Homer as we have upon Shakespeare, and as I have lately upon Milton." That this ingestive imagery was no dead metaphor appears from the sonnet on "The Human Seasons" (first version), where in the summer of his intellect man is said to

> . . . chew the honied cud of fair spring thoughts
> Till, in his Soul dissolv'd, they come to be
> Part of himself.

This ruminative process which is the essence of ideal reading is described at length in the February 19th letter to Reynolds. "A certain Page of full Poesy or distilled Prose" becomes the starting post for the reader's own voyage of conception; like the spider filling the air "with a beautiful circuiting," the reader "spins from his own inwards his own airy Citadel" of thought, tipping his web on a "few points" of the page before him. This "dissolving" of the poem in the imagination of the reader is no irreverence to the writer, Keats insists, but rather a demonstration of that "Benefit done by great Works . . . by their mere passive existence": for thus "by every germ of Spirit sucking the Sap from mould ethereal every human might become great, and Humanity instead of being a wide heath of Furse and Briars with here and there a remote Oak or Pine, would become a grand democracy of Forest Trees." In this dazzling fusion of images of spiritual nutrition and spiritual politics Keats suggests the vitally reciprocal relationship not only between the poet and his reader, but also between the poet and the tradition he is nourished by and helps in turn to create. The ideal community of the mind is a great ecosystem in which each organism lends vitality to all the others and eventually to the soil from which they all spring. And in the democratic emphasis of this image Keats strikes out his most characteristic definition of great poetry: by liberating the imaginative capacity in every man it acts to make every human great, making him as it were "more of an artist."

This definition, framed in a rare moment of creative calm and self-possession in February 1818, seems to have weathered the vicissitudes of uncertainty and self-dissatisfaction of the following year and a half to emerge as a dominant motive in Keats's last work. *The Fall of Hyperion* explores, among other things, the nature of the imaginative community between the poet and the ordinary man. For this theme to emerge, however, something was required to bridge the abyss which had opened up between Keats and his imagined readers in the latter part of 1818, some recovery of his earlier faith in his audience—not in the Public but in the countervailing force of the People, or what Keats had called his "fellows." The events of the summer and fall of 1819—the Manchester Massacre and Henry Hunt's triumphal entry into London in September, which Keats witnessed—seem to have effected this change. Writing to George in mid-September about "the present struggle in England of the people" against Government repression, he stated, "This is no contest between whig and tory—but between right and wrong." Evidently it was this resurgence of political concern that precipitated Keats's brief resolve to "write on the liberal side of the question"; more than this, the sight of thirty thousand people lining the London streets to welcome Henry Hunt revived his earlier idea of the "unnumber'd souls" ennobled by their applause of great art. "I am certain any thing really fine will in these days be felt," Keats wrote to Haydon a few weeks later. "I have no doubt that if I had written Othello I should have been cheered by as good a Mob as Hunt." In such a mood of renewed faith in the people he began recasting his epic of *Hyperion* as a dream-vision.[12]

The central theme of the new version is the transformation of the poet from mere dreamer to a "sage" and "humanist"—like "the human friend Philosopher." "Humanize" (II.2) may be taken as a key term for the poet's development from dreamy self-absorption to full awareness of "the giant agony of the world," in which he may join those "slaves to poor humanity" who "labour for mortal good." While the first version showed the youthful Apollo transformed into a god of poetry by a sudden access of divine power, *The Fall of Hyperion* portrays a much more protracted process, one that links the poet with his fellow mortals in all the pain and uncertainty of human growth. The induction, however ambiguous it may be on the precise status, ethical or metaphysical, of dreams, asserts unequivocally the universality of the dreaming faculty, of the gift of imagination itself. The visionary capacity is shared by "every man whose soul is not a clod"; the fully humanized poet, though set apart from other men by his gift of language, achieves the stature of greatness as the result not of a unique identity or special insight but of his ability to share "the miseries of the world," to take part in all other human existence. The manner in which this imaginative participation may work "for mortal good" is suggested by the climactic definition of the poet as "physician to all men." Bearing the freight of all Keats's early dedication to a medical career and the never-quite-resolved guilt he felt at giving it up, this image conveys the selfless concern of the being who has learned to confront human suffering in its fullest extent and, moved but not disabled by it, act somehow to ease it. This quality of interested disinterestedness is most memorably imaged in the gaze of Moneta, Keats's symbol of the superhuman consciousness that could sustain, as the merely mortal poet could not, the awareness of human history as the totality of human pain. Looking down from immense perspectives of time on the human drama, her "planetary eyes" (unblinking as a star's) filled with tears, Moneta provides an image of seeing "as a god sees" to the poet striving for insight into the human condition. To see in this fashion is not only to achieve a kind of immortality of the imagination in this life, as the poet moves beyond the limits of his own time and place into "a thousand worlds," but also to live on after death as an embodiment of the racial memory, the teller of those truths which other men sense without being able to speak them but will not willingly let die. It is significant that the act by which the dreamer-poet of *The Fall of Hyperion* is transported from the isolated garden of sensuous delight to the august Temple of Saturn with all its wreckage of human history, is a pledge which he drinks to "all the mortals of the world, / And all the dead whose names are in our lips": "that full draught," he tells us, was "parent of my theme." By recognizing his kinship with every man who has ever lived on earth, great or forgotten, by learning to share each man's dreams and help him confront his anguish, the poet is at last "fitted for verses fit to live" and becomes a sage and humanist, a friend to man.

So Keats conveys his final idea of great poetry as encompassing the awareness of all past experience standing behind and giving meaning to the present, and of all living beings in their struggle to make their souls within this world of painful circumstance. It was an insight that took on meaning only as Keats himself developed and the boundaries of his own imaginative experience widened. But not only did his growing apprehension of human experience transform his own poetry and his insight into the nature of poetry itself; his developing notion of greatness in poetry and what it demanded of the poet shaped his own selfhood. Few things are more characteristic of Keats than his attempt to sum up the meaning of his life in the face of the blank future that confronted him at the beginning of his last illness in February 1820. "I must make myself as good a Philosopher as possible," he wrote Fanny Brawne. " 'If I should die,' said I to myself, 'I have left no immortal work behind me—nothing to make my friends proud of my memory—but I have lov'd the principle of beauty in all things, and if I had had time I would have made myself remember'd.' Thoughts like these," he added, "came very feebly whilst I was in health and every pulse beat for you—now you divide with this (may *I* say it?) 'last infirmity of noble minds' all my reflections." It is a touching parenthesis, that "May *I* say it?" The thought of the great name which he had struggled to win and finally (as he now believed) had failed to attain, returned with the remembrance of Milton and his struggle in *Lycidas* to surmount the temptation of worldly fame. The irony with which Milton had admitted to "that last infirmity" spurred Keats to his last and finest *aristeia,* in which he disclaimed comparison with Milton's greatness even as he vied with him in self-annulling irony. It is a nobility of mind such as Keats believed the great poet could teach, and a final proof—if we need one—of the double immortality of poets.

NOTES

1. Ricks mentions this passage on page 162 of *Keats and Embarrassment* (Oxford: Clarendon Press, 1974) as a manifestation of "creativity," an example of the connection Keats sensed between physiological and artistic creation—a connection made explicit by William Howitt in his remark (in 1847) on Keats's "vivid orgasm of the intellect" (in *Keats: The Critical Heritage,* ed. G. M. Matthews [New York: Barnes & Noble, 1971], p. 311; quoted by Ricks, p. 160). But the tone of the statement to Woodhouse is more aggressive and emulative than erotic—like "the burning and the strife" which left Keats's forehead "hot and flushed" on seeing a lock of Milton's hair.
2. *The Diary of Benjamin Robert Haydon,* ed. Willard Bissell Pope (Cambridge: Harvard University Press, 1960), II, 107. The phrase "athirst for glory" occurs in the sonnet on "The Floure and the Leafe", l. 11.
3. *Essay on Man,* II, 245-46.
4. See A. O. Lovejoy, *Reflections on Human Nature* (Baltimore: Johns Hopkins University Press, 1961), Lecture IV: "Approbativeness as the Universal, Distinctive, and Dominant Passion of Man."
5. *An Essay upon False Vertue* (Dublin, 1716), p. 22; quoted by Lovejoy, p. 164.
6. *The Complete Works of Percy Bysshe Shelley,* ed. Roger Ingpen and Walter E. Peck (London: Ernest Benn, 1926-1930), VII, 76.
7. It originates, however, in Plato *(Republic,* iii. 400) and was echoed by Strabo: cf. M. H. Abrams, *The Mirror and the Lamp* (New York: Oxford University Press, 1958), p. 229.
8. *Poetical Works,* ed. Thomas Hutchinson, rev. Ernest de Selincourt (London: Oxford University Press, 1936), p. 953. Cf. also Hazlitt's remarks in his lecture "On the Living Poets" (which Keats heard on 3 March 1818): "Fame is the recompense not of the living, but of the

dead. . . . Those minds which are the most entitled to expect it, can best put up with the postponement of their claims to lasting fame" *(Works,* ed. A. R. Waller and Arnold Glover [London: J. M. Dent, 1906], V, 143-144).

9. So Robert Gittings corrects the identification of the recipient of Keats's letter of 9 June 1819 in his edition of *Letters of John Keats* (London: Oxford University Press, 1970), p. 402, n. 5.

10. As Donald Reiman has suggested, it is both ironic and touching that the work which, more than any other, was to keep Keats's name alive for the first quarter-century after his death was Shelley's *Adonais,* and that this tribute was based on an idea of the poet's immortality very close to Keats's. This is not just a matter of verbal coincidence, such as Shelley's description of Keats's fame as "a light unto eternity" (st. 1) echoing the phrase "a light unto posterity" in Keats's letter to Hunt of May 1817. Shelley's conception of "the thorny road" which the poet must tread "through toil and hate, to Fame's serene abode" (st. 5) and, still more, of the eclipse of the poet's reputation by lesser lights during his lifetime, to be followed by his emergence among "the immortal stars" after his death (st. 29, 44), is strikingly similar to Keats's insight into the cost of true achievement and of the difference between immediate and ultimate recognition.

11. Cf. the cryptic statement by an anonymous correspondent ("Y") in *The Morning Chronicle* of 27 July 1821 that Keats once intended to go to South America and "write a Poem on Liberty" (quoted by M. B. Forman, ed., *The Letters of John Keats* [London: Oxford University Press, 1952], p. 488 n.); also Keats's own remark in a letter to Dilke that he had two choices before him—"South America or Surgeon to an Indiaman" *(loc. cit.).* The date of Keats's letter is uncertain: Forman assigns it to May 1820, while Rollins less convincingly conjectures June 1819 *(The Letters of John Keats,* ed. H. E. Rollins [Cambridge: Harvard University Press, 1958], II, 114). The correspondent in *The Morning Chronicle* has been identified by Leonidas M. Jones as Keats's school friend Edward Holmes, and the conversation which Holmes records in his letter dated early in September 1820, when Holmes paid a visit to Keats just before he left for Italy ("Edward Holmes and Keats," *Keats-Shelley Journal,* 23 [1974], 119-128). Jones prints "Y's" letter in full and discusses it in detail; he dismisses the reference to South America, however, as "a sort of conventional daydream of adventurous escape" out of *Robinson Crusoe,* concocted by Keats to amuse his old school friend (p. 122). But contemporary readers of *The Morning Chronicle* would immediately connect the reference to South America and the cause of freedom with the daring and successful naval campaign in the Chilean War of Independence organized and led by Lord Cochrane from 1818 to 1821. On Thomas Cochrane, tenth Earl of Dundonald—a hero of the Napoleonic War, radical M.P. from Westmin-

ster, later commander of the Brazilian and the Greek fleets in their Wars of Independence, and leader of the movement for reforming the British Navy—see *Dictionary of National Biography.* By 1821 Cochrane's name had become a byword for courageous and decisive action—as in Byron's remark in a letter to John Murray castigating Bowles for abusing Hobhouse: "I will cut him out, as Cochrane did the Esmeralda" *(Letters and Journals of Lord Byron,* ed. R. E. Prothero [London: John Murray, 1922], V, 299). The *Esmeralda* was a Spanish frigate destroyed by Cochrane in a raid on Callao on 5 November 1820.

12. Leonidas M. Jones has recently challenged the traditional dating of *The Fall of Hyperion,* assigning the first 326 lines to September and October of 1818 ("The Dating of the Two *Hyperions,*" *Studies in Bibliography,* 30 [1977], 120-135). There is not room here to reply to Professor Jones's article, which I hope to do in another place. I am still convinced that a careful examination of all the evidence will assign *The Fall of Hyperion* neither to the fall of 1818 nor to the summer of 1819 (as in the three recent biographies of Bate, Bush, and Gittings), but to September through November or December 1819 (as Brown indicated: cf. *The Keats Circle,* ed. H. E. Rollins [Cambridge: Harvard University Press, 1948], II, 72) and that the *Hyperion* which Keats told Reynolds he had given up on 21 September 1819 (the same day he wrote Woodhouse quoting with evident satisfaction three passages from *The Fall* as though they were new), was in fact the first *Hyperion.* See my *John Keats: The Making of a Poet* (New York: The Viking Press, 1963), p. 433, n. 3 and p. 434, n. 15 for a summary of the evidence on this question; also pp. 313-314, 325-328, 338-341. To the reasons there given for this dating might be added the well-known fact of Keats's "unsteady & vagarish disposition"—"a creature of fits and starts," as Hessey called him (Edmund Blunden, *Keats's Publisher: A Memoir of John Taylor* [London: Jonathan Cape, 1936], p. 56). Keats may have silently changed his mind a few weeks later about giving up *Hyperion* (if in this remark he meant to indicate the revised version), just as he silently abandoned the journalism project. The record of the letters, we need constantly to remind ourselves, is incomplete.

"On Fishing Up the Moon": In Search of Thomas Love Peacock

William Walling

In a bowl to sea went wise men three,
  On a brilliant night of June:
They carried a net, and their hearts were set
  On fishing up the moon.
    ("The Wise Men of Gotham," *Paper Money Lyrics*)

Sooner or later anyone who embarks on a study of Thomas Love Peacock seems certain to risk foundering on two treacherous issues—the unusual nature of his reputation and the peculiar elusiveness of his personality. Fortunately, the unusual nature of Peacock's reputation requires a good deal less space to chart than his elusiveness. As an early reviewer remarked prophetically in 1829, as though mapping out the existence of a cultural iceberg, Peacock is a writer "whose general popularity bears the most insignificant proportion to the esteem in which he is held by the thinking portion of the reading public." [1] Thus, to confine ourselves only to the past half-century, three of the most prominent figures in the practice of literary criticism during that period—Edmund Wilson, F. R. Leavis, and Northrop Frye—have each found his own characteristic reason for praising Peacock highly. For Wilson, Peacock's prose style is "one of the best in English"; [2] for Leavis, in a book whose opening chapter casts dozens of established novelistic reputations back into the sea as so many minnows, Peacock remains safely and impressively over the limit, a writer whose works possess "a permanent life . . . for minds with mature interests"; [3] while for Frye, Peacock can be seen as someone who, from the perspective of Frye's own theory of genres, is as "exquisite and precise" in his kind of fiction as Jane Austen is in hers.[4]

Yet despite such praise, the size of Peacock's readership—in comparison to, say, Jane Austen's—surely remains small.[5] Moreover, a good deal even of that smaller readership probably finds its impulse for reading Peacock in reasons more scholarly and historical than aesthetic. To quote from the *Survey of English Literature* that Oliver Elton wrote nearly sixty years ago, Peacock's novels are "part of the comment of the 'romantic period' upon itself; we cannot fully understand it without them." [6] Or, to restate Elton's point more generally, part of the unusual nature of Peacock's reputation resides in what might be called his "reactive" quality: rather than being a writer who participates in creating the prevailing tone of the age, Peacock at his best provides an illuminating counterweight to its dominant characteristics. Hence, Ian Jack, in a survey a good deal more recent than Elton's, draws essentially the same conclusion Elton did, remarking that Peacock "is the great satiric commentator on the [Romantic] age . . . the Aristophanes of the period." [7] And this reactive conception of Peacock can clearly be taken further, for Howard Mills has recently argued that "Peacock's relationship to Shelley" is the key to his importance: "the friendship *made* Peacock," Mills writes; "it was the central fact in his development, the central condition of his quality." [8]

Unfortunately, whatever the merits of this latter approach (and surely it has many, including the creation of a richer context for the study of Peacock), the too-ready application of it does seem to relegate Peacock quite precipitously, as in Mills's treatment of him, to the limited role of a distinctly "minor" writer. What I intend to do in this paper, then, is to remain as faithful as I can to the kind of critical attitude reflected by Wilson, Leavis, and Frye—to grant, that is, as much primacy as possible to Peacock himself, without attempting to define him too quickly in terms of his apparent antitheses to Romantic themes and assumptions.

At the same time, to state my intention in such a fashion is to bring me inevitably to the second problematic issue involving

Peacock—his elusiveness. As G. D. Klingopulos observed some years ago, the lament concerning Peacock's "elusiveness" is a commonplace among his critics.[9] Thus Meyer Abrams, in commenting upon the ideas expressed in "The Four Ages of Poetry," warns that Peacock simply "cannot be pinned down" to an unambiguous position.[10] Similarly, Carl Dawson, in his impressive full-scale critical assessment of Peacock, points out how "for the most part" Peacock neatly "eludes" his first considerable biographer, Carl Van Doren.[11] Yet soon after this judgment even Dawson himself must concede that what is really needed with a writer as "elusive" as Peacock is "a fuller and richer study" of the biographical problems (p. 147). Unhappily, as Dawson also indicates, the materials for such a study are probably non-existent (pp. 139-147).[12]

Nor is all of this meant to suggest merely that Peacock, like any other writer of distinction, possessed a complex personality. On the contrary, the man whose obituary in the *Athenaeum* accorded him a high place in the "ultra-liberal literature" of the nineteenth century but whose two-column entry some twenty years later in the *Encyclopaedia Britannica* displayed an uneasiness about his "too earnest conservatism" is a subject who presents something more than an ordinary difficulty for his critics.[13] Indeed, Peacock's propensity for eliciting even the most extreme of contrasting judgments about him could easily be extended beyond the sphere of politics.

At its most comical, perhaps, we might initiate our own contrast by first considering the short-lived "career" Peacock had in the navy when he was in his early twenties. Placed in an important position aboard the H.M.S. *Venerable* through family influence (Peacock's maternal grandfather and two uncles had had distinguished naval careers of their own), Peacock found the ship a "floating Inferno," where he was "completely out [of his] element" (I, pp. xv-xvi, VIII, p. 162).[14] So uncongenial for Peacock was life aboard the *Venerable,* in fact, that at the end of his initial appointment he chose to abandon ship for good and begin a series of walking tours across the English countryside, as if to reassert his adherence to dry land in as concrete a fashion as he could (VIII, 167 ff.). Yet the episode, like a page torn from the libretto of the *Pinafore,* eventually disclosed its Gilbert-and-Sullivan-like ironies:

in later life, during the course of his distinguished career for the East India Company, Peacock played a highly important role in the development of steam navigation; was credited (at least according to family tradition) with being "the first man to say that iron would float"; and was paid the ultimate compliment of being told by his cousin that a pilot named "Bright" (who had made the sea his own career) "always thought 'Mr. Peacock was meant for an Admiral' " (I, clxxii, VIII, 487).

As for the more serious contrasts to be found in Peacock, one in particular offers itself as highly suggestive: the problematic nature of Peacock's relationship to some of the central tenets of utilitarianism. Consider, for example, the striking contrast to be found between the figurative judgments on "progress" in "The Four Ages of Poetry," Peacock's best-known essay, and those in *Gryll Grange,* his last and, possibly, finest novel. In "The Four Ages," as few of us who profess some aspect of literary studies are likely to forget, Peacock subjects the representative nineteenth-century "poet" to a sustained comic vilification, describing him as a "semi-barbarian" whose "march of intellect is like that of a crab, backward," all the while that "mathematicians, astronomers, chemists, moralists, metaphysicians, historians, politicians, and political economists" are steadily advancing "towards perfection" (VIII, 11, 20-21, 24). In *Gryll Grange,* however, it is this general "progress of intellect" and the overall "march of mind" which now get themselves likened to the "crab" of Hamlet's mad speech *(Ham.* II. ii. 207), as supposedly progressive "intellect" and the so-called "march of mind" continue to pursue their "backward" direction through the nineteenth century (V, ii).

Since it was around the very notion of "progress" that one of the most revealing divisions took place concerning the value of utilitarian ideals (a fact John Stuart Mill early pointed to in his remarkable essay of 1838 on Jeremy Bentham [15]), the contrast in Peacock's work would seem to indicate a significant change in his attitude towards utilitarianism. Yet the reversal in the *application* of an imaged pattern of thought is perhaps even more suggestive than the reversal of the judgment itself. For it hardly suffices merely to point out that essay and novel are separated by forty years ("The Four Ages" first appeared in *Ollier's* in 1820, *Gryll Grange* in *Fraser's* in 1860). Rather, the striking manner of Peacock's reversal—in which, as we have seen, precisely the same figurative pattern is used to indicate opposing judgments—deserves its own attention for what it suggests about the radical flexibility of his intelligence. In other words, the apparent change in Peacock's attitude towards "progress" may be a good deal less meaningful for his critics than the concomitant suggestion the change gives of a paradoxical integrity of verbal pattern coexisting with a seeming indifference to evaluative norms.

One further example from the same two works should clarify this particular aspect of Peacock's intelligence. In "The Four Ages of Poetry," in what is perhaps the most outrageous of several outrageous passages concerning the absolute worthlessness of poetry for a truly rational society, Peacock presents an indictment replete with metaphors drawn from infancy and childhood: "Poetry was the mental rattle that awakened the attention of intellect in the infancy of civil society: but for the maturity of mind to make a serious business of the playthings of its childhood, is as absurd as for a full-grown man to rub his gums with coral, and cry to be charmed to sleep by the jingle of silver bells" (VIII, 22). Yet in *Gryll Grange,* in one of the Reverend Dr. Opimian's many sweeping diatribes against contemporary civilization, the very cornerstone of a rationalistic faith in the improvement of society—as well, in truth, as the very heart of utilitarianism itself [16]—is condemned for reflecting nothing more than the essence of childishness: " 'Science is one thing, and wisdom is another. Science is an edged tool, with which men play like children, and cut their fingers' " (V, 186).

Unavoidably, then, the question of Peacock's "elusiveness" should concern every serious student of his work. For the habit of mind Peacock displays in this relatively early essay and this distinctly late novel—with their complementary indication of a capacity for the complete inversion of figurative judgments—suggests an extraordinary suppleness of sensibility on Peacock's part. (I stress "suppleness" as a deliberate rejection of indecisiveness: G. D. Klingopulos' claim that Peacock was constitutionally unable to arrive at "judgments of any finality" [17] seems to me thoroughly disproved both by Peacock's life and by his career.) Moreover, the subject of utilitarianism itself, which I have taken as a prototype of the difficulty of attaching Peacock firmly to any one ideological position, surely invites some further consideration in terms of the problematic relationship between romantic individualism (the subject of so much of Peacock's finest satire) and *laissez-faire* individualism (perhaps the central motive force, as so many commentators have suggested, for the success of the utilitarian creed in the nineteenth century [18]). What I propose for the remainder of this paper, therefore, is an approach to Peacock which I hope will make him a little more accessible to students of the nineteenth century. And since his relationship to utilitarianism has been my theme for the past several paragraphs, it probably will come as no surprise that my approach will also be attempting to relate Peacock to a rather longer period of literary history than one commonly encapsulated by the term "Romantic."

To begin, then, I turn to the poem which has already furnished me with both epigraph and title for my paper—"The Wise Men of Gotham," one of the *Paper Money Lyrics* Peacock first published in 1837. In this comic ballad (the sixth in the series), three obviously none-too-clever men set to sea in a bowl, hoping to fish up the moon. They sail on for some time, carried along by the current—until at last, when they are "Far, far at sea," they cast their net at the bright, round "prey" that has been glistening in the water:

And at the throw, the moon below
  In a thousand fragments flew.

The sea was bright with the dancing light
  Of a million million gleams,
Which the broken moon shot forth as soon
  As the net disturbed her beams.
(VII, 119-20)

No doubt the light-hearted parody of *The Rime of the Ancient Mariner* is evident enough (Peacock in fact lists "S. T. C., Esq., Professor of Mysticism" as the poem's ostensible author). But although, as a *Paper Money Lyric,* the even more central economic satire of "The Wise Men of Gotham" soon emerges—the "wise men three" are, in reality, "paper-money men," and the breaking up of "the imaged moon" is only a symbol for the "breaking of the bank"—I should like to seize upon the images of fragmentation I've quoted for a purpose a good deal more serious than any Peacock intended.

For, in truth, the concept of fragmentation itself ought to loom larger in any study of Peacock's work than it presently does. Consider, for one thing, the preface Peacock wrote in 1837 for the reissue of four of his novels *(Headlong Hall, Nightmare Abbey, Maid Marian,* and *Crotchet Castle)* in Volume LVII of Bentley's Standard Novels. There, in that preface, he pointed to the kind of "people" who inhabited his fiction:

> Perfectibilians, deteriorationists, statu-quo-ites, phrenologists, transcendentalists, political economists, theorists in all sciences, projectors in all arts, morbid visionaries, romantic enthusiasts, lovers of music, lovers of the picturesque, and lovers of good dinners . . . (I, 2).

Clearly, such a list implies a highly cerebral basis to Peacock's art. But it also puts into a rather different perspective his repeated mockery—from at least 1831 onward—of "the march of mind." Thus, a representative early Victorian like Tennyson might, as he did in his first public appearance as poet laureate in 1852, celebrate the nineteenth-century's fond vision of a "raw world" being magisterially transformed into moral grandeur by "the march of mind" ("Ode on the Death of the Duke of Wellington," l. 167). But Peacock, more than twenty years earlier (in *Crotchet Castle)* had already depicted another kind of rawness as it collided head on with that same "march of mind"—disclosing, in the process, the danger that the "raw world" unwittingly ran of being overcooked:

> "God bless my soul, sir!" exclaimed the Reverend Doctor Folliott, bursting, one fine May morning, into the breakfast-room at Crotchet Castle, "I am out of all patience with this march of mind. Here has my house been nearly burned down, by my cook taking it into her head to study hydrostatics, in a sixpenny tract, published by the Steam Intellect Society, and written by a learned friend who is for doing all the world's business as well as his own, and is equally well qualified to handle every branch of human knowledge." (IV, *CC,* 13)

And this farcical send-up of a century's faith in the developing majesty of "mind" receives its extended (now far more serious) orchestration in *Gryll Grange.* Indeed, one of the many sustained attacks in Peacock's last novel upon the so-called progressive advance of man's intellectual capabilities is probably today the most frequently cited passage from all his work, suggesting as it does not only an obvious "relevance" for our own time but a kind of eerie anticipation of the later Lewis Mumford as well:

> "Look at our scientific drainage, which turns refuse into poison [once again Dr. Opimian is the speaker]. Look at the subsoil of London, whenever it is turned up to the air, converted by gas leakage into one mass of pestilent blackness, in which no vegetation can flourish, and above which, with the rapid growth of the ever-growing nuisance, no living thing will breathe with impunity. Look at our scientific machinery, which has destroyed domestic manufacture, which has substituted rottenness for strength in the thing made, and physical degradation in crowded towns for healthy and comfortable country life in the makers. The day would fail, if I should attempt to enumerate the evils which science has inflicted on mankind. I almost think it is the ultimate destiny of science to exterminate the human race." (V, 187)

"Mind divorced from its traditional moorings," in short, might not be a bad way of describing the *un*-ironic underside to Peacock's witty deflations of the "march of mind." But more than that. For it might also be argued that the divorce of mind itself is the implicit donné of a good deal of Peacock's finest art, with "mind" in his novels usually presented as comically on the "march," in an absurdly diversified lock step of fragmented opinions. As one of the first reviewers of *Crotchet Castle* complained: "What [Peacock] shows are not characters, but *abstractions* of the follies of conceit." [19]

Of course much of what I've been claiming so far is meant to apply primarily to Peacock's first four novels of "talk"—the four, that is, which he had already published by the time of his 1837 preface for Bentley's: *Headlong Hall* (1815), *Melincourt* (1817), *Nightmare Abbey* (1818), and *Crotchet Castle* (1831). As for the other two novels of his which had appeared by that date—*Maid Marian*

(1822) and *The Misfortunes of Elphin* (1829)—their uncertain mixture of historical trappings and intermittent topicality removes them from the area of my chief concern. (It's also worth adding, at least in parentheses, that both of these latter books are notably less interesting as works of art than the four novels of "talk," despite the occasional triumphs of each, such as the brilliantly achieved Seithenyn ap Seithyn of *The Misfortunes of Elphin.)* Similarly, *Gryll Grange* (1861), although emphatically a novel of "talk," and (with *Nightmare Abbey)* one of Peacock's two thoroughly complete successes in the field of fiction, is a book whose beautifully balanced tone of autumnal mellowness and astringency achieves an effect substantially different from the other four novels.

But the idea of fragmentation which Peacock presents so comically in "The Wise Men of Gotham"—with the "imaged moon" shattering into "a millions gleams"—finds its semi-serious analogue in Peacock's work well before he wrote his preface for Bentley's Standard Novels. In *Headlong Hall,* Squire Headlong takes us on a tour of his grounds pointing out " 'the pedestal of a statue, with only half a leg and four toes remaining.' " Evidently, the shattered statue must once have been a Greek divinity, for elsewhere on the grounds " 'Neptune has been lying these seven years in the dust hole; Atlas had his head knocked off to fit him for propping a shed; and only the day before yesterday we fished Bacchus out of the horse-pond' " (I, 29-30). In *Nightmare Abbey,* Mr. Glowry speaks warmly to Mr. Cypress at his prospect of soon seeing " 'many a one-legged Venus and headless Minerva [during his tour of the Continent]—many a Neptune buried in sand—many a Jupiter turned topsy-turvy—many a perforated Bacchus doing duty as a water-pipe' " (III, *NA,* 101). And in *Rhododaphne* (1818), Peacock's last serious attempt at a long poem, the opening of the third canto presents us with a vision of a world from which all divinities have departed (along with the spiritual coherence their worship once supplied):

> In ocean's caves no Nereid dwells:
> No Oread walks the mountain-dells:
> The streams no sedge-crowned Genii roll
> From bounteous urn: great Pan is dead:

The life, the intellectual soul
Of vale, and grove, and stream, has fled
For ever with the creed sublime
That nursed the Muse of earlier time.
(VII, 29-30)

It would be easy enough, no doubt, to apply these passages solely to Peacock's sense of the unfortunate decline in the modern world's respect for Greek wisdom and art. After all, a man who could give names like *Pluto* and *Proserpine* to the first iron warships ever built, who made a habit of questioning new employees at the East India Company on "their classical proficiency," and who was known as "Greeky-Peaky" to the noted Platonist Thomas Taylor (I, xcviii, clxxi, clxxiii) is obviously a man whose attachment to the classical world is not to be lightly dismissed. Furthermore, in his unfinished "Essay on Fashionable Literature" (1818), Peacock virtually identifies true philosophical knowledge with the rigorous study of the classics (VIII, 272)—an identification he approximates soon afterwards in a letter to Shelley (VIII, 203)—while in both essay and letter he laments the contemporary indifference to classical studies.

Nevertheless, a deeper application of Peacock's several references to fallen and shattered divinities seems justified. He might—and of course did—write to Shelley with approval of the "mighty axe" which "Bentham has laid . . . to the root of superstition" (VIII, 206); a passage in *The Misfortunes of Elphin* can ridicule, almost as a foregone conclusion, the total inefficacy of the Christian religion in bringing about the moral improvement of mankind (IV, *ME,* 106); an early reviewer of *Gryll Grange* might point with justice to the "fine Pagan morality" of the novel, suggesting that its author seemed able to think "only as men thought before Christianity awoke them to the consciousness of sin, of suffering, and of immortality" (I, cci); and a remark attributed to him by Trelawny—"Ah, Trelawny, don't talk to me about anything that has happened for the last two thousand years!" (I, cxcvii n.)—can take on an unexpected resonance when we recall that the statement actually suggests (along with whatever else) the cancellation of the entire history of Christianity.[20]

But Peacock was much too intelligent an observer not to

perceive that the "intellectual soul" of nineteenth-century England, was, if not "fled," then at least in the process of a radical kind of transformation—however much he himself might approve of the "mighty axe" which was being laid "to the root of superstition." Indeed, his own passionate commitment to the study of Greek surely suggests at times the ardor of a near-religion.[21] Thus, as Squire Crotchet unwittingly indicates (and not merely by his name), the first decades of the nineteenth century have ushered in a whole new set of "intellectual" commitments, with few of them any longer bearing a discernible relationship to the ordinary concerns of Christianity:

> "The sentimental against the rational, the intuitive against the inductive, the ornamental against the useful, the intense against the tranquil, the romantic against the classical; these are great and interesting controversies, which I should like, before I die, to see satisfactorily settled."
>
> (IV, *CC,* 22)

And the intensity of the conflicts among these various abstract commitments is assured by the fact that, as Mr. Cranium puts it in *Headlong Hall,* "*his own system* is of all things the dearest to every man of liberal thinking and a philosophical tendency" (I, 146; my emphasis)—so much so that, as Sir Telegraph Paxarett remarks in *Melincourt,* in reply to an impassioned argument for the moral necessity of altruism, " 'Be that as it may, every man will continue to follow *his own fancy*' " (II, 44; my emphasis).

We have a traditionally serious name for what Peacock is comically suggesting, of course. And if "solipsism" is much too weighty a term to describe the ludicrous insulations of intellect which "talk" in Peacock's fiction, then the emphasis I have chosen to give the last two quotations may still remind us of one of the great moral and philosophical themes of the period—the potential of the imagination to transcend that sense of "subjective" isolation which rationalism implies in an "objective" world. For although Peacock enjoyed mocking the very notion of "subjective" and "objective" as a pair of pretentious German imports,[22] he would surely have been amused by the manner in which one of the most famous attempts at resolution of the subject-object dualism in all of later "romantic" philosophy—Kierkegaard's claim in his *Concluding Unscientific Postscript* of 1846 that "truth is subjectivity"—lends itself ironically to illuminating the characteristic Peacockian novel.

What I have in mind in particular is the large number of emphatically "subjective" eccentrics who inhabit Peacock's fiction. Onward from the first page of his first novel, *Headlong Hall,* in fact, we are never very far (at least in the first four novels of talk) from a pattern of these distinct "subjectivities" repeatedly colliding with one another "like two billiard-balls"—to borrow Peacock's own simile for the slapstick tumble Scythrop and Toobad take down the stairs in *Nightmare Abbey* (III, 25). Accordingly, by the second paragraph of *Headlong Hall,* we have already made our entry into a universe of continual, comic disputation. "A lively remark, that *the day was none of the finest,* having elicited a repartee of *quite the contrary,* the various knotty points of meteorology . . . were successively discussed and exhausted" (I, 5). And the continuing "lively" nature of all of this is assured, as I have already suggested, by the very discreteness of the minds engaged in the discussion, for of the four men who are on their way to Squire Headlong's country seat, one is a "perfectibilian," another a "deteriorationist," another a "statu-quo-ite," and the last "neither a philosopher nor a man of taste," save for his near-obsession with the table (I, 8-9). In brief, then, Peacock's characteristic strategy is to present us with a broad range of "subjectivities" (the more pronounced of them under the guise of comic monomaniacs), all of them coming up short against one another's crotchets in the course of the witty conversations that comprise so much of the "action" of his novels.

But more than that, if we continue to keep the spirit of Kierkegaard's aphorism in mind that "truth is subjectivity." For the really distinguished achievement of Peacock's fiction is to create an effect quite different from the apparent disparateness of its parts. As Edmund Wilson observed some thirty years ago, in his fine little essay on Peacock: "It is usual to treat him as a satirist whose power is more or less weakened by his scoring off both sides of every question; but the truth is that Peacock is an artist the aim of whose art is to achieve not merely a weaving of ideas but also an atmosphere—an aroma, a flavor, a harmony."[23] And it is exactly in this—the "harmony" of effect which so many of Peacock's best critics have noted in the novels—that we encounter a suggestive correspondence to the role "truth" plays in Kierkegaard's aphorism.

To be sure, the peculiar "truth" which is Peacock's is a good deal more self-authenticating than it can possibly be for a writer so morally conscious as Kierkegaard. Nevertheless, out of the fragmentation of a culture from which he clearly perceived the gods had departed, Peacock was able to distill a series of wonderfully self-contained little comic worlds of his own, peopling them with the obsessional splinters of consciousness that his own dispassionate intelligence had revealed to him as one of the signal consequences of a post-Christian "march of mind." To rephrase Kierkegaard's aphorism, then, in the light—or shadow—of Peacock's most characteristic fiction: "Truth" (that is, the realization of an aesthetic balance in which nothing is felt to be wanting) was achieved by Peacock through a paradoxical reliance on the extreme "subjectivities" of his comic gallery, the apparent discretenesses of which he was able to resolve, at his surest, into festive harmony by the close of the novel.[24]

From having reached such a point, however, we can perhaps see our way a little more clearly back to the problematic relationship between romantic and *laissez-faire* individualism in Peacock's work, not to mention the issue of his "elusiveness" with respect to utilitarian ideas.

We know, for example, how susceptible Peacock's best-known essay "The Four Ages of Poetry" might be to an interpretation as a utilitarian indictment of poetry—were it not for the essay's own unmistakable ironies of excess:

> The highest inspirations of poetry are resolvable into three ingredients: the rant of unregulated passion, the whine of exaggerated feeling, and the cant of factitious sentiment. . . . It can never make a philosopher, nor a statesman, nor in any class of life a useful or rational man. It cannot claim the slightest share in any one of the comforts and utilities of life of which we have witnessed so many and so rapid advances.
>
> (VIII, 21)

Furthermore, to consider these ironies more closely is surely to realize how many of Peacock's most striking effects in "The Four

Ages" reside precisely in this: his ability to create the tone of a maddeningly self-assured disciple of Bentham, unwittingly undercutting the master's own dictum that "all poetry is misrepresentation" [25] by the patently exaggerated faith such a disciple holds in the magisterial power of "rational" analysis.

Doubtless the Swiftian manner of "A Modest Proposal" will come to mind.[26] Yet Peacock's ironies are still further complicated by two personal issues: his ambivalent attitude towards Shelley's high poetic claims (simultaneous with work on "The Four Ages" Peacock was disagreeing with Shelley over the merits of *The Cenci,* as well as correcting the proofs of *Prometheus Unbound)* and the no-doubt conscious surrender on Peacock's own part of any further serious poetic ambitions for himself (the same year which saw the composition of "The Four Ages" also witnessed the beginning of Peacock's full-scale employment in the East India Company, a choice of career which was to continue for almost another forty years). Indeed, the easy familiarity with the utilitarian mode of argument suggested by the essay receives an added dimension through our knowledge of the curious interrelationship Peacock had with the three leading figures of British utilitarianism in the nineteenth century. For not only did Peacock indicate in later life that he had been on "extremely intimate" terms with Jeremy Bentham (presumably in the 1820s), "dining with him *tête à tête,* once a week for years" (I, clxxv), Peacock's own twenty years as Examiner for the East India Company (from 1836 to 1856) were sandwiched between the tenureship of that same post by the two men who probably played the most significant role in the post-Bentham development of utilitarian principles in England—James and John Stuart Mill.[27]

Nevertheless, Carl Van Doren's characterization of Peacock as "the Court Jester of Utilitarianism" [28] really fails to do justice to the ultimate seriousness of Peacock's objections to certain aspects of the utilitarian creed. We can pass over, as an early aside, the narrator's regret in *Headlong Hall* for the deleterious effect caused by the land improvements at Tremadoc upon the natural beauty of the Welsh coast—however much those same improvements might be praised by others for their "probable utility" (I, 74). We can note as well, in an article Peacock wrote for the *Westminster Review* in 1827, the significance of his linking one of the critical cornerstones of utilitarianism to the philosopher from the classical world he himself held in highest esteem: "Thus Epicurus first taught, that general utility, or as Bentham expresses it, 'the greatest happiness of the greatest number,' is the legitimate end of philosophy" (IX, 48-49). And we can hardly avoid the even weightier evidence of Peacock's thirty-seven years in the East India Company—with all the practical demands and practical accomplishments of that distinguished career—as indicating anything other than a fundamental sympathy with many of the central assumptions of utilitarianism.[29] Yet with every bit of this granted, Peacock's fundamental dissent from the utilitarian creed of the nineteenth century remains.

Briefly, that fundamental dissent had its origins in Peacock's resistance to the economic theories which had begun to intertwine themselves from the late eighteenth century onward with the basic philosophic position of utilitarianism. By 1815, in fact, the year of Peacock's first novel *(Headlong Hall),* utilitarianism had already completed the essential transformation which was to make it so powerful an influence in England during the next half-century. To quote from Elie Halévy's useful assessment of the intellectual climate: "By 1815 the theories of Malthus had been incorporated by Ricardo into the classical tradition of political economy. But contemporaneously Ricardo's teaching was itself incorporated into an entire system of philosophy whose action upon British public opinion would be profound and lasting, the philosophy of Bentham and his school." [30] Or, to restate Halévy's argument from a somewhat longer perspective, the tradition of utilitarian philosophy, which had held an important place in English thought from at least the middle of the eighteenth century (with the advent of David Hume into prominence),[31] received an enormous practical impetus forward some fifty and more years later through its amalgamation with certain critical notions about the nature of economic reality—most particularly as those notions were expressed by three men, Adam Smith (whose *Wealth of Nations* appeared in 1776), Thomas Malthus (whose *Essay on Population* appeared in 1798), and David Ricardo (whose *Principles of Political Economy and Taxation* appeared in 1816).

Accordingly, there is probably something of a distortion in the way so many of us are inclined to approach the history of utilitarianism in the nineteenth century: from the vantage point of John Stuart Mill's well-known characterization of Jeremy Bentham as, along with Coleridge, one of "the two great seminal minds of England in their age." [32] Bentham, to be sure, did exert a decisive influence. But, as the brief assessment from Halèvy suggests, it was the *conjunction* of Bentham's ideas with those of the *laissez-faire* school of economists which conspired so significantly to enlarge the appeal of utilitarianism over the next fifty years. And it was precisely against this school of economists that Peacock directed some of his most committed satire. Hence, to take only one striking example, Peacock described the followers of Ricardo as "that arch class of quacks" in his preface to *The Paper Money Lyrics* (VII, 99)—although, as we know, he prudently delayed publication of the remark until after the death of Ricardo's particular friend and adviser, James Mill.[33]

The interrelationship between romantic and *laissez-faire* individualism, then, provides a helpful means of approaching so extended a career as Peacock's. Clearly enough, the swarming variety of human opinion was a cardinal comic fact for him. "In the questions which have come within my scope," we find him writing reminiscently in 1861, "I have endeavoured to be impartial, and to say what could be said on both sides. If I have not done so, it is because I could find nothing to say in behalf of some specific proposition" (VIII, 253). And because of this, the imperious claims for an individualized consciousness that surface so often in romantic art generally become, in Peacock's hands, ludicrously inflated absurdities, weightless "billiard-balls" as it were, filled with hot air. (Perhaps no one who has truly experienced the delights of *Nightmare Abbey* can ever approach a poem like *Alastor* or *Childe Harold* in quite the same spirit again.)

At the same time, Peacock's sense of a consuming self-interest perpetually present in human behavior, coupled with his scorn for human credulity and ignorance, probably helps to explain better than anything else the increasingly negative attitude he held towards the kind of optimistic—and atomistic—individualism assumed by a *laissez-faire* philosophy. Thus, to take only two examples from the 1830s, the decade in which Peacock first made unmistakable his public departure from a strict utilitarian creed, we find him speaking with contemptuous irony, in the narrator's voice of *Crotchet Castle,* of "the *rational principle* of [enriching] oneself at the expense of the rest of mankind" (IV, 2; my emphasis), while in the Preface of the reissue of his novels in Bentley's series we hear the dry, sad indictment of "the Right of Might" as the "great principle" which continues—and apparently will always continue—to dominate human relationships (I, 3). As for Peacock's final novel, *Gryll Grange,* the criticism of utilitarian optimisms is so pervasive there that the very structure of the work is built around a challenge to what Leslie Stephen would later define as "the great error" of utilitarianism—its "rejection of history." [34] For, as readers of *Gryll Grange* will recall, what little plot there is in the novel arises from Mr. Gryll's decision to present an Aristophanic comedy during the Christmas season, one in which the values of contemporary Victorian society will be confronted by a recently awakened sleeper from the classical past.

Consequently, the tension between Peacock's amused attitude towards the excesses of romantic individualism and his increased concern for the unfortunate social consequences of *laissez-faire* individualism can be taken as a general guide to an overall view of his very long novel-writing career. On the one hand (and not through Shelley alone) he wittily confronted what was the major psychological event of the age: the growing self-consciousness of the individual sensibility. On the other hand (and not through his distinguished career at the East India Company alone) he significantly participated in—and significantly dissented from—an extraordinary effective movement of social transformation which had at its basis an abstract insistence on greater individual autonomy. In both cases, however, the result was the growth of fragmentation in Peacock's sense of society.

His finest novels, then, are paradoxical creations of community in a contemporary world where the possibility of community no longer seemed to exist. And if we can list, with some real degree of probability, the various personal stratagems by which Peacock was psychologically able to preserve his capacity for evoking a universe of comedy out of a far more likely occasion for tears,[35] the conclusion to the body of this paper will undoubtedly be better suited by a reminder of the most compelling reason for remembering Peacock: out of the extraordinary flexibility of his imagination he was able to write two totally successful comedies—*Nightmare*

Abbey and *Gryll Grange*—each of which points toward the other end of the social tensions of the first half of the nineteenth century.

NOTES

1. *Athenaeum,* 6 May 1829; cited in *The Works of Thomas Love Peacock,* eds. H. F. B. Brett Smith and C. E. Jones, 10 vols. (London: Constable & Co.; New York: Gabriel Wells, 1924-1934), I, cxli-cxlii. This, the "Halliford" edition, will be the source of all citations from Peacock's work.
2. "The Musical Glasses of Peacock," *Classics and Commercials* (New York: Farrar, Straus, and Giroux, 1950), p. 406.
3. *The Great Tradition* (New York: New York University Press rpt., 1964), p. 9n. Almost a half-century before Leavis, Richard Garnett was already asserting that "few novelists have a better prospect of permanence," ed. *Thomas Love Peacock: Letters to Edward Hookham and Percy B. Shelley* (Boston: Bibliophile Society, 1910), p. 4.
4. *The Anatomy of Criticism* (1957; rpt. Princeton: Princeton University Press, 1971), p. 309.
5. I make this judgment based on the evidence of readily available paperback editions of Peacock: only *Nightmare Abbey* (usually reprinted with *Crotchet Castle)* seems to command a steady audience, and that quite possibly because of the reason I advance above, in the next sentence of my text.
6. Cited by Eleanor L. Nicholes, "Thomas Love Peacock," *Shelley and his Circle,* ed. Kenneth Neill Cameron, I (Cambridge: Harvard University Press, 1961), 106.
7. *Oxford History of English Literature,* X (1963), pp. 213-214.
8. *Peacock: His Circle and His Age* (Cambridge: Cambridge University Press, 1969), p. 1.
9. "The Spirit of the Age in Prose," *From Blake to Byron,* ed. Boris Ford (Hammondsworth: Penguin Books, 1962), p. 138.
10. *The Mirror and the Lamp* (1953; rpt. New York: W. W. Norton, 1958), p. 126.
11. *His Fine Wit* (Berkeley: University of California Press, 1970), p. 139.
12. Although Felix Felton suggests that he has written the "fuller" biography Dawson called for *(Thomas Love Peacock,* [London: George Allen & Unwin, 1973], p. 16), his study, among other disappointments, fails to confront the challenges posed by Dawson (cf. for example, Felton, p. 281, with Dawson, p. 147).
13. *Athenaeum,* 10 February 1866, p. 208; cited in Carl Van Doren, *The Life of Thomas Love Peacock* (1911; rpt. New York: Russell & Russell, 1966), p. 263. Richard Garnett wrote the entry for Peacock in the

ninth edition of the *Britannica* (reprinted, with little alteration, in the eleventh edition).

14. Further details concerning Peacock's one-year term aboard the *Venerable* can be found in Nicholes, *Shelley and his Circle,* I, 97.
15. "Bentham," rpt. *On Bentham and Coleridge,* ed. F. R. Leavis (New York: Harper & Bros., 1962), p. 40.
16. "What is known as Utilitarianism . . . can be defined as nothing but an attempt to apply the principles of Newton to the affairs of politics and of morals," Elie Halévy, *The Growth of Philosophic Radicalism,* trans. Mary Morris (New York: Macmillan, 1928), p. 6; cf. p. 5.
17. *From Blake to Byron,* p. 138.
18. Halévy, *Philosophic Radicalism,* pp. 500-501; Leavis, *On Bentham and Coleridge,* pp. 31-32; John Plamenatz, *The English Utilitarians* (Oxford: Basil Blackwell, 1966), pp. 110-111.
19. *The Examiner,* 3 April 1831; cited in *Works,* I, cli; my emphasis.
20. Cf. the exchange between Mrs. and Dr. Opimian in *Gryll Grange*—Mrs. O.: "I think, Doctor, you would not maintain any opinion if you had not an authority two thousand years old for it." Dr. O.: "Well, my dear, I think most opinions worth maintaining have an authority of about that age" (V, 63).
21. "I think my good old friend, if he had worshipped anything, would have been inclined to worship Jupiter, as it was said that [Thomas] Taylor did," Grant Duff, *Notes from a Diary;* cited in Van Doren, *Life of Peacock,* p. 130. In his younger years Peacock liked to call Hogg and himself "Athenians" because of their whole-hearted devotion to things anciently Greek.
22. See, for example, the chapter entitled "Cimmerian Lodge," in *Melincourt (Works,* II), especially p. 338.
23. *Classics and Commercials,* p. 407.
24. One of the reasons many readers find *Melincourt* overlong may reside in Peacock's evident experiment in having the height of festive celebration occur in Chapters 27 and 28, with a full third of the novel yet to come (see Nicholas A. Joukovsky, "The Composition of Peacock's *Melincourt . . . ,*" *English Language Notes,* XIII, No. 1, September 1975, 18-25).
25. Cited in Mill's "Bentham," p. 95.
26. Howard Mills, for example, likens the style of "The Four Ages" to Swift's irony on at least two occasions in *Peacock: His Circle,* pp. 40-41, 45.
27. One of the most amusingly macabre illustrations of Peacock's refusal to follow the utilitarian creed to its logical extremes occurs in the anecdote of his advice to James Mill soon after Bentham's death. The elder Mill was struck by the notion of using the liquid exuded from Bentham's head in order to oil "chronometers which were going into high latitudes," but Peacock—with a straight face, we must assume—strongly advised Mill against it (I, clxxv).

28. *Life of Peacock,* p. 196.
29. As Peacock was to write to Shelley in 1821, two years after his career in the East India Company had begun in earnest: "There is nothing that would give me so much pleasure (because I think there is nothing that would be more beneficial to you) than to see you following some scheme of flesh and blood—some interesting matter connected with the business of life, in the tangible shape of a practical man" (VIII, 226).
30. *A History of the English People in the Nineteenth Century,* I, trans. Watkin and Barker (London: E. Benn, 1949), p. 577.
31. "All must admit that the essential doctrines of utilitarianism are stated by Hume with a clearness and consistency not to be found in any other writer of the century. From Hume to J. S. Mill, the doctrine received no substantial alteration," Leslie Stephen, *History of English Thought in the Eighteenth Century* (1902; rpt. New York: Harcourt, Brace & World, 1962), II, 73; and cf. Plamenatz, *English Utilitarians,* p. 1.
32. "Bentham," p. 40.
33. See *Works,* I, cxxxii-cxxxiii. It was James Mill who persuaded Ricardo to publish his major work, the *Principles of Political Economy,* a book which swiftly became "the economic Bible of the Utilitarians," Leslie Stephen, *The English Utilitarians,* 3 vols. (1900; rpt. New York: Peter Smith, 1950), II, 186.
34. *English Utilitarians,* II, 378.
35. Some of the more significant items which probably belong on any list of Peacock's personal "stratagems" in a whirling age: his near-religious veneration for the classical past; the seeming contradiction of his belief that human nature remained unchanged from era to era (see, for example, I, 2); the comforting self-assessment of his own stability—Peacock's seal bore the proud claim of a line from Horace: *Nec tardum opperior nec praecedentibus insto* ("I neither follow in the rear, nor pursue those who run before me," Van Doren, *Life of Peacock,* 275).

The Political Philosophy of Mary Shelley's Historical Novels: *Valperga* and *Perkin Warbeck*

Betty T. Bennett

In 1942, Kenneth Neill Cameron wrote an essay entitled "The Social Philosophy of Shelley" which has influenced Shelley scholarship to this day.[1] Arguing against the image of Shelley as an "ineffectual angel" who was out of contact with the actual events of his time, Professor Cameron demonstrates that Shelley was a realistic, however radical, social thinker, whose poetry and prose are permeated not by airy visions but rather by an organizing theory of historical evolution:

> The essence of this theory, as given in the first chapter of A PHILOSOPHICAL VIEW OF REFORM and other works, is that history is essentially a struggle between two sets of forces, the forces of liberty and the forces of despotism.[2]

Shelley's views, Professor Cameron stresses, were:

> the product of a mind shaped by the forces of the French Revolution and the English reform movement. They were views, moreover, shared in large part by such advanced political thinkers as Holbach, Condorcet, Volney, Paine, Godwin, Mary Wollstonecraft, Leigh Hunt, William Cobbett, Sir Francis Burdett and Jeremy Bentham.[3]

Scholars who examine Shelley as a political reformer so often turn back to this seminal essay that it seems appropriate to allow its basic methodology—the interpretation of the author's works with full cognizance of the social and political influences that helped shape them—to set the standard in reassessing the historical novels of another politically oriented, but too often misinterpreted, writer of the period: Mary Wollstonecraft Godwin Shelley.

Mary Shelley wrote two historical novels: *Valperga: or, the Life and Adventures of Castruccio, Prince of Lucca* (London, 1823) and *The Fortunes of Perkin Warbeck* (London, 1830). Several modern critics have acknowledged politics to be at the center of both novels but, failing to perceive the organizing philosophy which orders the novels, they have attributed to these works a variety of technical problems, ranging from structural to philosophical inconsistency. Jean de Palacio has suggested that Mary Shelley viewed history as a moral lesson, culling from it luminous examples of "individual heroism," and that the exemplary lives of her heroes serve to demonstrate the dignity of man. He contends that she modeled *Perkin* on the works of Sir Walter Scott, reshaping history to infuse her romantic attitudes into it and thereby producing a work calculated to be popular with the reading public of the day.[4] Sylva Norman also notes the influence of Scott and regards the "romantic flush" in Mary Shelley's novels as "imported" from the fashionable fiction of the period. Whereas Palacio recognizes political reformation as one of Mary Shelley's genuine goals, for Norman her political concerns are activated only when "some Shelleyan phantom" prods her.[5]

The problem with Palacio's suggestion is that his theory of "moral lesson," "individual heroism," and "dignity of man" is based solely on his reading of *Perkin* and does not hold up when we consider—as we must if we are to evaluate the politics of Mary Shelley's approach to history—*Valperga* (treated by Palacio primarily in terms of its Italian sources). Indeed, Palacio seems uncomfortable with his own theory, suggesting a structural dichotomy in which the "heroism" is made subordinate to the anti-monarchical theme.

The best rejoinder to Norman's assertion of the superficiality of Mary Shelley's political concerns, and clearly the most comprehensive discussion to date of the significance of politics in the works of Mary Shelley, is found in William Walling's *Mary Shelley* (New York: Twayne, 1972). Walling argues that "the conflict between political ambition and the desires of the human heart" is central to both novels. He regards *Perkin,* however, as unsuccessful because of an "ideational incoherence in the character of Richard," whom he describes as representative of both "outmoded chivalry" and "insurrectionary tactics . . . which eventually culminated . . . in the French Revolution." [6]

The resolution of the dichotomies of character and structure suggested by these critics, as well as the key to the organizing philosophy of the novels, can be found by examining the elements of Walling's proposed central conflict: specifically, what is the nature of the political ambition in both novels and what is the nature of the love theme in both novels? Such consideration will, I believe, demonstrate that for Mary Shelley, Richard's "heroism" is no more admirable than Castruccio's cruel tyranny, for both men are participants in, and victims of, destructive social systems. Furthermore, to dismiss Mary Shelley's "romance" as a fashionable imitation of Scott's idealized love stories is to fail to recognize that her novel owes far more to Shelley's Promethean ideal, in which love becomes the means of developing a viable alternative to the existing social structure, and to Godwin and Wollstonecraft, who advocated the need for alternative social structures. Finally, an analysis of the two novels will demonstrate that Mary Shelley's operative theme is political, that her criticism of fourteenth-century Italy differs little from her criticism of fourteenth-century England (and by implication, of nineteenth-century Europe), and that these works, whatever their stylistic shortcomings, are written in the tradition of social reform, particularly influenced—as were the efforts of so many other reformers of the time—by Godwin and Wollstonecraft.[7]

Mary Shelley carefully and extensively researched the historical framework of both novels.[8] Her habit of intensive study accords with Godwin's precepts.[9] Godwin had sent the same precepts to Shelley, along with his injunction on the necessity of studying history—an injunction Shelley immediately acted on.[10] That Mary Shelley was as much Godwin's protégé in this as Shelley is evident from her lifelong concern with historical subjects: she wrote historical novels; she contributed a series of volumes to Lardner's *Cabinet Cyclopædia* which rely on broad historical knowledge; [11] she offered to write for the publisher John Murray on any of a highly diversified list of historical topics, including the formation of the earth, the history of women, the history of chivalry.[12] In light of the depth and concentration of her study of history, we may safely set aside the notion that history served merely as background for her attempt at popular romance and look instead at the two histories she selected and the ways in which she altered the stories found in her sources.

The Preface and the opening pages of *Valperga* reveal much about the methodology and the purpose of the novel. Mary Shelley begins by citing a number of historical sources for the life of Castruccio (I, iii) but these provide only a skeletal plot.[13] Castruccio, a citizen of Lucca in the fourteenth century, was a member of the Ghibelline political faction which supported the Roman Empire and was in constant combat with the Guelph party, which advocated republican government.[14] Through a remarkable military career in foreign and civil wars, he became prince of Lucca. A cruel and tyrannical ruler (or, in Machiavelli's accounts, all powerful and successful), he died of a fever in middle age, at the zenith of his power.

In the Preface, Mary Shelley also discloses that the dates in her narrative differ from actual dates (I, iv). In a sense, this announces her intention to change the facts for her own purposes. Her changes prove significant, for she weaves into the life of Castruccio wholly fictional relationships with two women: Euthanasia, who combines Godwinian reason with Shelleyan love; and Beatrice, who embodies imagination misguided by superstition and religion.

Euthanasia's story is given as much attention as Castruccio's, and it is through Euthanasia that Mary Shelley superimposes on her material not mere "clever and amusing romance," [15] but rather the Shelleyan view of history as a struggle between two sets of forces. Mary Shelley reinforces and expands the role of Euthanasia as the symbol of liberty and democratic government by interconnecting her fate and that of her family's castle, Valperga. Valperga is presented as the historical, and ostensibly least vulnerable, citadel of the Guelph political faction. Valperga is situated by Mary Shelley partway between Lucca, the symbol of Ghibelline power, and Florence,[16] which was, in fact and in the novel, a Guelph republican city during this period. Its very locale suggests that it is the logical mediation point between the opposing factions. Mary Shelley emphasizes this with an incident from Castruccio's childhood. As a result of intense political strife, Castruccio's family faces death. His mother asks that he be conveyed to Valperga (I, 8-9) since, despite their political antagonism, Castruccio's and Euthanasia's families had formed close ties of friendship. This minor incident is intrinsic to the development of the central premise of the novel—that is, the necessity of the cessation of hostilities between the Ghibellines and the Guelphs and their mutual assent to government by the citizenry rather than by one ruler, be he foreign or native.

So, too, the title of the novel may be viewed as a statement of the central conflict of the novel. *Valperga; or the Life and Adventures of Castruccio, Prince of Lucca* suggests that the story is about one or the other. The two cannot coexist; confrontation must erupt. Victory for Valperga means universal liberty and the sharing of responsibility for government; victory for Castruccio means tyrannic government which arbitrarily subjugates and destroys the people for its own aggrandizement and perpetuation. The love story of Euthanasia and Castruccio is made analogous to chivalric one-to-one battle in which the fate of whole nations is dependent on the outcome. Euthanasia is resolute in refusing to support Castruccio's tyrannic government. However, if Castruccio can be won to Euthanasia's advocacy of liberty and freedom, their love would bring peace and liberty to all.

Carl Woodring has described the "conflict between advocacy of reform and faith in imagination" which troubled the romantics, maintaining that Percy Bysshe Shelley used imagination as the means to "mediate the dichotomy between love and revolution." [17] Mary Shelley's awareness of this potential conflict is demonstrated on the first page of *Valperga,* for she begins her story by speaking of Dante and his involvement in "political struggles and literature" (I, 2) and explicitly refers to Dante throughout the novel. Dante's dual concerns were also Godwin's and Shelley's, and we find them linked imaginatively in Euthanasia, who questions and challenges Castruccio's goals.

At several points in the novel, Castruccio is put into a situation in which he must reevaluate his quest for power and either alter or reconfirm his intention. For example, his dying father, seeming momentarily to question his own life committed to ambition and power, sends Castruccio to live with Guinigi, a former comrade-in-arms, with the injunction that Castruccio "be guided by his advice" (I, 38). Castruccio finds that the warrior has become a farmer who lives a simple life, close to nature. He is a man who "thought only of the duty of man to man, laying aside the distinctions of society" (I, 48); a man who is opposed to war and its results which "occasion such exultation to the privileged murderers of the earth" (I, 49). Mary Shelley's conception of tyrants as "privileged murderers" can be traced to Shelley, for as William Royce Campbell has pointed out, we find the idea as well as the phrase "legal murderers" in the *Esdaile Notebook* poem, "A retrospect of Times of Old." [18] We may, however, trace the source of this concept back yet another step, for Shelley's indictment of Sesostris, Caesar, Pizzaro, Moses, and Mahommed in "A retrospect" [19] seems to have been gleaned from Godwin's discussion of the "History of Political Society" in his *An Enquiry Concerning Political Justice.*[20] There, Godwin speaks of war as an "inseparable ally of political institution" and then cites, among others, Sesostris, Caesar, Mahomet, and "the Spaniards in the new world." Shelley adds Moses to Godwin's list and includes, in a footnote, the "legal murderers our own age affords": Frederick of Prussia, Buonaparte, Suwarroff, Wellington, and Nelson.

Ironically, Castruccio disobeys his father's injunction and rejects Guinigi's way of life in favor of the life of a soldier and politician as a direct result of the education and example his father himself had given him. Castruccio's overweening ambition, which prompts him to ask, "Is it not fame that makes gods?" grows naturally out of the society in which he was reared.[21] Castruccio's superior innate abilities (I, 14) are, in Mary Shelley's terms, channeled to the uses of destruction as he becomes the ultimate example of the political creed which countenanced the suppression and slaughter of subjects by rulers in order to keep power. Mary Shelley's descriptions of the destructive methods by which tyrants, and all monarchs, govern have their sources in Godwin's *Political Justice* and in Wollstonecraft's *A Vindication of the Rights of Woman,* which depict the British system as one which "grinds the poor to pamper the rich." [22]

Castruccio's education and moral code, the expected ones for a man of his class and time, contrast with Euthanasia's education and attitude, which represent the Romantic reformer's imaginative challenge to the established system. This challenge does, however, have an appropriate historical reference in the republican principles by which Florence was then governed. Euthanasia is educated to the beliefs of her father, paralleling Mary Shelley's own experience, and we find the fictional daughter repeatedly reflecting the philosophy of the author's father and mother. Euthanasia "saw and marked the revolutions that had been, and the present seemed to her only a point of rest, from which time was to renew his flight, scattering change as he went" (I, 29). Godwin stressed the necessity of a system of society which encouraged change rather than stasis.[23] Committed to support the republic of Florence, the center of Italian liberty of the period, Euthanasia pledges to put aside individual feelings, including her love of Castruccio, in order to do that which will benefit the most people (I, 169-170; 237), as Godwin asserted that "all private considerations must yield to the general good." [24] Euthanasia intends to abolish distinctions of rank within Valperga (I, 246), as both Godwin and Wollstonecraft advocated the abolition of class distinctions.[25] When Castruccio condemns Euthanasia to exile for her political activism (III, 253), we are reminded of Wollstonecraft's insistence that woman must become politically responsible.[26] Euthanasia denounces the remorselessness of those who rule (II, 154) as did both Godwin and Wollstonecraft.[27] Finally, and most significantly, Euthanasia perceives that:

> the essence of freedom is that clash and struggle which awaken the energies of our nature, and that operation of the elements of our mind, which as it were gives us the force and power that hinder us from degenerating, as they say all things earthly do when not regenerated by change (I, 197).

When Mary Shelley addresses the need to "hinder us from

degenerating," the tie to Godwin once again is clear. Godwin attacked government as the perpetuator of the status quo:

> Man is in a state of perpetual progress. He must grow either better or worse, either correct his habits or confirm them. The government proposed must either increase our passions and prejudices by fanning the flame, or by gradually discouraging tend to extirpate them.[28]

Thus we find rooted in Godwin the idea that "the essence of freedom is that clash and struggle which awaken the energies of our nature," an idea found in somewhat different form in Shelley's view of historical evolution. Euthanasia's statement on the necessary struggle is characteristically preceded by an enthusiastic speech stressing the importance of the study of history, a judgment recurrent, as noted earlier, in Godwin's precepts on education.

Mary Shelley writes of Euthanasia's death at sea: "Is not the catastrophe strangely prophetic," [29] referring to Shelley's death at sea on 8 July 1822. It is prophetic rather than coincidental because the character of Euthanasia is substantially based on Shelley; [30] Euthanasia is the embodiment of Godwin's theories as modified and partly lived by the poet.[31]

Mary Shelley's reflection on the prophetic nature of Euthanasia's death focuses attention on an issue which has seemed unresolvable regarding the published version of the novel. In 1822, having failed to find a publisher willing to meet her terms, Mary Shelley sent the novel to her father and gave him the right to have it published for his own financial benefit. This Godwin did, but not before altering the manuscript. Mary Shelley made no changes in the manuscript after sending it to Godwin and, in fact, expressed her concern to see, in the published version, the alterations he had made.[32] The question arises, therefore, as to the extent to which the work is Mary Shelley's or her father's,[33] a question particularly important to the evaluation of her view of history and politics. Godwin wrote to Mary Shelley that although he had "taken great liberties with the novel" what he had "done is merely confined to taking away things which must have prevented its success." [34] In fact, seventeen pages of Mary Shelley's manuscript of *Valperga* are extant and serve essentially but not completely to confirm Godwin's statements.[35] In comparing the manuscript with the published text, one finds that the main story line has in no way been altered by Godwin in the surviving pages. For example, the significant passage in which Euthanasia eloquently declares her intention not to marry Castruccio because of his political stance (II, 135-136), beginning "She remembered her vow not to unite" to "qualified her to complete the sacrifice," is as Mary Shelley wrote it, with the exception of the following changes made by Godwin: emendations in punctuation (substitution of periods and semicolons for dashes); ampersands replaced by "and"; a few word substitutions (such as "unite" instead of "join"; "upon" instead of "among"; "such a penalty" instead of "its censures"); and the inclusion of one phrase "habits of intercourse and mutual kindness" which has no parallel in the manuscript. Indeed, some of the word changes seem a bit arbitrary and unnecessary, such as the substitution of "qualified" for "befitted." The manuscript does have several lengthy passages in which characters are described, and these Godwin elected to remove. But it is important to recognize that Godwin's changes, at least on these seventeen random pages which correspond to printed pages in all three volumes, are stylistic rather than philosophic in nature. The reason Godwin found it unnecessary to alter the political ideology of *Valperga* is apparent. It seems appropriate to speculate, given Godwin's propensity for latinate diction and rather stiff prose style, whether the novel might not have been all the better before he changed it from the form it was in when Shelley so enthusiastically praised it.[36]

Euthanasia calls for "content of mind, love, and benevolent feeling" (I, 198) for all mankind. As Frederick L. Beaty has pointed out, Shelley's creed of benevolence, virtue, and universality emphasized love, whereas Godwin only recognized the "necessity of human affections as a concomitant of universal love"[37] after publication of *Political Justice.* Donald H. Reiman writes that "Prometheus' decision to turn from self-centered hatred to outgoing love marks the moment in human history that breaks the old meaningless cycle of oppression and retribution . . . ."[38] Prometheus' recantation of his curse, "I wish no living thing to suffer pain,"[39] therefore, is the beginning of a new order committed to love and forgiveness, even at the cost of personal suffering. Euthanasia is clearly a member of this new order. She forgives Castruccio for destroying her beloved Valperga (II, 285) and even seeks the means by which Castruccio might be changed. She is the personification of universal love and elects to suffer the loss of her love, and even the loss of her life, rather than capitulate to a political system based on power and revenge. Castruccio fails, Walling contends, because he preferred ambition to love,[40] but Mary Shelley goes further than setting up a simple choice between ambition and love. It is not Castruccio's rejection of love which determines the course of his life (for example, had he accepted Beatrice's love, she indicates that she would not have changed him), but the rejection of Euthanasia's love on her own terms—that is, his refusal to first accept the ideal of universal love and its responsibilities. In fact, Castruccio does not reject Euthanasia's love; it is she who rejects his. Their love relationship fails in political terms; a personal love would not suffice.

Euthanasia dies in a shipwreck, apart from all she loves: "Earth felt no change when she died; and men forgot her" (III, 261). Beatrice, victimized by superstition and by men, dies mad. Castruccio, a powerful but lonely figure, dies of a fever two years after Euthanasia's death. There is no happy ending which one would expect of a popular romance. Instead, *Valperga* depicts a cycle of historical struggle. Euthanasia declares her faith in a new era of freedom and liberty for Italy (I, 30), echoing the Shelleys' faith that the Europe of their day was entering into a similar era.[41]

Perkin Warbeck, Mary Shelley's second historical novel, illustrates even more clearly the inadequacy of personal love when linked to personal ambition. Though Richard, Duke of York, accepts the love offered to him by two women, he, like Castruccio, falls victim to the ambition inculcated by his society. The love, generously given and willingly accepted, does not prevent his participation in the destruction of others as well as of himself.

Mary Shelley indicates in her preface that the story of Perkin—the unsuccessful battle of Richard, Duke of York (or of someone pretending to be Richard, a man named Perkin Warbeck) to regain the crown from Henry VII—was suggested to her "as a subject for historical detail" but realizing "the romance" of the story, she decided that "it would be impossible for any narration, that should be confined to the incorporation of facts related by our old Chroniclers, to do it justice" (I, v).

Godwin had asked, "What rational man could possibly have given himself the least disturbance for the sake of choosing whether Henry the sixth or Edward the fourth should have the style of king of England?" and it may have been Godwin who suggested this historical topic to her, as he had others.[42] Certainly Godwin's attitude is reflected in Mary Shelley's narrative. Insofar as the characters participate in the feudal system by waging war for their hereditary "rights" to rule, whatever their personal attributes may be or the general welfare may require, they are considered unreasonable; for all humanity suffers through their failed reason. At the very outset of the novel, Richard's partisans pledge to restore the "rightful crown" and have either success and honor, or defeat and death (I, 19). This promise augurs suffering and death for thousands of innocent people, and by supporting it Richard chooses irrationality; he is as guilty of destroying innocent lives as Castruccio was. Like Castruccio, then, Richard has failed in universal love, that is, in making choices that benefit the most people.

Richard's failure is made amply clear to the reader. Mary Shelley details atrocities of war committed in his name (II, 303-307) and Richard renounces these acts: "let not the blood of my subjects plead against my right; rather would I pine in exile for ever, than occasion the slaughter and misery of my countrymen, my children" (II, 311-312). In the same mode: "the name and presence of a Plantagenet shall no longer sanction the devastation of his country. I would rather be a cotter on your wild Highlands, than buy the sovereignty of my fair England by the blood of her inhabitants" (II, 313). In a letter to his wife Katherine, he speaks of his ambition in terms of the influences which developed it:

> What am I, that I should be the parent of evil merely? Oh, my mother, my too kind friends, why did ye not conceal me from myself? Teaching me lessons of humbleness, rearing me as a peasant, consigning me to a cloister, my injuries would have died with me; and the good, the brave, the innocent, who

have perished for me, or through me, had been spared! (II, 316)

Despite this recognition, Richard continues to believe in his right to the crown and does not change his objective. When he is finally willing to give up his quest, he nevertheless leads his men into one last battle to "redeem his honour" (III, 80-81); losing that battle, he challenges Henry VII to meet him in single combat, his sole object being the recognition of his legitimacy (III, 110). The tragedy of *Perkin* is not that Richard is captured by Henry VII and executed—what matter, Henry VI or Edward IV—rather that Richard comes to recognize the necessary destructiveness of his ambition but is unable to act on his recognition. In this sense, Richard has far more dimension than Castruccio, for he does at least perceive. Unfortunately, his perceptions have been clouded by the standards of the chivalric social-political code, a code which was repugnant to Mary Shelley and to those who influenced her. Richard's "heroic" attitudes are more often foolish than admirable; for example, he wishes to gain the crown without bloodshed, while at the same time he actively recruits armies. His intended kindness to the people is dependent upon his attaining the throne. Mary Shelley's presentation of Richard shows her support of Godwin's contempt for the notion that good intentions are deserving of credit: "An action, though done with the best intention in the world, may have nothing in it of the nature of virtue." [43]

Richard, then, is neither the product of Walling's ideational incoherence nor an example of Palacio's individual heroism causing structural weakness in its conflict to the overall philosophy of *Perkin.* He is, rather, the product of erroneous education—a man of intelligence, grace, and ability, whose indoctrination into belief in the supreme rights of monarchs causes him to generate destruction "from mistake." By regarding Richard as the legitimate heir to the throne rather than as a fraud perpetrated by the Yorkists (most historical accounts credit the latter as true), Mary Shelley attacked the principle of "legitimate" monarchical power, an attack she repeats in 1844 in *Rambles in Germany and Italy.*[44] The philosophical bases of her attack on this benevolently inclined seeker of power are derived from the same sources as her attack on the tyrant Castruccio—the ideas of Godwin, Wollstonecraft, and Shelley.

The portrayal of Richard as product and victim of his social system is consistent with the thinking of those who opposed arbitrary power, whatever the source or intent of that power. As so many of Mary Shelley's views of history and politics stem from Godwin, so too does her model for Richard. If we look to *Caleb Williams,* we find the character of Falkland, a highly admirable man whose chivalric education misguides him into acts of deception and murder in order to safeguard the honor of his name. What occurs on an individual scale in *Caleb* is transmuted onto a national, even international, scale in *Perkin.* Walling correctly identifies Richard's objective in overthrowing Henry VII as reactionary, but there is little reason to see him as a precursor of anti-monarchical revolutionary tactics. Richard's avowed goal is not, like Euthanasia's, to found a republic, but rather to rule as a benevolent but absolute monarch. Richard is no more a hero than Falkland; indeed, they are both "from mistake" as culpable as Castruccio.

The other characters in *Perkin* sustain this view. The monarchs Henry VII and James III of Scotland ruthlessly and persistently seek power. They are depicted as men of talent schooled to lives of manipulation and destruction who contrast with Richard only to the extent that he occasionally recognizes the destructiveness of his own ambition.

Richard loves and is loved by his wife Katherine and his "adopted" sister Monina. Monina, like Beatrice in *Valperga,* is totally partisan and would support any action Richard might pursue (III, 159). She is active in political intrigue, and perhaps it is her love which blinds her to actual situations, causing her to misinterpret events in Richard's favor. For example, she summons Richard to invade England with the expectation that the Cornish men will serve as his conquering army when, in fact, his partisans are a small band of untrained soldiers (III, 69-71).

Katherine, on the contrary, supports Richard in his quest for the crown, but she early perceives the impossibility of his victory. Futhermore, though she does not speak out for republicanism, she "saw a vain mask in all the common-place pomp of palaces" and "she perceived that power failed most, when its end was good" (III, 60). She attempts, therefore, to convince Richard to give up his ambition: "Believe me, careful nights and thorny days are the portion of a monarch; he is lifted to that awful height only to view more clearly destruction beneath; around, fear, hate, disloyalty, all yelling at him" (III, 88). Although his love for Katherine is great,[45] Richard responds that he must fight on, now not for kingdom, but for honor (III, 90).

Richard is chained, by education and training, to the idea that he must fulfill the destiny of a legitimate heir to an unattainable throne. Under the circumstances, this destiny precludes any but a tragic ending for him. Nor does Katherine propose an alternative political role, such as Euthanasia, by argument and conduct, presented to Castruccio. Katherine simply suggests total abandonment of Richard's public role, thereby offering him a love ideal which is personal and restricted rather than general; an ideal which is as insufficient for him as it would have been for Shelley.[46] Katherine's monologue, which concludes *Perkin,* has been regarded as an apology for Mary Shelley's altered life style that followed Shelley's death,[47] but it is more than simply an apology. It sums up, through the voice of Katherine, a change not in final objectives but in the means of achieving those objectives—an attitude we find fully reflected in her last two novels, *Lodore* (1835) and *Falkner* (1837). The monologue represents a shift away from Shelleyan activism on a universal scale to Godwinian individual interaction, as expressed in Katherine's statement: "I must feel that my dear and chosen friends are happier through me" (III, 352). Katherine also speaks of "the angelic portion of us" which "teaches us to feel pain at others pain, joy in their joy" (III, 348); of the necessity to be "good and benevolent" (III, 352); of her need "to love and be loved" (III, 353); of her need to alleviate the suffering of others (III, 352); but it is clear that these objectives—which mesh with Wollstonecraft's and Shelley's—are now to be pursued on a one-to-one basis. In fact, neither Katherine nor Richard has Euthanasia's democratic, activist ideal of love. Rather, they envision themselves within the established power structure system and, like Falkland with the best of intentions, like Castruccio with the most self-seeking, they fail.

Valperga and *Perkin Warbeck,* therefore, are novels which present the same theme from different vantage points. In *Valperga,* a conscious struggle is depicted, in which the forces of liberty are pitted against the forces of repression. Although the forces of repression are victorious at the conclusion of the work, this is only one phase of an ongoing struggle. Mary Shelley's conclusion sets the stage for the next combatants, for Castruccio dies in recapturing Lucca from the Florentines (III, 265). In *Perkin,* the struggle is between forces both representative of monarchical government; that Henry wins and Richard loses has little impact for the citizens of England. Richard's character and actions indicate that, caught up as he is in the larger forces of history, he would have been no different from Henry once on the throne. His abiding commitment to his role as monarch would have caused him to make policies which would insure his power. The established system of government and society would force Richard into the role of repressive monarch.

Underlying both novels, then, is an exploration of the historical forces which shape the lives of individuals. When Norman and Palacio argue that Mary Shelley is merely writing romance calculated to appeal to readers with whom Sir Walter Scott was popular, they interpret both authors in the narrowest of terms. Edgar Johnson, on the other hand, effectively argues that Scott was far less concerned with the trappings of the past than with "the degree to which the individual and society are shaped by the historical past and the forces that have created social institutions." [48] Both Mary Shelley and Percy Bysshe Shelley expressed admiration for Scott's works,[49] and it seems appropriate to assume that it was this aspect of his work, together with his ability to weave events of the imagination into historical realities, which influenced Mary Shelley rather than either Scott's abiding Toryism or the colorful milieu in which he situated his novels.

Mary Shelley's journal entry of 21 October 1838 contains a counterattack against those who had faulted her for lack of political activity. In this entry (first published in full in 1969),[50] she sets forth her admiration for reformers only if they have "real disinterestedness, toleration, and a clear understanding." And such people, she says, were her "parents and Shelley." Though she does offer an apology for her nonactivist role, she argues that she had always written for the "liberal cause" and taken other actions in support of it: "At every risk I have befriended and supported victims of the social system." Her position is very much in accord with Godwin's philosophy though it differs from the more activist positions of Wollstonecraft and Shelley.[51] She disclaims the radicalism of "mere drivellers"—not radicalism itself.

Mary Shelley's historical novels express her belief in the "liberal cause"—in reform developed out of the struggle between the forces of liberty and those of repression—ideas which she did not originate, but which she incorporated into the fabric of *Valperga* and *Perkin.* Whatever quarrel her contemporaries may have had with her nonactivist position and however valid their arguments may be, it would be a critical error not to recognize in her historical novels how much a product of the reform movement she was. Indeed, in that very journal entry which has (no doubt in part due to its previously abridged published form) been read as a denial not only of radicalism but of genuine political commitment, Mary Shelley writes: "I wish no injury to any human being" and one must recognize in this the echo of *Prometheus'* most radical idea.

NOTES

1. *Sewanee Review* (1942), 458-466. See Bennett Weaver and Donald H. Reiman, "Shelley," *The English Romantic Poets,* ed. Frank Jordan, 3rd rev. ed. (New York: MLA, 1972), p. 356; and William Royce Campbell, "Shelley's Philosophy of History: A Reconsideration," *K-SJ,* 21-22 (1972-1973), 43-63.
2. "The Social Philosophy of Shelley," p. 458.
3. "The Social Philosophy of Shelley," p. 461.
4. *Mary Shelley dans son œuvre* (Paris: Editions Klincksieck, 1969), pp. 143-144.
5. "Mary Wollstonecraft Shelley," *Shelley and his Circle,* ed. Kenneth Neill Cameron (Cambridge: Harvard University Press, 1970), III, 409-411.
6. Walling, pp. 102, 104.
7. H.N. Brailsford, *Shelley, Godwin and their Circle* (London: Oxford University Press, 1913), p. 153.
8. See Walling, p. 52 and p. 101; and Palacio, pp. 141-142.
9. *The Letters of Mary W. Shelley,* ed. Frederick L. Jones (Norman: University of Oklahoma Press, 1944), I, 91.
10. *The Letters of Percy Bysshe Shelley,* ed. Frederick L. Jones (Oxford: Clarendon Press, 1964), I, 340-342. See also Campbell, p. 45.

11. *Lives of the Most Eminent Literary and Scientific Men of France,* 2 vols. (London: Longman, Orme, Brown, Green, & Longmans, 1838-1839); *Lives of the Most Eminent Literary and Scientific Men of Italy, Spain, and Portugal,* 3 vols. (London: Longman, Rees, Orme, Brown, Green, & Longmans, 1835-1837).
12. *Letters of Mary W. Shelley,* II, 362, 368, 369.
13. The following historical sources are listed in the preface to *Valperga:* Machiavelli's "The Life of Castruccio Castracani of Lucca"; J. C. L. Sismondi's *Histoire des Republiques Italiennes de l'age Moyen;* Niccolo Tegrino's *Life of Castruccio;* Giovanni Villani's *Florentine Annals;* Louis Moreri, *Grand Dictionnaire Historique.* See also Walling, p. 53.
14. Mary Shelley uses the same material in her short story, "A Tale of the Passions," *Mary Shelley, Collected Tales and Stories,* ed. Charles E. Robinson (Baltimore: Johns Hopkins University Press, 1976), pp. 1-23.
15. Walling (pp. 55, 58) quotes the review of *Valperga* in *Blackwood's Edinburgh Magazine*, XIII (March 1823) which viewed the fictional relationship of Euthanasia and Castruccio as "romantic" and "modern and feminine," failing to see the political significance. Walling, while he clearly credits Mary Shelley's political theme, speaks of "the feminization of her material in order to impose value judgments on what was actually a most unfeminine age."
16. In a letter of 7 August 1823 Mary Shelley suggests to Leigh Hunt that en route to England from Italy the Hunts will pass through the plains of Lucca and "see much of the scenery of Valperga," including the remains of Guinigi's and Castruccio's castles and the site of Valperga. *The Letters of Mary W. Shelley,* I, 190-191.
17. *Politics in English Romantic Poetry* (Cambridge: Harvard University Press, 1970), pp. 5-6.
18. Campbell, p. 45.
19. *The Esdaile Notebook,* ed. Kenneth Neill Cameron (London: Faber and Faber, 1964), p. 97.
20. London, 1793, I, 5-7.
21. Castruccio's challenge to the gods is a variation on the theme of *Frankenstein.* Clearly, both *Valperga* and *Perkin* are further explorations of the theme of human ambition and human limitation which was a focal center of Mary Shelley's earlier novel.
22. Ed. Charles W. Hagelman, Jr. (New York: W.W. Norton, 1967), p. 216. See also, *Political Justice,* I, 9-10.
23. *Political Justice,* I, 179-189.
24. *Political Justice,* I, 165.
25. *Political Justice,* II, 473; *Rights of Woman,* pp. 217-218.
26. *Rights of Woman,* p. 222.
27. *Political Justice,* I, 5-11; *Rights of Woman,* p. 44.
28. *Political Justice,* I, 185.
29. *Letters of Mary W. Shelley,* I, 224.

30. Mrs. Julian (Florence A.) Marshall, *The Life & Letters of Mary Wollstonecraft Shelley* (London: Richard Bentley & Son, 1889), II, 266.
31. Kenneth Neill Cameron, *The Young Shelley* (New York: Macmillan Company, 1950), pp. 61-69.
32. *The Letters of Mary W. Shelley,* I, 159, 171, 224.
33. Walling, pp. 54-55.
34. C. Kegan Paul, *William Godwin: His Friends and Contemporaries* (London: Henry S. King, 1876), II, 277.
35. The manuscript is in the collection of the Pierpont Morgan Library (quoted by permission).
36. *The Letters of Percy Bysshe Shelley,* II, 352-354.
37. *Light from Heaven* (DeKalb: Northern Illinois University Press, 1971), pp. 217, 258, 271; see also, Woodring, p. 233.
38. *Percy Bysshe Shelley* (New York: Twayne Publishers, Inc., 1969), p. 82.
39. *Prometheus Unbound,* I.306.
40. Walling, p. 66.
41. The personal disappointments which ensued did not tarnish Mary Shelley's hopeful vision of historical struggle and change, for we find her holding the same faith in her *Rambles in Germany and Italy in 1840, 1842, and 1843* (London: Edward Moxon, 1844), I, x.
42. *Political Justice,* I, 8; Walling, p. 56. Godwin had had correspondence about Perkin Warbeck as early as 1803; see the Abinger Collection, Duke Microfilm Reel 25. The story of Perkin was generally well known; see Palacio, pp. 148-149.
43. *Political Justice,* I, 103.
44. See, for example, I, 203-205.
45. Richard addresses her as his "best, my angel girl." In *Valperga* Castruccio's father addresses his wife as, "my best girl," I, 5-6. This is an interesting biographical touch since these were phrases commonly used by Shelley to Mary Shelley; see for example, *The Letters of Percy Bysshe Shelley,* I, 412, 415; II, 34, 414, 444. Mary Shelley, in turn, addressed Jane Williams as "my best girl" and "my best Jane," *The Letters of Mary W. Shelley,* I, 231, 236.
46. Mary Shelley's novels that follow, *Lodore* and *Falkner,* develop the theme of personal, domestic love.
47. Walling, p. 103.
48. Edgar Johnson, *Sir Walter Scott* (New York: Macmillan Company, 1970), II, 1252-1253.
49. *The Letters of Percy Bysshe Shelley,* I, 590; *The Letters of Mary W. Shelley,* I, 214; II, 15.
50. Palacio, pp. 630-633.
51. *The Young Shelley,* p. 68.

Miss Tina and Miss Plin: The Papers Behind *The Aspern Papers*

Marion Kingston Stocking

In the last twenty years of her life, from 1859 until her death in 1879, Claire Clairmont saw a great deal of her niece Pauline Clairmont (called Plin), first as an occasional visitor, then from 1870 as a paying guest in Florence, and finally in the last two years as a housekeeper without pay. As Claire's survival into the 1870s provided Henry James with the idea of Juliana Bordereau in *The Aspern Papers,* so the existence of the attendant niece provided the idea of Miss Tina. In my search for materials for my edition of the journals of Claire Clairmont [1] and the sequel edition (in preparation) of her letters and other family papers, I have also been able to learn quite a lot about Miss Plin, who might well be the heroine of a novel in her own right—but a very different novel from *The Aspern Papers.*

My purpose in this article is to share some of the story of my discoveries, with a promise of more detail in the edition under preparation.

I.

My trail to the Clairmont family papers began in 1946 when, at the suggestion of Newman Ivey White, I initiated a correspondence with Frau Alma Crüwell-Clairmont (1869-1946), Claire's great-niece, in Vienna.[2] As the custodian of the family archive, she had generously received Professor Herbert Huscher, later of the

University of Würzburg, and had provided him free access to the collection. Fortunately, he had completed and published the major part of his research [3] before her apartment suffered bomb damage and before her death, away from Vienna, in 1946. As soon as possible after the war, early in 1949, I went to Vienna, with the blessing and cooperation of Professor Huscher, to find out what had survived. I learned that some of the material he had used, including a section of Claire's Russian journal, had been sent by Frau Crüwell-Clairmont "to the country" for safekeeping; it has proved impossible to trace. The bulk of the papers, however, had been collected by the American military authorities and delivered to the next of kin, Dr. Walter Gaulis Clairmont (1868-1958) at Gauting near Munich. Dr. Clairmont received me graciously at Gauting in February of 1949 and allowed me full access to the materials recently delivered from Vienna.

It was a delight and a privilege to meet Dr. Walter Clairmont, then eighty-one years old—the very age that Claire had been at her death. He did not seem to me at all an old man, and in almost a decade of correspondence thereafter he maintained his keen intellectual curiosity and endearing good humor. Despite a fall from a tree when he was eleven, which had left him a partial cripple for life, Geheimrat Clairmont had had a distinguished career, for many years president of the Bavarian *Industriellenverband,* and a senator of the University of Munich. Throughout the war he had been relatively unmolested, partly because of his advanced years and partly because, like his father and grandfather before him, he had maintained his British citizenship. He had opposed the Nazi regime, and profound political differences had caused him some years before to cease communication with his sister Alma. Thus he had only recently learned of his family connection with the Shelley-Byron circle, an association he found both fascinating and disturbing. He had been eleven when his great-aunt Claire had died, and he recalled having met her. He spoke with great enthusiasm of his beloved Aunt Plin, a splendid linguist, who had taught him English and French and who spoke fluent Italian.

I stayed in Munich in March of 1949 long enough to organize and catalogue the jumbled manuscripts from Vienna and to have copies made of the three family portraits that had arrived with them (of Plin, Claire, and—probably—Mrs. Godwin). Since I did not have time to study the seven surviving volumes of Plin's *Lebensbuch* (nine volumes, I-VII, and IX-X, had apparently already been lost), Dr. Clairmont, with his characteristic generosity, allowed me to carry them back to London to peruse at my leisure. This I did, and returned them by post a few weeks later, having made twelve pages of rough notes. Today my distress at the sketchiness of the notes is matched by my relief that I was able to make any at all.

Dr. Clairmont had skimmed through his aunt's journals before allowing me to borrow them, and when they had still not been delivered by 16 June he wrote that I was not to worry about them. "The parting of a once beautiful and highly gifted woman from the better days of her youth is rather painful reading for one who was a witness of her inalienable devotion to her brother and his off-springs," he wrote. And when the parcels had still not arrived a month later he assured me again that I was not to be concerned. He regretted the damage the journals had done to his youthful ideal of his aunt: "That's why I hate reading old letters and consider diaries an infernal abuse" (letter of 19 July 1949). When the packages did finally arrive, in October, he admitted that the "eatables" I had sent along were "a lot more interesting than all the rubbish my good old Aunt wrote down so volubly in her journals" (letter of 13 October 1949).

After Dr. Clairmont's death, the family papers went to one of the two surviving heirs: Mary Claire Bally-Clairmont, in Grindelwald, Switzerland. In 1967, my husband and colleague David Mackenzie Stocking and I spent several days there as the guest of the gracious namesake of both Mary Shelley and Claire Clairmont. In her fairy-tale chalet, Träumli Hus, surrounded by the landscape that meant so much to both Byron and Shelley, we repeated the inventory that I had first made in Gauting eighteen years before. The tally was virtually identical, except that five of Plin's journals, Volumes XI-XV, were not to be found. Inquiries in the family have failed to produce any trace of these notebooks. It may be that Dr. Clairmont expressed his distaste at the "rubbish" by destroying them, though I cannot see any real difference between those volumes and the ones that survive.

What, then, have we lost? Of the sixteen or more original volumes, the seven I have seen were all about the same size, roughly 5″ x 8″, hardbound notebooks.

Vol. VIII. 6 May 1855 through 7 August 1857. In Australia, and the voyage back to London.

*Vol. XI. 6 August 1859 to September 1866. In Rakicsan, near Mura in Hungary; travels in Italy, Germany, the Netherlands, and England; some periods with her mother and brother in Austria.

*Vol. XII. 30 September 1866 to January 1868. In Vienna and Germany.

*Vol. XIII. 10 January 1868 through September 1868. In Baden.

*Vol. XIV. 4 October 1868 through February 1870. In Baden, with a visit to Hungary.

*Vol. XV. 2 March 1870 through October 1872. In Italy.

Vol. XVI. 17 May 1873 through October 1880. In Florence and Vienna.

(The asterisk indicates that the volume was missing in 1967.)

In her journals, Plin moves almost unconsciously from one language to another, as though the European languages were all one to her. Like Claire, she appeared to be writing as an aid to her own memory, not for other readers. Unlike Claire, she seems to have used her journal as an outlet for the expression of opinions she could not freely air to her more conservative friends and relations.

II.

What can we learn, then, about this unconventional woman—so great a delight and later embarrassment to her great-nephew? Christened Pauline [4] she was born on 28 July 1825, the eldest of the seven children of Claire's brother Charles and his Austrian wife Antonie (Tonie). When at the age of twenty she first went to England to visit her Aunt Claire, she was, by her father's description, a remarkably interesting and attractive young woman:

> A very pretty face, brown hair, dark eyes, neat, pretty round little figure 5 feet 2 inches high, English measure. She is a sweet good tempered girl, with an excellent understanding, but no inclination for literature; but to make up for this she speaks English, French and German almost equally well, and is besides, even here in Vienna (the very hot-bed of instrumental music) quite a proficient on the Piano. She is considered one of the best female dilettanti in our capital, and there is no doubt that in case of necessity she could earn her livelihood by it. She is consequently Beethoven mad.[5]

In December of 1852, Plin set out with her brother Willy for Australia, where he was to try out the agricultural methods he had been studying at the Greenwood Agricultural College at Stockbridge and she was to be a governess to Adelaide Bowler. There, at Brucedale, near Sydney, Plin had a passionate affair with the only man she claimed ever truly to have loved, Willie Sutton, nine years her junior, whom she lost to her own pupil, Adelaide. When in August of 1857 Plin and her brother returned to England, they, their mother, and their Aunt Claire were the only surviving members of the Clairmont family.

Plin seems to have concentrated into her small body all the vivacity and physical health and mental energy that had been lost in the four sisters and the brother who had died. Her journals reveal her as an emancipated woman—freedom-loving, high-spirited, and exuberantly sexual. More liberated and "romantic" than the Romantics, she recorded her intimate adventures with one man after another. Her journals show her as devoted to her brother and his children, deeply responsive to music (a Mendelssohn symphony "me délira presqu'aux larmes"), fond of horseback riding, drinking and smoking, traveling, and (her father would have been pleased) literature. Almost perversely she seems to have enjoyed Byron most, but her tastes extended to Longfellow and Thackeray, *Silas Marner* and Melville's *Mardi.* In 1859 she writes of planning an article, thinks of making her living by her pen, and visualizes herself as already a writer and famous, though I have not yet been able to identify anything that she had published. Her journals reveal an almost unflagging gusto for life, and she frequently congratulates herself on her knowledge of what most women of her day had missed. "Au fond," she wrote in 1859, "je suis née pour être courtisane mais non levée a ce metier."

It was in that year, 1859, after a visit to Claire in Croydon, she went first to Venice and then to Rakicsan as governess to the five children of a Countess Julia. But at the end of the year she left that position to visit Claire, now settled in Florence, and then drifted back to Vienna. In 1863 she was unwell and went to her brother's farm at Bobda, in Austria. Her problem turned out to be pregnancy, which did not seriously distress her, except as it made her a burden for a while on her beloved Willy. She stayed with him until the baby was almost due, then on 3 January went back to Hungary, where the baby was born on 21 January. On 29 January she walked melodramatically through a snow storm to offer the little girl, Johanna Maria Georgina Hanghegyi, to the Countess Amelie Karoly, who welcomed the infant into her household.[6] Plin's journals show that she was always delighted with the idea of this child, to whom she was deeply attached, and she never succeeded in keeping her wonderful secret very long from a person close to her.

Through the years until her mother's death in 1868, Plin did some traveling, spent a good deal of time with her mother, and wavered between a desire for the security of marriage and a relish for her freedom. She had a substantial income from her teaching. She rejoiced in her brother's family, and she made regular trips to Pest in Hungary to visit her daughter. After one such visit in February 1870 she wrote a self-revelatory account of the six-year-old girl:

> Altogether my heart is at peace about the child but the whole education the treatment is far from what I would wish to give her—she is too pale too tame too finnikin too timid too bourgeoise in short. I should like to see her flying about the house with ruddy cheeks her hair all loose, more wild more wilfull more daring but she has the English blood in her—slow of development. She is so primly dressed, with neat little stays & cuffs & little buttons, & keeps all her linen neatly tied up with little red bows. She speaks in a soft & low voice almost a whisper, & all her little wishes are modest & gentle. How unlike my wild gypsy nature!

> If the Almighty gives her health & life—& me the happiness to have her with me she will soon change.

In April of 1870 she took what was to prove the first step toward having her daughter with her: she went to Florence as a paying guest in the household of her Aunt Claire in the Palazzo Cruciato, Via Romana 73. In their earlier visits the two women had got on extremely well together; Plin had come to think of life with Claire as synonymous with freedom. But under the same roof they developed tensions, each one certain that she knew what was best for the other. Claire, for example, lectured Plin that cold baths and strenuous exercise were bad for her, and she forbade her to marry a rather unsavory young man named Pasquale.

One quality the two women had in common: they adored their children. The memory of the lost Allegra never dimmed in Claire's mind, and she even imagined that she might be alive still, in some convent. Finally Plin told her aunt about the existence of her own daughter. Looking back on Claire's reaction a short time later, Plin wrote:

> She received the news with some show of feeling & what ever the motive may have been she said—You will bring the child here, & I will adopt her. I remember day & place as well as possible when she said these words I felt as if a sudden spring had been touched in my soul & a powerful voice in me cried—No—No—I said nothing & it was only some time afterwards that she found out my quiet but firm resistance. (June 1871).

Plin's resistance gave way, however, and on 16 June the little girl arrived in Florence, disappointingly vulgar and snobbish, speaking horrible German with a Hungarian accent, interested only in Plin's clothes and rings, "in short not what any child of mine & free America ought to be." The journals of the next years show the child, now called Georgina or Georgie, torn back and forth like a favorite toy between her mother and the possessive Claire. The women grew farther and farther apart. Ironically, Plin cherished and absorbed into her own identity the "romantic" life of Claire's youth. On 8 March 1872 Plin took Georgina, timid and seasick, on a pilgrimage to Lerici and Spezia, clambering over storm-dashed rocks to visit the Byron and Shelley shrines. "How silly & weakminded," she mused at Lerici, "are those who dare not enjoy life."

As long as Claire was alive the tug-of-war went on. Claire in her own mind adopted the child as her own; Plin took Claire's possessiveness as personal malice: "*I* am the one on whom Aunt concentrates all her hatred—& strange to say—the very instrument she hoped to torture me with—à la Byron—escapes her—because the good little thing loves *me*—& obeys *me* for every feeling & sentiment & idea." (3 March 1874). Visitors to the house wondered that Claire should make such a fuss over a strange child, and Claire even brought herself to the point of offering her precious letters for sale if thereby she could raise money for Georgina's education.[7] When Claire died, the child was her chief heir.[8]

A new character enters the drama in October of 1872, when Plin's journal records the first visits from a man who was to spend a good deal of time in the next four years in the Clairmont household and unknowingly forge a new link between the Clairmonts and literary history. He was the Massachusetts sea captain Edward Augustus Silsbee (1826-1900), the "Shelley-mad" collector who was the original of the American narrator in *The Aspern Papers.* Plin's initial reaction was indignation that he spent all his time with Claire, who encouraged his enthusiastic curiosity. "Mr. Silsbee is with Aunt," wrote Plin to her brother (27 February [?1873]) "& she is quite happy & delighted I am not there to watch her funny ways with men—when she plays the *Gurli,* or the imbecile, which she does to perfection." [9]

Various accounts of Silsbee leave no doubt that he was a remarkable person. Richard Garnett describes him as

> much such an one as Trelawny might have been if Trelawny could have been made amiable and gracious without parting with any of his native force. He had travelled far and thought much. A grizzled, weatherbeaten veteran of fine physique, his discourse was mainly of poetry and art, on both of which he would utter deeper sayings than are often to be found in print. He was the most enthusiastic critic of Shelley the present writer has known, but also the most acute and discriminating.[10]

Vernon Lee related that he would "come and sit gloomily in an armchair, looking like some deep-sea monster on a Bernini fountain, staring at the carpet and quoting his favorite author with a trumpet-like twang quite without relevance to the conversation." [11] George Woodberry adds an account of the old sailor, reciting Shelley on the New England coast or fondling with an almost religious devotion the Shelley notebook which he had obtained from Claire.[12] Even without the powerful attraction of the Shelley manuscripts, Silsbee would have been drawn to the Clairmont household as a place where he could be sure of sympathetic responses to his Shelley worship. By the summer of 1875 he had become very much a part of the family, reading Shelley's poems, talking on literature and art, and flirting, according to Plin, with every female in Florence. Plin became increasingly jealous. With unconscious irony she wrote on 18 July 1875: "I cannot help wondering at the longevity of Envy & Jealousy in the human heart—There is Aunt at 77 so jealous that no man dare come into the house but what must be exclusively occupied with her—This morning Mr. Silsbee came at 11½ she talked with him till dinner time as soon as that was over she talked again till 4."

Eventually Plin made up her mind that she had finally found in Silsbee the man she would like to marry. When he made it clear to her that he was not interested in marriage, she accepted him for a short time as a lover. Her journal entries record all this, and also her mixed feelings:

> He is sometimes so charming so tender so charitable Christlike that one would like Magdalen sink down at his feet—& admire him like a spirit soaring high above human imperfections—& at other times so commonplace so ordinary not to say vulgar, so spiteful, that I don't wonder at Miss Trelawney's [sic] behavior to him. . . . It is true he is of a cold nation—Saxon, Anglo-American puritan become unitarian—what human love can there be left—

Despite this philosophical resignation, after Silsbee left the Clairmont household in 1876 to return to America Plin mourned for him in her journal as though for a lost husband.

On 5 September 1877, Plin became "housekeeper without pay," receiving her board and lodging free. Early in 1879, in her last surviving letter, Claire told her nephew Willy of their acute financial distress: "Mr. Silsbee helped us almost thro' last year—one cannot expect we [sic for he] shall do so this year." [13] On 19 March she died peacefully in her sleep. One chapter of literary history closed as another was unfolding.

III.

Through the medium of Plin's journal we now know some of the factual background to the gossip that Henry James was to transform into his exquisite novel. The story of how James heard of Claire, Plin, and Silsbee is too familiar to need extended quotation here.[14] Briefly, James's informant, Vernon Lee's half-brother Eugene Lee-Hamilton, told about Silsbee's going to lodge with Claire and her niece in the hope of obtaining the manuscripts on the death of the elder Miss Clairmont. According to Hamilton's account, Silsbee approached Plin after Claire's death and discovered that the price of the papers was marriage and "that Silsbee *court encore*." [15] But it was eight years after Claire's death that James heard this gossip, which, as a matter of fact, was mistaken in several details. Silsbee had been back in Massachusetts for over two years when Claire died, and on hearing from Plin that the papers were to be sold he at once returned to Florence in the hope of obtaining them. But by that time he was not alone in the field. H. Buxton Forman had engaged an agent, Henry Roderick Newman, to bid for them; later Forman sent in a second agent, Charles Fairfax Murray, a pupil of Burne-Jones.

The story of the ensuing struggle for the spoils is in a collection of letters by Newman, Murray, and Plin in the Berg Collection of the New York Public Library. Letters from Newman to Forman (18 and 24 June 1879) make it clear that Silsbee was on hand and desperate to buy the Shelley letters. But Silsbee had no cash—only promissory notes. On 31 July Plin noted in her journal that Silsbee had written "to say he could not give the price I asked for the letters—& begged to withdraw from the contest." She added cryptically, "If Mr. N. knew what a heroic step I took to secure him the letters, his devotion to me would be in proportion to his desire of having the letters." Can this possibly mean that Silsbee actually offered Plin marriage as a way of obtaining the sacred objects, and was refused? We can't know. We do know that Forman succeeded in acquiring what we are tempted to think of as the "Aspern papers."

We ought to resist speculation about correspondences between the fiction of the novel and the "real" story, to the extent that we can know it. Perhaps James heard more than he recorded in his notebook, perhaps not. He did make it clear that Hamilton had provided all that he needed to set his imagination to work, by "that odd law which somehow always makes the minimum of valid suggestion serve the man of imagination better than the maximum."[16] That is all we need to know to understand why the tremulous Miss Tina was so different from the vivid strong-willed Plin. It might be worth adding, all the same, that in 1888, when *The Aspern Papers* appeared in *The Atlantic Monthly,* both Plin and Silsbee were very much alive and possibly among the magazine's readers. For reasons of tact as well as art James had cause to avoid direct use of his material. By the time he published his illuminating Preface in 1908, he could reasonably and rightly assume that they were protected from offense.

Plin died as she would have wished—suddenly in a mountain-climbing fall on the Sonnenberg at Ohlam, in 1891. The story was carried by the Sydney papers, and her lover of thirty-five years before, Willie Sutton, wrote a shocked letter of sympathy to Plin's brother.[17]

IV.

As the "publishing scoundrel" of *The Aspern Papers* casts his shadow back over the actual events of Claire's last years, he also casts it ahead over the scholars who seek to publish the "Aspern papers" today. Was Miss Tina right to destroy the precious letters? In the context of the novel, she can only fulfill her character by doing so, and the deceitful scoundrel merits the reproof. But outside the novel, James takes a different tone. In the entry in his notebook where he records the Hamilton gossip about the Misses

Clairmont, he also notes that the occasion of Hamilton's story was a visit from the Countess Gamba, wife of a nephew of the Guiccioli and thus heir to a good many Byron papers. James reports in undisguised horror: "She says the letters—addressed in Italian to the Guiccioli—are discreditable to Byron: and H. elicited from her that she had *burned* one of them!" Even if Dr. Clairmont had destroyed some of his Aunt's journals (which I really doubt), should I hesitate to publish my notes from those journals? I have decided that all the documents of that vital and significant family deserve to be available to the readers who will care about them. Although the life that Pauline Clairmont recorded with such gusto and affection in her *Lebensbuch* was, as far as her family was concerned, largely a secret life, it was the life she lived and loved and wished to record. And her devoted great-nephew Walter, although confessing himself the product of a less liberal age, did appreciate that Plin and Claire were "pre-Victorians," to be judged by other standards, and he did encourage me to make my notes and to publish whatever I wished. In a letter dated 7 August 1951, he spoke of discouraging other scholars who wished to examine the family archives, adding: "Should *you*, however, ask for permission to publish anything about the family Clairmont you may consider it as granted before you ask for it." With respect and affection and gratitude, I am taking him at his word.

NOTES

1. *The Journals of Claire Clairmont*, ed. Marion Kingston Stocking with the assistance of David Mackenzie Stocking (Cambridge: Harvard University Press, 1968).
2. For the Clairmont family relationships, see "Genealogical Chart II: The Clairmont and Byron Families," ibid., p. 481.
3. Herbert Huscher, "Charles und Claire Clairmont," *Englische Studien* (Leipzig), 76 (1944), 55-117.
4. She was variously called Paula, Paola, Paolina, Plin, and—according to a letter from Professor Huscher—in the family she was usually referred to as "die Ampel" (i.e., a hanging lamp), a further contraction of "Aunt Plin."
5. Manuscript letter from Charles Clairmont to Claire, 23 November 1845, in the collection of Lord Abinger (quoted by permission).
6. Plin's journal refers to the child by a great many different names,

from "Dot," to Jane, Anna, Iana, and Georgie. Hanghegyi is an attempt to translate the name Clairmont into Hungarian, "*hang* being sound, especially clear or shrill sound (compare 'clarion') and *hegy,* mountain." Herbert Huscher, "Claire Clairmont's Lost Russian Journal," *Keats-Shelley Memorial Bulletin,* 6 (1955), 47 n.

7. Letter from Claire to Bartolomeo Cini, 11 August 1876, quoted in R. Glynn Grylls, *Claire Clairmont: Mother of Byron's Allegra* (London: John Murray, 1939), p. 287.
8. A translation of Claire's will, from the family archive, is in Huscher, "Claire Clairmont's Lost Russian Journal," pp. 46-47.
9. In the Clairmont family papers.
10. *Journal of Edward Ellerker Williams: Companion of Shelley and Byron in 1821 and 1822* (London: Elkin Matthews, 1902), introduction, p. 11n. See also the accounts of Silsbee in William Michael Rossetti, *Some Reminiscences of William Michael Rossetti* (London: Brown Langham & Co., 1906), II, 511-513, and Evan Charteris, *John Sargent* (New York: William Heineman, 1927), p. 14.
11. Quoted in Charteris, p. 14.
12. *The Shelley Notebook in the Harvard College Library* (Cambridge: Harvard University Press, 1929), pp. 20-21.
13. In the Clairmont family papers, 2 and 3 January 1879.
14. *The Notebooks of Henry James,* ed. F. O. Matthiessen and Kenneth B. Murdock (New York: Oxford University Press, 1947), pp. 71-72, and James's Preface to *The Aspern Papers* in The New York Edition (New York: Charles Scribner's Sons, 1908), XII, v-xiv.
15. The reference is to *maître Loup* in La Fontaine's fable of the dog and the wolf who discovered that the price of the dog's easy life was the wearing of a collar. Maître Loup is therefore still running.
16. Henry James, Preface to *The Aspern Papers,* p. vii.
17. In the Clairmont family papers, 4 September 1891.

Index

The following references appear alphabetically in this Index: names of persons; mythological or fictional characters that are not confined to a single literary work; historical events (and a few place names associated with them); a few general subjects. Titles of works appear under the names of their respective authors, and titles of characters specifically associated with a single literary work under the name of that work. (For Blake and Wordsworth, certain recurring characters appear in separate lists following the titles of works.) The following abbreviations appear in the Index: STC (Samuel Taylor Coleridge), JK (John Keats), MWS (Mary W. Shelley), PBS (Percy Bysshe Shelley), MW (Mary Wollstonecraft), WW (William Wordsworth).